Fourth Edition

An Introduction to Christian Ethics

Roger H. Crook

Meredith College

Prentice
Hall

Prentice Hall, *Upper Saddle River, New Jersey 07458*

Library of Congress Cataloging-in-Publication Data

Crook, Roger H.
    An Introduction to Christian ethics / Roger H. Crook. — 4th ed.
        p. cm.
    Includes bibliographical references and index.
    ISBN 0-13-034149-5
    1. Christian ethics.   I. Title.

BJ1251 .C79 2001
241'.0404—dc21   2001021256

Editorial/production supervision
    and interior design: Judith Winthrop
Acquisitions Editor: Ross Miller
Assistant Acquisitions Editor: Katie Janssen
Editorial Director: Charlyce Jones Owen
Cover Design Director: Jayne Conte
Manufacturing Buyer: Sherry Lewis

This book was set 10/12 Palatino by
Stratford Publishing Services and was printed
by Courier Companies, Inc. The cover was
printed by Phoenix Color Corp.

Printed in the United States of America
10   9   8   7   6   5   4   3

ISBN 0-13-034149-5

Pearson Education (UK) Limited, *London*
Prentice-Hall of Australia Pty. Limited, *Sydney*
Prentice-Hall Canada Inc., *Toronto*
Prentice-Hall Hispanoamericana, S.A., *Mexico*
Prentice-Hall of India Private Limited, *New Delhi*
Prentice-Hall of Japan, Inc., *Tokyo*
Pearson Education Pte. Ltd., *Singapore*
Editora Prentice-Hall do Brasil, Ltda., *Rio de Janeiro*

Dedicated
to
Mary Ruth Crook

Contents

Preface

This book is a college-level introductory textbook in Christian ethics. This statement indicates three important facts. First, the book is based on the Christian faith and is written for people who stand within that faith. The text recognizes as viable options a number of other systems and indeed, because of their significance, describes some of them briefly without attempting to assess their strengths and weaknesses. Yet this book is an effort to state a Christian ethic—a Christian method of making moral decisions. It makes certain assumptions, which are proper subjects of debate in Christian theological discussion, that reflect the theology of Protestant Christianity. Although in the field of ethics there is a significant mutual influence between Protestant and Catholic thinkers, there are also significant differences. At many points, therefore, my own Protestantism is clearly revealed.

Second, this is an introductory textbook. It is intended to acquaint beginning students with both the field of ethics in general and varieties of Christian ethical systems in particular and to assist them in formulating an approach that they will find valid for themselves. It is further intended to help them consider from a Christian perspective a wide variety of ethical issues, both personal and social, with which modern men and women must deal.

Third, this text is written for college students and is designed to help them develop a method of dealing with the thorny moral issues that they face not only as students but also as people involved in the life of the broader community. It does not, therefore, assume either the experience or the preparation of students at the graduate level.

The plan of the book is clearly indicated in the part and chapter titles. Part I (Chapters 1 through 3) introduces the field of ethics and a variety of approaches to its study. Part II (Chapters 4 through 6) describes my own method for making ethical decisions. Part III (Chapters 7 through 15) deals with some of the issues that demand attention today. No attempt is made to draw a line between "personal" and "social" issues because most issues have both personal and social implications, and the two aspects are therefore considered together.

To assist the students, I have prepared a glossary of unusual terms and common terms that are given a distinct meaning in the study of Christian ethics. The first time those words are used in the text they appear in boldface. All quotations of scripture are taken from the New Revised Standard Version of the Bible.

I am grateful to Meredith College for the sabbatical that enabled me to complete the major portion of the actual writing of the first edition of this book. I am deeply indebted to three long-time colleagues at Meredith College, B. H. Cochran, Allen Page, and Bob Vance, for continuing discussion and debate, the fruits of which are reflected in much of what I have written. I am further indebted to the students who have taken my course in Christian ethics and have criticized this work in both oral and written form. Hugh T. McElwain at Rosary College, Dean M. Martin at Campbell University, and Emmanuel K. Twesigye at Ohio Wesleyan University made valuable suggestions that were incorporated in the second edition. In making revisions for the third edition I benefited greatly from suggestions made by Rev. Mark A. Duntley, Jr., at Lewis and Clark College; Charles L. Kammer at the College of Wooster; Ronald A. Smith at Hardin-Simmons University; and Edward R. Sunshine at Barry University. In this fourth edition I have taken into account the suggestions of these additional reviewers: Akin Akinade at High Point University, NC; Pamela K. Brubaker at California Lutheran University, CA; and James B. Martin-Schramm at Luther College, IA. While I have updated material throughout the book, the most significant revisions are found in Chapters 2, 7, 8, and 9.

Introduction:
To the Student

Every day we make decisions on ethical issues. Even routine, everyday choices often involve judgments about good and bad, right and wrong. Sometimes the issues are clear, and one simply has to decide whether or not to do the right thing. More often, however, it is not quite so apparent what "the right thing" is, and one has to weigh the options, examine the implications, and choose the better way. The more one's choices affect other people, the more urgent the moral problem becomes.

Students, for example, live and work in a setting in which their conduct is regulated by many rules. Certain expectations about preparing for class, participating in class, writing papers, and taking tests and examinations demand self-discipline and involve students in relationships with the subject matter, their fellow students, and their instructors. Most students, sometimes for reasons beyond their control and sometimes because of their own neglect, occasionally find themselves in situations in which a violation of the rules seems a viable alternative. In such situations they have a simple decision to make: Will they follow the rule? If a rule is unclear, however, what are they to do? How are they to write their research papers, for example, when the members of the faculty do not agree with one another on what constitutes plagiarism?

Not all teachers use a grade curve. Yet in every class the students who do the best work are likely to be given an A, most students will receive a C, and students whose work is significantly inferior to that of others in the class will get a D or an F. Whether they like it or not, students are competing with one another. What should a student do if he or she becomes aware that a classmate is getting good grades by plagiarizing, turning in work done by another student, or cheating on tests?

Every student makes decisions about sexual activity. Those who believe that intercourse is to be reserved for marriage face challenges to that conviction over and over again. Those who do not share that conviction nevertheless have to make choices about partners and circumstances. Many people, married and single, have to decide what to do about unplanned pregnancies. Many people have to deal with the unfaithfulness of marital partners. Those who discover that they are homosexual have to decide how they will deal with that fact.

The marketplace demands decisions that are surprising not in their frequency but in their variety. What should an employer do, for example, when a worker who earns a minimum wage requests payment in cash rather than by check? The salary is not enough to meet the needs of the employee's family, but payment in cash facilitates cheating on income taxes and perhaps welfare. What is the responsibility of the employer for seeing that the needy employee abides by the letter of the law?

Consider another marketplace situation. A department store advertises a low-priced lawn mower. The clerks, however, are instructed to pressure customers to buy a more expensive one. Can a clerk appropriately urge all prospective customers to buy a more expensive mower, no matter what their needs and whether they can actually afford to pay more?

Students often ask their professors to write recommendations for them as they seek employment or entry into a graduate or professional school. Should the professor be completely honest in the recommendations? If a student did not take seriously the responsibilities of academic life, should the teacher say so? If a student had been guilty of academic dishonesty, should the teacher report that fact? If the teacher thinks that the student is really not qualified, should the teacher say so?

As knowledge of the natural order increases and as our ability to manipulate it grows, new moral issues are raised. How can we balance our increasing need for energy with our need for a clean and safe atmosphere? What are the moral implications of genetic screening, in vitro conception, and surrogate motherhood? What are the moral implications of organ transplants and artificial organs? What are the bases on which we can decide about the best use of our scanty resources?

These matters are not moral issues only. They are scientific, political, religious, and economic as well. They are sociological, psychological, and philosophical. They are theoretical and practical. They are emotional, rational, and volitional. They are, in short, matters that involve the whole person. They require value judgments in personal life, in vocations, in social relationships, in politics. Precisely because they involve the whole person, the fundamental issue is morality. Morality is not concerned with a limited number of specific matters; it is concerned with every course of action that involves human beings. In this book you are invited to examine this wide range of issues from the perspective of Christian ethics, to ask, "In light of my Christian faith and commitment, what is the right thing for me to do in the circumstances in which I live?"

1

An Overview of Ethics

Most of us think of the natural order as characterized by a high degree of certainty. The very term *order* implies regularity, dependability, and predictability. We assume that there are certain laws of nature that are immutable and to which there are no exceptions. We talk of cause and effect, of predictability, of doing certain things so that we can obtain certain results. We believe that once we have discovered the cause of a disease we can treat it, perhaps cure it, possibly even prevent it. The more we know about genetics, the more we can improve plants and animals and human beings. The more we discover about energy, the greater the possibility of harnessing energy to suit our own purposes.

When we think about the social order, however, we are much less likely to think in terms of certainties. Although the disciplines of psychology and sociology, for example, require the use of scientific methods, these methods are necessarily different from those of the physical sciences. Social scientists cannot experiment in the same way that physical scientists do. The accuracy of their predictions is much more open to question. There are more variables than they know what to do with. Social scientists are acutely aware that dealing with persons is radically different from dealing with things.

Both the natural sciences and the social sciences, however, are concerned with giving an accurate description of what exists. Both deal with objective reality. Scientists in both areas observe how specific entities act and react. They describe those entities, compare notes with one another, evaluate the work of their colleagues, and debate conclusions. They create images and discuss the reality so represented. They describe processes and speculate on why things operate as they do.

We move out of the realm of science when we speak of *good* and *right*, of *value* and *duty*. Science does not know what to do with such qualities because it can neither describe them nor experiment with them. As a person, the scientist has values and feels obligations. Those values and obligations, however, cannot be subjected to the kind of empirical examination used in the study of physics or chemistry or psychology or sociology. Much less can the scientist examine the values and the sense of obligation of a fellow scientist.

Although the methods are different, the study of value and of duty is no less rigorous a discipline than is the study of the natural or the social sciences. Good work in the study of ethics requires that one be well informed, think carefully, and be open to additional information and insight. Because the ethicist does not have the same tools as the scientist, and because the work of the ethicist is not subject to the same type of objective verification, one can appear to be thinking logically and critically when in fact such is not the case. A conscientious student learns that there are no quick and easy solutions to the difficult problems of moral judgment.

Most, if not all, studies are oriented to the future. To attain some desired goal, we analyze what has been and what is. We study the cause of a disease in order to find a cure and ultimately to find a means of prevention. We study soils and seeds and chemistry to provide more adequate food and fiber. We study history to understand how we got to where we are so that we can move into a better future. Certainly some study is not immediately practical; much research is abstract rather than utilitarian. Because human beings care about the future, however, the utilitarian issue is ever-present.

The study of ethics is entirely at home with this utilitarian approach. Ethics is not fundamentally concerned with evaluating past actions and therefore with assessing guilt or innocence or with attaching blame or credit. Instead, it is interested in the formation of character and in guidance for decision making. It is concerned with helping people answer the question, "What is the good or right thing for me to do?"

Many different types of questions can and must be asked about any problem. The economic situation in Mexico during the 1990s, for example, led people by the thousands to enter the United States, some legally but others illegally, seeking employment. Their presence in the United States has forced our nation to face a number of questions: How can we best meet the immediate needs of those people for food, clothing, and shelter, and what long-term provision can we make for them? This is an economic issue. How can we prevent people from entering illegally, and what are we to do with those who are intercepted in the attempt? These are legal questions. How are we to relate to the government of another country that has failed to cooperate effectively with our efforts to deal with the traffic of illegal drugs? This is a political question. What is our moral obligation to the people who leave their own country for economic reasons? This is an ethical issue the answer to which must take into account all the other questions but also will go beyond them.

Another issue that continues to demand a great deal of attention in the United States is the rapid spread of AIDS. Many questions are appropriate: How extensive is the problem? What are the most effective methods of treatment? Who will pay for them? Who will finance the necessary research to discover more effective methods of prevention and treatment? To what extent may those who discover effective methods of treatment profit financially from them? How can we make treatment available to all who need it? Since our resources are limited, should we concentrate our efforts on some other disease that affects a larger number of people? And underneath all these questions is the ethical issue: In the interest of the AIDS victims, and in the interest of the larger community, what is our moral responsibility?

These two illustrations deal with social issues. All social issues, however, entail individual decisions and actions. It is individuals who are involved in political issues, who vote and hold public office. It is individuals who buy and sell, who work and who employ other people, who live in communities, who are involved in institutional life. It is individuals who, within the context of a social order, influence that order by their own actions. It is individuals who suffer. In our complex society we all deal both with the structure and with individuals within it. As individuals living in society, we interact with it, affecting it and being affected by it. At times we find ourselves at home in society; at other times we find ourselves standing in judgment over it. The final question is neither legal nor scientific nor political nor economic but moral. It is not "What do I think?" but "What action shall I take?"

DEFINITIONS

Ethics is a systematic, critical study concerned with the evaluation of human conduct. This evaluation, as has been noted, is oriented toward the future. That is, it is concerned with the making of decisions. Its basic question is not "Did I do right?" or "Was my conduct good or bad"—although to raise the ethical question, of course, is to take the past into account. The evaluation of past conduct, however, is not for the purpose of creating a sense of guilt but of helping make decisions about the future. Its concern is "What am I to do now?" Such evaluation requires some standard, some canon by which to measure. The beginning point in the study of ethics, therefore, must be the choice of some worldview, some philosophy of life. Ethics does not stand on its own feet but rather is based on a philosophy. The person who decides that something is good must be prepared to justify the decision. What makes this good and that bad? Why is this value superior to that one? The answer to the question why is determined by one's basic view of life.

Christian ethics is the critical evaluation of human conduct from a Christian perspective. The Christian ethicist stands within the Christian faith and makes Christian assumptions about human nature, about the relationship of human beings to one another and about their relationship to God. The Christian community provides the supportive context for such deliberation and action. Christians share some beliefs with adherents of other religions and some with nonreligious ethicists. Whether they agree with these ethicists on a particular idea, whether they reach the same conclusions, is not the definitive matter. The definitive factor is the starting point. The Christian faith defines the motives from which the Christian ethicists act, the generalizations they may make about value and duty, and the conclusions they reach about a proposed course of action.

The word *morals* is used freely in discussions of ethics. Indeed, in popular discussion *ethics* and *morals* are often used interchangeably. There is a distinction, however, that should be maintained. Properly understood, *ethics* refers to theory, whereas *morals* refers to conduct. This distinction, however, is not always maintained either in popular usage or in academic discussion.

SUBJECT MATTER

In the study of ethics, one is concerned with making value judgments. *Value* literally means "worth, importance." We are accustomed to evaluating almost everything in terms of money. We understand that many factors, in addition to the cost of materials and labor and distribution, enter into a decision about the price to be placed on an object. One such factor is its desirability, the willingness of the public to pay a high price. For many items this factor appears to be the major one. Put in simple terms, the question is this: Would you rather have this object than the money needed to pay for it? The issue is therefore one of establishing priorities. If one thing must be sacrificed (or paid) for another, what will you hold on to? In the study of ethics we do not think primarily in terms of money. Yet we are dealing with the question, What is the value of this proposed course of action? The way of answering this question is the subject of the study of ethics.

Some thinkers insist that the proper approach to the making of ethical decisions is to begin by determining what is the highest good in life. If this is true, we must look for the one thing for which we would sacrifice everything else. Discovering it, we can understand what will determine our lesser decisions. Everything else will have value in relationship to our movement toward that highest good. In simple terms, the question is, What do we want out of life? Happiness? Power? The approval of someone else? A sense of accomplishment? A sense of being true to ourselves? Once we have answered this question we can evaluate things in terms of whether they would help us attain our objective or would interfere with attaining it. This approach is **teleological**, concerned with movement toward an ultimate objective. Duty is derived from value; we ought to do what helps attain the goal.

Other thinkers, however, put duty first and say that value is derived from it. The word **duty** refers to an obligation that is based on a relationship or that results from one's station in life. It is closely related to the word *responsibility*, which implies an action prompted by a sense of loyalty to something outside the self. The person who acts from duty acts not in order to attain a goal but because of an inner commitment. The focus is on the motive rather than on the objective. Satisfaction comes from doing one's duty; the good life is the life of response to this inner sense of compulsion. In that sense, value is derived from duty. Such theories are **deontological**, concerned with movement from a basic obligation.

Whether Christian ethics is teleological or deontological can be debated. In either case, however, it is concerned with norms or standards. It is not interested simply in describing the patterns of people's actions, in analyzing their moral beliefs, customs, and practices. That is a function of the social sciences, which try to avoid making value judgments. They are not in the business of saying that this way of acting is good and that way is bad. The most that they will say is that this way of acting achieves certain results and that way of acting achieves other results. The essence of ethics, however, is the making of value judgments. Its nature is to be prescriptive rather than descriptive. It is to recommend a way of acting either for the achievement of certain desirable goals (teleological) or as a response to certain fundamental relationships (deontological). Like the natural and the social sciences, ethics recognizes the fact that we are not merely individuals; we are also individuals in society. The ethicist does not try to impose standards upon a person or upon a group, but rather tries to find and to recommend to individuals in society a valid way to make sound decisions about moral issues.

ASSUMPTIONS

In every discipline students are required to make certain assumptions. Whether the discipline is history or biology or mathematics or economics or music or physics, the study does not proceed from a vacuum. The assumptions of one discipline may well be a proper field of investigation in another. Indeed, within the same discipline there may be debate about what assumptions are necessary. Agreed upon or not, however, no work proceeds without them.

It has been observed that the study of ethics is based on a worldview and that the worldview on which Christian ethics is based is the Christian faith. This, then, is the first assumption that underlies this particular study of ethics. In every religion there is a distinctive understanding of value and duty, of right and wrong, of good and bad. At many points Christian ethics and the ethics of other religions overlap, and at many points they differ. Nonreligious philosophies have their own understanding of value and duty, right and wrong, good and bad. In their conclusions they, too, have much in common with Christian ethics, as well as much in variance. Moreover, within Christianity there are differences both in theology and in ethics. Recognizing all of this, the Christian ethicist stands within the Christian faith and draws conclusions from it.

A second assumption underlying this approach to the study of ethics is that there is an orderliness in the universe that is independent of our knowledge of it. This assumption, in fact, is made in all scientific investigation. Patterns are observed and on that basis predictions are made with a high degree of accuracy. The more we know these patterns, the more we can use them to our own ends. In this study of Christian ethics the assumption is made that there is a pattern, an orderliness, that underlies human relationships. In these relationships, therefore, we can talk about cause and effect, about consistency, and thus about norms. We can make predictions with a reasonable degree of accuracy.

A third assumption is that human beings can know something about that orderliness. We cannot know everything; that is no more possible in the realm of ethical concerns than it is in scientific investigation. An honest scholar in any discipline maintains a spirit of tentativeness about discoveries and conclusions. Information may be incomplete, data may be misinterpreted, and later discoveries may alter thinking about what is now believed to be true. This spirit of tentativeness keeps the scholar going; there is always more to be learned. To learn, one must proceed on the basis of what is now known or believed. This is the spirit that the Christian ethicist is asked to maintain. The quest is for truth that will be the basis for moral decisions. The ethicist can act confidently on the basis of present insight and at the same time be open to new understandings that are yet to come.

A fourth assumption is freedom of the will. Human beings do in fact make choices and act on them of their own volition. No one assumes that people are totally free. We live under the restrictions of the natural order and of the social order, some obvious and some not so readily apparent. Within these restrictions, however, we make choices. While we cannot violate the law of gravity, for example, we can use it in a wide variety of ways to accomplish our purposes. Although we cannot choose our parents, we can make decisions about how we deal with them. We cannot choose whether to be sexual beings, but we can decide how to deal with our sexuality. We recognize, therefore, that certain conditions and influences restrict our choices even though they do not determine them. We can talk about why a person is a criminal, for example, and recognize that a poor family setting, bad companions, personality problems, and so on influence that person. At the same time we recognize these factors as influences, not determinants, and we know that the individual makes independent decisions.

The final assumption is the responsibility of the individual. In one sense this responsibility means that having made a decision, a person must live with it. The consequences of an action are the logical result of the choice. We are not free to choose an action and to refuse its consequences. Nor can we attribute the results of a choice to some other person or some other set of circumstances. This responsibility means that a person who chooses is held accountable. Our choices and actions often come under judgment by some external authority. That authority may be as informal as group pressure or as formal as community law. From a Christian perspective, the final authority to which we are accountable is God. At this point the concept of duty becomes involved in Christian ethics. We have a duty to ourselves and to the communities of which we are a part. This duty, however, is contingent. The Christian's ultimate duty is to God, and moral choices are made in response to God.

PURPOSE

To maintain a careful objectivity and to maintain the integrity of their study as an academic discipline, many ethicists stress the fact that they aim at knowledge and not at behavior. John Hospers, for example, says that "ethics is concerned to find the truth about these moral questions, not to try to make us act upon them." Hospers is not indifferent to behavior, and he hopes that people who find the truth will act on it. He insists, however, that ethics "is concerned not directly with practice but with finding true statements about what our practices ought to be" (*Human Conduct*, p. 9). Such affirmations, however, are overstatements of the need for objectivity. It is probably true of all disciplines, and it is certainly true of ethics, that knowledge is not sought for its own sake; it is sought so that it can be used. No knowledge of goodness, of course, can make one good. To know the good is not necessarily to do the good. Armed with the best information available, one may nevertheless make bad decisions. Knowledge, however, provides a necessary tool for action. One learns an approach to decision making in order to make good decisions.

In the pursuit of this objective the student faces a number of serious problems. First, there is no consensus on the nature of good and bad, of right and wrong, of value and duty. At the starting point is the question of whether there are indeed any absolutes. Is it possible to say "always" or "never" about anything? This is, of course, a question about the nature of truth. Is truth simply within the human mind or does it exist independently of human thought and knowledge? Neither philosophers nor theologians agree among themselves on whether there is objective truth in the moral realm. Those who believe that there is such truth do not agree on its content. They do not agree, therefore, as to whether there are any reliable universal criteria of judgment, and they do not agree on what makes something good or right.

A second problem is the fact that many views that once were generally accepted are now being challenged. No longer is there a consensus on sexual morality, including premarital and extramarital relationships, abortion, and homosexuality. Although there was never a time when the rules were universally followed, those who ignored them knew that they were violating the standard. Now the question is not so much whether to violate the standards as whether the standards are valid. The same thing is true concerning the use of violence in the achievement of good ends. Until quite recently it was generally agreed that only the state had the right to use violence in that way and that it was wrong for individuals to do so. Individuals were expected to work within the system to correct what they considered to be unjust. Increasingly, however, people are insisting that violence may be a correct way to bring about change. Thus some people suggest that mob violence, while always regrettable, may be an understandable reaction to racial injustice in this country. Some believe that terrorism may be a necessary, and therefore valid, tool in the struggle of a minority people against an oppressive government. Some think that a battered wife may be justified in killing her abusive husband. Some insist that private citizens are morally right in carrying weapons for self-protection and in firing them when threatened.

Another difficulty one encounters in the effort to develop a pattern of right conduct is the fact that few problems are simple, clear-cut choices between right and wrong. Most problems that people face are highly complex, and one is aware that any decision will bring certain undesirable consequences. The pressure to establish racial balance in the public schools in the South, for example, was an effort to prevent certain injustices of the past from being perpetuated and to prepare young people for life in an integrated society. At the same time it placed many people in emotionally stressful situations; it created problems of discipline in the schools; and it undermined the neighborhood concept, which many people found meaningful. Busing was an effective way to achieve the goal of desegregation in the schools, but it required many children to take an unduly long ride to reach their school. The quota system in the employment of teachers guaranteed a racial balance but worked a hardship on many individuals and brought emotional stress to children and teachers of both races.

The same difficulty troubles people in making certain intensely personal decisions. Suppose that by doing honest work on a test you earned a C, whereas your friend cheated and got an A. Your knowledge of the cheating inevitably will affect your relationship with your friend, even if you say nothing. The relationship will also be affected if you confront your friend with the cheating. Furthermore, your friend's action has a bearing on the teacher's curve. If it were true that your friend's cheating hurt no one else in the immediate situation, what about the long run? Decisions about conduct, whether on a social issue or on a personal matter, are rarely simple choices between right and wrong.

Convinced about what is an appropriate thing to do in a given situation, we may find ourselves frustrated when we try to do it. Consider, for example, the efforts of a middle-class family to help some poverty-stricken neighbors. An elderly widow lives in a two-room shack with four grandchildren, the sons and daughters of her own unmarried daughter. The daughter lives in another city. The widow's only source of income is public welfare.

She is too old to work, and if she did work there would be no one to care for the children. The shack in which she lives is heated with a wood stove and is a firetrap. The children are ill fed, ill clothed, ill educated, and have inadequate medical care. She frequently asks for help from her middle-class neighbors, playing on their sympathy as much as she can. In the face of such obvious need, they cannot refuse assistance. Yet by helping her they contribute to the perpetuation of the pattern in which she is living. The problem is personal and individual: This woman and her grandchildren have immediate and urgent needs, which they cannot meet. But the problem is also social: Our society has not learned how to deal with poverty. People often respond spontaneously to cries for help, particularly when they feel that the victim is worthy, but they know that such a spontaneous response leaves tremendous unmet needs. They deal with the symptoms of a social problem without knowing how to cure the disease. Although the welfare system is an important effort to meet the needs of the people, it is subject to abuse. We believe that we must provide for the poor in our land—and in our neighborhood—but we are not satisfied with any method that we have devised.

One further difficulty complicates our efforts to make moral decisions. All of us are subject to a variety of influences and we act from mixed motives. No one has one loyalty only: All of us are members of families; we have friends; we are citizens; we belong to social clubs and churches and political parties. We learn the news from the mass media and we are entertained by the same media. We are pressured by advertisers who want to sell us something and by exhorters who want us to do something. Bombarded on all sides by merchandisers and charities, we find it difficult to look objectively at value and duty.

In spite of all the difficulties, however, in this study we shall try to establish a pattern for making sound moral decisions. A part of our work will be theoretical: We shall try to formulate a system for dealing with the moral issues. We have already made it clear that our system will be developed within the framework of the Christian faith. We shall look briefly at certain non-Christian alternatives, without trying to evaluate them, because we need to understand the basis on which many of our contemporaries operate. But we shall move from them to a Christian approach.

Another part of our work will be practical: We shall attempt to cultivate an uneasy conscience. We shall raise questions about commonly accepted practices. Although we cannot deal with all ethical issues, we shall raise questions about a wide variety of personal and social activities, and we shall cultivate the practice of raising questions that will invade every realm of life.

QUESTIONS FOR DISCUSSION

1. What is the relationship between personal morality and social problems?
2. What is the relationship between *value* and *duty*?

3. In dealing with ethical issues, what difference is made by one's religious beliefs?
4. How can we speak of *right* and *wrong* in a world where there are so many different religious and philosophical perspectives?

RECOMMENDATIONS FOR FURTHER READING

ARTHUR, JOHN, ed., *Morality and Moral Controversies*. 4th ed. Englewood Cliffs: Prentice Hall, 1995.

BROWN, MARVIN T., *The Ethical Process*. Englewood Cliffs: Prentice Hall, 1998.

HARMON, GILBERT, *The Nature of Morality*. New York: Oxford, 1994.

STOUT, JEFFREY, *Ethics after Babel*. Boston: Beacon Press, 1990.

WILLIAMS, BERNARD, *Morality: An Introduction to Ethics*. Cambridge: Cambridge University Press, 1993.

2

Alternatives
to Christian Ethics

Making decisions about relationships with other people is of central concern to Christians. Wishing to make those decisions on the basis of their faith, they look both at personal issues and at social concerns from that perspective.

Christians have no monopoly on ethical concerns, however. Many other people have a powerful concern for issues of morality. They think just as seriously about values and obligations as do Christians, and they have just as strong a sense of ethical compulsion. We turn, therefore, to a discussion of some of the most viable alternatives to Christian ethics current in American society. Rather than examining classical philosophical systems, we are examining some ways of looking at life that are characteristic of people in our day. The representatives of the systems that we cite are not necessarily formative thinkers. Rather they are people who give clear statements of systems by which many people live.

RELIGIOUS SYSTEMS

Approximately two-thirds of the people of the United States identify themselves with some faith group, and most major religions of the world are represented here. While the large majority of American people of faith are Christian, four other religious groups claim a large number of adherents. There are nearly four million religiously active Jews, and another two million people regard themselves as cultural or ethnic Jews. The Muslim population numbers more than five million. There are approximately nine hundred thousand Hindus, and approximately seven hundred and eighty thousand Buddhists in the United States. Each faith has its own distinctive approach to morality.

Judaism

Fundamental to the Jewish religion are three convictions: First, the God of the Hebrews, the one and only God, created the heavens and the earth and continues to govern them with mercy and justice. Second, the **Torah** is God's word to humankind. Third, God's word came—and comes—to Israel, the children of Abraham, Isaac, and Jacob (Jacob Neusner, "Judaism in the World and in America," in Neusner, ed., *World Religions in America*, pp. 153–154). To this last conviction many Jews add that "As a part of the original covenant with Abraham, God promised the Jewish people an eternal homeland, the Land of Israel" (Wayne Dosick, *Living Judaism*, p. 8).

Within American Judaism there are wide differences in the observance of rituals, in theology, and in ethical emphases. Orthodox Jews believe that "the entire Torah, oral and written, comes from God, in exactly the words in which we now have it" (Neusner, p. 170). Consequently they try to observe every detail of the Torah, both its ritualistic requirements and its ethical teaching. In *Living Judaism,* Wayne Dosick summarizes the orthodox understanding of ethics: "Judaism's ethical *mitzvoh* are standards of human behavior that lead people to lives of decency, kindness, righteousness, justice, goodness, and compassion." He adds:

> The Jewish ethical code is based on the *authority of the Author*.
> This code is called ethical monotheism—for the ethic, the standard of behavior, comes from the One Lord God. God, who created humankind, has declared how his children are to behave. God's ethical commandments are not affected by time or place. They are eternal and universal—for all time, for all people, for everywhere.
> Right is right; wrong is wrong—*because God said so*. (p. 35)

In a great body of traditional interpretation (the **Talmud**), Orthodox Judaism finds guidance in applying the teachings of the scripture to virtually every contemporary moral issue.

Orthodox Judaism concentrates on personal issues and on individual decision and action more than on social problems and corporate action to change the social structure. In *Jewish Personal and Social Ethics,* for example, Louis Jacobs devotes most of his attention to such matters as self-improvement, peace of mind, humility, health, honesty, speech, gambling, and sexuality. When he discusses such issues as animal rights, justice, war and peace, and ecology, he focuses on individual decisions relative to those matters.

Reform Jewish thinkers approach ethical issues from a very different stance. They still adhere to the Pittsburgh Platform adopted by the American Reform rabbis in 1885, which affirms:

> We recognize in the Mosaic legislation a system of training the Jewish people for its mission during its national life in Palestine, and today we accept as binding only its moral laws and maintain only such ceremonies as elevate and sanc-

tify our lives, but reject all such as are not adapted to the views and habits of modern civilization. (Quoted in Neusner, *Understanding Jewish Theology,* p. 171)

While Reform Jews take the Torah seriously, therefore, they take into account the cultural situation out of which it arose. Describing Judaism from a Reform perspective, Samuel S. Cohon says, "Jewish ethics starts with the principles of Judaism, i.e., with the monotheistic view of the world and of life, with Torah and with Israel, and with man as a free and responsible agent" (*Judaism—A Way of Life,* p. 103).

Believing that the law of the Torah is consistent with natural law, Reform thinkers talk about universal ethical concepts that can be discovered through the exercise of human reason. The moral laws of the Torah thus have their counterparts in the laws of nature. Like the laws of the physical world, they are not invented by humankind but rather are discovered. They reflect a natural order that operates according to the will and purpose of God. They are not merely a description of social patterns, but are rather a revelation of the will of God.

The ethic of reform Judaism concentrates more on social issues than on personal morality. Reform ethicists talk of building a moral world, saying that such a world must be based on the concept of justice. Observing that justice was a basic concern in the Torah, Cohon adds, "Under the prophetic teaching, justice came to be the touchstone of religion. Conceived as an attribute of God and the ideal pattern of human behavior, it was identified with righteousness, the all-inclusive moral category of Judaism" (pp. 193–194). He interprets the **Messianic** ideal in terms of building "the Kingdom of God on earth," seeing it as "the flower of Jewish optimism, growing out of the undying conviction of the ultimate triumph of justice over wickedness, of love over hate, and of social harmony over chaos" (p. 226). His final paragraph on ethics succinctly states the belief in social progress which is the hallmark of liberal thought:

> Human progress grows real when it moves toward an ethical end. Humanity advances to perfection by making God its goal and righteousness its path. An ideal social order need not forever remain a visionary Utopia. It may become an inspiring reality when men will venture to live by the ethical and religious ideals which they profess, and consecrate their skill and intelligence to the creation of proper instrumentalities and techniques for the establishment and preservation of conditions in which the noblest ideals and values of humanity may flourish. Faith in man as well as in God furnishes the ground for the belief in the ultimate realization of the Kingdom of God on earth. (p. 233)

Between the authoritarian stance of Orthodox Judaism, which says that "right is right and wrong is wrong *because God said so,*" and the rationalism of Reform Judaism, which says that ethical concepts are properly established on the ground of human reason, is the middle ground of Conservative Judaism. In *Jewish Social Ethics,* for example, David Novak talks of enunciating the "underlying principles" that are behind the laws. He says that "the task of

Jewish social ethics is not to deduce conclusions from the rules at hand but, rather to perform the more imaginative intellectual task of attempting to gain insight into the principles that inform and guide the whole normative Jewish enterprise in dealing with social issues." (p. 5). For him, Jewish ethics begins with a concern for what is lawful. Tradition, he says, regards law as an indispensable requirement of human life. He moves quickly beyond the idea of human law to that of natural law, however. Recognizing the fact that for many contemporary problems there are no precedents and no regulations, he says that one must try to determine the overall purposes of the law and the good that the law intends. One may take the traditional rules into account and combine them in such a way as to give insight into current problems. Jewish law, therefore, is never fully formulated but is always changing.

Islam

Numerically Islam is second only to Christianity in the United States. Like Christianity, it draws heavily from the Hebrew prophets, and indeed it respects Jesus as one who stood within the prophetic tradition. For Muslims, that great tradition of God's self-revelation through the prophets is completed in the work of Muhammad. "There is no god but God, and Muhammad is his prophet" is the fundamental affirmation in Islam; everything else is based on that conviction. The appropriate response of people to the will of Allah is affirmed in the name "Islam," which means "submission."

The importance of the Qur'an for Muslims cannot be overemphasized. Muslims do not think of the Qur'an as the work of Muhammad, but as the revelation from Allah given to people through Muhammad. It is literally the words of Allah, given over a period of twenty-three years and preserved unchanged from that time (the first part of the seventh century c.e.) to the present. Fazlur Rahman gives two reasons for following a Qur'anic ethic: "First of all, Muslims believe that the Qur'an is the Word of God. Second, they believe that the Qur'an contains, actually or potentially, the answers to all the questions of life" ("Law and Ethics in Islam," in Hovannisian, *Ethics in Islam*, p. 14). Since the Qur'an is without error, its teachings cannot be questioned. The obligation of the believer is to know the will of God through the Qur'an, and to submit to that will.

The teachings of the Qur'an presuppose a union of religion and the state, and therefore a state governed by the laws of Allah. It is certain, says Rahman, "that the Qur'an views the establishment of a Muslim community as essential for its task and will not be content with good individuals only; further, the community is charged with the task of establishing a sociopolitical order" (p. 15). That union, of course, does not exist in the United States, and Muslims in this country do not seek to establish it. Yet they do seek to live and function as persons of faith in this society. How do they manage to do that?

The opening *surah* of the Qur'an, repeated in the daily prayers of the Muslim, includes the petition,

> Guide us in the straight path,
> The path of those on whom Thou hast poured forth Thy grace,
> Not the path of those who have incurred Thy wrath and gone astray.

In traditional Islam that path is defined by the "Five Pillars of Faith," one of which is almsgiving (the other four are the creed, prayer, fasting, and a pilgrimage to Mecca). Nowhere in the Qur'an are the demands of "almsgiving" described in detail, and nowhere is a systematic ethic spelled out. Over and over again, however, exhortations occur and examples are given. Rahnam observes that a large part of the Qur'an

> is full of statements on the necessity of justice, fair play, goodness, kindness, forgiveness, guarding against moral peril (*'adl, qist, ihsan, taqwa,* and their equivalents), and so on. It is clear that these are general directives, not specific rules. But they are not abstract moral propositions either; they have a driving power, a compelling force, which abstract propositions cannot yield. (p. 8)

From these teachings about personal virtues one may draw implications about contemporary issues that the ancient writings never addressed. Frederick M. Denny observes:

> Although the Qur'an provides no systematic legal corpus, there is much in it pertaining to how humankind should rightly live in the Ummah: marital relations and family life, inheritance, commercial activities and relations, social welfare (e.g., *zakāt*), slaves, punishment for crimes, and so on, all of which and more are to be understood as implicit in the 'urging what is reputable and restraining from what is disreputable,' a key phrase for Qur'anic ethics. (Frederick M. Denny, "Ethics and the Qur'an: Community and World View," in Hovannisian, *Ethics in Islam,* p. 117)

While most of the ethical teachings in the Qur'an deal with matters of personal morality, much attention is given to broad social issues. Huston Smith identifies four such areas:

1. Economics: the basic principles require that "material goods be widely and appropriately distributed."
2. The status of women: the Qur'anic teachings represent a significant advance beyond the standards of Muhammad's day.
3. Ethnic relations: the Qur'an stresses the racial and ethnic equality within the faith community.
4. The use of force: while the Qur'an does not counsel "turning the other cheek," it does teach forgiveness. (Huston Smith, *The World's Religions,* pp. 248–257).

Kemal Faruki summarizes his understanding of what he calls "the main purpose of the Islamic message here on earth":

> to help bring about in ever-increasing measure the role of conscience in the ethical and legal regulation of men's lives, whether collectively or singly, and to do so not merely outwardly but also inwardly, when only the Most Merciful and Just God and the individual concerned know of the thought and even the act. ("Legal Implications for Today of the Five Values," in Hovannisian, *Ethics in Islam*, p. 7)

Hinduism

So varied are Hindu beliefs and practices that it is almost impossible to define. Hinduism has no founder, no creed, no authoritative book, no leader or governing group of leaders. It is a religious movement or way of life that arose in India around 2000 B.C.E. and continued to develop for centuries. It is concerned both with the rituals of worship and with the ordering of human relationships.

Trying to summarize the Hinduism as it exists in the United States, The Himalayan Academy identified nine generally accepted beliefs:

1. That there is "one, all-pervasive Supreme Being";
2. That there are "endless cycles of creation, preservation and dissolution" (that is, a cyclical view of time and history);
3. That "all souls are evolving" toward or seeking "Moksha" or "liberation";
4. That there is a "law of cause and effect" known as Karma;
5. That there is "reincarnation";
6. That there are "divine beings and forces" that require "temple worship" and "personal worship," or Puja, in the home;
7. That there is a need for "an awakened Master of Sat Guru" (that is, a reliable, personal teacher) for one's personal and ethical life;
8. That "all life is sacred" and that one should pursue "*ahimsa* or non-violence"; and
9. That "no particular religion teaches the only way to salvation above all others, but that all genuine religious paths are . . . deserving (of) tolerance and understanding." (Jacob Neusner, *World Religions in America*, p. 197)

If there is any unity to Hinduism, it is to be found in its questions more than in its answers. In a broad sense, however, it is possible to identify four philosophical concepts that are fundamental to Hindu ethical thought. The first is the idea of the *transmigration* of souls, or *reincarnation*. Individual souls, which are never identified with the bodies they occupy, are subject to an indefinite cycle of life, death, and rebirth. The second is the law of *karma*, which teaches that our present circumstances were determined by the soul's past deeds and that our current actions determine our future circumstances. Third, the divine is not separated from the human, but rather is within our very being. Fourth, the ultimate destiny of the soul is liberation from the journey of the soul from one life to another, and absorption into the divine.

Of theses four concepts, the one most pertinent to ethical concerns is the law of *karma*. It holds that there is a moral causation that operates in this life and that is related to both the past and the future of the soul. It assumes that the soul gets what it deserves, either in this current incarnation or in some future one. This means that ultimately, justice is always done. The moral implication is that in this life one must act in such a way as to progress toward that ultimate liberation from the sense of individuality and toward a oneness with the divine that is so elusive that only a few rare souls ever achieve it.

This goal is pursued by doing one's duty (*dharma*), what one should do because of one's lot in life. Although Hindu ethics recognizes other values, duty is the highest. It is the careful performance of obligatory actions and the avoidance of forbidden ones. Roy W. Perrett calls it "the cosmic ordering principle that guarantees the harmonious evolution of the universe." He adds that "This cosmic ordering principle is concretely expressed in the social and moral order as agents' ceremonial, moral, and legal obligations" (Roy W. Perrett, *Hindu Ethics,* p. 50). The individual operates with two types of responsibility which determine specific duties. The first consists of the universal obligations of honesty, respect for the property of other people, respect for the well-being of other people, patience, and so on. The second consists of the demands of one's station in life, the chief factor of which is caste. The function of the priestly caste is to teach, of the warrior caste is to preserve order, of the merchant caste is to provide for the economic well-being of society, and of the servant caste is to assist the other three to operate properly.

Saying that "Hindu ethics are mainly subjective and personal," Albert Plotkin summarizes the essential elements of the system by saying:

> Its purpose is to eliminate such mental impurities as greed and egotism for the ultimate attainment of the highest good. Hindu ethics are based upon the Hindu conception of Dharma or duty, related to a man's position in society and his stage in life. Objective ethics, according to the Hindu view, are a means to an end, its purpose being to help the members of society rid themselves of self-centeredness, cruelty, greed, and other vices, and thus to create an environment helpful to the pursuit of the highest good that transcends society. (*The Ethics of World Religions,* p. 147)

Buddhism

Although Buddhism is not numerically strong in the United States, claiming only three-quarters of a million adherents, its influence has been and continues to be significant. That influence is found not only in popular culture, but also in the wide circulation of the writings of the Dalai Lama and of Thich Nhat Hanh. Acknowledging that most Americans do not really understand Buddhism, Malcolm David Eckel says, nevertheless, that "there is no doubt that Buddhism has crept into our culture in surprising and delightful ways" ("Buddhism in the World and in America," in Neusner, *World Religions in America*, p. 204).

Buddhism arose out of the Buddha's profound dissatisfaction with Hinduism as it existed in the India of his day. Huston Smith observes that that Hinduism had come to "clog its own works." Onto the religious scene in India, says Smith, "corrupt, degenerate, and irrelevant, matted with superstition and burdened with worn-out rituals—came the Buddha, determined to clear the ground that truth might find new life" (Smith, *The World's Religions*, p. 94). Smith characterizes the Buddha's religion as devoid of authority, devoid of ritual, skirting speculation, devoid of tradition, requiring intense self-effort, and devoid of the supernatural. The basic elements in the Buddha's religious system are summarized in the "Four Noble Truths":

1. Life is suffering (all human existence is characterized by instability, dissatisfaction, suffering).
2. Suffering is due to desire.
3. Desire must be extinguished.
4. In seeking salvation, one must walk the "Noble Eightfold Path."

Walking in the Noble Eightfold Path requires:

1. Right belief
2. Right purpose
3. Right speech
4. Right conduct
5. Right effort
6. Right mind control
7. Right meditation

Entirely missing from this description of the system and from the detailed explanation of its implications is any reference to ritual or to worship. Indeed, there are no references to the divine. The Buddha refused to involve himself in speculation about the nature of the divine and about the origins of the material world. Everything in his teachings has to do with the way one deals with life in the intensely personal quest for nirvana.

Yet the steps which the Buddha prescribed fall within the category of what is normally identified as "the ethical." There was a distinction between the requirements for the monks and those for laypeople. For the monks, who were seriously engaged in the quest for Nirvana, he laid down "Ten Precepts." The monk has to promise:

Not to destroy life
Not to steal
Not to engage in sexual misconduct

Not to lie
Not to drink alcoholic beverages
Not to eat after midday
Not to take part in amusements such as dancing, singing, and the theatre
Not to wear ornaments, use perfumes, or dress extravagantly
Not to sleep on comfortable beds
Not to accept money

For laypeople, only the first five precepts were required. Laypeople were allowed to marry and live a normal family life, to engage in daily work, and to be involved in community life. In that normal daily life they were to be guided by a multiplicity of instructions for getting along with other people. While this kind of acting would not bring them to nirvana, it would ensure them of a rebirth into a better life.

HUMANISM

Of all current alternatives to Christian ethics, one of the most influential is that offered by humanism. In essence, this approach to moral issues affirms that our basic obligation is to the human race, to humanity. One form of this approach is properly called "secular humanism." The current careless and even malicious misinterpretation of this phrase should not blind us to the credibility of this philosophy of life. Its emphasis on the centrality of persons and on the possibilities of human achievement commend it to the modern mind and provide for many people a way of making sense of an otherwise morally chaotic world.

Morris B. Storer is an excellent representative of secular humanism. He identifies as humanist those persons who "have set aside faith in revelation and dogmatic authority (if they ever had it), and have settled for human experience and reason as grounds for belief and action, putting human good—the good of self and others in their life on earth—as ultimate criterion of right and wrong, with due concern for other living creatures" (*Humanistic Ethics*, p. 2). Humanism, therefore, emphasizes the centrality of humankind in the universe. This means both that the human race can control its destiny and that human beings are of supreme value. Humanists do not find any belief in a divine power necessary to explain either the origins of the universe or its operation. They see human beings both as a part of the natural order and as unique in that order. What people do in manipulating it should be done for the benefit of humankind. Judgments about good and bad, right and wrong, must be made in relationship to their impact on human beings.

Another secular humanist, Paul Kurtz, characterizes humanism as based primarily on science, committed to the use of critical intelligence and rational inquiry in understanding the world and solving problems, and an ethical philosophy (*In Defense of Secular Humanism*, pp. 8–9). Since he stresses the scientific approach to all of life, for him ethical philosophy is based on scientific concepts. The humanist, he says, tries "to lead the good life on his own terms and to take destiny in his own hands." He is committed to the defense of individual freedom, to "the right of the individual to make up his own mind, to develop his own conscience, and to lead his own life without undue interference from others." The moral problem—and therefore the great challenge of life—is "to actualize one's talents and satisfy one's needs, while also developing moral awareness and a sense of moral responsibility to others" (p. 9).

But not all humanism is secular. Indeed, the *Humanist Manifesto* issued by leading American humanists in 1933 has a strongly religious note. A humanist understanding of religion, however, is quite different from that of traditional Christians. One item in the manifesto defines religion as "those actions, purposes, and experiences which are humanly significant." The manifesto insists that scientific knowledge "makes unacceptable any supernatural or cosmic guarantees of human values" (Item 5). Most of the fifteen items in the manifesto affirm faith in the scientific method and deny the affirmations of traditional religion. They insist that humankind can and must cope with life without any assistance from the supernatural.

Forty years after the publication of this document, in October 1973, more than 275 philosophers, psychologists, and sociologists issued *Humanist Manifesto II*. Like the first manifesto, this one gives a good deal of attention to a denial of traditional religious affirmations. It differs significantly from the earlier one, however, in that it is more explicitly secular. Its first affirmation, while acknowledging that "religion may inspire dedication to the highest ethical ideals," states, "We believe, however, that traditional dogmatic or authoritarian religions that place revelation, God, ritual, or creed above human needs and experiences do a disservice to the human species." The second manifesto differs from the first also in that it is centered on morality. Its first four affirmations deal with religion; the other thirteen deal with the individual, democratic society, and world community.

Humanism, then, is committed to a high moral ideal of respect for the person, of individual responsibility, and of the establishment of a social order that operates for the benefit of all people. It has faith in the ability of humankind to deal effectively with personal and social problems by using the same methods that have proved successful in dealing with the natural order.

One matter with which humanists struggle is the establishing of an adequate basis for their moral concern. Although they differ among themselves about the process by which they reach their conclusions and about the proper way to implement their decisions, they seem to agree on a kind of twentieth-century utilitarianism as the basis for making moral judgments. They think of moral imperatives as focusing on the consequences of one's action. Those moral rules are valid that will lead to the best possible life for all concerned. Humanists do not eliminate self-interest, but they recognize that all personal well-being is dependent on an orderliness that makes it possible for all human beings to achieve desired goals.

What are these goals? The humanist assumes that happiness and self-awareness are fundamental human goods and that pain and suffering are never desirable in themselves. The only way that human beings can be assured of a social climate in which they can achieve these fundamental goods is to cooperate with other human beings in their quest. The *sine qua non* for such cooperation is a community in which each person is recognized as deserving respect and in which each one's interests are given equal consideration. Max Hocutt says,

> I think we are obliged . . . to give consideration to the needs and interests of others—not because doing so is right according to some transcendent standard of morality laid down by some almighty deity, but because doing so cannot be avoided if we wish to pursue our own ends effectively in a world that contains people. ("Toward an Ethic of Mutual Accommodation," in Storer, p. 147)

Humanism, then, sees humankind as central in the universe. Although we are a part of the natural order, we are supreme within it. No supernatural force is in charge of the destiny of the world; there is no power to which we may or must relate. All that we have to deal with is the natural order, and our most effective way of doing so is through the scientific method. We human beings are preeminently rational creatures, and the scientific method is the tool by which we cope with our environment. Our personal goals cannot be achieved in isolation. Because we exist in community, our goals can be achieved only in community. Community, furthermore, cannot be defined in terms of immediate and direct contact alone. It must include the entire human race. That is the ground of all moral obligation. As we deal with our environment we establish rules that move us toward our goals. These rules are never absolute; they are always subject to change as circumstances change. All moral values, therefore, are created rather than discovered. They are always relative, always tentative, always to be tested by usefulness.

OBJECTIVISM

Another alternative to Christian ethics is the idea that one's primary obligation is to oneself. From that perspective, the basis for decisions on moral issues is the effect of an action upon oneself. Although this attitude has probably been present in all cultures, it is a major characteristic of our society. For most people it is not a carefully worked out system but rather a subconscious disposition. Its most thoughtful and eloquent literary expression is Ayn Rand's philosophy of objectivism. Best described in her novels *The Fountainhead* and *Atlas Shrugged*, this philosophy is more systematically delineated in her nonfiction works, *For the New Intellectual, The Virtue of Selfishness,* and *Capitalism: The Unknown Ideal.*

Rand vigorously attacks altruism, which is a central element in most traditional ethical systems. She considers it fundamentally evil because it is contrary to human nature. It is totally irrational, she believes, because there is no sound basis to support the sacrifice of one person for another. She calls the doctrine of altruism "moral cannibalism" and "anti-self ethics." Instead of altruism as the fundamental moral obligation, she proposes selfishness. She recognizes that in popular thought this word is synonymous with evil, but she stresses its basic meaning: concern with one's own interests. That definition makes no moral evaluation; it merely describes. It is traditional ethics, she says, that has designated such a concern as evil and has insisted on renouncing self-interest for the sake of others.

Rand recognizes that her use of the word *selfishness* is unusual. She does not use it to mean immediate responses to irrational desires, emotions, and whims. She means rather a "rational selfishness," which seeks the values necessary for human survival. The ultimate value, she insists, is human life, and our final responsibility is to preserve life. She does not believe that the quest for this value will bring rational people into conflict. She claims that "there is no conflict of interests among men who do not desire the unearned, who do not make sacrifices nor accept them, who deal with one another as traders, giving value for value" (*Selfishness,* p. 31). Her basic idea is that "the actor must always be the beneficiary of his action and that man must act for his own rational self-interest" (p. x).

Rand does not believe that an action is made right merely by the fact that one chooses to act in a given way, and she does not imply that there is no objectivity to the concepts of right and wrong. Quite the contrary, she insists that people often make wrong choices. One's judgment is not the criterion of right and wrong; it is the means by which one determines one's actions. Rand insists that one must validate one's choices by reference to some principle. She defines ethics, therefore, as the discovery and definition of "a code of values to guide man's choices and actions" (p. x).

For Rand, a value is whatever a person acts to gain or to keep. In this sense, the ultimate value is life. One's senses enable one to identify the experiences that threaten life and those that enhance life, and one's reason identifies and integrates the material that the senses provide. Reason, therefore, is one's basic means of survival; whatever is appropriate to the life of a rational being is the good, and whatever opposes or destroys it is evil (pp. 17–25).

But what of social responsibility? The one such responsibility that Rand recognizes is to live in a way that does not interfere with the well-being of other people. She says that "every human being is an end in himself, not the means to the ends or the welfare of others." "Each person must live for his own sake, neither sacrificing himself to others nor sacrificing others to himself." One additional sentence sums up her perspective: "To live for his own sake means that the achievement of his own happiness is man's highest moral purpose" (p. 27).

This objectivist philosophy is popularly expressed in the affirmation that "I have to be myself." This implies that each person must be independent of all external controls. One understands one's personhood not in terms of what one has in common with other people but in terms of one's own unique interests and abilities. The search for self-understanding is the quest for individuality. Rather than looking outward to other individuals to get in touch with them, one looks inward to get in touch with oneself.

In contrast, traditional society imposes certain external restraints. Certain rules are laid down by the great institutions: the state, the family, the educational system, religion, business and industry. These rules define the good life and point the way toward its achievement. The rules are the same for all, the objectives are the same for all, and the rewards are the same for all. The person who does not play by the rules is a misfit and is subjected to a wide variety of sanctions in the effort to pressure him or her into conformity. These rules are the major social force.

The reaction against external restraints became prominent on college campuses in the 1960s, particularly in the protest against American involvement in Vietnam. By the 1970s this reaction had spread into all segments of society and was challenging more and more of the commonly accepted values and standards in the areas of sexuality, marriage and the family, personal objectives, national loyalty, and so on. It expressed itself in new lifestyles, in liberation movements, in protest movements. It took on big government and big business in the interest of the rights of the individual. The dominant mood was one of questioning what for so long had been taken for granted. By the 1980s all social institutions were seriously affected by a sharp decline in support from a generation that had grown up with questions rather than answers and with a spirit of self-assertion rather than commitment. During the 1990s that lack of support degenerated into a general cynicism about all social institutions and a lack of interest in public affairs.

This reaction against restraints was more of a revolution than a reformation. A reformation deals with weaknesses within a structure and seeks to correct them, even when drastic steps must be taken to do so. It does not challenge the validity of the system; it merely seeks to make the system operate properly. A revolution, however, challenges the system itself. It assumes that the system is intrinsically evil and must be replaced by a new one. It questions the very assumptions on which traditional institutions are based.

In traditional American society the concept of self-denial has been regarded as fundamental. Christians recognize it as an ideal taught by Jesus. Through the influence of Christianity it has been made an essential element in our way of relating to all social institutions. That ideal, in simple form, insists that we put the interests of other people ahead of our own.

The emphasis on individualism, however, rejects the ideal of self-denial and substitutes for it the insistence that one must do what is right for oneself. This change is based on the conviction that self-denial results in frustration, insecurity, and a wide variety of other negative and life-destroying emotions and attitudes. "I must be true to myself" is therefore the theme of this view of life. "I must be an authentic person, not governed by the attitudes of others, either other individuals or others in society, but by my own inner nature. I will not stand in judgment over other people, and I will not allow myself to be judged by them. I insist on my freedom to live by my own decisions, and I will not restrict the freedom of other people to do the same thing."

This view of life has led to a radical challenge in such areas as the status of women, the mores regulating relationships between the sexes, and attitudes toward homosexuality. It has led to an increasing unwillingness of people to remain in marriages that have gone sour, to remain in jobs that they do not find personally rewarding, to pursue courses of study in which they are not interested, or to participate in institutional activities that do not seem relevant to the direction their lives are taking.

Objectivism, then, along with its popular expression in individualism, involves a radically different understanding of morality. The locus of authority for one's actions is entirely internal, not any external social structure. One is obligated first of all to oneself; only secondarily is there a sense of duty to anyone else other than the duty to respect that person's freedom and individuality. One's goal is to be an authentic, self-directed person. Because this approach is so intensely personal, the social problems that once claimed the attention of a large segment of society are ignored by all but those who are the victims.

BEHAVIORISM

Behaviorism, yet another alternative to Christian ethics, conceives of human behavior not as a matter of free choice but as one of conditioning. People do what they do because of social, cultural, and economic circumstances, personal history, genetic factors, or some other factor over which the individual has no control. This way of thinking essentially eliminates any consideration of morality. It sees human activity as reaction more than response.

The best statement of this alternative is that offered in the work of B. F. Skinner. Skinner eloquently and effectively reaffirmed the concept developed in the early part of this century by J. B. Watson, who insisted that the proper study of psychology is not mental processes but human behavior. Obviously Skinner does not merely repeat Watson; fifty years of scientific investigation cannot be ignored. Skinner, however, does agree with Watson about both the basic subject matter for the study of psychology and the proper approach to that study.

Behaviorism is an understanding of human nature, and as such it has profound implications for the study of ethics. Skinner affirms that all human behavior can be understood in strictly scientific terms. While he recognizes the existence of thoughts, feelings, and sensations, he insists that they are best understood by studying one's genetic and environmental history (*About Behaviorism*, p. 117). A person is "an organism . . . which has acquired a repertoire of behavior" (p. 167). Because no two persons have the same repertoire, no two will behave in precisely the same way. Furthermore, each person's repertoire is constantly being altered by changes in the world in which that person lives. Behavior patterns are therefore constantly changing. And in the last resort one's actions are determined by that cumulative history. Skinner says, "A scientific analysis of behavior must, I believe, assume that a person's behavior is controlled by his genetic and environmental histories rather than by the person himself as an initiating, creative agent" (p. 189).

According to Skinner, then, we are not autonomous creatures but ones who respond to the total environment. We are animals—more complex than other animals, with certain abilities that other animals do not possess, and with a self-awareness not characteristic of other animals—but animals nevertheless. We can manipulate our environment in a highly effective way and thus affect our way of life. That does not mean, however, that either individually or as a species we are autonomous. We are the product of the culture that humankind has devised (*Beyond Freedom and Dignity*, p. 206). Although every person is unique, each is "merely a stage in a process which began long before he came into existence and will long outlast him" (p. 209). For Skinner, therefore, there is no such thing as freedom in the sense in which most students of human nature conceive of it. He insists that human beings are not autonomous; they merely react to their environment. There is no such thing as individual responsibility or achievement. Any improvement in the human situation will result not from the effort to free people from controlling forces but from an alteration of the kinds of control to which people are exposed (p. 43).

With this understanding of human nature, what, then, is the nature of morality? It is merely action in conformity with the patterns of conduct set by the total environment. One does not make decisions and act as an autonomous person; rather one merely reacts to the environment in such a way as to be comfortable within it. Society labels certain actions as good and certain actions as bad, reinforcing the one and punishing the other. People accept those labels as rules, learn to live by them, and feel good (or "rewarded") when they do so (*About Behaviorism*, p. 193).

The highest good, according to Skinner, is survival, which becomes the basis on which moral judgments are made. Whatever promotes survival and well-being, either individually or socially, is good. Skinner does not think of the kind of blind struggle for survival that Darwin talked about, however. Rather he thinks in terms of the possibility of things being put right by explicit design. "The behavior of the individual," he says, "is easily changed by design-ing new contingencies of reinforcement" (p. 206).

Skinner does not avoid the thorny question of who is to determine the design. He sees that as the function not of any leader but rather of "the cul-ture as a social environment." He foresees the evolution of a culture in which individuals are not concerned with themselves but with "the future of the culture." No one person, therefore, really intervenes in the process. Persons are simply a part of a slow and even erratic development of an environment in which they live with some degree of personal satisfaction (p. 206).

In this kind of setting, how do we make decisions on moral issues? Skinner does not discuss this question, nor should he be expected to do so. He is, after all, a psychologist rather than an ethicist. From his perspective, however, the question is nonsensical. Moral decisions can be made only by autonomous individuals, and the autonomous individual, according to Skin-ner, is nonexistent. Our choices are hedged in by our personal history; we do not act, we react. As we react, of course, we affect our environment, changing it to provide greater comfort. The change, however, is not decided either by any individual or by divine purpose. "No one steps outside the causal stream. No one really intervenes," says Skinner. Humankind evolves "slowly but erratically" (p. 206).

Skinner sometimes talks about values and ideals, but he always thinks of them as socially determined. He makes free use of such words as *should, must,* and *need.* He raises questions about what is "ethical" in the treatment of people. He talks about the conditions that must be met before a person is subjected to the methods of behavior modification. All of this discussion, however, is shaped by his conviction that such values and ideals are socially determined.

QUESTIONS AND TOPICS FOR DISCUSSION

1. How does one's goal affect one's thinking about morality?
2. Can differing philosophies lead to the same conclusions about moral behavior? Why or why not?
3. On what basis can one choose among differing philosophies of life?
4. What philosophical system seems to you most compatible with Christian faith?

RECOMMENDATIONS FOR FURTHER READING

Ashmore, Robert B., *Building a Moral System.* Englewood Cliffs: Prentice Hall, 1987.
Brown, Montague, *The Quest for Moral Foundations.* Washington: Georgetown Uni-versity Press, 1996.
Gensler, Harry J., *Ethics: A Contemporary Introduction.* New York: Routledge, 1998.

HUNT, ARNOLD D., CROTTY, ROBERT, and CROTTY, MARIE, *Ethics of World Religions.* Rev. ed. San Diego: Greenhaven, 1991.

KIDDER, RUSHWORTH M., *How Good People Make Tough Choices.* New York: Simon and Schuster, 1996.

KUNG, HANS, and KUSCHEL, KARL-JOSEY, *A Global Ethic: The Declaration of the Parliament of the World's Religions.* New York: Continuum International Publishing Group, 1994.

PLOTKIN, ALBERT, *The Ethics of World Religions.* Lewiston, N.Y.: Mellen, 1993.

STOUT, JEFFREY, *Ethics After Babel.* Boston: Beacon Press, 1988.

3

Alternatives within Christian Ethics

One cannot talk about *the* Christian ethic because there has never been unanimity among Christians on moral judgments. Christians differ on such individual questions as whether honesty is an absolute requirement and on such broad social issues as civil rights. There is no one Christian position on nuclear disarmament, reverse discrimination, abortion, health care, or any other moral issue.

One reason for the lack of unanimity is the difference among Christians on the approach to the making of decisions. On what basis do we determine values? What makes something good or bad, right or wrong? What procedures do we follow in deciding what to do? Several distinctly Christian approaches to the decision-making process can be delineated. We need to be aware of these alternatives not only to know that there is variety but also to know how to establish a method that will serve our own needs. In this presentation no attempt is made to evaluate or to criticize the various systems. All that is attempted is a careful and accurate description of alternatives. In Chapters 4 to 6 I will delineate my own approach.

ROMAN CATHOLIC MORAL THEOLOGY

Vatican II was a major turning point for the Roman Catholic Church. The significance of the deliberations and the decisions of that council, which met from 1962 until 1965, can hardly be overemphasized because they have brought about some radical changes in the life of the Catholic Church. One area in which the impact of the council has been most important is Christian ethics.

To understand current trends in Roman Catholic ethical thinking, we must understand the approach that dominated the Roman Catholic Church until Vatican II and to which many Catholic moral theologians still subscribe. (An excellent example of the traditional approach is Robert H. Dailey's *Introduction to Moral Theology*.) This approach assumes a dualism in which the human spirit is thought of as bound up in the less important (though not evil) body. The salvation of the soul is achieved through a rigorous spiritual discipline in the pursuit of theological, intellectual, and moral virtues. These virtues, however, can be attained only with the help of God. God's **grace**, which gives one the necessary strength for Christian living, is mediated by the church through the sacraments. The sacraments, therefore, are indispensable to the good life.

For the person who tries to live a moral life, there are two basic sources of guidance. The first is the law, which is clear and precise. The law falls into three categories: (1) **Natural law** is communicated through human reason and is available to anyone who submits to the discipline of careful observation and logical thinking. Its implication is clouded, however, by the fact of human sin. This law, since it was written by God into the natural order, is universal and unchanging. (2) *Divine positive law* is recorded in sacred scripture and is available to those who give themselves to the discipline of that revelation. Because it is the law of God, no human power can alter it. (3) *Human positive law* is made by human beings and includes both civil law and ecclesiastical law. Ecclesiastical law, created by the church to guide its members in making decisions, is an application of the first two types of law to the specifics of time and place. Since it is made by the church it can be changed by the church when appropriate.

The second source of guidance is the conscience. Whereas the law is general, the conscience is individual. Conscience is the judgment one makes about the moral goodness or badness of a contemplated action. It is the conclusion one reaches through reason in the attempt to apply the principles of morality to specific actions. The conscience must be informed by the law, instruction, experience, reason, worship, and the inner voice of the Holy Spirit.

A crucial point in traditional Catholic morality is the conviction that there are certain moral absolutes, that certain actions are intrinsically evil. Nothing can justify the violation of those absolutes. In making decisions about specific courses of action, the individual must take three principles into account: (1) the action itself cannot be intrinsically evil; it must be either intrinsically good or morally neutral; (2) circumstances can change an action that is ordinarily permissible into a sinful one; and (3) the purpose that the individual contemplating the action has in mind must be good. An action may be moral if all three conditions are satisfied, but it is immoral if any one of them is not met.

When right and wrong are clearly defined, there is little problem in deciding which course one should follow; one's responsibility is to learn what is right and do it. No circumstances can make an intrinsically evil action good. An intrinsically good action, however, can be made evil by improper motivation or by complicating circumstances. Furthermore, few actions entail single results; most have many consequences, some of which are good and some bad. In such circumstances, how does one know what to do? Here the principle of the twofold effect may be applied: An action that will have both good and evil results may be considered moral if that action is not intrinsically evil, if the good effect and not the bad one is intended, and if the good effect is not produced by means of the evil one.

In this traditional approach, an objectivity in morality makes possible the determination of whether an action is good or bad, right or wrong. The responsibility of the believer is not so much to *decide* as it is to *discover*. The route one follows in that discovery is clearly marked, and the conclusions one reaches are, for the most part, valid not only for the one making the choice but also for other persons as well. What one finds to be the right thing to do in a given circumstance would be the right thing for others in the same situation.

Since Vatican II, some Catholic moral theologians have taken a new tack. Vatican II did not bring these changes into being, however; rather it opened the door to an approach that had already begun to appear. Before the end of the nineteenth century certain German theologians had begun to explore a number of options, and their influence was felt throughout Europe and America in the first half of the twentieth century. In the mid-twentieth century Bernard Haring's influence was critical in giving a new direction to Catholic moral theology. His most important work, *The Law of Christ*, first published in 1954, stressed the importance of Scripture for making moral decisions and interpreted the moral life as the believer's response to the gracious gift of God in Christ. In contrast with the traditional effort to determine whether specific acts were sinful, Haring concentrated on the whole life of the Christian, the Christian's call to the faithfulness of love. This approach was taken up by many, though by no means all, post-Vatican II moral theologians.

Timothy E. O'Connell, who takes this new approach, defines moral theology as the attempt to answer the question, "How ought we, who have been gifted by God, to live?" (*Principles for a Catholic Morality*, p. 7). Because for him the *person* is far more important than the *act*, he begins his work with an analysis of what it means to be a moral person. Although he does not reject Catholic tradition, this emphasis moves him in a new direction. Discussing what it means to act humanly, he emphasizes the centrality of knowledge and freedom. "For one can only be morally responsible," he says, "when one has knowledge and freedom, when one is fully in control of the events that transpire" (p. 53). Acknowledging the reality of certain impediments to free and informed decision making, he nevertheless asserts that human beings live in situations where they must make real choices between viable alternatives.

O'Connell says that one's "fundamental stance" gives direction to the choices one makes (pp. 72–74). That stance expresses and affirms the person that one has chosen to be. Rather than dictating answers to moral questions, it provides the basis for making decisions. Even after one has assumed a basic stance for God, therefore, one still must make specific decisions about sin and virtue. Christians are capable of sinful actions, in other words, just as sinners are capable of good actions.

According to O'Connell, the conscience is crucial in Christian decision making. Following Catholic tradition, he does not think of conscience as a feeling of guilt about past actions, but as a guide to decision making in concrete situations. As traditional theology conceives it, there are three levels of the conscience. The first level is the general sense of value and the awareness of personal responsibility. The second level is the exercise of moral reasoning, and here the church has its greatest role in the realm of the conscience. The third level is the actual making of judgments and taking action in specific situations (pp. 109–113). At this level individual responsibility comes to the fore because the making of judgments is the final norm for a person's actions (p.112). Because human beings are fallible, their judgments may be objectively wrong. Yet we must do what we believe to be right and avoid what we believe to be wrong.

Acknowledging that many Catholics have been led to believe that when their conscience conflicts with church authority they should follow authority, O'Connell insists that this is not the authentic tradition of the church. Authentic tradition, he says, teaches that while the church "has an important and responsible role in the process of moral education," that role is limited by "the possibility of error, the possibility of incompleteness, and the possibility of inadequacy." Acknowledging that the truths taught by the church in the realm of faith "are perduring truths, touchstones of unchanging belief," he affirms nevertheless that

> The truths asserted in the realm of morals are quite different. They do not describe an unchanging reality such as God is, but rather the consummately changing reality of the human world. They are tools for the illumination of contingent realities. Thus they hold within themselves the potential for that mutability which is the destiny of all contingent things. (p. 117)

O'Connell succinctly summarizes his understanding of the importance of the conscience in the simple statement: "It is the quintessence of human morality that we should do what we believe to be right, and avoid what we believe to be wrong" (p. 113).

Right and wrong, says O'Connell, are objectively valid truths and therefore are not determined by what human beings believe. They are not created by human beings but are there to be discovered (p. 132). O'Connell characterizes these truths in four ways. First, they are real, not figments of our imagination. Their validity depends neither upon our feeling nor upon the law of the land or the law of the church. Second, moral values are often in conflict with one another. Most often, the choices that one must make are not between good and bad but between mutually exclusive goods (p. 167). Third, because we make choices within a constantly changing historical context, moral values are subject to change. Fourth, moral values are grounded in reality in such a way that some actions "are either integral to or antithetical to the very essence of morality" (p. 171). The moral challenge lies in making specific decisions in such a way as "to do what is right," to do "as much good as possible and as little evil as necessary."

Whether something is good or bad, right or wrong, then, does not depend on what one thinks or believes. Doing good and avoiding evil require the practice of certain virtues (honesty, justice, chastity, reverence for life, and so on) and the avoidance of certain vices (cruelty, lust, contempt, injustice, and the like). These virtues are not usually defined in terms of laws but of "norms." "Material norms" are specific, dealing with particular actions: tell the truth, do not kill, pay your debts. "Formal norms" are general, describing "the form, the style, the shape that one's life should have in a particular area of ethical concern." O'Connell distinguishes between the two types of norms by saying that "although material norms tell us what we should do, formal norms tell us who we should be" (p. 180). Formal norms are absolute, describing the kind of person we ought to be (pp. 174–186). Material norms "formulate the script" and tell us what to do. They are "concrete, informational, instructive" but also "debatable, often tentative, open to the possibility of exceptions" (p. 186).

What, then, is the place of law in Christian morality? For O'Connell, the natural law is fundamental. Our understanding of that law is always partial, our formulations are always inadequate, and our affirmations are always tentative. Yet the limited knowledge that we have provides the basis for our moral judgments. Human law, on the other hand, is a helpful but not authoritative guide. Because we are weak and sinful, we need its instruction and direction. But in no sense is it an ultimate; it is only a tool for use in decision making. When it meets our needs and the needs of others, "we obey it with joy and a cooperative spirit" (p. 238). When, on the other hand, it does not properly serve us, we are not bound by it and we cannot allow it to distract us from the good. "If the law guides us to the good, so much the better. But if it does not, then the law must be forsaken, it must be violated, it must be ignored. The good must be sought, always and in all things. For the good, after all, is where God is finally to be found" (p. 238).

Aware that his discussion has often been "more philosophical and phenomenological" than distinctly religious, O'Connell concludes with a consideration of what is necessary for a distinctly Christian morality. He observes that the "Christian, Catholic ethic" differs from philosophical ethics in two ways. First, he says, the Christian vision is unique: Christians "are gifted with a profoundly Christian view of the meaning of the world. This worldview functions as a basis and context for all our concrete moral judgments" (p. 248). At the heart of that worldview is the doctrine of the resurrection.

Second, he says that the motives of Christians are unique. They have "a whole complex of peculiarly Christian motives" (p. 249). Although Christians may do the same good things as their non-Christian neighbors, "They see their behavior as profoundly religious." They see the Christian life as "a life of Eucharist, of thanksgiving, of response to divine initiative" (p. 250).

THE ETHICAL CENTER OF PROTESTANTISM

For the most part, contemporary Protestant ethicists give more attention to social issues than to personal ones and talk more of influencing social policy and practice than of individual decision making and acting. It is neither desirable nor possible, of course, to separate the two types of concern. The individual lives and moves within the context of the community, affects the community, and is affected by it.

Today most Protestant ethicists apply fundamental theological concepts to the making of moral decisions in the social realm. People as different in their particular emphases as H. Richard Niebuhr, John C. Bennett, James Sellers, Paul Ramsey, James McLendon, James M. Gustafson, and many others have made and are making significant contributions to the ongoing discussion of moral issues. In Protestant Christian ethics, however, the single most influential theologian of twentieth-century America was Reinhold Niebuhr.

From the beginning of his career to the end, Niebuhr focused on the significance of the Christian gospel for life in modern, industrialized society. He was firmly convinced that a knowledge of human nature, including a recognition of human sinfulness, was essential to an understanding of the relevance of the gospel to life in the world. His view is epitomized in his statement that the human "capacity for justice makes democracy possible, but [the human] inclination to injustice makes democracy necessary" (*The Children of Light and the Children of Darkness*, p. xi). He had discussed that understanding of human nature in an earlier book, *Moral Man and Immoral Society* (1932), and a decade later he explored it in depth in his two-volume work *The Nature and Destiny of Man* (1941, 1943).

Early in his career Niebuhr published *An Interpretation of Christian Ethics* (1935), in which he outlined what he considered a valid application of the gospel to social issues. In that book he called Christian love an "impossible possibility" and spoke of "the relevance of an impossible ideal." He said,

> The religion of Jesus is prophetic religion in which the moral ideal of love and vicarious suffering, elaborated by the second Isaiah, achieves such a purity that the possibility of its realization in history becomes remote. His Kingdom of God is always a possibility in history, because its heights of pure love are organically related to the experience of love in all human life, but it is also an impossibility in history and always beyond every historical achievement. Men living in nature and in the body will never be capable of the sublimation of egoism and

the attainment of the sacrificial passion, the complete disinterestedness which the ethic of Jesus demands. (pp. 36–37)

For Niebuhr, the ideal of justice was the necessary guide for the expression of love. In his preface to the 1956 edition of *An Interpretation of Christian Ethics*, he expressed some "embarrassment" at the republication of something he had written twenty-five years earlier, noting that he had changed his mind on a number of points. He said, however, "I still believe, as I believed then, that love may be the motive of social action but that justice must be the instrument of love in a world in which self-interest is bound to defy the canons of love at every level" (p. 9). He concluded:

> The primary issue is how it is possible to derive a social ethic from the absolute ethic of the gospels. The gospel ethic is absolute because it merely presents the final law of human freedom: The love of God and the neighbor. A social ethic must be concerned with the establishment of tolerable harmonies of life, tolerable forms of justice and tolerable stabilities in the flux of life. All this must be done, not by asking selfish people to love one another, neither by taking their self-love for granted. These harmonies must be created under "conditions of sin." That is, a social ethic must assume the persistence of self-regard, but it cannot be complacent about any form of partial or parochial loyalty or collective self-interest. (pp. 9–10)

In *Basic Christian Ethics*, first published in 1950 and still in print, Paul Ramsey defines an approach to Christian ethics that many people consider more helpful than any other option. In the introduction to this book Ramsey states his thesis: "The central ethical notion or 'category' in Christian ethics is 'obedient love'—the sort of love the gospels describe as 'love fulfilling the law' and St. Paul designates as 'faith working through love'" (p. xi). This love, according to Ramsey, is not a universal quality known and understood by persons everywhere, like "blueness or fatherhood." It is known only as Christ is known. Ramsey is therefore thoroughly **Christocentric**: "Analyzing ethical problems from the viewpoint of Christian love simply means that Jesus Christ is the center" (p. xvii).

According to Ramsey, Christian love is rooted in two sources. The first is the righteousness of God, by which Ramsey means God's way of dealing with people. In biblical terms, the righteousness of God is essentially the same as "justice." It is rooted in God's nature and God's activity, not in human nature. It is not what human beings deserve because they are human but what God does for humankind because God is God. The covenant that God has established with humankind is the standard by which human justice is measured. God's righteousness is seen essentially in Jesus's work of redemption. The human response to this redemptive work is called "grateful obedience or obedient gratitude." The meaning of Christian love can therefore be understood only "by decisive reference to the controlling love of Christ" (p. 21).

The second source of Christian love is the kingdom of God. Ramsey acknowledges that the teachings of Jesus about the kingdom must be understood in eschatological terms. He observes that Jesus expected that soon God would suddenly and catastrophically bring an end to this present age and inaugurate a new kingdom of righteousness. Jesus's belief in the imminence of this eschatological event gives added urgency to all of his teachings.

The bearing of the eschatological hope on the content of Jesus's ethical teachings varies, says Ramsey. Some maxims are obviously universally valid: "Be not angry, avoid inward lust, decide once and for all time, with singleness of purpose, for some cause allegiance to which will be superior to all other duties and all other goods" (p. 33). Some, however, such as nonresistance, unlimited forgiveness, and returning good for evil, seem to suit only an apocalyptic perspective (p. 34). Regardless of the eschatological factor, however, the ethical teachings remain valid. They are not valid in the sense that they work or in the sense that they solve human problems or in the sense that they will bring in the kingdom. Indeed, Jesus did not suggest that these things would result from following his teachings. Rather, he taught a way of life that was the vocation of his disciples. The fact that he assumed the imminence of the kingdom does not minimize the import of his teachings, which should be considered on their own merits or demerits alone and not by reference to the conditions out of which they arose (p. 41).

Ramsey calls the Christian ethic "an ethic without rules." He summarizes Jesus's attitude toward the Law by saying, "A faithful Jew stayed as close as possible to observance of the law even when he had to depart from it. Jesus stayed as close as possible to the fulfillment of human need, no matter how wide of the sabbath law this led him" (p. 56). Ramsey focuses on Jesus's love and respect for persons, particularly for those in need; on the essential inwardness of morality, with an emphasis on motive rather than overt action; on Jesus's summary of the requirements of the Law in the commands to love God supremely and to love one's neighbor as oneself; and on Jesus's "ethic of perfection which transcends any possible legal formulation." He considers Paul to be a sound interpreter of the ethical teachings of Jesus. In a section entitled "What the Christian Does without a Code," he summarizes Paul's view: "Everything is lawful, everything is permitted which Christian love permits" and "everything is demanded which Christian love requires" (p. 79).

Ramsey sees the Christian life as one of faith rather than one of cultivating virtue. Christian goodness, therefore, is not self-conscious and not an end in itself. It is not even the consequence of the life of faith; it is one of the ways in which the life of faith invariably expresses itself. He sums up the implications of love by saying that it creates and preserves community, that it teaches us to attribute value to persons, and that it works through power systems for justice (pp. 234–248).

The last of these three works of love is the basis for applying the ethic of love to social problems. Ramsey believes that the fact of sin must be taken into account in any effort to deal with social institutions, just as it is taken into account in dealing with individual matters. Every social institution is affected by it, and no plans for any institution can ignore it. Yet "obedient love" on the one hand and realism about human nature on the other can guide us in government, education, business and industry, and the like. They can help us formulate social policy. The Christian operates within the social structure on the basis of love and tries to bend social policy in the direction that love requires.

SITUATION ETHICS

In the 1960s and early 1970s, discussion of Christian ethics was dominated by debate on situation ethics. The most eloquent spokesperson for that approach was Joseph Fletcher. In his early writings Fletcher had operated from that perspective, even though he had not defined it in any precise manner. In 1966, however, he described and defended his position in a book entitled *Situation Ethics*. The central affirmation in his "nonsystem," as he called it (p. 11), is that the only ethical absolute is love. "There is only one thing that is always good and right, intrinsically good regardless of context," says Fletcher, "and that one thing is love" (p. 60). "When we say that love is always good," he adds, "what we mean is that whatever is loving in any *particular* situation is good" (p. 61).

Fletcher devotes a great deal of attention to an argument against the legalistic approach, which he thinks dominates Christian ethics. The situationism that he espouses bases solutions to specific problems not on prefabricated rules but on doing the loving thing. He says that the situationist fully respects the traditional ethical maxims and uses them to illuminate problems. Yet the situationist is always prepared to compromise those maxims or to set them aside in any situation in which love seems better served by doing so (p. 26).

Fletcher states his presuppositions in terms of four working principles. The first is pragmatism, by which he means that the criterion by which an action is to be judged right or wrong is love. The second is relativism, the idea that one cannot use words like *never, perfect, always, complete,* and *absolute.* The third he calls positivism, by which he means that Christian ethics reasons out what obedience to God's commandment to love requires. The fourth is personalism, which, Fletcher says, considers people rather than things. On the basis of these working principles Fletcher concludes that the only universal requirement is the commandment to love. All other so-called commandments are at most only maxims, never infallible rules. He insists, "For the situationist there are no rules—none at all" (p. 55).

Because love alone is always good, whatever is loving in any situation is good and whatever is unloving is bad. No action is intrinsically good or evil;

all actions are good or evil in terms of whether they help or hurt persons. Not even the Ten Commandments can be taken as absolutes; any prohibited action might, in certain circumstances, be the right thing to do because it would be helpful to someone. While laws are necessary for community living and are helpful in personal relations, they are always to be ignored when human welfare is better served by ignoring them than by obeying them.

Fletcher believes that one cannot decide in advance of a situation what is the right thing to do. "Love Decides Then and There," he says (Chapter 8). Every decision-demanding situation is unique, and one cannot know all the facts of any situation until it has arrived. One always has the benefit of experience and of the accumulated wisdom of the past. At the same time, however, there is no precedent for any situation. One must decide *in the situation* what is the loving thing to do.

Paul Lehmann, whose *Ethics in a Christian Context* was published in 1963, is very much at home with Fletcher's approach. His book does not have the popular style that Fletcher's does, and it is more carefully reasoned and more detached. Lehmann includes one element that if not missing from Fletcher at least does not play a prominent role. He talks about faith in Jesus Christ and about involvement in the Christian community. He defines Christian ethics as "disciplined reflection upon the question and its answer: *What am I, as a believer in Jesus Christ and as a member of his church, to do?*" He says, "Christian ethics is not concerned with *the good,* but with what I, as a believer in Jesus Christ and as a member of his church, am to do. *Christian ethics, in other words, is oriented toward revelation and not toward morality*" (p. 45).

For Lehmann, the concept of community is fundamental. He stresses the idea of the church as the body of Christ, calling it "the *fellowship-creating* reality of Christ's presence in the world." This fellowship cuts across all barriers and creates a new race of people. The goal of the individual who is a part of this new Christian community is "mature manhood." Lehmann says that "Christian ethics aims, not at morality, but at maturity" (p. 54). It is within the church that one strives for this maturity. Although the **koinonia** (or fellowship) is not the same as the visible church, it is intimately related to it. Thus one makes decisions on the issues of life within the context of this fellowship. In the decision-making process, the Christian is guided by the question, "What is God doing in the world?" Within the fellowship we learn that what God is doing is relating people to one another.

Like Fletcher, Lehmann says that love is the only absolute. Beyond that, he insists, one cannot generalize about Christian behavior. Decisions about conduct must be made in a particular situation. But a major element in that situation—even the dominating factor—is one's response to what one perceives to be God's work in the world. For the Christian the basic context of any moral decision is the fact of life within the Christian community. The formative factor for the Christian community is the fact that God is incarnated in it and through it is at work in the world.

ABSOLUTIST ETHICS

The kind of legalism against which Fletcher and Lehmann protest so vigorously is advocated by Robertson McQuilkin in his book *An Introduction to Biblical Ethics*. For him "Christian ethics" and "Biblical ethics" are synonymous terms. He calls the Bible "a revelation by God of his will for human behavior" and says that "we shall treat the Bible as our final authority" (*An Introduction to Biblical Ethics*, revised edition, p. ix). He adds: "Our approach is that universal biblical norms are absolute and that these absolute norms, properly understood, will not conflict one with another. Technically stated, then, the position of this book is nonconflicting absolutist, transcendental, theological ethics" (p. xiii). To interpret Scripture, therefore, he assumes that "only Scripture is the final authority in ethical matters and that every ethical teaching of Scripture is normative for us unless Scripture itself limits the audience to others or modifies the teaching" (p. xiv).

McQuilkin justifies his rejection of the ceremonial laws of the Old Testament by saying that that system was completely fulfilled in Christ. The moral laws, however, with a few exceptions specified in the Scripture itself, he considers to be permanently valid. He says:

> The Mosaic economy indeed has been surpassed by the incarnate Son of God (John 1:17; Luke 16:6), but the Decalogue is a touchstone to discern, among all the recorded Old Testament laws of all varieties, what is the enduring will of God for his people of all ages. Those laws or other teachings that derive from, interpret, or reinforce one of the Ten Commandments should thus be recognized as having enduring authority. (p. 52)

In his interpretation of "Love" (Chapter 1) and of "Law" (Chapter 2), McQuilkin finds the two to be completely compatible. He thinks of the law as an expression of God's love and as a guide for human expression of love for God and for other human beings. He calls love "the essence of God's law" and adds that "By saying that love summarizes the law, neither Christ, John, Paul, nor James meant that it was a substitute for the law" (p. 68). It does not empower such human expression, but it describes it. He says, "Law leads us to grace, and grace then, in turns, enables us to obey the law" (p. 69).

In his "Introduction," McQuilkin states that he proposed "to survey all essential ethical issues, classical and contemporary, personal and social," and that in doing so he would examine "all texts that deal with each ethical question" (p. x). In Part Two of his book he deals with a large number of contemporary ethical issues, though hardly all of them. He is thoroughly consistent in his approach: He tries to find a biblical answer for each contemporary moral problem with which he deals. He does not struggle with those issues, but gives what he believes to be God's solutions. He pays little attention to information from the physical and social sciences, because, in his judgment, they shed no light on moral considerations. For him, the moral problem is not to find out what God wills, because he believes that the Scripture is quite clear on that; the moral problem is to do what we know to be right.

EVANGELICAL ETHICS

A large segment of American Christianity identifies itself as "Evangelical." Ethicists within this tradition are aware of the impact of situationism and indeed are not totally unaffected by it. For the most part, however, they do not argue with situationism; they simply reject it as an effort to operate without principles and as therefore offering little help to the Christian trying to make moral decisions. They clearly are not legalists as Fletcher defines the term. They see the Christian life as the response of the believer to God. God, the final authority, does not leave humankind to make decisions without guidance. Scripture is the unique and authoritative record of God's self-disclosure, Christians are God's covenant people, and the Holy Spirit guides them in their effort to live in the world as God's children. On the basis of the truth, which God has made known, Christians decide what to do in moral situations.

The work of Lewis B. Smedes illustrates the Evangelical approach. In the introduction to his book *Mere Morality,* Smedes states the proposition that morality is a basic component of human life. All people have a sense of morality, he says, and there is in fact a consensus on certain fundamental moral judgments. Morality is not to be identified with Christian devotion, or even with religious devotion. It is a matter of universal concern. Yet Smedes states his position in terms that are distinctly Christian—and thus in terms that would not be accepted by all people. He says that morality "has to do with what God expects of all people, regardless of whether they believe in him." One is not exempt from God's moral demands, he says, simply because one does not believe in God. These demands can be understood by any reasonable person who will try to understand them. Morality, therefore, is not sectarian; it is human and ecumenical. It is obligatory, not just for Christians but for everyone (p. vii).

Smedes begins with the assumption that the Bible is authoritative on matters of morality. He focuses on the **Decalogue**, which he believes summarizes the moral duty of all people. He says that the law that Jesus fulfilled was the law of the Ten Commandments and that the modern Christian must find out what they say about the will of God today (pp. 4–5). While he does not think that God's moral will is spoken only through the commandments, he does think that there it is spoken "most urgently and clearly" (p. 50).

Smedes makes a distinction between "direct commands" and "abiding laws." Direct commands were given to specific individuals in specific circumstances and did not incorporate universal truth. God's command to Abraham to sacrifice Isaac, for example, cannot be translated into a general obligation. Abiding laws, however, although given to specific people at specific times, are properly translated into universals. The "Thou shalts" of the Decalogue clearly can be translated into "Everyone ought." But how do we know which command falls into which category? Smedes says that the abiding laws "fit life's design," or are appropriate to human life as God has planned it; that they embody an abiding law of human life; that they tell us to do what we already know we should do; and that they are indicators of the kind of life that the Christian lives (pp. 7–10).

Smedes stresses the importance of both justice and love. He defines justice as respect for the rights of others, and love as caring for what one needs in order to function as a member of the community. He does not identify justice with love, speaking as if they were simply two terms for the same thing. Neither does he separate them, speaking as if the one could exist without the other. Rather he speaks of them as inseparably connected. Assuming that the Decalogue is an authentic, abiding commandment from God, Smedes concentrates on the question of how people today can fulfill its requirements. He does not try to assess whether a person who has violated a law has sinned but rather tries to show how the commandment can guide one in making decisions about what to do. Rarely does he take an absolutist stand and say that it is never right to do so and so. But he does say that there must be compelling reasons to make an exception to any rule. On the question of abortion, for example, he acknowledges the difficulty of determining just when a fetus becomes a person, and he acknowledges that the mother as well as the fetus must be considered in any decision (p. 144). He concludes, therefore, somewhat reluctantly, that laws forbidding abortions are not good laws (pp. 144–145).

Smedes takes this approach to each commandment. He sees all of them as speaking authoritatively to modern people, as giving sound guidance for the good life. He concedes that for any commandment there can be exceptions. He focuses not on the exception, however, but on the directive. He believes that the requirements of the commandments are fundamental not merely for Christian living but also for a meaningful life for all people. They are valid because they tell us how God has ordered human existence.

The first word in the title of each of Smedes's chapters on the commandments is *respect*. In Smedes's approach this concept of respect is vital. Although he does not define the term, he uses it to convey the idea that in each commandment there is a givenness that people must acknowledge and to which, indeed, they must be true. It is not to be debated; it is to be understood. Once understood, it is to be lived out. It does not give specific directions for all problems, but it does provide the framework within which one can reach valid conclusions. Individual decisions within that framework may vary; the individual, however, is not free to abandon the framework. One's freedom must be exercised within the guidelines of the commandment. Although the commandments do not tell us everything we need to know in making decisions, they tell us the most important kinds of things we ought to do. While we can get help from reason and from intuition, we are to test everything by the teachings of Scripture (pp. 239–240).

THEOCENTRIC ETHICS

James Gustafson, one of the most influential thinkers in the field of Christian ethics during the past three decades, has produced a number of volumes in which he has developed the concept of "theocentric ethics." His most comprehensive statement is the two-volume work *Ethics from a Theocentric Perspective,* published in 1981 (vol. 1) and 1984 (vol. 2).

Gustafson believes that both Christian and philosophical ethicists base their work on an unacceptable assumption: the idea that everything that happens in the universe takes place for the sake of humankind, that humankind is the central reference point for all that exists. He finds that assumption both in Roman Catholic and in Protestant thought. Beginning at an entirely different point, he draws a radically different conclusion about the basis for moral judgments. He asserts that God's concern extends beyond humankind to the whole of creation and that "we are to conduct life so as to relate to all things in a manner appropriate to their relations to God." Rather than being sovereign over the created order, humankind is an integral part of it. Our purposes and our conduct must be evaluated not simply on the basis of what is good for humankind but also on the basis of God's purposes for the whole of creation (vol. 1, p. 113).

Gustafson recognizes that all claims about knowledge of God's purposes are both tentative and risky. He asserts, however, that the experience of "the Other," which for him is the context of moral decision making, has certain characteristics common to all the historic religious communities and traditions. He designates three such elements: (1) a sense of a powerful other; (2) piety, or "an attitude of reverence, awe, and respect which implies a sense of devotion and of duties and responsibilities as well"; and (3) a belief that all human activity must be ordered properly in relation to the purposes of God (vol. 1, pp. 129–133).

On the basis of his discussion of the traditional theological concepts of human nature, the fall, and redemption, Gustafson describes his theocentric ethic. He attempts to establish a perspective in which "we come to some certitude (but not always certainty) about what God is enabling and requiring, and about the appropriate relations of ourselves and all things to God" (vol. 1, p. 327). Such discernment, he says, begins with an awareness of the facts, a judgment about which facts are morally relevant, and an understanding of what the possibilities are. Although such discernment is reflective and rational, it is also "an informed intuition." After this exercise of human reason there comes a "final moment of perception that sees the parts in relation to a whole, expresses sensibilities as well as reasoning, and is made in the conditions of human finitude" (vol. 1, p. 338).

In what sense is this approach theocentric? Gustafson does not believe that the will of God is revealed in moral details in Scripture because Scripture is historically conditioned. What one discerns through the Bible is the fundamental requirements for individual, interpersonal, and social life. General and formal in character, these requirements provide the basis for individual moral decisions.

If moral decision is individual, however, is not ethics completely relativistic? Gustafson insists that that is not the case. Certain actions and relationships are always wrong, he says. Certain absolute prohibitions set the outer limits of moral conduct and leave to the individual the resolution of specific issues. Gustafson illustrates by saying that slavery and murder are always wrong because they violate respect for the individual. Yet we have to grapple with the question of how to deal with political and economic systems that dictate the conditions of life for masses of people (vol. 1, p. 340). Within this context we are responsible for avoiding moral evil insofar as possible. We cannot do so totally, however, because many of the good choices we make will involve evil. A war may be just, for example, but the suffering and death it brings are no less evil. Although an abortion may be justified, a potential human being is destroyed. Economic stringencies may be necessary to a nation, but that does not ease the deprivation and suffering of the poor. The persistence of evil does not lessen our responsibility to strive for the good (vol. 1, pp. 340–342).

A theocentric perspective, says Gustafson, requires a reordering of values and ethical concepts. The basic moral question is, "What is God enabling and requiring us to be and to do?" To ask this question is to recognize that our ultimate responsibility is "to relate ourselves and all things in a manner (or in ways) appropriate to their relations to God" (p. 3). The chief emphases of theocentric ethics, therefore, are these:

1.   Humankind is not central in creation.
2.   Human life and the rest of creation are interdependent.
3.   Rather than standing in judgment over natural impulses, the moral directs them.
4.   Piety is the natural response to the experience of the ultimate power.
5.   Everything must be described within the context of the larger whole.
6.   A concern for the common good is essential.
7.   Theocentric ethics requires an awareness of the moral ambiguity in life, and thus an awareness of the tragic character of particular choices.
8.   A strong emphasis is placed on self-denial and sometimes even self-sacrifice. (vol. 2, pp. 4–29)

Gustafson argues that the basic point for moral thinking is "the interpretation of God and God's relations to the world, including human beings." He develops his own thought around the central idea that human beings are not spectators of the life process and not proprietors of it but participants in it. Humankind is a part of the larger whole (p. 144).

THE ETHICS OF LIBERATION THEOLOGY

Although its themes are at least as old as the ancient Hebrew prophets, liberation theology arose as a distinct theological movement in Latin America in the early 1970s. When the European powers lost control of their colonial possessions in Africa and Latin America after World War II, most of the emerging nations became neither democratic nor economically independent. Instead they were ruled by repressive military dictatorships that maintained rigid control of all social institutions and sought to suppress all dissent. The masses of people in those countries continued to be oppressed both economically and politically. Consequently armed uprisings broke out in many countries, seeking to overthrow the ruling capitalistic dictatorships and to install socialist-inspired regimes (Boff and Boff, *Introducing Liberation Theology*, p. 67). The churches became involved in the revolutionary movements, particularly the dominant Roman Catholic Church, and many priests and theologians became leaders in those movements. Among the most ardent and eloquent of them was Gustavo Gutierrez, whose foundational work, *A Theology of Liberation*, first published in Spanish in 1971, was translated into English and published in the United States in 1973. Another spokesperson, better known in this country, was Salvadoran Bishop Oscar Romero, whose increasingly vigorous criticism of the Salvadoran government resulted in his assassination in March 1980.

While liberation theology has not become a major Christian theological stance outside Latin America, it has made a worldwide impact. Robert McAfee Brown, perhaps its most influential proponent in the United States, says that

> liberation theology exists wherever there is oppression, and there are few parts of the globe, as a consequence, where movements for liberation are not this very day growing in size and intensity—South Africa, the Philippines, Sri Lanka, Singapore, China, Pacific rim nations, India, not to mention articulations of liberation theology within our own shores by African Americans, feminists and womanists, Hispanics, gays and lesbians, and many others." (*Liberation Theology*, p. ix)

Instead of following the time-honored pattern of systematic theology, liberation theology begins with people, and especially with the poor and oppressed. It assumes that God is working for the liberation of those people and that the Christian community is called to work for that same cause. Writing from a Protestant perspective, Brown identifies four recurring themes in liberation theology:

1. Commitment—taking a
2. Hope—the anticipatior
3. God's presence—the re midst, in other persons
4. A preferential option for the poo. which will bring greater justice into the world (Brown, pp. 2~-~~,

Writing from a Catholic perspective, Leonardo Boff and Clodovis Boff identify the following as key themes of liberation theology:

1. Living and true faith includes the practice of liberation.
2. The living God sides with the oppressed against the pharaohs of this world.
3. The kingdom is God's project in history and eternity.
4. Jesus, the Son of God, took on oppression in order to set us free.
5. The Holy Spirit, "Father of the poor," is present in the struggles of the oppressed.
6. Mary is the prophetic and liberating woman of the people.
7. The church is sign and instrument of liberation.
8. The rights of the poor are God's rights.
9. Liberated human potential becomes liberative. (*Introducing Liberation Theology,* pp. 49–63)

As liberation theology does not follow the usual patterns of systematic theology, so its ethic does not follow the usual patterns of moral responsibility. Liberation theologians insist that to be moral is to engage in the struggle against the forces that oppress people. They engage in that struggle armed with the teachings of the prophets and of Jesus and drawing upon the teachings of the church. They cite the stories of martyrs in the cause of justice and forcefully employ the powers of logic and persuasion. More than that, however, they live and work with the oppressed and use the methods of popular, political, and economic pressure. Many of them, though not all, take part in a military struggle for freedom. For them, to be moral is to act.

African-American Themes

In the United States, the work of a number of African-American theologians centers on the theme of liberation. Among these, James H. Cone shows the closest affinity to Latin American liberation theology. His book, *A Black Theology of Liberation,* first published in 1970, was reissued in 1986 without revision but with articles of "critical reflections" written by a number of American theologians. In the preface to the 1986 edition Cone said of his 1970 work, "I was completely unaware of the beginnings of liberation theology in the Third World" (p. xii). Yet how similar was the theme! The preface to the 1970 edition begins:

The reader is entitled to know what to expect in this book. It is my contention that Christianity is essentially a religion of liberation. The function of theology is that of analyzing the meaning of that liberation for the oppressed so that they can know that their struggle for political, social, and economic justice is consistent with the gospel of Jesus Christ. Any message that is not related to the liberation of the poor in a society is not Christ's message. Any theology that is indifferent to the theme of liberation is not Christian theology. (p. v)

Cone discusses the traditional theological concepts: revelation, God, human nature, Jesus Christ, the church, the world, and eschatology. From beginning to end, however, he interprets those concepts from the perspective of a black person, that is, as a member of an oppressed group.

Over the years Cone has broadened but not significantly altered his perspective. In *God of the Oppressed,* published in 1975, he uses the word *liberation* in four of his ten chapter titles. He calls *For My People,* published in 1984, a "critical assessment" of the black theology movement. Highly critical of traditional American theology, he observes that "white theologians and preachers denied any relationship between the scriptures and our struggle for freedom." He dismisses "white theology" as irrelevant to African-Americans and observes that "We black theologians contended that if God sided with the poor and the weak in biblical times, then why not today? If salvation is a historical event of rescue, a deliverance of slaves from Egypt, why not a black power event today and a deliverance of blacks from white American racial oppression? (*For My People,* p. 65).

Cone concludes his survey and interpretation of black theology with some suggestions for "the new vision of freedom":

1. The new vision will need to include an emphasis on black unity through an affirmation of the value of black history and culture. There will be no freedom for blacks without black unity.
2. After black unity has been achieved, the new vision will need to include the best in the integrationist tradition as articulated by Martin Luther King, Jr., in his dream of the "beloved community."
3. The vision of the new social order must be antisexist.
4. The new social order should be democratic and socialist, including a Marxist critique of monopoly capitalism.
5. The new black perspective must be a global vision that includes the struggles of the poor in the Third World.
6. Any new vision of a just social order must affirm the best in black religion and embrace the creative elements in the religions of the poor who are struggling for freedom throughout the globe. (pp. 202–204)

Less strident than Cone in his criticism of white churches and white theologians, J. Deotis Roberts nevertheless cites the fact that American theology has been firmly rooted in North-European thought and that it has been predominantly white and male. He says that we are in a new era into which have come new "liberation theologies, including feminine, black, and Hispanic programs" (*Black Theology in Dialogue*, pp. 11–12). In this new era we must address the issues of "racism, poverty, the feminization of poverty, and discrimination against women and homosexuals." We must deal with these issues, he says, "with full exposure to the accumulated knowledge of the historic faith. But there should also be an encounter with the real world where witness is to take place" (pp. 14–15). In his elaboration of his ideas about how theological reflection should develop, he stresses ecumenicity, the importance of the Bible, the long tradition of theological discussion, and the life and work of the church. He also says that we should be "political but not partisan," "particular but not provincial," and "passionate without being irrational" (pp. 16–19). Unlike Cone, who sees the white church as a part of the oppressive power structure, Roberts essentially ignores the white church and focuses on what he thinks the black church and black theologians need to do to deal with the collective evils that characterize our society.

Feminist Themes

A number of feminist writers also express the central theme of liberation theology. Feminism itself is not a religious movement but a social one in which some people of religious faith participate along with others who do not have such faith. Many Christians, however, find the concern with the liberation of women to be not merely compatible with their faith but a logical outgrowth of it. Although Christian feminist writers do not use the rhetoric of liberation theology quite as explicitly as do African-American liberation theologians, they do accept its basic assumption that God is on the side of all who struggle for liberation.

Using historical and sociological material, feminists review the patriarchal character of our culture from the beginning of our nation to the present. They cite evidence from the intimate life of the family, the formative activities of educational institutions, the informal relationships in social and recreational activities, the demanding life in the economic realm, and the combative world of politics. Even the church—many feminists would say *especially* the church—reflects this characteristic. Sharon Welch says, "My participation in a community of faith has evoked an awareness of my oppression as a woman" (*Communities of Resistance and Solidarity*, p. ix).

As feminism is a reaction against the patriarchal character of society, so is feminist Christian ethics a reaction against the traditional male-dominated way of doing Christian ethics. Feminist writings, says Lois Daly, "are attempts to envision a different world, one in which patterns of domination and subordination, of hierarchy, of injustice are replaced by reciprocity, coalition, and justice" (*Feminist Theological Ethics*, p. xiii).

Eleanor Humes Haney describes feminist ethics as the effort to articulate a vision of a new community and to make that vision real ("What Is Feminist Ethics?" in Daly, ed., *Feminist Theological Ethics*, pp. 4–5). The effort, she says, is shaped by commitment to "the good," which she describes in terms of nurture for all and friendship with one another, with the earth, and with "all that is and can be" (p. 6). While this commitment entails concern for the liberation of all oppressed people, she says, "Our primary responsibility is the liberation of and by women, liberation from an ethos that corrupts our hearts and minds, from the religious and philosophical constructs that support and reflect the ethos, and from the concrete institutional and physical expressions of that ethos" (p. 7).

Recognizing that feminist ethics is not per se an expression of Christian ethics, Haney says that it is "appropriately related to traditional Christian ethics as a critique and an alternative" (p. 10). She thinks that a feminist perspective on Christian ethics will enrich traditional Christianity. She does not regard Jesus as the final and definitive model for human excellence. Instead she sees him as one who redefined God for his time and whose relationship with women was consistent with that redefinition. She says that for Christ "God was not the Holy One who demanded exclusion and purity, so much as the Gracious One with Whom the self could be on intimate terms." She interprets the crucifixion of Jesus as the result of his loyalty to feminine values such as "nurturing and serving the needs and well-being of the neighbor" (p. 11).

Much of the work of Christian feminist ethicists is a critique of traditional male-dominated ethics and an effort to reeducate the church and the general public. They give a great deal of attention to biblical studies, offering corrections to translations and to traditional interpretation. They cite historical evidence to show how the church has traditionally reflected the culture in which it has existed. They challenge the theologians and the social reformers, showing how they have overlooked women in their thought and their action.

Like male scholars in their discussion of other issues, feminists call attention to the social context within which biblical narratives and teachings were developed. They call attention to the irrelevance of certain teachings and the basic immorality of certain practices. They point out the inconsistency between certain biblical passages that denigrate women and other material that is clearly more respectful and appreciative of women. Feminist writers do not try to claim a modern perspective for ancient writers. They do show, however, that modern readers do not always interpret the Bible properly and that certain passages of scripture normally cited in support of patriarchal traditions actually do no more than describe current practice.

Feminists are sometimes caustic in showing that twentieth-century Americans are still bound to undemocratic and un-Christian practices. Anne McGrew Bennett points out that in the progress resulting in part from the Social Gospel movement of this century—the eight-hour day, the right of labor to organize, the establishment of Social Security, civil rights, human rights, and so on—women either have not been included at all or have been relegated to an inferior status ("Overcoming the Biblical and Traditional Subordination of Women," in Daly, ed., *Feminist Theological Ethics*, p. 135).

Yet many feminist writers acknowledge their own involvement in the very structures of oppression that they condemn. Sharon Welch says,

> There is another aspect, however, to my experience of faith, one identified by the terms *white, middle-class,* and *American.* For me, to be a Christian is to become aware of the degree to which I am a participant in structures of oppression, structures of race, class, and national identity. As a woman, I am oppressed by the structures of patriarchy. Yet as white, I benefit from the oppression of people of other races. As a person whose economic level is middle-class, I am both victim and victimizer of others. As an American I live within a nation whose policies are economically, politically, and environmentally disastrous for far too many of the world's peoples. (p. ix)

Many African-American women are not involved in the feminist movement because they believe its orientation is basically white and middle-class. Feminists tend to focus on the patriarchal system as a system in which women are oppressed by men. But many African-American women see white women as an integral part of the patriarchal system, under which white people, both women and men, keep African-Americans in subjection. White women are a part of the white-controlled American institutions. Although they seek liberation, they do so within the context of those oppressive institutions, in which, from the viewpoint of African-Americans, they are privileged persons. White American patriarchy, says Delores S. Williams, has "provided white women with the education, skills, and support (and often financial resources) they need to get first chance at the jobs and opportunities for women resulting from the pressures exerted by the civil rights movements in America" ("The Color of Feminism," in Daly, ed., *Feminist Theological Ethics*, pp. 47–48). Essentially ignoring the mainstream feminist movement, Williams talks primarily of the task of the black church as "the business of casting out the demonic—the socially, politically, economically, and spiritually demonic rule that threatens the life of black people and the life of the human spirit." A part of the mission of the black church, she says, is to enlighten its people "so that the oppression of women in the church is alleviated—so that black male imitations of white manhood and white male patriarchy are discarded" (p. 56).

Seeing their struggle as different from that of white feminists, some African-American women ethicists talk of "womanism" rather than of "feminism." They talk of the problem of "the demonic governance of black women's lives by white male and white female-ruled systems using racism, violence, violation, retardation, and death as instruments of social control" (Williams, p. 50). Katie G. Cannon, writing about the direction in which she thinks black liberation ethics should move, says that it should (1) be moved by a vision that includes black women, (2) examine the contributions of black women in all fields of theological studies, (3) gather the evidence on women's contributions to the black church community, and (4) recognize and condemn the sexual discrimination in the institutional church ("Hitting a Straight Line with a Crooked Stick," in Daly, ed., *Feminist Theological Ethics,* pp. 37–38).

While feminist ethicists, womanist ethicists, and African-American ethicists all employ the basic concept of liberation theology, they take very different approaches. All three groups try to cope with the oppressive forces in our society. Feminist ethicists, dealing with the middle-class white establishment, are trying to change the social conventions. Womanist ethicists, dealing with a white-dominated system in which both women and men play a part, are looking to the black church as the place in and through which they can make an impact on the lives of African-American women. Black liberation theologians, regarding the entire structure of white-dominated society as oppressive, are going their own way to confront rather than to interact with the white power structure.

QUESTIONS AND TOPICS FOR DISCUSSION

1. In what ways do all systems of Christian ethics agree? In what ways do they differ?
2. How can we explain the fact that Christians, using the same sources of guidance, often reach radically different conclusions on moral issues?
3. Compare the traditional Catholic concept of guidance from the conscience with the post-Vatican II approach.
4. What is the place of conscience in Protestant ethics?

RECOMMENDATIONS FOR FURTHER READING

BROWN, ROBERT MCAFFEE, *Liberation Theology.* Louisville, Ky.: Westminster/John Knox, 1993.

CONE, JAMES H., *A Black Theology of Liberation.* Twentieth Anniversary Edition. New York: Orbis, 1990.

———, *God of the Oppressed.* New York: Orbis, 1997.

———, *Speaking the Truth.* New York: Orbis, 1999.

DALY, LOIS K., ed., *Feminist Theological Ethics.* Louisville, Ky.: Westminster/John Knox, 1994.

GUSTAFSON, JAMES M., *Protestant and Roman Catholic Ethics.* Chicago: University of Chicago Press, 1980.

IHAUERWAS, STANLEY, and WILLIAM H. WILLIMON, *Resident Aliens.* Nashville: Abingdon, 1989.

MAY, WILLIAM E., *An Introduction to Moral Theology.* Our Sunday Visitor, Publishing Division, 1995.

RAY, SCOTT B., *Moral Choices.* Grand Rapids: Zondervan, 2000.

SANDERS, CHERYL J., *Empowerment Ethics for a Liberated People. Minneapolis:* Fortress, 1995.

SMEDES, LEWIS B., *Choices.* New York: Harper Collins, 1991.

TILLMAN, WILLIAM M., *Understanding Christian Ethics.* Nashville: Broadman and Holman, 1994.

TRULL, JOE E., *Walking in the Way: An Introduction to Christian Ethics.* Nashville: Broadman and Holman, 1997.

WILKINS, STEVE, *Beyond Bumper Sticker Ethics.* Downers Grove, Ill.: InterVarsity Press, 1995.

4

Sources of Guidance

The choice between right and wrong sometimes seems so clear-cut that no decision appears to be necessary. Most students, for example, do not claim that cheating on tests is morally right. In desperation, some do cheat, admitting to themselves that it is wrong but seeing no alternative. Others do it as a matter of course, with no concern for the moral issue at all. Knowing that they can get away with it, they simply do what they can to raise their grades. They do not regard cheating as morally right; they simply ignore moral considerations. The same sort of thing might be said about murder or theft or adultery. In extreme circumstances even a person with strong convictions might succumb to temptation and resort to any one of these actions. A person without such convictions might do so much more casually. In any case, performing such actions does not mean that the perpetrator thinks that they are right but only that other factors override moral judgments.

From a moral perspective, therefore, some judgments are easily made because the right action is quite apparent. One simply has to choose whether to act morally or immorally. Having chosen and acted, one lives with the consequences. In the aftermath of an immoral action one may be repentant, defiant, scornful, sorry for having been caught, embarrassed, or relieved that the offense has not been detected. In the aftermath of a moral action one may be happy, self-satisfied, pleased with social approval, or assured of God's approval. In either event, one's thinking about right and wrong has not been challenged.

Most decision making, however, is much more complicated. Cheating, for example, is not a clearly defined term. What one student or one instructor might consider to be plagiarism another student or instructor might consider to be the proper use of source material. Murder is defined as one person

Relativity

deliberately taking the life of another. Does that include **euthanasia**? Abortion? Capital punishment? Warfare? To steal is to take someone else's property without that person's consent. Does that include charging a high price for a scarce object? Does it suggest anything about how much one may pay for a meal on an expense account? Does it have anything to do with the use of ideas learned from someone else? The difficult task of decision making is found in areas where choices are not clearly indicated, where lines are not sharply drawn, where all choices are bad or where all choices are good, or where all alternatives are a mixture of good and bad.

In such difficult situations, how is the Christian to decide? It is not enough to say that one must decide for oneself. That truism simply reaffirms the idea that a choice must be made. Of course, if I face a problem I am the one who must act. Of course, therefore, I have to decide what to do. But can I prepare for making decisions? Is there a basis on which I can operate? Is there help for me as I struggle with the decision? Are there guidelines by which I can make moral judgments?

As we have seen, there is no consensus either among philosophers or among theologians on how one should go about making decisions, on whether there are guidelines, and if there are, on what those guidelines are. Some Christian ethical systems, as we have seen, structure an approach around the goal to be attained, assuming that certain desired or desirable objectives dictate actions. In one way or another, these systems suggest that if we act in a given way we move in the direction of our objective, usually spoken of in such terms as the Kingdom of God, universal peace, the growth of the church, or the welfare of humankind. Other systems, as we have seen, structure an approach around a sense of duty or of obligation, assuming that there are general principles of conduct rooted in the character of God and in the nature of God's creation. These systems focus more on motive than on result. Still other Christian systems focus on Christian morality as the response of an individual to God in Christ. Although I have not argued the merits and demerits of the systems that I have described, the reader should know that the last approach is the one taken in this book. Although I am influenced by ethicists who take other approaches, my basic stance is that Christian morality is decision and action emanating from character that is shaped by a faith relationship with Christ.

That faith relationship is not amorphous. It does not ask that one make decisions without any wisdom from the past, without any teachings, without any reference to other circumstances. No human experience is a *de novo* matter. No choice is made without a precedent; no one is cut off from the broader human communities, including the community of faith. While each person is unique, each also has a history, an environment, and a future. For this reason, the basic doctrines of the Christian faith, and our own interpretation of them, shape our thinking on moral issues. At this point, therefore, we turn our attention to those sources of guidance available to us for making moral decisions.

THE BIBLE

Because the Bible is basic to the life of the church, it is also basic to a Christian approach to decision making on moral issues. A fundamental principle of Protestant Christianity, as a matter of fact, is the authority of Scripture in matters of faith and practice. Many Christians agree with the affirmation in the Westminster Confession of Faith that Scripture is "given by inspiration of God, to be the rule of faith and life," and that its authority "dependeth not upon the testimony of any man or church, but wholly upon God (who is truth itself), the author thereof."

Christians do not agree, however, on what is meant by "given by inspiration of God." Some subscribe to a biblical **literalism** that affirms that the very words of the Bible were given by God to the writers and that the words of the Bible are therefore the words of God. In looking for guidance on moral issues they turn to the Scripture for answers. Since in the Scripture there is no direct reference to certain contemporary issues, such as abortion or environmental pollution, they interpret those issues in terms of matters to which the Bible does speak. They do not consciously reject or reshape the teaching of the Scripture; rather, they interpret the issues in light of what they understand to be the clear teachings of the Bible. Other Christians say that the fundamental concepts or principles found in the Scripture came from God, but that the authors wrote the material in their own way. These Christians, acknowledging the influence of the culture out of which the writers spoke, try to sort out the eternal truths from that which reflects the circumstances of time and place. Grasping those principles, they try to apply them to the moral issues of our day. Still other Christians think that the Bible reports humankind's best thinking about God and about the life of human beings in God's world. They see in the Scripture a record of humankind's constant struggle with moral issues and of the constant growth in the human understanding of moral responsibility. They think of themselves as taught by the Scripture in making moral decisions but not limited by it.

Although today the idea of **inerrancy** is debated in some circles, most people who take the Bible seriously do not use that term. They accept the authority of the Bible because they believe that in some way the people who wrote it were acting under the inspiration of God. Yet they think of God, not the Bible, as the final authority. How we understand the Bible to have been inspired determines how we interpret it and how we attempt to apply its teachings to daily life. Although this is not the place to debate theories of inspiration and of biblical authority, the understanding of the Bible that is in the background of this study needs to be stated.

An important tenet of the Christian faith is the conviction that God works in history and that God's character and purpose are revealed in that work; that is, God is known by what God does. Although there are problems with such particularity, this doctrine affirms that in a unique way God chose the Hebrew people and worked through them, that the history of the Hebrew people is therefore God's self-disclosure, and that God's self-disclosure reached its climax in the person of Jesus. As the only record of that history, the Bible is a unique source for the knowledge of God. The Old Testament was written by people who participated in the unique encounter of the Hebrew people with God. The New Testament was written by people whose encounter with God was shaped by the person of Jesus Christ. Through what those people wrote, God continues to speak.

This encounter with God in history is a dynamic reality. God is not an object to be seen and described, as one might describe a building or another human being. God acts. God takes the initiative to reach out to people; God moves upon individuals and upon communities of people. God speaks not in words but in actions.

How then is the Bible related to what God says? In what sense is it "the word of God"? There are two important ways in which the Bible is understood to be the word of God. First, a word is a message that conveys a specific idea. The Bible is the word of God in the sense that it contains the insight of those persons who participated in the encounter with God in historical events. What they wrote conveys definite ideas to the reader, ideas concerned with what God has done in the world, with God's purposes for people, with God's will for the manner in which people relate to one another. Thus we have in the Bible more than a report of what certain individuals have thought and written. We have a report of God's self-disclosure. We have something that transcends the time and circumstances in which it was written. That statement does not make absolute the words of the Bible, its historical statements of fact, or its specific formulations of laws. It recognizes the cultural conditioning of the documents. It acknowledges the tendency of people to invoke divine sanction upon what is merely social custom. Behind that recognition of cultural conditioning, however, is the conviction that God spoke, that God was made known to people in a disclosure of truth and meaning that transcends time. What the Bible teaches, therefore, is taken seriously as a guide for life in the modern world.

Second, a word is a means of effecting an encounter between persons. To say that the Bible is the word of God is thus to say that it is a means by which people are confronted by God. A common expression of this idea is that "the living Word comes through the written word." Through Scripture one meets God and is required to decide how to respond. The truth of the Bible is not so much in the accuracy of its statements as in the reality of the encounter with God that it produces. Revelation is not something that long ago was made known to the writers of the Bible but something that today is made known to people who read the Bible.

What use, then, does Christian ethics make of the Bible? How are biblical teachings applied to contemporary issues? A negative statement must be made at the outset. We cannot go to the Bible to look up answers to all ethical questions. If we could do so there would be no need for decision making; the decisions would be already specified and we would only have to follow the outlined procedures. As a matter of fact, the manner in which the Bible treats some issues (warfare, the status of women, the attitude toward people of other ethnic groups, and so on) creates rather than solves moral problems for us. In addition, the Bible does not discuss many ethical issues of today: abortion, organ transplants, nuclear energy, environmental pollution, genetic engineering, behavior modification, and so on. We cannot, therefore, find in the Bible predetermined, clear-cut directives for all the problems of contemporary living.

The abandonment of this literalism, however, does not mean the abandonment of the Bible. Rather it means that the proper use of the Bible is a demanding undertaking. It requires the careful and honest use of the best methods of biblical interpretation. It requires the best use of critical thinking about the circumstances of our lives. And it requires imagination and intuition to apply ancient truths to present issues.

Thus far we have avoided the word *authority* in relation to the Bible because in popular usage it has a legalistic connotation. It conveys the impression that something is commanded and that what is commanded is obligatory. It is closely related to the idea of the will of God, which is right for people to follow and wrong for people to ignore. The word suggests that there is a power that compels, with which there is no give and take, from which there is no escape. It suggests that the actions of people are regulated and regimented. The God of such authority is feared but not loved, obeyed but not trusted. The subject of such authority is neither free nor responsive, but subservient. The best that such a person can hope for is to escape the notice of such immutable power.

That description, of course, is a caricature. The root meaning of the word *authority* is "one who is an author" or "an originator" or "a source." The literal meaning of the Greek word that is translated *authority* is "from one's own being." An authoritative declaration, therefore, comes from one who is the source, who has the power to originate. In this sense, authority is characteristic only of God, and it is not appropriate to speak of the Bible as authoritative. Whatever else is said about the place of the Bible in Christian life and thought, it cannot be a substitute for God.

In practical terms, however, people who accept the Bible as in any sense authoritative do so because they believe that in some way God inspired its writers. Their acceptance is a personal response, not merely a creedal affirmation. The Bible is authoritative only for those who acknowledge its authority, and it is significant for them only to the extent that through it they encounter the living God. For them it is not enough to say, "The Bible says," as if that were the last word. For them the authority is in the God who speaks through the Bible *to those who will hear.*

THE CHRISTIAN COMMUNITY

Because Christians do not exist in isolation from other Christians, the church plays a vital role in their moral decision making. The community of faith is the context within which one comes to know Christ and to live as his disciple. As members of the church, Christians face moral issues and the church helps to shape their moral judgments. This does not negate individual responsibility or imply that within the church there is a consensus on all moral issues. It does mean that the church provides invaluable resources that we may use in making sound moral decisions.

The Nature of the Church

The word *church* is derived from the Greek *kuriakon,* which means "of or belonging to the Lord." It therefore implies that the reality with which we are dealing does not belong to the persons who are a part of it. It is of divine origin, not human, and ultimately its destiny is not in the hands of people but of God. Whatever organizational structure a particular church might have, that church is ultimately responsible to God, and its obligation is to learn what is right and good and to make decisions on the basis of what it learns. The church is the instrument of God's continuing self-revelation and of redemption for the world.

For this reason, Paul's picture of the church as "the body of Christ" is significant (1 Corinthians 12:4–31; Ephesians 4:11–16). The term suggests that the church is a continuation of the incarnation. It is through a body that one acts, relates, accomplishes, and expresses oneself. It is difficult, if not impossible, for us to conceive of a person without a body. The body is how one lives in the world. When Paul called the church "the body of Christ," he was saying that through the church Christ lives in the world.

Another term that Paul used for the church is "the temple of God." When he wrote to the Corinthian Christians about their divisiveness, he asked, "Do you not know that you are God's temple, and that God's Spirit dwells in you?" (1 Corinthians 3:16). A temple, for the Hebrew people as well as for others in the ancient world, was the place where God dwelt. Although the Hebrews believed that God was present everywhere, they also believed that in a special and unique sense God resided within the Temple in the Holy of Holies. Paul was therefore saying to the Corinthians that they, the church in Corinth, were where God lived.

The idea of a covenant community is part of Paul's spiritual heritage. Having been reared Jewish and educated as a rabbi, he believed that God had chosen the Hebrew people, that through Abraham God had established a covenant relationship with them. The covenant phrase "I will be your God and you shall be my people" was engraved on the minds and hearts of the Hebrews. According to their faith, they lived in that relationship by the grace of God. In his letter to the Galatians and in his letter to the Romans, Paul insisted that the covenant relationship was continued with the disciples of Jesus. These disciples, said Paul, were the new Israel, the new people of God. To be a Christian was to be a part of that new covenant community, to learn from it, to be sustained by it, to be faithful to it.

A term often used to refer to the church is *koinonia*. This Greek word stresses the idea of community, of fellowship, of unity, of belonging together. Early in the book of Acts that idea is emphasized in the description of the life of the disciples when it is said that they "had all things in common" (Acts 2:44, 4:32–35). Paul often spoke of the body needing all its parts, and his strongest criticisms of the Corinthian Christians were for actions that divided and disrupted the fellowship. His strongest praise was for actions that demonstrated their love and care for one another. This unity of the church is not something that exists for its own sake and it is not something that people create. Rather it is created by the common commitment of believers to Christ. It is the unity into which they enter when they become disciples. Individuals may violate it or respect it, disrupt it or maintain it, ignore it or treasure it. But it does not draw its reality from them; it draws its reality from God in Christ.

The reality of *koinonia* overrides the differences among the churches. There are historic reasons for the origins of the denominations, and both organizational and theological concerns sustain them. Because of these differences some Christians have difficulty in worshiping with other Christians, in communicating with them, and in cooperating with them in the mission of the church. Yet most Christians have a feel for *koinonia* that cuts across differences, and they do not allow denominational divisions to stand as barriers to fellowship. They share a common Scripture, their heritages overlap, their worship influences one another, and they recognize a common concern for what is happening in the world.

The Function of the Church

Religion is basically the response of people to the God who created and sustains the universe and who is the source of life. The appropriate response is a spirit of awe, reverence, praise, and gratitude. All else in a person's religious experience grows out of that response. The basic function of the church, therefore, is to worship. When the community gathers for that purpose it provides some structure through which the believers may express this spirit. The structure itself is not of major significance, but the reverent encounter of the worshipers with God is. From a Christian perspective, to separate moral responsibility from this experience is to deprive morality of its foundations.

A second function of the church is to teach. The relationship of this function to morality is obvious. At the heart of the teaching work of the church is the Scripture. The early church acknowledged the Old Testament as its sacred writings. In time, it produced the New Testament as a means of sharing the faith with people who were not Christian and of instructing Christians in the content and the implications of their faith. The books of the New Testament were written for specific groups in specific circumstances, and their content was determined in part by the needs of the groups to which they were addressed. The truth of the gospel and its application to the fundamental issues of life that are reported in the New Testament have been used by the church from the beginning to the present. Although the church has taken many forms, although there has always been theological ferment, and although the problems of human existence have been expressed in many different ways, the church has used the Bible in the instruction of the faithful because it has found that it speaks to the human condition.

The teaching of the church, however, is not limited to instruction in the content of Scripture. The church looks at the world in light of Scripture. It makes judgments about the life of the world in both personal and social matters. It speaks what it understands to be the purposes of God for the world. In some groups the teaching takes the form of authoritarian pronouncements; in others it takes the form of recommendations. In some judgments the church is quite traditional and supportive of accepted ways of life; in others it challenges the commonly accepted stance of society and of government. Some judgments have been verified by history and some have been shown to have been incorrect. But always the church has taken seriously its responsibility to instruct its followers on matters of morality.

A third function of the church is to prompt the believer into action. No other agency is committed in quite the same way to making us ask questions about accepted practices. No other agency elicits quite the same fervor for righting wrongs, for building good relationships, for accepting personal responsibility. No other agency is quite so concerned about what is "good" except in a selfish sense, about what is "right" except in a legal sense. While much of the teaching of the church is indoctrination, much also is stimulation. The believer is made to examine moral issues and is helped to make moral judgments. Even when the moral judgment reaffirms a traditional view it does so on the basis of a sensitive conscience, and when it challenges a traditional view it does so within the commitment of the community of faith.

The Christian in the Church

Everything said so far about the nature and function of the church is related to the concept of community. As community, the church is a major part of the total context within which the individual makes decisions on moral issues. Because the church helps to define our environment, it plays a major role in establishing the conditions under which we think, feel, and act. This means that we make decisions with careful attention both to the teaching of the church and to the impact of the decision upon the life of the church.

All of this presupposes that we share in the life of the church. This sharing is not simply an organizational matter, although it is difficult to understand how one can share without some such involvement. Louis B. Weeks asks, "Can a Christian exist without belonging to a congregation? Theoretically, yes. One can remember communities of Christians or look forward to occasions of gathering and sharing. But in practice, the community is part and parcel of real Christian life" (*Making Ethical Decisions*, p. 33). We are not talking about the church in organizational terms but as a fellowship of believers. In that sense, the church existed before it was organized. Jesus said, "Where two or three are gathered in my name, there am I in the midst of them" (Matthew 18:20). Community with one another and with Christ is the reality of the church. Organization is merely the means of achieving certain results, of doing certain things effectively. It is necessary, but it is not the essence of the church. With that understanding, we may reaffirm the idea that Christian moral decisions are made within the context of involvement in the life of the church. This involvement is actual rather than formal. It is a matter of relationships—of feeling, of attitude, of personal identity. It is the acceptance of the reality that what happens to one happens to all, that what one does affects all. It is what is conveyed by Paul's exhortation to the Roman Christians, "Rejoice with those who rejoice, weep with those who weep" (Romans 12:15).

To come to God in Christ, then, is to enter into a spiritual fellowship with all other people who have had the same experience. There is no option, no possibility of doing the one but not the other. As there can be no such thing as a string with only one end or a coin with only one side, so there can be no such thing as relating to God without relating to God's other children. In practical terms, this means that although it is possible to be in spiritual fellowship with other Christians without being a part of a church, it is extremely difficult to do so. We learn from one another, we discern the will of God together, we make decisions in relationship with one another, and we act together. This does not mean that within the church there is no room for differences. It does not mean that the majority rules, that whatever conclusion the group reaches is right. Indeed, some of the most profound insights have come from persons who rejected the judgment of the group. It does mean, however, that the individual believer lives within the fellowship, is taught by the fellowship, is prompted into action by the fellowship, and acts with concern for the fellowship.

PERSONAL JUDGMENT

When we speak of Scripture and of the church, we speak of objective realities. Although their nature and characteristics and significance are open to discussion and interpretation, they are there to be observed, argued with, accepted or rejected. Personal judgment, however, is subjective and thus is more difficult to deal with. Here we are concerned with something that cannot be argued. Just as beauty is in the eye of the beholder, so judgment is in the mind of the judge. That is not to say that there is no objective reality to a judgment, no good or bad, no right or wrong. It is only to say that no one can argue with me when I say, "This is what I think." They can question whether my thinking is sound; they cannot question whether I think it. Here the responsibility falls ultimately on the individual. We shall consider three factors involved in making personal judgments: the sense of the leadership of the Holy Spirit, the use of human reason, and the prompting of the conscience.

The Leadership of the Spirit

The New Testament is full of references to the working of the Holy Spirit, and for Christians that work is vital to the process of decision making. The chief function of the Spirit, reflected both in the New Testament and in the continuing experience of the church, is that of teaching—not the imparting of information but the prompting of a person or a group of believers to move in a specific direction. Such teaching is the development of the conviction that "We ought to do this" or "We ought not to do that." It is the gift of insight, the creation of a sense of concern, the renewal of hope, the provision of inner resources for doing what needs to be done. It is the assurance of God's presence with the person or with the church and the evocation of reverence and awe.

Some Christians accept the idea of the leadership of the Spirit as the final authority. Many people who have difficult decisions to make pray for such leadership and often have a sense of assurance that their prayer is answered. For some the idea of the leadership of the Spirit is so related to daily activities that it is commonplace for them to speak of "being led" in the routine decisions of daily life. Historically the Quakers have given primacy to the "inner Light" as God's word to them. Although most Christians do not speak quite so freely of divine leadership, the idea is implicit in the concept of prayer. Prayer is communion with God in such a way that our spirits are opened up before God so that God can speak to us through the Bible, through the church, through other people, and through the workings of our own mind. This openness enables us to receive insight from God, a perspective on life, an understanding of what has happened and is happening, so that we say, "God has done this" or "God is moving me in this direction." Although we do not attribute to God's purposes everything that happens, we recognize God's working in our lives in all circumstances and we avail ourselves of God's grace as we deal with the issues of life.

The leadership of the Holy Spirit, then, does not usually come in the form of clear and explicit instructions for dealing with a specific problem. It comes more often in an encounter of a person with Person. By such an encounter one can move beyond preoccupation with self and into concern for neighbor. One's character and personality may be changed by a continuing encounter with the divine presence. That change will be reflected in deliberation on difficult decisions and in action in difficult circumstances.

The leadership of the Spirit, therefore, is not an occasional matter, a "first-aid" experience to which we resort when we are in trouble. It is a cumulative matter, one incorporated in all of our worship, both private and corporate. Certainly there are times when we are unsure about the best course of action and when we are therefore more aware of our need for help. Then we are most likely to ask for guidance and may be more responsive to God's presence. Yet unless we are always sensitive to God's presence, we are not apt to recognize divine leadership in emergencies. As we store our understandings of the will of God, our feelings of "oughtness," our experiences in which we feel good about what has happened—as we operate with an awareness of God's presence, in other words—we are responding to the leadership of the Spirit.

Many Christians think of this leadership in purely personal and individualistic terms. They think of God dealing with one person, so that what that one person is led to do might be quite different from what another might be led to do. Although it is true that God speaks to individuals and that individuals respond to God in their own way, we do not exist in isolation from a community. Our experience with the Spirit of God therefore comes within the context of the community of faith. We come to faith through the church, read Scripture as a part of the church, and worship as a part of the church. By the same token the Spirit leads us within the context of the church. Under the influence of the Spirit we may speak to that community of faith, but we will also listen to it. The Spirit may work through us to change the direction that the church is taking; the Spirit may also work through the church to change the direction that we are taking. To be led by the Spirit, in other words, is to share in the life of the community of faith.

To stress this community aspect of the leadership of the Spirit is not to minimize individual responsibility. Of course every person has to decide for himself or herself because there is no such thing as a group mind or a group will. The identity of a group depends, in part at least, on the individuals who make it up. But emphasis on this community aspect does mean that God's work in the world is not spasmodic or chaotic and that God does not lead people to ignore one another. Life in the Spirit entails awareness of the presence of God, a sense of fellowship with other believers, and a common commitment to the truth that unites people under the presence of God.

Human Reason

A second factor in making personal judgments is the use of the ability to reason. In most discussions of human nature it is assumed that this ability is the most distinctive human characteristic. Philosophical speculation, at least, always assumes that reason has the final word. The Christian ethical systems that we have discussed assume the possibility of the mind getting in touch with reality. Even when they talk about humankind being created "in the image of God," they approach the subject in rational as well as mystical terms.

Faith and reason are not incompatible. It is not correct to assume that philosophical systems are based on logic and religious systems on faith. Philosophers make assumptions, accepting the validity of certain concepts that they have not demonstrated to be true. Theologians attempt to state their faith in a logical, intelligible fashion. Both philosophers and theologians, therefore, operate on the basis of faith and employ the best logic they can command. Both faith and reason are functions essential to coming to grips with life.

Neither are faith and reason two supplementary ways of arriving at truth. A popular approach is to suggest that we go as far as we can through the rational method and then allow faith to take up where reason leaves off. As neat as that package is, it does no justice either to faith or to reason. It implies that the two approaches ask the same kinds of questions, that both seek factual information. It implies further that as the knowledge gained by the scientific method increases, the realm of the unknown diminishes and therefore the realm of faith diminishes. If this were true, we could expect that some day the need for faith would disappear completely. The fact of the matter is that a person who tries to come to grips with reality operates on the basis of both faith and reason. It is not a matter of using now one and now the other; the two are used at the same time. Just as the organs of one's body all function at the same time while the individual lives and works, so faith and reason function at the same time while the individual deals with meaning in life.

Thus it is not correct to say that we learn one thing by reason and another by faith, that we accept by faith what we cannot understand, or that one thing is subject to rational examination but another is not. It is not correct to say that by faith we accept without question a divine edict or that by reason we have the right to say no to God. In Christian ethics faith and reason combine in our effort to understand our place in the universe, to understand human obligation, and to respond to the divine in making decisions.

Reason is therefore a necessary faculty for making moral decisions. Reason is finite and limited; it is corrupted by sin; it is not the sole criterion for truth; it is not God. Yet like other human faculties it is a gift of God, a part of human nature, and therefore a vital part of the decision-making process. It serves as a critic of our attitudes, a restraint on our emotions, an evaluator of our mystical experiences. It analyzes and reflects on our personal encounters and our religious experiences and helps us relate them to the rest of life. As a sound theology uses reason to give coherence to religious experience and conviction, so a sound ethic uses reason to give coherent expression to a sense of value and duty.

To put this in simpler terms, reason is not the ultimate criterion of value and duty. That is the place of God. But reason is a God-given tool necessary for making sound decisions. Reason operates at its best when it is illuminated by faith; faith gives reason the impetus to search for meaning. Faith needs reason in its quest for truth. Reason functions as the instrument of faith.

The Conscience

The conscience is a third factor in the process of making personal judgments. The nature of conscience, and therefore its reliability as a guide, is an open question. The root meaning of the word *science* is "knowledge." The prefix *con-* means "together," "jointly," or "thoroughly." In this word the prefix intensifies the basic meaning. *Conscience*, therefore, literally means "a thorough knowledge." The term refers either to a sense of the moral goodness or blameworthiness of one's actions or to a feeling of compulsion to do what one judges to be good or right. It is a powerful feeling that "I should have done this" or "I should not have done that" or that "I ought to do this" or "I ought not to do that."

The fact of conscience seems to be universal. All people have feelings of guilt about certain actions and feelings of rightness about others, feelings of compulsion to act in a given way and feelings of aversion to acting in another way. There is, of course, no universal agreement on the specific content of conscience; that is, there is no action that all people agree should be done and no action that all people agree is wrong. The content of conscience varies from one culture to another and within a given culture from one individual to another. The disagreement, however, is not on whether one ought to act morally but on what that moral way is. The sense of compulsion is there and the sense of aversion is there. The only difference lies in what is compelled and what is prohibited.

The force of conscience is extremely powerful. Not always is it recognized, for it may operate through the subconscious. Not always is it rational, for one's mental processes often lead to different conclusions from those dictated by conscience. Yet it speaks in an authoritative voice, its dictates seem final, and the person who violates its demands suffers remorse.

The content of the conscience is learned within the context of our social relationships, just as other attitudes are learned. The formal institutions of the home, the school, and the church are major factors in the moral education of children and young people. The peer group is more important in the process than most of us are willing to admit, and the experiences we have in all of our social contacts have an impact. Two important facts about the content of the conscience emerge from this understanding of where it comes from. First, the consciences of individuals vary because their cultural settings vary. And second, a person's conscience is never permanently fixed but is constantly changing.

If the conscience is so unreliable, how can it have any significance for the Christian in the process of decision making? The conscience is like any other human faculty. It can be used or abused. It can be given direction or it can be allowed to take its content from all sources without discrimination. Conscience can best be understood as a call to wholeness. In terms of morality this means that conscience is the pull of the right and the good, an aversion to the wrong and the bad. It will be a valuable guide for the Christian to the extent that it matures through faith. The Christian can evaluate the conscience through the gathering of information, the study of Scripture, the sharing of the life of the *koinonia,* and the worship of God.

In *Conscience and Caring* Geoffrey Peterson discusses the mature Christian conscience, saying:

1. The Christian conscience is liberated by God's acceptance and forgiveness, which have been made humanly visible and tangible in Jesus Christ. No longer is the Christian devastated by guilt and fear of rejection.
2. The conscience is shaped and developed by sharing in the Christian community of faith, the chief social influence in the life of the believer. Although that community is the *koinonia* rather than the institution, the two are in fact closely related to each other.
3. The Christian conscience is continually growing. New experiences within the *koinonia* and within society at large bring new information, new insight, and new sensitivity.
4. Conscience is an integration of all of the various levels and facets of one's being. Rational and emotional factors are integrated with one another, and judgments about the past are integrated with decisions for the future.
5. The mature conscience calls us to care about our neighbor. Although caring can be interpreted simply as liking or having sympathy for or wanting to help, it means more than that here; it means the actual acceptance of another person into a warm personal relationship.
6. A mature Christian conscience accepts social responsibility. It works through organizations and responsibility to them. (pp. 68–75)

In the last resort, Christians follow the dictates of conscience, the compulsion to seek the good and the right. We feel an obligation to enlighten our consciences with the best information available, to bring to them all of the resources of the community of faith, and to listen for the voice of God rather than the voice of social structures. The prompting of an informed and sensitive conscience, then, we understand to be our response to God's gracious action in Jesus Christ and to God's continuing activity in the world around us. Although at times we will make errors of judgment about the best course of action, we respond to the divine imperative when we follow a conscience so directed.

QUESTIONS FOR DISCUSSION

1. In what sense do you "believe" the Bible?
2. What is the impact of generally accepted social views on the moral teaching of the church?

3. What is your responsibility when your moral convictions differ from what your church teaches?
4. What is the relationship between conscience and reason?

RECOMMENDATIONS FOR FURTHER READING

BROWN, MARVIN T., *The Ethical Process*. Englewood Cliffs: Prentice Hall, 1998.

HAUERWAS, STANLEY, and WILLIAM H. WILLIMON, *Resident Aliens*. Nashville: Abingdon, 1989.

KIDDER, RUSHWORTH M., *How Good People Make Tough Choices*. New York: Simon and Schuster, 1996.

SMEDES, LEWIS B., *Choices*. New York: Collins, 1991.

WEEKS, LOUIS B., *Making Ethical Decisions*. Philadelphia: Westminster, 1987.

5

Biblical Ethics

Because the Bible is a historical record of God's self-disclosure, one cannot understand the thought and work of the church without at least some knowledge of its teachings. Because the Bible is a collection of material written by many different people over a long period of time, the reader cannot expect to find in it a cohesive and consistent approach to moral issues. Yet because God continues to speak through Scripture, one who approaches contemporary issues from a Christian perspective must attempt to understand what God is saying there. Although biblical ethics and Christian ethics are not identical, each requires the other. The study of biblical ethics is an attempt to understand what Scripture teaches on moral issues. The study of Christian ethics is an attempt to look at the world in light of the Christian faith. Informed by biblical teachings, it examines specific issues and tries to determine the best course of action.

THE OLD TESTAMENT

One cannot understand the moral teachings of Jesus without knowing the context within which they were expressed. Jesus was a Jew, a member of a covenant community, an heir to a great tradition, and a student of a vital religious literature that he treasured and revered. This literature was produced over a long period of time by many different people living in widely varying circumstances. The writers vary a great deal in their viewpoints; they reflect differing values, express differing attitudes, and recommend differing procedures. The documents reflect significant development in thought from the earliest stage of Hebrew history to the latest.

General Characteristics of
Old Testament Morality

We begin with a number of general observations about the morality taught in the Hebrew Scriptures. First, in the Old Testament, morality and spirituality are mixed in such a way that they cannot be separated. Communion with God involves morality; morality is obedience to the will of God. No distinction is made between the sacred and the secular. All of life is lived in the presence of God; everything is sacred and thus subject to God's direction. Laws governing rituals of worship and laws regulating neighborly relations appear side by side. Hymns of praise to God stand next to songs urging righteous conduct. The prophets denounce people who try to separate piety from morality and assume that one can please God by the proper observance of rituals.

Second, Hebrew moral obligation is a part of the covenant relationship. The traditional covenant phrase is, "I will be your God, and you shall be my people." In historical terms this relationship was established by deliverance of the Hebrew people from bondage in Egypt. God broke the power of the Pharaoh, delivered the people at the Red Sea, gave them the Law at Mount Sinai, and established them in the promised land. In their national festivals they celebrate the mighty works of God. In their worship they commit themselves to obedience to God. In times of national strength and prosperity they give thanks to God, and in times of danger and disaster they anticipate that God will once again save them. For them righteousness consists of grateful obedience to the will of God.

Third, the Hebrew sense of moral obligation results from the understanding that God is the absolute sovereign. God is the ruler beyond whom there is no other authority. God is responsible to no one, but all persons are under the governance of God. Whatever God wills is right; whatever God forbids is wrong. One can never question God's decisions; one can never speculate on whether an action of God is just or unjust. God's doing it makes it just and right. God's commands, therefore, are to be obeyed not because they are inherently just or good but because God commands them.

Fourth, Old Testament morality is legalistic. What God requires and what God prohibits are specified in the Law. Law, however, is not arbitrary regulation but instruction. Its purpose is to teach the way of life that is right and good. It states in clear and precise terms what God expects, giving careful direction both for the rituals of worship and for moral obligations.

Fifth, Hebrew morality has a distinctive concept of justice. It does not begin with a concept of human nature but with the character of God. The central issue is not what people deserve because they are human but how God acts because God is God. Whatever God does is right or just. For people, to be just is to deal with other people in the way God deals with them. If justice were rooted in a concept of human nature, it would be rooted in something that is badly flawed. Human beings are sometimes good and sometimes bad, sometimes just and sometimes unjust. It is erroneous to assume that they are true to their nature when they are good and just but untrue to their nature when they are bad and unjust. Because God alone is constant, only God's character can be the standard of justice.

A final general characteristic of Old Testament morality is the centrality of the community. God deals not with individuals but with the Hebrew people. Of course individuals make up the community, and of course certain individuals appear either as leaders or as representatives of the group. Yet it is the nation with which God has established the covenant, not the individuals. It is the nation that is seen as obedient or disobedient, that worships God or that turns to other gods, that sins and is punished. This sense of corporate identity is a helpful way to deal with social evils. The problems of war, for example, are not merely the problems of David or of Hezekiah; they are also the problems of a nation trying to survive in a world of turmoil. The conditions of the poor are not merely the problem of individuals whose lands are unfertile, and the sins of the rich are not merely the problems of individuals who inherit large estates. They are also problems in the economic system itself. Apostasy is not merely the turning of some individuals to other gods; it is also the nation yielding to social pressures favoring the worship of other gods. The judgment of God, therefore, falls not on individuals but on the nation.

The Requirements of the Law.   The Law, or Torah (the first five books of the Old Testament), is a mixture of narrative and legislation. Because these books are not a single work produced in a short time but rather the product of a long and complicated process of writing and editing covering several centuries, the laws reported in them come from various periods in Hebrew history. The several codes found in the Law, therefore, reflect changing circumstances and reveal developing concepts.

The *Covenant Code* (Exodus 20:22–23:33) dates from the establishment at Mount Sinai of the covenant between God and the Hebrew people. It is notable for the high value it places on human life and for the absence of any distinction between classes of people. It reflects a concern for persons and an interest in protecting the rights of individuals to life, to well-being, and to the ownership of property. Attention is given to the protection of certain people who are often victimized in society: slaves, women, the poor, and orphans.

The best-known set of laws in the Old Testament is the Ten Commandments (Exodus 20:2–17, cf. Deuteronomy 5:6–21). These laws encapsulate the requirements of the Covenant Code, and indeed of the entire legal system of the Hebrew people. The first three commandments concern the human orientation to God: The first requires absolute loyalty to God; the second prohibits the use of unworthy means to worship God; and the third requires reverence and respect for the name of God. The fourth commandment sets aside the seventh day as holy to God; it provides for a basic human need, however, in setting that day aside for rest. The other six commandments concern fundamental human values and needs: The fifth provides for the stability of the family; the sixth protects human life; the seventh protects the sanctity of marriage and of the sex relationship within marriage; the eighth recognizes and protects the right to private property; the ninth protects the reputation of persons; and the tenth (which in some ways comes close to the meaning of the first) warns the individual against an attitude that disrupts relationships. The basic principles set forth in this code are fundamental both to personal conduct and to national life.

A much later set of laws, the *Holiness Code* (Leviticus 17–26) spells out the requirements of being a people, a people "cut off" or "separated" for the service of God. Dating from a period when the Hebrews were in danger either of turning to the gods of other peoples or of allowing their faith and practices to be influenced by an alien religion, the Holiness Code magnifies certain ritualistic practices that set the Hebrews apart. Yet because holiness cannot be separated from morality, the code requires a moral purity that is dictated by the God who is pure. The central statement of the code is Leviticus 19:2: "You shall be holy; for I the Lord your God am holy." The code intermingles ritualistic and moral requirements, as if they were all in the same category. In Hebrew thinking, that is exactly the case; all regulations come from the one God, to whom the Hebrews are bound by covenant. God is the source of that holiness that distinguishes the Hebrews from other peoples both in the way they worship and in the way they relate to one another.

The *Deuteronomic Code* (Deuteronomy 12–26) is entirely in keeping with the rest of the book of Deuteronomy. Its ideal is generally regarded as Hebrew religion at its best, and the morality specified in it is illustrated in the history recorded in the book. In both spirit and content it has much in common with the Covenant Code and the Holiness Code. It has, however, a stronger emphasis on love than is found in either of them. God's love for Israel is stressed, and Israel's love for God is revealed as the basic motive for obedience to God's Law. In speaking of God's love for Israel, the mighty acts of God in directing Israel's history are emphasized. In speaking of Israel's love for God, the note of gratitude is emphasized. The commands of God are given as commands of mercy and grace, and the people find that obedience to them is for their own good.

The other Old Testament books presuppose the ethical content of the Torah. Although the Law is not thought of as describing all moral obligations of the Hebrew people, other obligations cannot be discussed without reference to it. The Law is the starting point, the ingredient common to all Hebrew morality, the standard by which decisions can be made. Without it one cannot comprehend the ideal of the Prophets or of the Writings.

The Ethical Monotheism of the Prophets. Although there were precursors, the great prophetic movement among the Hebrew people arose in the eighth century b.c.e. A prophet is one who speaks for God, one who declares God's judgment on historical developments. The Hebrew prophets interpreted the nation's past and spoke to contemporary issues. They dealt with the future in terms not of prediction but of guidance. Usually appearing in a time of national crisis, they spoke in an authoritarian way, claiming, "Thus says the Lord." Unlike priests, they were nontraditional and noninstitutional. They were "raised up" for a specific purpose or time. Often using radical and even inflammatory language, and sometimes using dramatic symbolism, they called on the nation to return to God.

The message of the prophets is sometimes summed up in the term **ethical monotheism**. We are not sure how early the Hebrew people reached the understanding that there is only one God over the entire universe. We can be sure that they were tempted to worship other gods until long after the period of the Exile in the sixth century B.C.E. The prophets, however, proclaimed a faith in which monotheism was fundamental. After their work, any recognition of the existence of other gods was understood as inconsistent with Hebrew belief.

The ethical emphases of the prophets were the logical conclusion of their faith in the one God who ruled the whole earth. Proclaiming the oneness of God and functioning as the heirs of a long tradition of allegiance to the Law, they focused on those laws that regulated the relationships of people with one another. Each prophet began his work in response to some problem that he perceived in the life of the nation. In high places and in low, to persons in authority and to the ordinary people in the marketplace, the prophets announced "the word of the Lord." They dealt with economic injustice, militarism, sexual immorality, domestic violence, and corruption in government and religion. For the most part they did not attack religious institutions, but they observed the inconsistency between devotion to religious observances, on the one hand, and violation of the basic laws of God, on the other. For them the essence of religion was obedience to God's command that we strive for the good of our neighbors. The words of Micah (6:8) summarize this emphasis:

> He has told you, O mortal, what is good;
>> and what does the Lord require of you
> But to do justice, and to love kindness,
>> and to walk humbly with your God?

The prophets brought to the Hebrew faith an important insight into the universality and impartiality of moral law. As we have seen, the early Hebrews recognized a responsibility for one another but were limited in their sense of responsibility for other people. The prophets, however, with some exceptions, saw that the one God who rules the universe is concerned about the welfare of all people, makes the same moral demands of all people, and deals in the same way with all who fall short of these demands. This emphasis should not be overstated, for the exclusivist and nationalistic spirit of the Hebrews continued to be a problem in the time of Jesus. Some prophets, indeed, such as Nahum and Obadiah, were quite bitter in their attitude toward other nations. Yet the logical conclusion of the concept of monotheism is that God's love and concern are universal, and most prophets recognized that implication. The prophetic stress on God's demand for righteousness is complemented by an emphasis on judgment and punishment, on the one hand, and the possibilities of divine forgiveness, on the other. The prophets insisted that God would not permanently tolerate the immorality that characterized the life of the nation, and they generally saw as imminent some expression of divine wrath. At the same time, however, they saw God as gracious and forgiving, ready to receive the people when they repented. Because the prophets thought of judgment and restoration as taking place within the historical process, they believed the fortunes of the nation rose or fell on the basis of its response to God.

Only rarely did the prophets hint that God deals with the individual. It was almost always the nation that acted morally or immorally, the nation that God held accountable, and therefore the nation that suffered disaster or experienced restoration. Within the corporate identity there was individual responsibility of course. Yet it was the nation to whom God spoke through the prophets, and it was the nation that reacted to the message.

The Prudential Character of the Writings.   Among the Writings, only the **Wisdom literature** contains material explicitly concerned with morality. This literature is essentially down-to-earth, practical advice for everyday living. It applies the doctrines of the faith to the experience of the individual. Often it has the flavor of good, sound common sense, and often it seems to have no religious character. Although Hebrew wisdom is more like philosophy than anything else in the Old Testament, it does not engage in abstract speculation. Indeed, philosophy focuses on asking questions; Wisdom literature, in contrast, focuses on giving answers. Philosophy asks, for example, "What is wisdom?" This literature affirms, "The fear of the Lord is the beginning of wisdom."

The assumptions underlying this Wisdom literature are those of the Hebrew faith. God is the source of all that exists. God has established the moral and social order in which humankind lives. God is wise, just, and merciful; God is the defender of the poor and the helpless; and God is the guide to the righteous. The proper response of people to God is trust, reverence, patience, righteousness, kindness, and generosity. God will deal kindly with those who make the proper response and punish those who do not. The distinctive character of the morality of the Wisdom literature is its emphasis on individual responsibility. Its prudential advice is directed to the individual in the contemporary social setting. The virtues recommended and the vices cautioned against are individual ones. The good fortune that comes to the virtuous and the disaster that strikes the wicked are directed toward the individual. The statement of the virtues and vices is based on divine law;

actions are good or bad because of divine decree. The life of virtue or the life of vice is the choice of the individual, and the chosen way determines the consequences.

JESUS AND THE GOSPELS

Contemporary biblical scholarship deals with many critical questions about the gospel reports of the person of Jesus. Who were the authors of the gospels? Where did they get their information? What were their purposes in writing? How are the gospels related to one another? What can we know about the life of Jesus? To what extent do the gospels report accurately what he said and did? To what extent are they colored by the cultural setting? By historical developments? By personal memory and oral tradition? Long the subject of debate in the scholarly world, such questions were dramatically brought to the attention of the general public by the publicizing of the work of the Jesus Seminar in the mid-1990s (see Robert W. Funk and Roy W. Hoover, *The Five Gospels*). Although this is not the place to deal with these issues, we must indicate how the gospels are used in this approach to Christian ethics.

Each gospel affirms in its own way the incarnation of God in the person of Jesus. Each makes its own emphases on the nature and the meaning of the ministry of Jesus. Each reports his teachings and the events in his life in a manner consistent with its own approach, its own interests and concerns. All of the gospels, however, talk about the same person. The synoptic gospels often describe the same incidents and report the same teachings. Although a comparative study of the gospels raises questions about details, a picture of one person emerges. The character of that person is shown in the way he dealt with people and by what he taught. What we learn about him is central to our approach to Christian ethics because in one way or another Christian ethics takes Jesus as the norm.

Jesus and Judaism

Jesus was thoroughly Jewish. He lived in Galilee, a section of Palestine more free of Gentile influence than the rest of the country. He knew and revered the Scripture, he participated in the rituals of worship, and he accepted without challenge the fundamental doctrines of the Jewish faith. His sharp criticism of religious leaders was not directed against any basic tenet of Judaism but against the abuse of its concepts. He did not see himself as the founder of a new religion but as a devotee of the ancient faith of his fathers.

This faith undergirded the ethical teaching of Jesus. Like other Jews, Jesus made no distinction between ethical concepts and other religious teachings. He did not divide life into categories, calling this matter theological and that one ethical, this sacred and that secular, this a religious matter and that not. For him, all human activity was life in the presence of God, under the direction of God, subject to the judgment of God. The idea that one could be religious without being moral would have made no sense to him, nor would the idea that one could be moral without being religious. What made sense was the recognition of God's presence at all times and in all the affairs of life.

Jesus, then, shared the basic assumptions of Judaism: ethical monotheism; the covenant relationship with the Hebrew people; God's involvement in and control of the historical process; God's judgment on human sinfulness; God's mercy, loving kindness, and faithfulness, which worked for the redemption of humankind. Yet he was not just another rabbi. Standing within the Jewish tradition, he criticized it as it was practiced in his day. He was critical of many religious leaders, using sharp language to point out their pride and self-righteousness; their insensitivity to human need; their "hardness of heart," which kept them from acknowledging any failure. He differed from them in his attitude toward women, his rejection of nationalism and his openness to Gentiles, his consideration for little children, and his self-identification with the poor. He was different from them in his emphases: Rather than focusing as they did on matters of tradition, ritual, and personal purity, he stressed "the weightier matters of the Law"—justice, mercy, and faith.

Was there anything new in the ethical teaching of Jesus? Some writers insist that everything he said can be paralleled either in the Old Testament or in the words of other rabbis. Although the basic issue is not whether a teaching is new but whether it is true, Jesus did make distinctive emphases. Ideas that are found only rarely, if at all, in the teachings of other rabbis are frequent in his. One such point of emphasis is the worth of the individual. This emphasis is found in such teachings as the statement that "even the hairs of your head are all counted" and "you are of more value than many sparrows," as well as in the parables of the lost coin, the lost sheep, and the lost son. It is found also in the reports of his obvious respect for such differing persons as Nicodemus, a ruler of the Jews; Zacchaeus, the tax collector; the "woman in the city who was a sinner" who anointed his feet; and the "little children" whom the disciples were about to send away.

A second emphasis is God's love for all people. As we have seen, the neighborly obligations spelled out in the Law were usually interpreted to refer to other Jews. Although not everyone agreed with them, the Pharisees (who indeed had great influence with the masses of people) refused to have anything to do with Gentiles, thinking that contact with such people rendered them unclean and therefore unacceptable to God. Yet Jesus moved freely and naturally through Samaria, he visited the region of Tyre and Sidon, he spent time in the area of Caesarea-Philippi, he healed the child of a Roman centurion, and he made a Samaritan the hero of a story illustrating neighborliness.

A third emphasis in Jesus's teachings is flexibility in dealing with the Law and with religious institutions. At times many people, while insisting that they were obeying the requirements of the Law, bent it to achieve their own purposes (see Mark 7:9–13). The kind of flexibility that characterized Jesus, however, put human need above allegiance to institutions and to established procedures. With this kind of concern, Jesus could declare, for example, "The sabbath was made for humankind, and not humankind for the sabbath" (Mark 2:27).

Jesus's response to the eschatological element in contemporary Jewish thought is an inevitable issue in a consideration of his ethical teachings. In a broad sense eschatological thinking is found throughout the Old Testament, for the Hebrew people consistently thought of history as being in the hands of God and of the Hebrew nation as having a special place in God's purposes. They were convinced that both their present circumstances and their final destiny were in God's hands. In a stricter sense, Old Testament eschatology is apocalyptic in character. Apocalyptic material speaks of God's sudden intervention in history to bring an end to the present order and to create something new and different. This kind of eschatology characterizes those periods in Jewish history when the situation of the nation was most dangerous and there seemed little prospect of improvement. In a broad sense, therefore, eschatology deals with significant changes in the historical process in which a new and different state of affairs emerges. In a stricter sense it refers to the end of history and to the beginning of a different kind of existence for the people of God.

According to the apocalyptic literature popular in the time of Jesus, the end was close at hand. There was to be a period of distress for the faithful, a period of trials and woes in which they would be caught up in the struggle between the cosmic forces of good and evil. In the end, however, God would triumph and render a final judgment in which the wicked would be destroyed and the righteous admitted to an ideal life in a world to come. Using elaborate and often bizarre imagery, which probably was not intended to be taken literally, the writers speculated on when the events would take place and generally concluded that the time was at hand. As signs that the end was near they often cited the distress of their present circumstances. Born out of despair, their message is one of hope for the future. It expresses the confidence that God is in control, that God has a purpose that ultimately will be realized, and that God's faithful people will participate in the new order.

The extent to which Jesus shared this apocalyptic vision is debatable, and the extent to which it influenced his ethical teachings is not at all clear. Even if we take the apocalyptic discourse in Mark 13 at face value, we cannot be certain about how important this way of thinking was to Jesus. Clearly he assumed that the end was near (Mark 1:15, 9:1; Matthew 10:23). Yet he did not speculate about when it would occur; rarely did he speak of "the signs of the times," and he did not describe the glories of the new age. Once, when asked directly about the time of the coming of the kingdom, he replied that it would not be "with things that can be observed." Rather, he said, it was already present (Luke 17:20f.). Asked the same thing on another occasion, he merely cited his own actions (Matthew 11:2–6).

Jesus's vision of the future magnifies rather than minimizes the significance of the present. The present is not merely preparation for the future; it participates in the future. God's future for the world is salvation, and that future is being worked out in the present. God's victory is not a hope to be achieved in the future but a reality now being achieved. The appropriate response of the believer is a life of obedience. Citing Jesus's words "Take heed, watch!" Gunther Bornkamm says, "Jesus' message demands that we reckon with the future, lay hold on the hour, do not calculate the times. Those who wait in the right way are therefore called to fulfill the will of God now with all their might" (*Jesus of Nazareth*, p. 95).

If Jesus did not give up on this world, he intended his teachings to be significant for life in it. If he did not deal with the question of when the world would end, that question must not have been important to him. Certainty that the end is in the hands of God gives a quality of urgency to his message; disinterest in the date gives it a quality of timelessness.

Characteristics of Jesus's Ethical Teachings

Jesus's faith in God is the basis for his ethics. He stood within a great religious system and he did not think of himself as in any sense abandoning that faith. He talked about one's relationship to God and about the expectations that God has of people. He spoke of the love of God and of the desire to please God. Even when he was at odds with the usual interpretations of the faith, he worked in response to his understanding of his relationship to God. At the heart of his teaching is his urging that people act on the basis of their sense of oneness with God.

The teaching method that Jesus employed was quite different from that to which modern students are accustomed. Jesus was occasional rather than systematic. That is to say, he did not organize discourses on given topics and move progressively from an introduction through carefully ordered steps to a logical conclusion. His ideas on a given topic are not concentrated in one place in the Scripture to which one can turn to find out what he taught about God, human nature, sin, the family, or the state. Rather, his teachings were responses to specific situations, given to fit the circumstances. He answered questions. He reacted to criticism. He commented on what he saw. He dealt with problems that were brought to him. He visited synagogues and shared in the study of Scripture. He engaged in conversation with friends. This non-systematic approach, however, did not result in a fragmentation. Instead, there was an inner unity that resulted from Jesus's understanding of God and of God's purposes for people.

Jesus seems always to have talked in terms of the ideal pattern of human relationships. When one considers what he taught about love; about anger, lust, and greed; about divorce; and about any number of other matters, one is disposed to look for exceptions, asking, "But what if . . .?" If people find it difficult to control their actions and to live in accordance with the law, do they not find it impossible to control their emotions and attitudes and to live in accordance with the ideal that Jesus taught? Jesus was not insensitive to human frailty, however, and he always dealt redemptively with people when they fell short of the ideal. Yet he regularly and consistently held up the ideal as God's will for people.

Jesus was not legalistic. He stated fundamental truths and either explained them or illustrated them. Had he legislated, his teachings would have been limited in scope and in time. They might have helped people in his day, but they would have had no more permanent value than any other legalistic system. By presenting ideals of moral living, however, and leaving the application to his disciples, he offered something of permanent worth.

The fact that the teachings of Jesus are based on his religion means that they were intended for his disciples. At many points Christian ethics overlaps with other religious and philosophical systems. Truth is truth, regardless of who holds it or on what ground it is held. Yet from Jesus's point of view, value and duty derive their meaning from God. One who knows and loves God holds to those values and acknowledges those duties that one sees to be derived from God. God is the believer's reason for thinking and acting in a given way. What Jesus taught was directed to those who shared his understanding of the character and purposes of God. No other appeal for moral conduct was necessary and none was valid. Jesus's ethics does not commend itself to all people; it is a way of life to be accepted by people who know God.

Basic Concepts in Jesus's Ethical Teachings

The Kingdom of God.   The idea of the kingdom of God is central in the teachings of Jesus and basic to his ethics. Mark introduced his narrative of the ministry of Jesus's by summarizing his message: "The time is fulfilled, and the kingdom of God has come near; repent and believe in the good news" (Mark 1:15). Everything that Jesus taught about God and human beings, about the institutions of religion, about the practices of personal piety, and about morality must be understood in light of the concept of the kingdom.

Although the phrase "the kingdom of God" does not occur in the Old Testament, it was readily understood by Jesus's hearers. It denotes the rule of God over the covenant people, an idea that is at the heart of the Hebrew faith. The Hebrews believed that God had established a unique relationship with the Hebrew people, had given them the Law by which they were to live, and had guided their history to keep them close to God. Even when they were governed by a king, that king's power was not absolute; he was the agent through whom God governed. The Law, the Prophets, the Writings—all assumed the sovereignty of God and interpreted history as controlled by God.

With that understanding, the Hebrew people had a special way of interpreting events that other people would have regarded as disastrous. They believed that such events are God's judgment, intended to rebuke the people and to bring them back to the covenant. That judgment, however, is in no sense final; God is looking beyond the immediate situation toward the redemption of the people. No matter how bad a situation might get, there is always a future. In that light the subjugation of the Hebrews by the Romans, beginning in the first century before Christ, was viewed as a temporary problem. In due season God would expel the Romans and the nation would be free again. The nation would indeed be the kingdom of God.

But how would God free the people? Three views can be distinguished. Some people anticipated a military movement led by the Messiah, which would result in the restoration of national independence. This view is associated with the Zealots, a revolutionary group active at the time of Jesus. Others also anticipated the establishment of national independence but expected it to come as an expression of God's control of history. God would intervene not through a struggle by the people but by directing the affairs of the nations. For them, the best course was to hold on to one's faith by a strict observance of the Law. When the Law was perfectly kept, God would act. Still others cherished the apocalyptic hope, the expectation that God's intervention would take the form of a catastrophic end to the present order and the creation of a new one over which the Son of Man would rule.

One thing common to all forms of the expectation was the anticipation of a new order over which God would rule through the Messiah. The New Testament documents affirm that in Jesus the historic hope of the Hebrew people has in some way been fulfilled. They do not agree on how Jesus fulfilled that hope, and the effort to find in them a single, unified view of the person of Christ is doomed to failure. Yet they do come together in the proclamation that Jesus is the Christ, that his advent was the decisive event in the coming of the kingdom, and that people are called to affirm the new age by responding to him. In him, hope has become a reality; anticipation has become fulfillment. The claims of God on people are made not in terms of what is yet to be but in terms of what already is. The kingdom "has come near," the Scripture "has been fulfilled," and what all ages have longed to see is here. While we must deal with the futuristic aspect of the kingdom, it does not contradict the reality of what has occurred. The early church insisted that the new age dawned with the coming of Christ and that the disciples were already living in it. They were living with new duties, new loyalties, and new motivations derived from the reality of what had already occurred. A Christian sense of right and of good is rooted in this conviction that the new age has dawned.

Yet the disciples of Jesus knew that they were still living in the "old age." They worked at their trades, lived with their families, participated in traditional religious activities, dealt with neighbors, bought and sold in the market, saw Roman soldiers patrolling the land, and longed for a better world. Many of Jesus's teachings reflect his belief that the present order would soon end (Mark 9:1; Matthew 16:28; Luke 9:27). Some interpreters insist that all of his teachings were shaped by that belief. Although this is probably too broad a generalization, his teachings were certainly affected by it. His awareness that the completion of the kingdom was yet to come gave significance to what was happening in the old order and freed his disciples from bondage to it. In terms of ethical responsibility, this awareness focused allegiance beyond the social order but placed responsibility within it.

Such language may seem abstract. What is the significance of the kingdom of God, so understood, for ethical living? At the heart of the matter is the fact that citizenship in the kingdom imposes on the disciples of Jesus a radical demand for obedience. Those who accept God's offer of forgiveness and become a part of the community of faith have a responsibility to obey. Right and wrong, good and bad are defined by the purposes of God. Every way of acting must be evaluated not in terms of whether it is expedient or logical but in terms of God's will. The believer's decisions about day-to-day activities must be based on the sovereign will of God.

God's will is not a matter of whim or caprice. It is an expression of God's character and is therefore consistent, orderly, reliable, and predictable. In the thought of Jesus, however, there is no standard beyond God by which God's decisions can be evaluated; God is the standard by which all judgments are made. We understand right and wrong from our knowledge of God. Loyalty to God is what determines our decisions, and these decisions are good or bad, right or wrong, as they relate to God. The ethic of Jesus, then, is a radical demand for obedience to the will of God.

The Law.   Against the background of Jesus's teachings about the kingdom of God we may consider his attitude toward the Law. Because of who he was, he could not have ignored the Law. He was reared in a typically pious Jewish family. His hometown was located in the heart of the most traditional section of the country. His education, like that of other Jewish boys, was based on the Law and the prophets. The synagogue, where Scripture was taught, was an institution second in importance only to the home. The Pharisees, whose devotion to the Law was unmatched by any other group, had considerable influence in the area. Jesus's own teachings reflect a thorough knowledge of the Law and a deep appreciation for it. Saying that he had come to "fulfill" the Law, he regarded his teachings as fully harmonious with its fundamental truth.

Several generalizations may be made about Jesus's attitude toward the Law. First, he made a distinction between the Law of Moses and the rabbinic interpretations of it, which had come to have the force of unwritten law. He often challenged these interpretations, pointing out how ridiculous some of them were. He always spoke with respect, however, when he dealt with the Law of Moses. Even when he rejected a specific regulation, he gave what he understood to be the reason for that rule and stated his reason for rejecting it (see Mark 10:2–9).

Second, Jesus considered some parts of the Law more important than others. In general, he was more concerned about moral laws than about those having to do with rituals. His failure to say much about rituals may signify only that he was more concerned about something else. His comments on laws having to do with morality, however, clearly indicate that for him morality was a major concern. They show also that he did not have equal regard for all moral laws. He was quite demanding in his interpretation of the laws on murder, adultery, and false swearing, for example. Yet his comments on the law of divorce essentially negated that regulation (Matthew 5:21–32).

Third, Jesus stressed motive and intent more than overt action. His interpretations indicate that moral wrong lies in one's attitudes toward other people (Matthew 5). That emphasis is in keeping with his statement on prayer, fasting, and almsgiving, the traditional deeds of piety (Matthew 6). It is also in keeping with his comments on the widow's gift of her "two small copper coins" (Mark 12:41–44).

Fourth, Jesus broadened the scope of moral responsibility. Although the Law specifies certain duties of the Jews in their dealings with Gentiles, its primary concern is the duty of Jews toward one another. In traditional interpretation, Gentiles were given less consideration. Jesus, however, removed such ethnic limitations.

The Central Imperative.   The central imperative in Christian ethics is summed up in the term *obedient love* (see Ramsey, *Basic Christian Ethics*, p. xi). The word *obedient* ties Christian morality to the idea of the sovereignty of God, which we have discussed. Related to the morality expressed in the Law and in the prophets, and to a less extent in the Wisdom literature, it is tied in with Jesus's heralding of the kingdom. It associates the concepts of justice, right, duty, value, virtue, and calling to one's relationship to God. It gives an objective reference to the Christian life by suggesting that its requirements are established by God, not by human decision. It says, in short, that what is just, right, valuable, and good is discovered by human beings rather than determined by them. This does not mean that people do not make decisions about conduct; rather it means that these decisions must be made in light of the sovereignty of God. This is thoroughly familiar because it is completely in keeping with Old Testament morality.

Tying obedience to love, however, is not quite so familiar. It is not correct to say that the concept of love originated with Christian morality. The idea of the love of God is presented in the Old Testament as the basis for God's dealings with the Hebrew people. Both the Law and the Prophets cite

God's love, and Deutero-Isaiah forcefully and beautifully expresses its sacrificial and redemptive character. At best, the obedience of God's people is their response to God's grace. Yet nowhere in the Old Testament is love as central to the human response to God as it is in the thought of Jesus. For him, love is that response. Although he did not always use the word, the concept is never missing. Because he considered it central in one's response to God, he considered it central also in one's response to other people.

For us the word *love* has a variety of meanings. We love our parents and our brothers and sisters. We love our boyfriend or girlfriend. We love our roommate. We love certain kinds of music or certain kinds of food. We love our dog. We love to work. All of these uses of the word convey specific attitudes or dispositions. They describe normal and legitimate relationships. None, however, is in the same category as love for God, and none is in the same category as love for one's neighbor or love for one's enemy. No lengthy discussion of Greek terms is necessary at this point. It is enough to say that in Greek the term *philia* is used for comradely affection, *storge* for a sense of family unity, and *eros* for desire or for response to the beautiful. *Agape,* rarely used in other Greek literature, is the distinctive New Testament word for that attitude that Jesus considered to be the appropriate relationship between people and God and between people and other people. Its meaning can best be explained by an examination of its use. Since here we are discussing the ethical teachings of Jesus, we shall limit our consideration to the use of the word in the gospels.

One of the best passages for understanding the concept of *agape* is Matthew 5:21–48 (cf. Luke 6:27–31). After having commented on several other laws, Jesus said, "You have heard that it was said, 'You shall love your neighbor and hate your enemy'" (v. 43). Neither Leviticus 19:18, which he was citing, nor any other Old Testament law says that one should hate one's enemy. The words in Leviticus, however, stand in the context of a statement of the Israelite's obligations to fellow Israelites. One who did not wish to do so would certainly not be compelled to find there any obligation toward non-Israelites. Other Old Testament passages do permit hostility toward one's enemies. Thus the latter part of Jesus's "quotation" is an accurate summary of generally accepted attitudes. Jesus challenged that common hostility toward outsiders by saying, "But I say to you, love your enemies." In his view one has the same obligation to an enemy that one does to a neighbor.

On the basis of this passage, several things can be said about the character of love. First, love is the opposite of hatred. As hatred is divisive, love is a unity-creating force. Jesus's comments on the law against murder (Matthew 5:21–26) bring further insight into this idea. Anger and contempt fall into the same category as hatred and therefore may also be seen as opposites of love. Second, love is active, expressing itself in some positive way. Jesus urged his disciples to "pray for" and to "greet" their enemies. In the same way, in his comments on the law against murder he spoke of actively seeking reconciliation. Third, love is an impartial concern for other people, making no distinction between the good and the bad, the just and the unjust. This is the character of God's love, which serves as the pattern for the disciples of Jesus. This characteristic leads to a fourth, which is that love is universal. If God loves both the just and the unjust, the evil and the good, then God loves everyone. Jesus concluded this observation by cautioning his disciples to be perfect as God is perfect. The word *perfect* means "complete" or "mature." Jesus's disciples are therefore to be complete in their love, loving all persons.

In another brief statement in the Sermon on the Mount Jesus speaks of love in terms of service: "No one can serve two masters; for a slave will either hate the one and love the other, or be devoted to the one and despise the other" (Matthew 6:24). This verse is a statement about one's priorities and therefore about one's relationship to God. It uses the phrase "be devoted" as a synonym for *love.* To be devoted is to cling to, to give oneself to. This statement calls to mind the ancient Hebrew conception of devotion as setting a person or an object aside for the service of God.

The most dramatic statement of the centrality of love in the teachings of Jesus is found in the so-called twin commandments: "'You shall love the Lord your God with all your heart, and with all your soul, and with all your mind.' This is the greatest and first commandment. And a second is like it: 'You shall love your neighbor as yourself.' On these two commandments hang all the law and the prophets" (Matthew 22:37–40; cf. Mark 12:28–34 and Luke 10:27–37). This is Jesus's answer to the frequently discussed question, "Which commandment is the greatest?" Many rabbis looked for ways to sum up basic religious obligations in one or two simple, easily remembered statements. Jesus's answer is such a summary.

Jesus's summary is a skillful blending of Leviticus 19:18 and Deuteronomy 6:4. Although Jesus was not the first to make this combination, for him it summarizes the essence of religious obligation. In it the inseparability of love for God and love for one's neighbor stands out. The question asks for one commandment; the answer cites two, as if they were two sides of the same coin, as if one could not exist without the other. A right relationship with God entails a right relationship with one's neighbor. A right relationship with one's neighbor is based on a right relationship with God. The significance of this concept cannot be overemphasized. The way one relates to a neighbor is determined not by the worth of the neighbor but by the character of God.

Another word of great importance in this statement is *neighbor.* While acknowledging the obligation to love one's neighbor, one may limit responsibility by restricting its definition. Jewish people in Jesus's day used the word much as we do: Our neighbor is someone who lives near us who is like us, someone of the same race, class, religion, education, socioeconomic status, and so on. In Luke's report of this conversation (10:25ff.), Jesus answered the question, "Who is my neighbor?" by telling the parable of the good Samaritan (vv. 30–37). Although that story offers no definition, it removes all limitations from the obligation to love. With this story Jesus suggested that love recognizes no distinctions between people.

Another important understanding of the nature of love is brought out in the action of the Samaritan in the parable. One gathers that he did not pause to consider what his duty might be. Rather he reacted spontaneously and quickly to the need of the victim. The word *compassion* describes his feeling for the victim, and the words that follow describe his efforts to relieve the situation. To love is to do something. In the New Testament the word *love* is almost always a verb, almost never a noun.

The Character of the Disciple.   Jesus was not a systematic teacher of theology or of ethics. He did not engage in the kind of discourse that may have characterized the teachers of his day and that certainly has characterized Christian thinkers since. He would not have been at home with Greek philosophers, who spent a great deal of time discussing the virtues to be cultivated and the vices to be avoided. Rather he wanted to bring people into a relationship with God that would reshape their character. He assumed that the kind of person one is determines the kinds of thing one does: "Either make the tree good, and its fruit good; or make the tree bad, and its fruit bad; for the tree is known by its fruit" (Matthew 12:33). "Figs are not gathered from thorns," he said, "nor are grapes picked from a bramble bush" (Luke 6:44). "For out of the abundance of the heart the mouth speaks" (Matthew 12:34). While he did not assume that a good person automatically does good things, he did assume that character determines conduct.

The character formation on which Jesus focused is not simply an individual matter; a person does not enter into a solo relationship with God. Jesus never seemed to believe that one could know God apart from a community of faith or that one could maintain a relationship with God while isolating oneself from other believers. Although he did not discuss this matter, he lived in community with his disciples and invited others to join them. He was not concerned merely with the conversion of the individual, in other words, but with people living and functioning as a part of the family of God. While individuals made their own decisions about their involvement in the community and their life of faith, they made them within the context of a fellowship.

The key question for conduct, therefore, is this: What kind of person are you? Jesus never described an ideal person. Yet he consistently recommended certain ways of thinking and feeling, ways of acting, ways of relating to other people, ways of regarding oneself, and ways of regarding God. As we read the Sermon on the Mount and the other collections of the teachings of Jesus, as we read his parables, the reports of his conversations, or his scattered comments, we discover certain themes and begin to get a feeling for the kind of character that can be designated "Christian."

One quality of character that Jesus stressed is *humility,* the way in which people must see themselves before God. It describes their response to the awareness that they live in the presence of God. It recognizes an ideal that is beyond them, that they have not yet attained and may never attain. Recognition of one's failure before God leads to a sober assessment of one's status in relationship to other people. The person who is humble before God, according to Jesus, cannot be arrogant with other people. The humble person does not seek preferential treatment, does not impose on other people, does not presume an unwarranted status. The humble person does not make claims about personal achievement or personal abilities. When Jesus's disciples asked about greatness in the kingdom, he replied, "Whoever becomes humble like this child" is the greatest in the kingdom of Heaven (Matthew 18:1–3).

A second quality of character that Jesus praised is *sincerity.* Although he did not use the word *sincere,* as far as the record goes, he often spoke of a life that can stand up under the closest scrutiny. Frequently he condemned hypocrisy, deliberate deception, the pretense that you are one thing when you know you are something else. He spoke in harsh terms of certain scribes who "devour widows' houses and for the sake of appearance say long prayers" (Mark 12:40). He talked about people who honestly thought that they were correct when they were self-deluded. "If then the light in you is darkness," he warned his disciples, "how great is the darkness!" (Matthew 6:23). He denounced the Pharisees who blindly stressed minor matters and neglected major ones (Matthew 23). In contrast, he urged his disciples to be openly and simply honest (Matthew 5:33–37), "pure in heart" (Matthew 5:8), generous (Matthew 5:42), and "as wise as serpents and as harmless as doves" (Matthew 10:16).

A third quality of character that Jesus often praised is *faithfulness.* He insisted that people are stewards of possessions entrusted to them by God and that they owe unlimited service to God. He said that "whoever is faithful in a very little is faithful also in much; and whoever is dishonest in a very little is dishonest also in much" (Luke 16:10). Even his eschatological teachings emphasized not the time of the end but the need for faithful service until that time comes. Faithfulness was for Jesus a quality of character that reflects one's basic loyalty to God.

The Example of Jesus

"The imitation of Christ" is an ideal that has loomed large in the minds of the disciples of Jesus throughout the history of the church. In spite of the fact that a discovery of the historic Jesus is extremely difficult, if indeed it is possible at all, most Christians accept as their model the portrayal of Jesus that they find in the gospels. R. E. O. White says that "the imitation of Christ is, in truth, the nearest principle in Christianity to a moral absolute." He continues,

> The law of love may be held a second Christian absolute: but without the example of Jesus, the law remains an abstract form rather than a concrete ideal, while without devotion to the person of Christ the law lacks incentive and enabling moral energy. When all allowance is made for varying interpretation, the imitation of Christ remains the heart of the Christian ethic. (*Christian Ethics,* p. 109)

What we learn from the example of Christ reinforces what we learn from his teachings. There is no inconsistency, no failure on his part to be true to the insight that he has voiced. He announced the coming of the kingdom of God and he lived as one joyfully acknowledging the sovereignty of God. Proclaiming love as the fulfillment of the Law and the prophets, he expressed that love in his way of life. Without being self-consciously good, he exemplified in his own life the qualities of character that he urged upon his disciples.

The example of Jesus conveys one idea that is more implicit than explicit in his teachings: Every individual is of infinite worth and is to be treated with respect. The reports of his work show that he made no distinctions among people. Men and women, Jews and Gentiles, righteous people and sinners were all respected as individuals, as people with whom God was concerned. Jesus did not deal with all people in the same way; what he did was conditioned by circumstances and by the responses of individuals. But never did he act as if anyone were worthless or beyond God's concern. He treated the rich young ruler and the blind beggar with equal respect. He dealt graciously with a Pharisee who invited him to his home for a meal and with the woman of the city who entered that same house and anointed his feet. He was concerned about people who fell through the cracks of society: widows, little children, lepers, demoniacs. Although he did not idealize them, neither did he turn aside from them. He looked on them all as children of God.

For Jesus, life in response to God was a life of active effort to meet the needs of people. The word *compassion* is often used to describe his emotional reaction to people in distress—the sick, the poor, the social outcast, the moral reprobate—and he always tried to help them. If there is a keynote for his ministry, it is Isaiah 61:1–2, which he read and discussed in a service in the synagogue in Capernaum early in his ministry:

> The Spirit of the Lord is upon me,
>   because he has anointed me
>   to bring good news to the poor.
> He has sent me to proclaim release to the captives
>   and recovery of sight to the blind,
>   to let the oppressed go free,
> To proclaim the year of the Lord's favor. (Luke 4:18–19)

The story of Jesus's career is the story of an active ministry to the kind of people described in this passage.

THE ETHICAL TEACHINGS OF PAUL

Paul identified himself completely by his relationship to Jesus Christ. He thought of Jesus as the long-awaited Messiah, though his understanding of messiahship was quite nontraditional. He talked about Christians as the New Israel, and he used Jewish Scripture freely to bear witness to Jesus as the

Christ. He did not see himself as the creator of a new system of theology or of ethics but as a proclaimer of the gospel of Jesus as the Christ.

Rather than reporting the facts of Jesus's ministry, Paul discussed the implications of the gospel for Jesus's disciples. As he faced problems and dealt with issues, he tried to make the kinds of judgments that he thought Jesus would make. Whether he was in fact consistent with the spirit of Christ can be debated. Whether he added to the teachings that he believed came from Jesus is an open question. Whether he was entirely free of the legalism against which he protested is not at all clear. For his moral judgments he was clearly more indebted to his Jewish background than he realized. Yet there can be no doubt that he believed that everything he taught was true to the gospel. For him, it was Jesus and not the Law that was basic in morality.

Theology and Ethics

For Paul, as for Jesus, the starting point in thinking about human life was the sovereignty of God. This fundamental Hebrew conviction was the basis for all his thinking about the place of human beings in the world and about human responsibility. God is the creator, the sustainer, and the judge. God is the one who makes demands of people, who gives people the power to meet those demands, and who stands in judgment over them for their failures. This concept of the sovereignty of God shaped all of Paul's statements about moral obligation. Although he gave full play to human responsibility for decision making, Paul never left the impression that he thought that human decision determines the good or the right. Good and right are rooted in the sovereign will of God.

Paul believed in the universality of sin. His statement that "all have sinned and fall short of the glory of God" (Romans 3:23) affirms his deep-seated conviction that no one has escaped the corruption of evil. He thought of sin as a basic alienation from God, a failure to be true to the insight that one has into God's purposes and demands. This alienation results in a wide variety of actions that demonstrate people's self-love, their determination to do what they wish rather than to obey the will of God. This self-love is so deep-seated that no individual can overcome it. According to Paul, therefore, human beings are victimized by their own sinful nature. Although he talked about powerful spiritual forces of evil at work in the world, he did not think of them as being responsible for sin. It is people themselves who are responsible.

For Paul, Christ is the solution to this human predicament. In Christ God acts to redeem people. In Christ God takes the initiative to make people true sons and daughters of God. For Paul the incarnation, the life of Christ, the death on the cross, and the resurrection constitute one redemptive act. In all that he was and did, Christ was the revelation of God's love, the work of God in redeeming people. Paul summed up Christ's work in his affirmation that "in Christ God was reconciling the world to himself" (2 Corinthians 5:19).

This new life becomes a reality in the person who responds in faith. Paul insisted that one is saved "by grace through faith." Jews, who had the Law, and Gentiles, who did not have the Law, he thought, were equally helpless. Because Jews and Gentiles were on an equal footing in their need, they could both be reconciled to God in the same way, by accepting God's love offered in the person of Christ. They could do nothing to effect their salvation; salvation came to them as the gift of God's grace. The appropriate human response to God's initiative is to acknowledge one's sinfulness and helplessness and to throw oneself on the mercy of God. One who does so is assured of God's forgiveness and enters into a new life.

This new relationship to God, according to Paul, entails a new way of living. Believers are not merely forgiven for their sins; they are also given the power to overcome sin. Paul constantly urged his readers toward Christian conduct, saying to them, in effect, "You *are* Christian; now *act* like it." He urged them to resist evil and to do good, to work out their own salvation. Sometimes he was quite specific in his judgment about what they should or should not do, and at other times he spoke in more general terms. Always he conveyed a sense of moral urgency, however, as if one constantly has to make decisions. His understanding of new life in Christ is the framework for his ethical teachings.

An Ethic of Responsible Freedom

This new way of living into which the Christian enters requires the responsible use of freedom. Paul's statement that "you are not under law but under grace" (Romans 6:14) sums up his understanding of how one is saved, and it has significant implications for the moral life. If we are not under the Law in receiving God's gift of salvation, are we then under the Law in moral obligation? Once we have been saved without obedience to the Law, does the Law dictate how we are to act?

For Paul, the moral standards expected of the disciples of Christ were higher than those expressed in the Law. Even as he insisted that the believer is free from the Law, so also he insisted that freedom should not be used as "an opportunity for self-indulgence" (Galatians 5:13). He talked about "the works of the flesh" as "fornication, impurity, licentiousness, idolatry, sorcery, enmities, strife, jealousy, anger, quarrels, dissensions, factions, envy, drunkenness, carousing, and things like these." In contrast, "the fruit of the Spirit is love, joy, peace, patience, kindness, generosity, faithfulness, gentleness, and self-control" (Galatians 5:19–23). Paul rejected the idea that Hebrew rituals were obligatory for Christians, but he did not actually discuss the relationship of the Christian to the Old Testament moral laws. Had he been asked to do so he probably would have remained consistent and argued that they were not obligatory either. Yet he was convinced that certain ways of acting are inconsistent with the new life of the believer and that other ways of acting are a natural consequence of one's relationship to Christ (cf. Ephesians 4:22–5:14; Colossians 3:1–17). He was not hesitant to specify which was which.

In most of his letters Paul spoke on moral issues, some personal and some social. He said more about such matters in his letters to the Corinthians than in any other, perhaps because of the special problems faced by Christians in that large city, notorious for its immorality. On the basis of what he said, we may state several considerations that guide the Christian in responsible decision making.

Respect for the Church.   Paul had a profound respect for the church, as indicated by his figures of speech referring to it: the body of Christ, the temple of God, the household of faith, the household of God. He stressed the dependence of the members of the church on one another and the importance of the contribution of each person. In a passage dealing with divisiveness within the church in Corinth, he appealed to the Christians there to overcome their differences. He asked, "Do you not know that you are God's temple and that God's Spirit dwells in you?" (1 Corinthians 3:16). Although he did not say, "Surrender your own judgment to the church," he did say, "Remember that what you do affects the temple of God."

Respect for Yourself.   When one makes decisions on the basis of a legal system, one asks, "Is there a law against it?" If there is no law, presumably the conduct in question is legitimate. Because Paul insisted that "we are not under law but under grace," some people concluded that moral considerations are irrelevant and that any conduct is permissible. Their view is summed up in the statement, "All things are lawful for me." Paul suggested, however, that another affirmation should be used as a guide in moral issues: "Not all things are beneficial" (1 Corinthians 6:12). Thus we might ask, "What good results are to be expected from this way of acting?" If results are considered good because they move us toward a desired goal, what is the goal of the Christian life? While the goal can be described in various ways, our answer must deal in some way with our relationship to God in Christ, to our commitment to the will of God as that will is known in Christ.

To this suggestion Paul added another affirmation: "I will not be dominated by anything" (1 Corinthians 6:12). In pondering a moral issue we might therefore ask, "Does it tend to get control of me, to dominate my actions?" If so, it endangers the very freedom that is so important to us.

Applying to sexual activity their line of reasoning that all things are lawful, some people had apparently concluded that any natural conduct is legitimate (1 Corinthians 6:13). Paul rebutted that idea by affirming that for the new life of the Christian, "immorality" is neither natural nor normal. While he had other comments about extramarital sexual activity, his basic position was that it is not appropriate to the new life in Christ. His concluding argument was, "Or do you not know that your body is a temple of the Holy Spirit within you, which you have from God, and that you are not your own? For you were bought with a price; therefore, glorify God in your body" (1 Corinthians 6:19–20).

Respect for Fellow Christians.   Paul's understanding of the church as the body of Christ and as a fellowship of believers involved a sense of concern and respect for the members of that fellowship. While he did not think Christians were responsible only for fellow Christians, he believed that such a special relationship entailed a special responsibility. Much of what he said had to do with the way Christians deal with one another. In 1 Corinthians 8, he concluded a discussion of a divisive issue in the church, whether a Christian could eat meat that had been offered to an idol: "if food is a cause of their falling, I will never eat meat, so that I may not cause one of them to fall" (8:13). He did not intend to surrender his conscience to anyone else, as he made clear in the next chapter. He was unwilling to make rules for anyone else and he was unwilling for anyone else to make rules for him. But his sense of responsibility for his fellow Christians was a principle by which he made decisions about what he would do. The church in Rome had a similar question: How do you deal with the fact that members of the church reach differing conclusions about what is appropriate personal conduct? Insisting that people ought not to pass judgment on one another, Paul said, "it is good not to eat meat or drink wine or do anything that makes your brother or sister stumble" (Romans 14:21). This is not the place to discuss eating meat or drinking wine. It is important, however, to stress the concern for what happens to a brother or sister.

The same consideration is found in Paul's exhortation to Christians to "love one another" and "care for one another." The "strong ought to put up with the failings of the weak" (Romans 15:1). Christians are to "bear one another's burdens" (Galatians 6:2). They are to pray for one another, to share with one another, to exhort one another, to "rejoice with those who rejoice and weep with those who weep." They are even to suffer wrongs from a fellow Christian rather than seek justice in the courts (1 Corinthians 6:7–8). They are to submit themselves to one another out of reverence for Christ. Their actions, therefore, are to be determined, in part at least, by how they will affect fellow Christians.

Respect for Outsiders.   Paul's basic objective for people who were not Christian was their conversion to Christianity. For him, a Christian's chief responsibility for other people was the presentation of the gospel to them. If anyone was overtly hostile to them, Christians should not retaliate. He urged the Roman Christians, for example, to "bless those who persecute you," not to "repay anyone evil for evil," to "live peaceably with all," to forego vengeance, and even to give food and drink to the enemy who needs them (Romans 12:14–21).

An Ethic of Love

Paul was faithful to the teachings of Jesus in making love the central imperative. He said, "Owe no one anything, except to love one another; for the one who loves another has fulfilled the law" (Romans 13:8). He stated the same idea in Galatians 5:14: "For the whole law is summed up in a single commandment, 'You shall love your neighbor as yourself.'" These exhortations echo Jesus's statement that all the Law and the prophets depend on the requirement of love for God and love for neighbor (Matthew 22:37–40).

In several significant passages Paul probed the deeper meaning of love, which in his judgment was at the heart of the life of the Christian. The best-known such passage is 1 Corinthians 13. This magnificent poem, unlike most of Paul's writings, is a polished literary product. The first three verses speak of the value of love, verses 4 through 7 speak of the characteristics of love, and verses 8 through 13 speak of the permanence of love. The second section (verses 4 through 7) most fully tells what love is like. An examination of the things that Paul says love does, and of the things that he says love does not do, brings out the fact that love creates and maintains a unity between people. The works of love draw people together; the things that love avoids separate them.

Romans 12 is another important chapter in which love is characterized. This passage begins a section in which Paul gave practical advice on several matters of conduct. Although he did not use the word *love* until he reached the middle of the chapter, its use there makes it clear that this is the concept he was discussing in the entire passage. In this chapter he talked about the importance of humility, of concern for the unity of the fellowship, of diligent service to one another, of sharing, and of nonretaliation. Within that broad and unorganized collection of exhortations Paul said: "Let love be genuine; hate what is evil, hold fast to what is good; love one another with mutual affection; outdo one another in showing honor" (Romans 12:9–10).

Most of what Paul said about love refers to the relationship of Christians to one another. For him it seemed self-evident that Christians belong to one another and have a responsibility for one another. If love of fellow Christians did not actually characterize the churches, it certainly should do so. Sometimes, therefore, Paul praised churches because they showed this quality (see 1 Thessalonians 4:9). At other times he rebuked them for not acting on the basis of love (see 1 Corinthians 1–3). At all times he spoke as if those who acted in love for fellow believers were acting in the spirit of Christ. So significant was the church for him that he thought one of the worst things a Christian could do was to act with disrespect for it. In rebuking the Corinthians for the way they were celebrating the Lord's Supper, he exclaimed, "Do you show contempt for the church of God and humiliate those who have nothing?" (1 Corinthians 11:22).

An Ethic of a New Life

For Paul the essence of ethical behavior was the new life in Christ. He was convinced that in Christ people enter into a new relationship with God, that they become new persons as a result of this relationship, and that as new persons their lives are different. As we have seen, he cited certain actions as "works of the flesh" and others as "fruit of the Spirit" (Galatians 5:22). By using these terms he implied that people are fully responsible for the evil they do but that they deserve no credit for doing good. The new way of life of the Christian is the result of faith. As God's work in the person, it is the natural, expected expression of Christian character.

At the same time, however, Paul constantly dealt with moral issues and urged believers to act in a Christian way. The members of the church at Corinth, for example, were at odds with one another over their allegiance to different leaders. They were going to court to settle issues between them. They were indifferent to a case of sexual immorality within their fellowship. Paul felt compelled to instruct them in the right way of dealing with these matters and to urge them to act properly. Again, the fact that he warned the Galatians about the sins of the flesh suggests that they were having difficulty at that point. His words to the Ephesians about "fornication and impurity of any kind, or greed" and "obscene, silly, and vulgar talk" (Ephesians 5:3–4) suggest that their lives were not entirely above reproach. His plea to the Colossians to "clothe" themselves with certain characteristics and to "let the peace of Christ rule in your hearts" (Colossians 3:12–17) suggests that they needed prodding in that direction. Paul recognized that a new way of living was not an automatic consequence of becoming a Christian.

For Paul, therefore, a moral life was a consequence of Christian faith and was possible only within the context of the Christian community. Christians, he believed, always have to struggle with the forces of evil and therefore with pressures toward immoral conduct. Trying to be faithful, they are nevertheless always vulnerable. Apart from the grace of God, he believed, they can have no success in the effort to be moral. Realistic enough to recognize failure, Paul talked about the continuing need for forgiveness. Recognizing the possibility of success by the grace of God, he continually urged people to rely on the Spirit of God. He knew that the struggle would go on as long as time lasted, and he anticipated the final victory of good over evil only at the end of time. The anticipation of that final victory, however, was not an escape into otherworldliness but a reason for faithfulness in the present struggle. For him, therefore, the moral struggle was an essential ingredient of faith.

Far from being concerned only with the world to come, salvation was for Paul essentially a moral concept. Although it is a gift of God's grace and in no sense is earned, it is quite directly related to conduct. Paul considered it sheer nonsense to think that what one does is unimportant. One who is justified (i.e., a Christian) is expected to maintain rigorous self-discipline, to live a life far more exemplary than that spelled out in the Law. Justification is not a substitute for righteousness but a precondition for it. Although Paul did not expect the Christian to live by the Law, he expected of the Christian a righteousness that exceeds the Law. The lordship of Christ means following the example of Christ and obeying his word. Redemption means moral transformation, so that the Christian is a new person in Christ Jesus. The sharp break with the past is not simply a matter of belief and of worship. It is a new way of acting that results from a new character and draws on newly discovered resources. For Paul, life *in Christ* is life *like Christ*. His crowning statement is, "For to me, living is Christ" (Philippians 1:21).

QUESTIONS AND TOPICS FOR DISCUSSION

1. Jesus once said that he had not come to destroy the Law but to fulfill it. In what sense did he fulfill the Law? How was his approach to ethical issues different from that of the Old Testament?
2. Compare Paul's approach to ethical issues with that of Jesus.
3. What is the relationship of apocalyptic thinking to moral concern?
4. How can a person who lived two thousand years ago be an example for people who live in the twenty-first century?

RECOMMENDATIONS FOR FURTHER READING

BRUGGEMANN, WALTER, *Interpretation and Obedience*. Minneapolis: Augsburg Fortress, 1991.

HAYES, RICHARD B., *The Moral Vision of the New Testament*. New York: Harper Collins, 1996.

HOULDEN, J. L., *Ethics and the New Testament*. New York: Oxford University Press, 1977.

MOTT, STEPHEN CHARLES, *Biblical Ethics and Social Change*, Part 1. New York: Oxford University Press, 1982.

WIIITE, R. E. O., *Christian Ethics*. Macon, Ga.: Mercer University Press, 1996.

WILLIMON, WILLIAM H., and STANLEY HAUERWAS, *The Truth About God*. Nashville: Abingdon, 1999.

6

Faith Working Through Love

In the discussion thus far, a general approach to ethical decisions has begun to emerge. Chapter 1 outlined the field of ethics, Chapters 2 and 3 described some alternative approaches, and Chapters 4 and 5 presented some theological and biblical concepts. We can now draw these concepts together and propose a system for making decisions on ethical issues. The framework for this approach is provided by Paul's statement, "For in Christ Jesus neither circumcision nor uncircumcision counts for anything; the only thing that counts is faith working through love" (Galatians 5:6).

PREMISES OF THE FAITH

As noted in Chapter 3, the Christian ethicist stands within the Christian faith and makes Christian assumptions about human nature, about the relationship of human beings to one another, and about their relationship to God. We cannot separate ethics from theology. That is not to say that we must first develop a theology and then consider its ethical requirements. Indeed, ethical insight and theological understanding usually grow together and influence each other. Logically, however, our theology shapes our ethic. Although details of a basic Christian theology are beyond the scope of this study, it is important to call attention to certain premises of the faith that are directly related to ethical considerations.

Beliefs about God

The theological starting point for Christians is the belief in God. When we attempt to state this belief, we can speak only in human, and therefore inadequate, terms. We use images, no one of which can say all that we believe and no one of which is intended to be taken as literal truth.

The first image is *person*. We do not think of God as an impersonal force, an insensitive power, or an unresponsive system. Rather we conceive of the Divine Being as possessing certain characteristics: thought, feeling, willing, self-awareness. It is these qualities we think of when we read the Genesis statement that we are made "in the image of God." By recognizing these qualities in God, therefore, we understand that we can have a personal relationship with the divine.

The second image is *creator*. The biblical writers portray God as creator and all else as creature. This means that God was behind the beginning, the "First Cause" that set things in motion. More than that, however, it means that God is continually creating. We do not say that God *was* creator but that God *is* creator. Creation is a dynamic process; the world is constantly changing, with some things ceasing to be and new things coming into being. This continuing creative process is orderly, reliable, and understandable, and thus a reflection of the character of God.

Closely related to the image of God as creator is the image of God as *sovereign*. People in the ancient world attributed the dependability of the natural process to the power of the divine. The modern concept of natural law, unknown to the ancients, may lead to the assumption that the world is a self-perpetuating system that operates without any interference from God. But as the world continues to evolve and change in ways that we do not understand, Christians believe that God is involved in the process and gives direction to it. This idea is particularly important for ethical consideration. Human beings, as a part of creation, are subject to God's continuing activity in the world. God directs the processes at work in the realm of morals as well as in the natural order. The ultimate standard of human conduct, therefore, is determined by God's character and purposes for humankind. That is the burden of Jesus's teachings about the kingdom of God.

The image of God as *judge* follows naturally from the image of sovereignty. Accustomed to emphasizing divine love, we tend to say little about divine judgment. Consequently we are uncomfortable with the Old Testament portrayal of a God who destroys or redeems a nation because of its actions, who blesses or punishes individuals according to their faithfulness. We are even a bit troubled by Jesus's portrayal of a last judgment in which the sheep are to be separated from the goats. Yet we know that certain ways of acting bring about certain consequences. We understand that we cannot delay indefinitely the consequences of our actions. And if we see God at work in history and in our own lives, we realize that those consequences are the judgment of God.

Beliefs about Humankind

The second element in a theological system important for the study of ethics is a perspective on human nature. Our understanding of humankind can be summed up with four affirmations. First, *humankind is a part of the natural order.* We are not divine; we are creatures, brought into being by divine activity. Made "from the dust of the earth," we are kin to all other creatures; we have a place in the natural order, as does everything else. We are not above the natural order; we are a part of it. As all else in creation is finite, limited, dependent, fragile, so are we.

Second, *humankind is unique in creation.* According to Scripture, we are at the climax of the creative process. We are made "in the image of God." Into our nostrils was breathed "the breath of life." As the Psalmist said, therefore, we are "a little lower than God." This fact does not set us apart from the rest of creation but affirms that within creation we have a unique responsibility.

Third, *human beings are social creatures.* We live in community. We interact with one another, from the simplest level of existence to the most exalted. In a significant sense, we draw our identity from the community. While we never lose our individuality, neither do we lose our need for other people.

Fourth, *human beings are sinners.* To use the biblical image, we are the man and the woman eating the forbidden fruit in the Garden of Eden. We are Cain, jealous of our brother and ultimately killing him. We are the people of Babel, building a tower of pride and self-assertion. Unfortunately, we have a long tradition of trivializing the concept of sin. We picture it as specific actions that are often rather petty and that we can overcome if we really set our minds to it. But the problem of sin is much more deep-seated. Its essence is pride, a rebellion against the sovereignty of God and an assertion of our own sovereignty. It pervades and contaminates all of our relationships, personal and social. As Waldo Beach says, it is "the sinister, all-pervasive infection of will that disrupts the community of the created order and sets persons or groups against each other" (*Christian Ethics in the Protestant Tradition*, p. 27). Any realistic consideration of moral issues, both personal and social, must take into account the fact that all of us are by nature self-centered.

Beliefs about History

A basic theological question for all religions concerns how one is able to know God. That is, how are the divine nature and purpose disclosed to human beings? In some religions, such as the fertility cults that the ancient Hebrew people encountered in the land of Canaan, the divine is revealed in the realm of nature, in the cycle of the seasons. In some, such as the ancient religions of Hinduism and Buddhism, the divine is encountered through mystical experiences in which people transcend the material world. In Judaism and in Christianity, history is the arena of the divine self-disclosure. For the Jewish people, this means that God is seen in the historical acts that are reported, celebrated, and interpreted in the Old Testament. For Christians, this means that God's supreme self-disclosure is seen in the person and work of Jesus Christ, whose life, death, and resurrection are reported and interpreted in the New Testament.

Christian faith assumes a continuity in the historical process. Human beings are not in full control of this process, holding the destiny of the world in their hands. Neither are they mere victims of it, dominated by events that are totally beyond their control. Rather they interact with history, participating in decisions and actions that affect all of creation.

For this reason, eschatology is important to the study of ethics. This term, literally meaning "the doctrine of the end," concerns the direction of human history. In the first century of the Christian era there was among both Jews and Christians a fairly common expectation of the imminent end of the present world order, and there was considerable speculation about the evidence that that end was near at hand. Most modern Christians, however, do not really expect the world to come to an end during their lifetime or even at some date in the future. Rather they act as if history will continue indefinitely and that their responsibility is to do their best to live a reasonably normal and happy life.

Jesus himself did not indulge in speculation about the end. He talked about "the last days" only when questioners pushed him to do so (see Mark 13). Yet his teachings reflect the belief that the world is not permanent, that time is limited, that judgment awaits, and that his disciples must be prepared for the end. All of the documents of the New Testament show some influence of these beliefs on the life of the early church. Most New Testament writers tied the idea of the end of the world to that of the return of Christ. In all New Testament thought about the end, the significance of that event is the final victory of God over the forces of evil.

Our clue to understanding the relevance of eschatology to ethical considerations lies in this New Testament approach. As long as the world lasts, there will be conflict between good and evil in the lives of individuals and in the structures of society (see the Parable of the Tares in Matthew 13:24–30). We do not struggle with evil believing that we can arrive at permanent solutions. Rather we realize that we are always seeking to resolve particular issues. We try to deal with problems in the way that God intends us to live. We try to respond to God's purposes for us and to make a similar response possible for other people. We work in the knowledge that whatever the specific problems of the present and whatever the outcome in these situations, the ultimate victory is God's. For Christian action, the final question is not whether we are successful in overcoming evil but whether we are faithful to the God who placed us in this world.

FAITH

At the heart of one's religious life is faith in God. Faith is not something that one possesses as one owns a book or a piece of apparel. Neither is it something that one does, as one utters a word or writes a check. Rather it is an attitude or a disposition, like love or fear or admiration or resentment. Its nearest synonyms are *trust* and *confidence.* In this sense, faith is a condition, a way of life.

Paul often spoke of faith as if it had a starting point. He looked back on the time, vivid in his memory, when he first believed in Christ. For him, however, that initial act was the beginning of a relationship, not an action complete in and of itself. Furthermore, he did not make his own experience standard for everyone, insisting that only his way had validity. He recognized that people enter the relationship in many different ways; for him it was the relationship and not the manner of entry that was significant.

Faith and Salvation

Salvation is God's gracious act of deliverance from sinful selfhood into newness and fullness of life. The word salvation literally means "health" or "wholeness." Deliverance is thus liberation from the dark, destructive forces of sin, guilt, and death—all of which involve pain, loss, and estrangement. It is a movement into the fullest and truest realization of one's own powers and values and into rich and creative relationships. While the concept of salvation is broader than the ideal of morality, it clearly has significant implications for Christian ethics.

The Christian understanding of the way people are saved presupposes two beliefs about human nature that we have just affirmed: All human beings are made in the image of God, and all human beings sin. These contrasting ideas explain the tension we feel between good and evil. Because the image of God is in all of us, both the desire and the potential for good are in all of us. Yet we are attracted to evil, are indeed capable of massive evil, and find that even our best efforts are tarnished by our self-centeredness. An awareness of this dual character of human nature should prevent us from being judgmental toward others and self-righteous about our own actions.

The solution to this human dilemma is the grace of God, which we receive through faith. Grace is God's loving, kind, merciful outreach to human beings. In classical Greek the word refers to whatever affords joy, pleasure, or delight. In the New Testament it is used for the one thing that affords human beings the greatest possible good: God's action on our behalf. God is constantly at work in the world and in our lives to restore the harmony and peace broken by our sin. Although we cannot correct our own problems, we are not doomed to the chaos that we create by our sins. Divine grace reaches out to us, not as an easy indulgence, ignoring the problems and the consequences of our actions, but as a force of restoration and renewal. This action is completely unearned and totally undeserved and is, therefore, an unconditional gift. It is God's acceptance of us in spite of our sinfulness and without our having done anything to persuade God to look on us with favor.

God always acts redemptively toward the world and toward human-kind. The Old Testament story of the Hebrew people is the picture of God working in history to make God's self known to the people and to enable them to find peace. There are, of course, many moral and ethical problems in the Old Testament narrative, problems that we cannot simply overlook. Yet the essence of the story is that God never leaves the people alone, never leaves them to their own devices, but constantly interacts with them and with the rest of the world.

For Christians, God's redemptive work is seen uniquely and supremely in the person of Jesus Christ. The "good news" of the gospel is the story of the life, the death, and the resurrection of Christ. In what Jesus said and did and in what happened to him we experience redemptive love. Through Christ, God's grace comes to us and through faith we are brought back to God. Although there are many theories about how our salvation is achieved by the person and work of Christ, all Christian theology affirms that it is so. In Protestant theology, salvation is in no sense earned or merited but is the gift of God. This salvation turns us from our self-centeredness into a new life of dependence on God. This new life, made possible by the grace of God, is one of moral responsibility. The essence of the gospel, therefore, is found in the declaration that "in Christ God was reconciling the world to himself" (2 Corinthians 5:19).

The result of Christ's work in us is a transformation of character. Our nature, which has been marred by self-love, is transformed into a new Christian nature. The sense of oneness with God, made possible by being created in the divine image but broken by our sinfulness, has been renewed. In Christ God has done for us what we could not do for ourselves. Faith is our response to that grace. Prompted by what God has done and is doing, it is our constant "Yes" to God.

This transformation of character, however, is not a sudden, radical, complete change, at least not for most people. Rather it is a process that takes place within the context of the Christian community and under the influence of the community as a whole and of individuals within that community. It takes place through private and group study of the Scripture, through personal prayer and meditation, through corporate worship, through conversation with other believers, and through cooperative efforts to deal with personal and social problems. It takes place in interaction with other individuals and groups outside the Christian community. It takes place within the social institutions of which we are a part. Because we are always interacting with persons and groups and institutions, our character is always being reshaped. But for Christians the shaping is not a random process. Rather it is a learning, growing process directed by a fundamental commitment to the God whom we know in Christ, a sharing in the life of the Christian community, and a responsiveness to the leadership of the Spirit of God.

Salvation, then, entails a new way of life. We are saved, says Paul, "for good works" (Ephesians 2:8–10). One consequence of our relationship with God is the development of a new pattern of action that expresses concern both for personal purity and for the well-being of others. For Paul, at least, the difference made by salvation was sharp and clear: "For once you were darkness, but now in the Lord you are light" (Ephesians 5:8). You once walked in an earthly way, he said to the Colossians; you were guilty of fornication, impurity, passion, evil desire, greed, anger, wrath, malice, slander, and foul talk. But now you have "put on the new nature," which involves compassion, kindness, humility, meekness, patience, forgiveness, love (Colossians 3:5–17). A new moral nature, therefore, is an essential ingredient of salvation. One who acknowledges the sovereignty of Christ becomes a new self. New motives compel one to new decisions, and new resources make it possible to implement them. A new goal integrates one's life and gives direction for moral development.

Life in the Christian Community

By virtue of being Christian, one has a special relationship with other believers. The church is the community of people who believe in Jesus Christ. As the central figure, Christ makes the distinction between the church and all other communities of faith. Long before it was organized, the church existed as a community. It came into being when people began to associate themselves with Christ, and it grew as other people became his disciples. People were a part of the church not because they joined something but because they acknowledged Christ as Lord. That kind of relationship continues to the present, transcending time and place, ignoring cultural and ethnic differences, paying no attention to theological niceties, and disregarding organizational considerations.

Within the context of the Christian community, the goal of life is "the unity of the faith and of the knowledge of the Son of God," which Paul called "maturity" (Ephesians 4:13). The idea that the believer can mature within the church acknowledges the possibility that the believer may fall short of the ideal. Paul urged Christians to give careful attention to basic moral ideals and to grow in their love for one another. Only occasionally does the New Testament hint that one who falls short of certain standards should be excluded from the fellowship. Far more often it speaks of helping one another, of striving for goals not yet attained, of seeking forgiveness for failure, and of asking for strength to resist temptation. The Christian life is a pilgrimage toward a goal that has not yet been achieved. For Christian ethics, the significance of this life in the community of faith cannot be overemphasized. The church is the context for our living, the environment in which we develop toward "mature manhood." For the Christian, all questions about behavior are to be asked and answered in the context of the community of faith, with regard both to the judgment of that community and to the impact of a decision on that community.

How does the community of faith affect us? First, we become believers through the community, the group through whom the faith has been perpetuated. Extending back to the time of Jesus, the community provides the basic information about the person and work of Christ. Moreover, in it Christ is now present in the world and through it speaks to the world, in worship, in religious instruction, and in reaching out to others.

Second, we understand Scripture through the church. Scripture is uniquely the possession of the church. The community of faith makes it available to the world and is concerned that it be understood as a vehicle for the living word. Although we may study the Bible in the same way that we study other literature, that is not quite enough. We can understand Scripture best by reading it as a part of the community of faith.

All of this means, third, that we learn from the community of faith. We do not surrender judgment to the church, because it does not have all the answers. Like all other institutions it changes, and its judgments change. The church must acknowledge its fallibility. It must be open both to the critic on the outside and to the prophet within. Yet it is the community of faith, it is devoted to the truth, and it acknowledges the leadership of the Holy Spirit. As conscientious believers seeking to make moral judgments, we will do well to consider carefully what the church teaches.

Fourth, as believers in Christ we share in the life of the church. Because there is a corporate identity, we who constitute the fellowship are involved in corporate actions. We are a part of the brokenness of the church, its racial segregation, its discrimination against women, its investments in corporations in our own country and abroad that employ unjust business practices. We are also a part of its ministry to the poor, its championing of oppressed minorities, its efforts to bring peace to all nations. The silence of the church is our silence, and its moral judgments are our moral judgments. At times we would like to dissociate ourselves from something that the church does; at times we wish to speak when it is silent. But we are always a part of that community to which we speak and to which we listen.

Finally, as a part of the church we are responsible for its well-being. Its spiritual and moral health is our concern. If we are aware of insensitivity on its part, ours must be the word that irritates. If we are aware of inappropriate action, ours must be the word of alarm. If we are aware of division, ours must be the healing word. Always we must speak the truth in love.

The Instruction of Scripture

Although the sole authority of the Scripture is a basic Protestant principle, Protestants are far from united on the meaning of this idea. Beliefs range from the idea of "inerrancy" through "where the Bible speaks, we speak; where the Bible is silent, we are silent" to "we take the Bible as our starting point." In spite of these differences, however, we all take the Bible seriously and think that in some way it has a bearing on our life in the world.

A proper use of Scripture in making moral decisions must take into account the nature of the Bible. In simple terms, it is the written record of God's self-revelation. Basic to an understanding of that record is a knowledge of the circumstances in which it was written, the literary forms in which it was written, and the situation of the people for whom it was written. The writers encountered God in the historical process and reported that encounter in their own way. Who they were affected what they said and how they said it. A vital part of who they were was their encounter with God both in day-to-day living and in unusual circumstances. The truth of the Bible is therefore not to be found in its specific statements about what God said or did but in the response of those ancient persons to God—and in the response to God that is evoked in the modern reader.

The Bible, then, is a vehicle of God's self-revelation. Regardless of the experience of the writers, if we do not encounter God as we read the Bible, revelation has no meaning for us and the teachings of the Bible are irrelevant. If, on the other hand, the living word comes through the written word, then for us the Bible is authoritative.

But authoritative in what sense? If the words of the Bible are not directives, or specifications about what must be done or not done, is it authoritative at all? If the Bible is not intended to secure compliance, why bother with what it teaches? The encounter with God that the authors reported was real. It was not merely an emotional experience, an amorphous feeling of being in the presence of God. It provided a sense of divine judgment and divine compulsion. In ethical terms, it led to an understanding of a way of life that pleases God, as contrasted with a way of life that displeases God. The details of how one is to act in specific circumstances vary because the conditions of life vary, but the perspective is constant. This perspective was stated in a dramatic way by Micah: "What does the Lord require of you but to do justice, and to love kindness, and to walk humbly with your God?" (Micah 6:8). It was summed up by Jesus: "You shall love the Lord your God. . . . You shall love your neighbor as yourself" (Mark 12:30–31). It was summarized by Paul: "For the one who loves another has fulfilled the law" (Romans 13:8). It was reiterated by James: Pure and undefiled religion is "to care for orphans and widows in their distress, and to keep oneself unstained by the world" (James 1:27).

This simple and comprehensive summary of the requirements of true religion does not end all discussion of moral responsibility but opens the way for learning how to implement it. We can understand this stated norm more fully by noting how people of biblical days responded to it or failed to respond to it. Because many of our problems, though not all of them, have parallels in the experience of people of biblical days, we can be enlightened by a knowledge of their thoughts and experience. The ways in which they responded to their encounter with God instruct us and give us clues for responding to God's call in our day.

Worship and Morality

A major function of the church, and of the individuals who make up the church, is worship. To worship is to acknowledge God's supreme worth, to present ourselves before God in praise and adoration, to acknowledge our dependence, and to express our devotion. We can do these things both in the company of fellow believers in a planned service of worship and in solitary and intensely private experiences. Worship does not depend on a mood, although a spirit of expectancy is conducive to it. It does not require our presence in any particular place or the use of any particular symbols, although accustomed places and symbols may facilitate it. It does not require a given pattern, although familiar procedures may be the means by which we turn our attention to God. Places and symbols and patterns are valuable to the extent that they enable us to offer ourselves to God.

Isaiah's description of his vision of God in the temple (Isaiah 6:1–8) brings out the elements that are common to most worship. First was an awareness of God's presence: "I saw the Lord sitting on a throne, high and lofty." God's presence is awesome, for God is the transcendent, sovereign creator and sustainer of the world and all that is in it, whereas we are dependent creatures. The second element was an acknowledgement of sinfulness: "Woe is me! I am lost, for I am a man of unclean lips, and I live among a people of unclean lips." The awareness of God, in all of God's purity, makes us aware of our own sinfulness and leads to a confession of sin and a petition for forgiveness. The third element was an experience of renewal. Because Isaiah's mission was to be one of the spoken word, his confession of sin focused on his "unclean lips," and his experience of forgiveness involved a sense of his lips having been cleansed and purified. When the burning coal touched his lips he was told, "Your guilt has departed, and your sin is blotted out." The final element of worship was a willingness to do the will of God. Only after being cleansed could Isaiah make that kind of commitment. As his initial reaction to his vision was an awareness of his own unworthiness, his final reaction was an offering of himself.

Worship, then, involves us in a reciprocal relationship with God. God reaches out to us, and we respond by offering ourselves. This offering is the connection between our praise of God and our work in the world. Worship is not a preparation for work, nor is work a substitute for worship. Work and worship are so inseparably united that together they constitute the life of faith.

We are affected by worship in three basic ways. First, worship incorporates us in the Christian community. In worship, both corporate and private, we function as a part of the body of Christ. We are united in prayer and service with all other people who share in the community. Even private, individual experiences of worship unite us because we enter these experiences as a part of a broader fellowship. We come to private worship from involvement with other Christians and we return to such involvement. Even in our solitude, therefore, we continue to worship with them. Corporate worship, however, unites us in a unique way. When we worship together, the shared experiences of praise, confession, renewal, and commitment strengthen the bond between us.

Second, worship gives us insight into the meaning of faith. Whether private or corporate, it almost always involves the use of Scripture, the basic document of our faith. It involves meditation, in which we try to make some sense of life, rationally and/or emotionally. It involves prayer, in which we place ourselves before God and open ourselves to God's leadership. The essential function of the Holy Spirit is to teach. That does not mean to impart facts but to give insight, to prompt movement in a given direction, to urge action in a given way. A person torn by emotion and unable to make a decision on a purely rational basis may learn through worship what is the best course of action.

Third, worship renews. Although we do not worship to gain strength but to praise God, one consequence of the experience is a sense of personal renewal of commitment and of the ability to fulfill that commitment. Because God is the source, we draw from God through worship. Worship is therefore a sacrament, a means by which God's grace reaches us.

The word *liturgy* comes from the Greek *leiturgia,* which is sometimes translated as "worship" and sometimes as "service." Indeed, when Paul wrote to the Roman Christians about their *leiturgia,* he referred to what they did when they gathered in worship, to their personal relationships with one another, and to their responsibilities in the community at large (Romans 12). The fact that one word can be used to cover all three activities indicates that the three are not so different from one another as we imagine, that they are in fact parts of one whole. From a Christian perspective, then, morality cannot be considered in isolation from worship.

LOVE (*AGAPE*)

If a relationship to God is at the heart of our religious life, so is a relationship to other people. So intimately connected are the two, in fact, that they cannot be separated. When Jesus was asked, "Which commandment is the first of all?" he replied, "The first is, 'Hear, O Israel: The Lord our God, the Lord is one; you shall love the Lord your God with all your heart, and with all your soul, and with all your mind, and with all your strength.' The second is this, 'You shall love your neighbor as yourself.' There is no other commandment greater than these" (Mark 12:29–30). Asked about one commandment, he cited two as if they were one. Love for God is incomplete without love for neighbor; love for neighbor is not a freestanding relationship but depends on love for God. For Jesus, one side of the coin is faith; the other side is love.

The Nature of Love

In the command to love God, the word *love* implies the concept of faith. It also involves grateful obedience to God's will: "For the love of God is this, that we obey his commandments" (1 John 5:3). When we love God we are in a relationship in which what we want most is to do God's will.

God wills that we love our neighbor. Here the word *love* means an unselfish concern for the welfare of another person. It is not primarily an emotion that, like all other emotions, changes in response to external factors. It is a rational, deliberate acceptance of responsibility for another person. Neither is it a response to certain desirable qualities in another person. The reason for it is not to be found in the object of love. Jesus said nothing about people deserving our love but a great deal about our responsibility to love. Christian love therefore does not depend on reciprocation. We must love regardless of how the other person acts. Although love may turn an enemy into a friend, that does not always happen. When it does not, we are still under the obligation to love.

To love someone is to seek what is good for that person. This does not necessarily mean doing what that person wants, because what one wants may not be what is best. We are not required to surrender our judgment. Acting in the interest of other people, we may even alienate them. Yet we cannot refrain from seeking the best for them.

Love is a personal relationship. It is not regard for people in general but for persons in particular. There is no such thing as "the poor" or "the sick" or "the criminal." There are individuals who are poor, sick, or criminal. To love is to deal with these persons. We find the perfect illustration of such love in the ministry of Jesus.

Love in universal in its range. When Jesus said, "Be perfect, therefore, as your heavenly Father is perfect" (Matthew 5:48), he was concluding a statement about God's love for everyone. The Old Tesament command, "You shall love your neighbor as yourself," was well known to the Jews of Jesus's day. But in practice they limited their obligation by restricting the meaning of "neighbor" to other Jews. In the parable of the good Samaritan Jesus removed that restriction. The Christian obligation to love extends to all people.

Love creates a community between persons. All of the actions of love that Paul cites in 1 Corinthians 13 bind people together; all of those actions that love avoids divide them. Thus love ignores all artificial barriers such as race, wealth, class, nation, and the like.

The Source of Love

These demands of love are impossibly difficult. The person who takes faith most seriously is the one who is most aware of failure. Talking in the abstract about what love demands is easy, but dealing with unlovely people is an entirely different matter. A legalistic morality is relatively simple because we can measure our achievements by the code and catch ourselves where we fall short. But the radically unselfish concern and the constant self-giving demanded by love are entirely beyond our grasp. We cannot act with utter and complete disregard for ourselves.

In this radical sense, then, love is a quality that only God possesses. It is God's way of dealing with people, a way in which we are utterly incapable of acting. But if this is so, what becomes of our duty to love? Why did Jesus say, "You shall love your neighbor as yourself"? Although love cannot originate with us, it does come from God through us to our neighbor. The First Epistle of John elaborates this idea, which is summarized in this simple and direct statement:

> Beloved, let us love one another, because love is from God; everyone who loves is born of God and knows God. Whoever does not love does not know God, for God is love. God's love was revealed among us in this way: God sent his only Son into the world, so that we might live through him. In this is love, not that we loved God but that he loved us and sent his Son to be the atoning sacrifice for our sins. Beloved, since God loved us so much, we also ought to love one another. No one has ever seen God; if we love one another, God lives in us and his love is perfected in us. (1 John 4:7–12)

That love that cannot originate with us, then, comes from God through us to our neighbor. We can act in love even though we cannot originate love. Although we cannot by our own will begin to love our neighbor, we can respond to God's call. We can be instruments of God's love at work in the world. Whether God's love reaches our neighbor depends in a sense on our willingness to permit the divine love to flow through us into the world.

The essence of the covenant God has made with us is summed up in the Old Testament declaration, "I will be your God and you shall be my people." It is caught up in Jesus's statement about the wine at the Last Supper: "This is my blood of the covenant." As people of the covenant, we participate in God's work in the world. We learn what reason alone cannot tell us, we are motivated by the love of God, and we are enabled by the spirit of Christ embodied in the community of faith.

The Demands of Love

The specific demands of love are endless, varying with the circumstances in which we live. On the basis of the New Testament teachings, however, we can generalize. The first requirement is an attitude of concern and respect for other people. Jesus's interpretation of the Law of Moses consistently focused on attitudes rather than actions. While he did not suggest that what we do is not important, he insisted that what we think and feel is primary. Even a "good" action based on a wrong motive is un-Christian. Conversely, although it is no guarantee that our judgments are wise, a right attitude means that we are trying to act in the best interests of the other person.

A second requirement is that love must be expressed. We cannot love and leave alone. To ignore someone is to act as if that individual were not really a person. When Jesus talked about the responsibility to love, he always spoke of doing something. When, for example, he said, "Love your enemies," he added, "do good, and lend, expecting nothing in return" (Luke 6:35).

Love requires forgiveness and the pursuit of reconciliation. The only phrase in the Lord's Prayer that Jesus interpreted was the petition, "Forgive us our debts, as we also have forgiven our debtors" (Matthew 6:12). Jesus commented, "For if you forgive others their trespasses, your heavenly Father also will forgive you; but if you do not forgive others, neither will your Father forgive your trespasses" (Matthew 6:14–15). He even said that unreconciled differences with a brother prevent one from truly worshiping God (Matthew 5:23–36). When Peter asked how often he should forgive an offending brother, Jesus replied that there should be no limit to forgiveness (Matthew 18:21–22). This principle for dealing with an enemy is not merely nonretaliatory. It is an active, generous treatment of wrongdoers in a positive effort to establish a good relationship with them.

Jesus had a special concern for the unfortunate. He saw his mission as a ministry to the poor and neglected (see Luke 4:18–19). Often he used such service as an illustration of the true character of neighborly love. Obviously he saw deeper needs, needs of the spirit, and these he did not neglect. But an indifference to the physical and emotional needs of the unfortunate is utterly foreign to his religion and therefore to the religion of his disciples.

Jesus's demand for love involves the demand for justice. In this emphasis he was the heir of the great prophetic tradition. Although he did not often use the terms *just* and *justice*, the concept was fundamental to his thought. When, for example, he said, "You shall love your neighbor as yourself," he implied a standard by which we might measure our obligations to our neighbor. When he discussed either the value of the individual or the will of God, he was talking about a standard of right conduct to which his disciples owe their allegiance. In Christian thought, therefore, justice is not merely giving all persons their due. Rather it is acting toward them as God acts.

Love and Justice

When we think of Christian responsibility we tend to think in individual terms. We think of our relationships with other people and of what we should or should not do in dealing with them. We are concerned about matters such as whether to give money to a poor person who asks for help, whether to retaliate when someone does something to offend us, or whether to take advantage of the ignorance of a person with whom we are doing business. We concentrate on personal matters like keeping our temper, speaking the truth, or using drugs. We deal with intimate questions such as whether to have an abortion, whether to become romantically involved with someone already married, or whether to withdraw life-support systems from a family member who is terminally ill. We see Christian responsibility, in other words, as having to do with individual conduct.

There is, of course, some justification for this way of thinking. Jesus's teachings were directed to individuals, and they dealt with personal responses to all kinds of circumstances. Whether his teachings are valid or applicable to present-day living or relevant to social policy can be debated. But that they are intensely personal is clear. Jesus talked about loving one's enemy, about returning good for evil, about going the second mile, and so on. But can a nation love? Can a race of people deal with another race? People do not function as a nation or a race or even as a family. They function as individual citizens of a nation, as persons of a given racial group, as members of a family. It was to such individual functioning that Jesus spoke.

Is there, then, a Christian responsibility for the social order? Can we deal as Christians with social issues? Can we deal with racial discrimination in any way other than trying as individuals to be fair and honest and accepting of all people? Can we deal with the problem of war other than by praying that it will never break out again? Can we deal with the disintegration of the family other than by trying to maintain the stability of our own family life? Can we deal with the second-class status of women other than by ignoring stereotyped roles and double standards?

Most Christians believe that they do have some responsibility for the social order, although there is no general agreement on what it entails. Many Christians, perhaps most, believe that the way to build a better world is to work through individuals. At the simplest level this is interpreted to mean the effort to proselytize. Many people assume that someone who becomes a Christian undergoes a change in character and begins to act morally. The more Christian people there are, the better society will become. At a deeper level this individualistic approach assumes that the more one is imbued with the spirit of Christ, the more one is likely to act in a Christian way. Experiences of worship, the teachings of the church, and association with like-minded Christians will coalesce to bring a deeper insight into the character of the Christian life and more compelling motivation to follow the example of Jesus. At both levels this individualistic approach assumes that because better individuals make for a better world, the Christian solution to social problems is simply to help individuals to become Christian and to help Christian individuals to become more Christlike.

This approach, however, fails to come to terms with serious social problems. It ignores the fact that people do not fall into the neat categories of "good" and "bad." The continuing problem of Christians is that they are continually torn between good and evil, constantly struggle with choices, and do not always follow the way they believe to be right. Furthermore, an honest Christian acknowledges that many people who do not have Christian convictions share the same concerns and often follow courses of action that are good and just. The fact that one is a Christian, in other words, is no guarantee that one's decisions are correct or that one's actions are moral. Nor does the fact that one is not a Christian mean that one's decisions are wrong or that one's actions are immoral.

In addition, this individualistic approach fails to get at the root of many problems. We are what we are in a social context. We have a biological and cultural heritage, we are members of families, we are influenced by our peers, we are subject to the laws of the state, and we are affected by what we see and hear. Acceptance of the Christian faith does not automatically result in a correction of our attitudes on social problems. The values and ideals of a white, Protestant Christian are not always the same as those of Christians who are not white and Protestant. The values and ideals of a Roman Catholic from Boston are different from those of a Catholic from Charleston or San Francisco. Our habits and traditions affect our judgment on educational, economic, political, religious, and moral issues. Our decisions are not made on the basis of our faith alone but are powerfully conditioned by other loyalties as well.

The individualistic approach fails to recognize the character of social institutions. The functions of the state are not individual but corporate. The state, for example, builds roads and maintains a postal system and goes to war. The state deals with criminals, takes care of the poor, and sends people into outer space. Individuals may approve or disapprove of state actions, they may express their opinions, and they may try to alter the course that the state is taking. But however responsive or unresponsive the state is to individual opinion, the state acts. In varying ways the same situation exists with respect to the economic system, religion, education, and social custom. It even exists with the specific company for which a person works, the local school a person attends, or the congregation to which a person belongs. Individuals act in the social context, but the social context also acts on the individual.

This last fact points toward a conclusion about Christian responsibility in dealing with social issues. If we care about feeding hungry people, we must work through the structures of society—the economic order and the government—to deal with the causes of poverty. If we are concerned about peace between peoples, we must work through the political structure of which we are a part. If we are concerned about the mistreatment of any group in our society, we must work through the agencies that perpetuate discrimination. This approach in no way minimizes personal relationships. It recognizes, however, that individual problems are often symptoms of a much broader social situation and that the structure must be corrected if the situation is to be improved.

When racial segregation in public facilities was being challenged in the 1950s and 1960s, one cry often heard was, "You cannot legislate morals." The people making this protest were ignoring the fact that the laws requiring segregation, enacted in the post-Reconstruction era, had in fact done that very thing. Experience since those laws were struck down, furthermore, has proved that legislation can do a great deal in changing not merely practices but attitudes as well. In the 1970s and 1980s the status of women in society and the attitudes of people toward the rights of women were altered in the same way. This is not to suggest that all problems can be solved through legislation. It certainly is not to suggest that Christians should try to impose their moral standards on others by having them enacted into law. Many of the moral issues we face are social in nature, however, and the appropriate and effective way to deal with them is to work through the structures of power.

Here the relationship between love and justice becomes crucial. We have said that many Old Testament passages express a concern for justice. We have observed also that Jesus focused on the concept of love, even to the extent of saying that all the requirements of the Law and the prophets are summed up in the commandments to love God supremely and to love one's neighbor as oneself. Since he said little about justice, are we to conclude that it is not a Christian concern? If a Christian ethic entails concern for both love and justice, how are the two related to each other?

Joseph Fletcher insists that "Love and justice are the same, for justice is love distributed, nothing else" (*Situation Ethics*, p. 86). He speaks of justice as "Christian love using its head, calculating its duties, obligations, opportunities, resources." For him, love and justice are simply synonymous terms. Neither is superior to the other, neither is derived from the other, neither is in conflict with he other, and neither uses the other. The two words should create the same image in our mind.

Interestingly enough, Fletcher agrees with Paul Ramsey on this point. Ramsey says that "obedient love" is the central category in Christian ethics. He defines justice as God's way of dealing with people, or God's "righteousness," which is neither "corrective" nor "distributive" but "redemptive" (*Basic Christian Ethics*, p. 14). The standards of human justice, he says, are drawn from the righteousness of God and are therefore redemptive. Taking Paul as his model, he avoids giving a simple definition of love. He says that

1 Corinthians 13 "defines by *indication*, pointing not to anything generally experienced by all men everywhere, like blueness or fatherhood, but, as we shall see, to Jesus Christ" (p. xvi). He describes love as neighbor-centered, nonpreferential, nonresistant, obedient, and universal. He observes, therefore, that the concept of obedient love focuses on the ideas of covenant and the reign of God, concluding that the two are the same thing, that to obey the covenant is to do justice (p. 388).

DECISION

To make good decisions on specific issues, one needs guidelines for determining what love requires. One cannot make sound decisions without some criteria to serve as a basis for saying, "I ought to do this" or "I ought not to do that." As a matter of fact, most people do have certain patterns of conduct, whether they are explicitly stated or not. A person who has deliberately chosen and rationally stated principles by which to operate is in a position to make good decisions.

Accepting love as the essence of Christian moral obligation, then, one needs to ask, "What does love lead me to do?" The following general principles are offered as guidelines:

1. The human race is one. The differences that exist between people (in race, class, culture, education, and so on) are of only secondary importance.
2. Every individual is of infinite worth. Everyone, therefore, is to be dealt with not as a tool or a thing but as a person, as an end and not as a means.
3. Material values are secondary to personal values. *p/ last week*
4. Every person has certain basic human rights that must be respected at all times. At the least, these rights include life, physical well-being, reputation, and property.
5. Each person has a responsibility to seek the good of other people.
6. Often one value or duty must be sacrificed to another.
7. Because the universe is orderly, it is often (though not always) possible to anticipate the consequences of a given course of action.

These principles are not rules of conduct. They say nothing directly about cheating on tests, about premarital or extramarital sexual intercourse, or about working for an institution with whose policies one disagrees. They say nothing directly about caring for aging parents, cleaning up the slums of the city, eliminating discrimination against minorities, dealing with corruption in government, or addressing the political and economic situations in Eastern Europe, Africa, and the Near East. They say nothing about national defense or nuclear energy or protection of the environment. Can we use these principles to make decisions about these kinds of situations? Certainly we can predict with some degree of accuracy the results of contemplated actions. We can be sure that good is more likely to be attained by one course of action than by another. Although each situation is unique, there is a regularity or similarity in the patterns of human relationships that allows us to be more specific about what we should or should not do. That is, we can establish certain patterns of conduct.

Are these patterns of conduct "rules"? We might draw a parallel with the concept of the laws of nature. A law of nature is simply a prediction based on an observed regularity. It says, "This is the way things operate." On the basis of this regularity we can say, "If we want to get that result, this is the way we should act." A pattern of conduct, or rule, in the realm of morality is the same sort of thing. It is a generalization or a prediction based on observation. It does not control; it is not arbitrary; it is not without reason. Since we can observe that a given way of acting brings certain results, we can say, "This is the way we should act." Such formulations are tentative, always subject to correction by additional information, but they offer useful ways to make day-to-day decisions.

Our social order presupposes such moral generalizations, and we can best seek the good of others by giving critical allegiance to them. As a case in point, consider the academic community. It is the responsibility of an instructor to share information with students as completely, honestly, and objectively as possible, to stimulate their thinking, to test them fairly, and to evaluate their work carefully. It is the responsibility of the students to do their own work as effectively as they can. The instructor cannot seek the good of the students, as love requires, by neglecting the basic responsibilities of the position. The student cannot seek the good of the instructor and the good of fellow students, as love requires, by cheating on tests. Although this academic system may not be the best of all possible systems, it is the one within which we live and work, and within it we implement our love by following certain rules. Circumstances may sometimes arise that call for a suspension of a rule, but in the long run the normal procedures provide the framework for serving the best interests of all concerned.

In addition to such general rules covering social relationships, there are also rules of personal conduct that we choose on an individual basis. Although we cannot generalize these personal rules and try to force them on other people, we can respond to God's leadership by choosing for ourselves a particular pattern of acting. Using Paul Lehmann's terms, "as a believer in Jesus Christ and as a member of his church," we might choose to act in this way or not to act in that way (*Ethics in a Christian Context*, p. 45). The establishment of such personal rules is not only permissible but inevitable. Either deliberately or by default, we do in fact establish for ourselves a pattern of conduct. Sound decisions are best made by careful and deliberate choice.

These rules, or patterns of conduct, are concerned with action rather than with motive. They are guidelines for the expression of those principles that we have just discussed, and which are in turn extensions of the concept of love. They are thus instruments of love. They serve as norms or standards by which we can make loving decisions and choices day by day. They are not directives or preset solutions. Rather they are norms, guides for acting in normal situations, and patterns for making decisions in abnormal ones. They provide a standard by which we can evaluate the new, the different, and the challenging in terms of what is familiar. They are not absolutes, which permit no variation; we can readily make exceptions when they are warranted. Indeed, only because we have rules for the usual situation can we know when extraordinary measures are called for.

This approach can be illustrated with examples from the ministry of Jesus. In his day the written law prohibited work on the Sabbath. By traditional interpretation, or oral law, a large number of activities that were unlawful on the Sabbath were identified. In addition, custom decreed attendance at synagogue services. Even the most casual reader of the gospels will observe that Jesus respected the Sabbath and the purposes for which it was intended. He frequented the synagogues, and he rested on that day. He acknowledged that the Sabbath was created for the benefit of humankind (Mark 2:27). When the occasion called for it, however, he worked on the Sabbath (see Mark 3:1–5). In keeping with a basic principle of Jewish law, he saw no contradiction between observing the Sabbath, on the one hand, and making exceptions to meet human need, on the other.

Furthermore, since rules are always closely related to life in a given context, the rules must change as the context changes. This, too, can be illustrated from the teachings of Jesus. Once Jesus was asked about the Old Testament law that apparently gave men unrestricted freedom to divorce their wives (Deuteronomy 24:1). Whatever the reason for the law in its original form, in Jesus's day it worked to the disadvantage of women. In the first century women were almost totally dependent on men. A divorced woman, therefore, may very well have had no one to care for her and no means of caring for herself. Jesus's alteration of the Old Testament law (Mark 10:2ff.; cf. Matthew 19:3ff.), whether it was unique to him or not, represents his awareness of the necessity of changing rules that prove to be damaging.

Thus far, although the concept of living by rules has been discussed, nothing has been said about *whose* rules these are. It has been implied, however, that moral rules are not imposed on us by an external authority. Rules are valid for us when we deliberately give our allegiance to them. That rule is valid for me, as a mature Christian person, whose guidance I choose to accept.

This is not to say that we start from nothing and arbitrarily create a set of rules by which to govern ourselves. We could not do so, even if that were best, because of all the influences from the past that have made us what we are now. Each of us has learned a great deal from our family, from our peers, from the church, from educational institutions, and from all our experiences. Those teachings have become a part of us. As adults, we have both the freedom and the responsibility to examine critically what we have received from the past. Our examination of any rule should take into account the reason for its creation, its adequacy for dealing with the issue, and the relationship between the present situation and the past. The rules of conduct that we have received from the past may indeed represent the wisdom of experience. If they do, we will do well to preserve them in some fashion. If they do not, we will do well to abandon them. The fact that a rule is old does not make it either true or false. The fact that it has survived, however, does suggest that it merits examination.

One fact that makes the creation of rules of some sort both possible and necessary is the universality and permanence of certain qualities of human nature. Certain desires, needs, and drives characterize all people, regardless of time and place. These universal characteristics give rise to a variety of patterns in personal and social relationships. Moral rules have come into being in various societies as embodiments of human experience. Of course, individual differences must be taken into account in all human relationships. It is the similarities, however, that make it possible for us to approach each new experience with some degree of confidence based on the experience of others.

In Christian thought, the rules by which we operate are cast within the framework of our relationship to God. Christians talk a great deal about "the will of God." The starting point for their understanding of the will of God is the Bible. Now, quite obviously, Christians vary widely in their view of how the Bible was written, how it is to be understood and interpreted, and consequently how its authority is to be accepted. All Christian thinkers, however, take it seriously as a record of God's self-disclosure. For this reason Christian ethicists of all schools of thought try to show that their approach to ethical issues is essentially in keeping with the spirit of Scripture.

It is furthermore generally assumed that God is reliable and orderly, not whimsical or capricious. We can talk about love and justice and righteousness, about honesty and fidelity and integrity because of the unchanging nature of the One upon whom the whole structure of the universe rests. The rules that we make for ourselves are properly those that we find to be the logical conclusion of this understanding of the way God deals with the world.

Another element in the concept of the will of God is the idea of the discipline of the Holy Spirit. Whatever else we mean by the leadership of the Spirit, we mean that God is at work in the world and in our lives. This is not to suggest that in all circumstances, or even in any circumstance, we might get a clear vision of the will of God, a vision that will lead us in an entirely new direction. But as we use the best that is available from Scripture, the wisdom from the past, and a knowledge of present circumstances, we may be further enlightened by the presence of the Spirit. In this way we can establish helpful patterns of acting. Rules of conduct so established are not matters of whim or of prejudice but of personal decision, commitment, and acceptance.

Rules, then, can serve well as guides for day-to-day conduct. We do not need to try to make every decision in life as if we have never before encountered a similar situation. Once we have decided that we are going to be honest, for example, and once we have decided that honesty prohibits us from using someone else's work as our own, for us the matter is settled. We do not have to approach every book with a mental debate about whether we will or will not use the author's material as if it were ours. We do not have to debate before each test whether or not to copy answers from the person beside us. One decision can settle the issue.

Rules can also be helpful in preventing us from making decisions on the basis of self-interest rather than of love. If we are threatened in any way, our first thought usually is to save our own skin. Most of us are willing to do so even at the expense of someone else. A student who for any reason has delayed to the last minute the preparation of a paper, for example, is at that point hardly able to debate the morality of plagiarizing or of using a paper acquired from someone else. All that the student can think about is the urgency of turning in a paper. The last minute is not the time to debate issues of personal integrity; it is the time to act on decisions made more deliberately in other circumstances.

Rules help us avoid the undue influence of emotions. Our emotions are an integral part of our total makeup and therefore are an important element in the decision-making process. They often lead us to take actions that are quite unwise, however. Some of the stronger emotions, not merely the negative ones such as fear and anger but also the positive ones such as compassion and desire, tend to disrupt the reasoning process. Since love is concerned with what happens to people, this urgent impulse of self-giving needs the direction of careful thought and decision. Rules arrived at in a careful manner are more reliable than impulsive reaction.

In addition, rules help us preserve the wisdom of experience. They help us incorporate in future actions what we have learned from our mistakes and successes. Indeed, because many of the rules by which we operate are those taught by our parents, by educational experiences, by the church, and by wise men and women of history, we are the beneficiaries of a sort of collective wisdom. Certainly its content varies, and obviously not everything that has been passed on is properly called wisdom. Furthermore, even if something were valid for the past, it may have no relevance to the present. The process of determining our own pattern of action, however, makes it quite possible for us to examine what we have received and apply the good and the relevant to our own day-to-day living.

Such rules protect the rights of other people. If it is a fact that each individual has inherent rights that we must not violate, the rules help us to identify these rights. They give some clue about what we need to do to help secure these rights and what we should avoid doing so as not to interfere with other people's pursuit of those things that are properly theirs. Some regularity in our day-to-day conduct, then, some pattern of behavior or norm by which we can regularly operate and from which we can vary when love so dictates, is essential. Rules carefully arrived at by deliberate consideration, made our own through personal acceptance and commitment, and used conscientiously under the discipline of the Spirit of God can indicate the way of love.

QUESTIONS AND TOPICS FOR DISCUSSION

1. Comment on the idea that you can't legislate morality.
2. How can we know what the will of God is in a given situation?
3. Since love is directed toward persons, how can it be relevant to problems in the structure of society?
4. Discuss the idea that moral action and worship are inseparable.

RECOMMENDATIONS FOR FURTHER READING

BEACH, WALDO, *Christian Ethics in the Protestant Tradition*, Part 1. Atlanta: John Knox, 1989.

BLOESCH, DONALD G., *Freedom for Obedience*. New York: Harper and Row, 1987.

HAUERWAS, STANLEY, *A Community of Character*. Notre Dame, Ind.: University of Notre Dame Press, 1994.

HAUERWAS, STANLEY, *Character and the Christian Life*. Notre Dame, Ind.: University of Notre Dame Press, 1994.

HIGGINSON, RICHARD, *Dilemmas*. Louisville: Westminster/John Knox, 1988.

SMEDES, LEWIS B., *Choices*. New York: Harper and Row, 1991.

SMEDES, LEWIS B., *Love Within Limits*. Grand Rapids: Eerdmans, 1995.

7

Human Sexuality and the Marriage Relationship

William, twenty-two years of age, and Mary, twenty-one, knew each other in high school but did not date. They lived in the same neighborhood and their families were acquainted with each other. They attended the same church and for a time were involved in some of the youth activities. In late high school years, however, both of them gradually became less involved in the church. After he graduated from high school, William continued to live at home and attended the local university. Mary went to a nearby college and lived in the residence hall. They began dating when he was a senior and she a junior. After he graduated he found employment in another state. She completed college, secured a position in the city where William was living, and moved into an apartment with him. Neither set of parents initially knew about the living arrangement, but gradually they sensed the situation. They were troubled when they realized what was happening and did not understand why William and Mary did not marry. The couple had toyed with the idea of marriage but decided that they were unwilling to make a permanent commitment. They simply entered into a living-together relationship with no strings attached.

This story is not an account of a real couple but a composite constructed from the lives of several couples. Such living-together arrangements, increasingly common, raise a number of questions that are important from a Christian perspective. What is the nature of human sexuality? What is the place of sex in the man–woman relationship? What is the nature of marriage? What are the appropriate constraints under which Christians live?

THE CURRENT SCENE

The family of a generation ago is often sentimentalized and idealized. The man is portrayed as the breadwinner and the woman as the homemaker. They married because they were in love, and they entered into marriage knowing what would be expected of them and what they could expect from their mates. As mates they were loving and faithful; as parents they were wise and kind. Their children were dutiful, they accepted the values their parents passed on to them, and they had a bright future.

This portrait, of course, is a caricature. Never has any one family pattern been characteristic of even a majority of the people. There have been differences between black families and white ones, between working-class families and upper-class ones, between southerners and midwesterners, between Christians and Jews, and between people of other religions and those of no religion. There have been male-dominated and female-dominated families, childless couples, single-parent families, and extended families living in the same household. There have been families created and maintained by people legally married and families created and maintained by people whose relationship was never legalized. There have been happy families and unhappy ones. But never has there been a "typical" family.

Sociologists, however, once could generalize about such matters as the age at which most people marry, the percentage of marriages that fail, the percentage of women who work outside the home, and the average size of the family. They could describe patterns of behavior, discuss factors that contribute to success or to failure in marriage, and predict the consequences of certain ways of acting. Such generalizations are now more difficult. The most significant single element in the present is the fact of rapid change. The way men and women relate to each other, the way they make decisions about marriage, what they expect in marriage, how they adjust to each other, how their marriage affects the other aspects of their lives, how they deal with their children, what they do if they find their marriage to be unsatisfactory—all of this is so varied and is changing so rapidly that no pattern is discernible.

With change the order of the day, there seems to be no place for absolutes. Earlier generations of Americans assumed that right and wrong were defined by generally accepted standards of conduct. Not everyone lived by those standards, but most people acknowledged them as right and proper. At present, however, the validity of the standards themselves is challenged. Although people have to make choices about their own conduct, and although they choose what seems to them to be right, most are unwilling to say that other people should make similar decisions. As in the period of the Judges in the Old Testament, all people do what is right "in their own eyes."

Nowhere is change more evident than in man–woman relationships. The widespread movement of women into employment outside the home has given them a great deal of independence. An increasing number find great personal satisfaction in their careers. Many delay marriage, and many others choose not to marry at all. In marriage, the income of women is becoming more and more important in order for the family to have all the things they consider important. Furthermore, no longer economically dependent upon men, an increasing number of married women are deciding not to remain in marriages that they find unsatisfactory. No longer, therefore, do women identify themselves exclusively, or even primarily, in terms of their families.

This change in the status of women involves important role changes for both women and men. These changes are reflected most obviously in the more casual and equalitarian relationships between unmarried people. As yet, however, they have not materially altered the pattern of relationships within marriage. In few marriages is the woman's career given equal consideration with the man's. In few do men share fully in household responsibilities and in child care. The slow pace of change within the family is not due simply to the unwillingness of men to change; it is due also to the unwillingness of women to relinquish their traditional functions. But changes outside the home inevitably will result in changes within.

Another factor that affects the pattern of man–woman relationships is the development of safe and effective methods of contraception. In an earlier day the possibility of an unwanted pregnancy was a significant deterrent to sexual activity both before marriage and in marriage. With the development of more effective contraceptives, however, the possibility of an unwanted pregnancy has been greatly reduced. Furthermore, the availability of simpler and safer methods of abortion has allowed the termination of unwanted pregnancies at little cost, with little loss of time, and without disclosure to other people. The development of "sex without fear" has had a profound impact on the man–woman relationship.

The possibility of contracting AIDS, however, has reintroduced the element of fear. First assumed by the general public to affect only men involved in homosexual activity, it is now known to afflict both men and women without regard for sexual orientation. The danger of contracting AIDS and the absence of effective treatment have combined to affect the way men and women relate to each other. In this new atmosphere people still live and function as sexual beings, and many do so without any sense of certainty about their sexual nature. They are subject to the pressures of the sex drive, to the influence of their peers, to the concepts presented by the media, to the teachings of their family, and to the ideals enunciated by the church. Since most people are not accustomed to thinking philosophically, most never arrive at a rational and morally defensible position on sexual behavior. The establishment of one, however, is an integral element in the formation of a Christian ethic.

Our understanding of our sexuality must be developed in the context in which we live. Sexuality is not isolated from the other aspects of life; it is involved in all of our relationships with other people, and thus it affects our political, business, educational, religious, and recreational activities. While it is not the determining factor in all that we do, we do not cease being sexual beings when we do business or play or pray or engage in political activity.

One aspect of our sexuality is the biological factor. Indeed, one can think of sex as a biological function only. In that sense the sex drive, like hunger or thirst, is a physically based need. It is oriented immediately toward pleasure and the release of tensions and ultimately toward procreation. For the satisfaction of this drive sex partners may be interchangeable. In this sense sex functions among human beings exactly as it does among the lower animals. Although an adequate understanding of sex cannot stop with this biological aspect, no discussion of human sexuality can ignore it.

A second element of sexuality, one that plays a major role in our society, is the game in which many, perhaps most, men and women engage. When two people are attracted to each other, they may flirt with each other and tease each other. At the outset they may have no serious interest in each other, though that may develop. For the moment they simply enjoy playing the game. The game does not necessarily involve sexual intercourse, although it may. If it does, the intercourse does not necessarily entail any commitment beyond the present moment. Indeed, for many people a part of the game is to avoid commitment.

A third element of sexuality is romantic love. In our marriage mythology we assume that love is the only sound reason for a couple to marry, that it is all they need to create a good marriage, that if they are in love they should marry and if they are not in love they should not marry. This kind of love idealizes the other person. It has been called a gross exaggeration of the difference between one person and everyone else in the world. It is a response to all the attractive features that one finds in the other person and it is a desire to possess that person for one's own. The highly charged and unrealistic situations depicted in the television soap operas and R-rated films tend to confuse both the married and the unmarried about personal relationships in and out of marriage.

Against this background, the traditional Christian understanding of sexuality and of marriage represents a difficult ideal. Stated in simple terms, this ideal calls for chastity before marriage and fidelity within marriage. It considers marriage to be a permanent relationship and divorce for any reason to be a failure. Because of the power of the sex drive, one must be extremely careful about personal relationships. Because the games that men and women play are so highly sexual, a married person must not indulge in them. Even if romance and excitement disappear from a marriage, a couple must remain true to their vows. The period of courtship is the time for fun and games; the period of marriage is the time for more serious matters.

In this traditional concept of marriage, romance matures into a deeper and more meaningful love. Sex has a more profound meaning than the satisfaction of a biological urge. The security of marriage is more satisfying than the uncertainties of romance. Marriage, indeed, is seen not as restricting but as liberating. Even those people who fail to achieve a satisfying marriage think of their failure as a personal matter, not as a sign that the institution is flawed.

A CHRISTIAN INTERPRETATION OF SEXUALITY

A Theological Perspective

It is ironic that Christianity, which professes to help people relate to God and to the world, has actually given little assistance in dealing with a reality so basic to human nature that some people consider it to be the driving force in all human activity. In the late fourth century the great theologian Augustine expressed a negative attitude toward sexuality. Because of his own personal spiritual struggle he came to believe that the sex drive was in itself evil. Grudgingly admitting that sexual relations were permissible to married couples who wished to have children, he insisted that celibacy is the holiest way of life. His view came to dominate the thinking of the early church, and his influence is still felt. Until quite recently it expressed itself in our country in a Puritanism that drew a curtain around sexuality. Sex was a taboo subject, not to be discussed in polite society and certainly not in mixed company. "Dirty" jokes were jokes about sex. Children were taught nothing about sex, neither at home nor at school and certainly not at church. Although some Christian theologians tried to discuss sexuality in a relevant way, they could not alter the thinking of the church as a whole. When the sexual revolution struck with full force in the middle of the twentieth century, therefore, the church was ill-prepared to guide its members. At the beginning of the next century the subject was no longer taboo, but the church seemed not to know what to say.

In sharp contrast, the Bible is quite open in its treatment of sex. Without deifying it, as some ancient religions did (and, in a sense, as modern society does), Scripture recognizes sex as a normal and important part of human life. Without titillating, it reports many facets of the sex life of the people of the Bible. Without any hint of naughtiness it reports their immoralities.

On the basis of biblical teachings we can make several affirmations about human sexuality. First, sex is a part of our God-given nature. In biblical terms, all creation is the work of God and God has made us the way we are. In the older creation account, God's creation of humankind was not complete until woman was created as a complement to man (Genesis 2:7, 18–22), and the climax of the story is the statement of the couple's unity (Genesis 2:24). In the later creation account, humankind was made "male and female" (Genesis 1:27) and was commanded, as were the other creatures, to "be fruitful and multiply."

Sexuality, therefore, is characteristic of all human beings. The power of one's sex drive is unrelated to one's attractiveness. A physical or mental handicap does not make one immune to the sex drive. Older people do not cease to be sexual beings, nor do those who take religious vows. The strength of the sex drive is unrelated to marital status. We are all human beings whose sex drive is affected by circumstances but not destroyed by them.

Second, our sexuality is good, not evil. God made us the way we are, and all of God's work is good. Like everything else that God made, we can abuse and corrupt it. We can even use it to destroy ourselves, doing something evil with what God has created as good. The importance of this affirmation lies partly in the fact that it stands in sharp contrast to the view long held by the church. It lies also in the fact that although the present generation is quite open and free in its enjoyment of sex, the sad consequences of the abuses of our sexual nature are all too common. The goodness of sexuality is affirmed in spite of the guilt that many people feel about normal and legitimate sexual feelings and activities, the damage caused by the use of sex in the power struggle between men and women, the violation of human beings by other human beings, and the jealousies, frustrations, and insecurities that disrupt personal relationships. The goodness of this aspect of our nature needs to be understood by a generation that in its frantic search for pleasure finds little joy in self-expression.

Third, sexual intercourse is best understood as a relationship rather than as something that two people do. The vulgarisms often used to refer to coition speak of one person doing something to another. The most common biblical term for the legitimate sexual relationship, "to know," conveys a very different attitude. Knowledge does not simply mean an awareness of facts, an intellectual acknowledgment that something is true; it is an experience of reality. To know someone is to be involved with that person at the deepest possible level. A man and a woman who know each other sexually enter into a communion that is far more than physical. From a Christian perspective, the mutuality of this relationship is of major significance. This concept is implicit in the older creation narrative, which focuses on the man's need of companionship (Genesis 2:18–25). It is more directly affirmed in the later creation account, which speaks of humankind being created as male and female, as the two essential parts of the one entity (Genesis 1:26–28). No biblical writer, however, states this idea more forcefully than the apostle Paul, who said to the Corinthians,

> Each man should have his own wife and each woman her own husband. The husband should give to his wife her conjugal rights, and likewise the wife to her husband. For the wife does not have authority over her own body, but the husband does; likewise the husband does not have authority over his own body, but the wife does. (1 Corinthians 7:2–4)

In a later statement about the total man–woman relationship, he said, "Be subject to one another out of reverence for Christ" (Ephesians 5:21). While his discussion of mutual submission was not limited to the sexual relationship, it did include it.

Fourth, the sexual relationship has two basic functions. One is reproduction. This function, affirmed in the command to "be fruitful and multiply," is assumed throughout the Scripture. The other is the creation and the maintenance of the personal union of two individuals. While other factors are involved, such unity is incomplete without coition. This function is affirmed in the words of the older creation account which Jesus cited, "and they become one flesh" (Genesis 2:24; Mark 10:7–8). Once a man and a woman have come together in coition, their relationship can never be the same as before. For this reason Paul warned, "Do you not know that whoever is united to a prostitute becomes one body with her?" (1 Corinthians 6:16). Undoubtedly he overstated his case. There is nothing magical about coition, and two people who have no intention of a relationship beyond a temporary physical contact are not necessarily changed by that act. Yet coition does create a kind of identity between two people who come together to express their love and their acceptance of each other. In addition, it continues to express this union. When a man and a woman who love each other come together sexually they do not merely satisfy sexual desire. They come together because their lives are united, and coition is the most meaningful expression of that oneness.

Fifth, the sex drive needs to be regulated. Just as there are good and legitimate means for satisfying the hunger for food, so are there good and legitimate means for satisfying the sex drive. As hunger can be satisfied in ways that harm, so the sex drive can be satisfied in ways that are damaging. The fact that sex is a natural, God-given function does not imply that no limits are to be set on its expression. While sexual repression is demonstrably dangerous, sexual license is no less so. The voluntary establishment of limits and the exercise of restraint are sound ways of dealing with the sex drive.

This does not mean that one must turn to an external authority that has prescribed what may and what may not be done. It means rather that the Christian has to make decisions about how to channel the sex drive to make it a positive and constructive and creative force in life. We have already observed that in making decisions the Christian uses a number of resources, one of which is Scripture. Three general principles permeate biblical teachings about sex. First, casual and promiscuous sexual encounters are prohibited. Second, so central is the sexual relationship in marriage that to have intercourse is to enter into a union that amounts to marriage. Third, any kind of forced relationship is a violation of a person and thus a violation of the will of God.

A final theological affirmation is that personal integrity is not so much a matter of action so much as one of motive and attitude. Jesus employed this principle in interpreting the commandments concerned with murder, adultery, divorce, honesty, and justice (Matthew 5:21–48). Thus it is persons rather than actions that are moral or immoral. This is not to say that actions do not matter; they matter a great deal, as Jesus affirmed when he said that "you will know them by their fruits" (Matthew 7:20). But whether one is loving or unloving determines how one acts, and there are many ways of expressing both kinds of attitudes. Sexual purity, therefore, concerns not merely what one does but also one's attitude toward other people.

Questions about the Relationship

Sex and Freedom. One of the most important forces for social change in recent history has been the development of safe and reliable methods of contraception. Before this development, the possibility of an undesired pregnancy was a basic factor in setting the standards for sexual conduct, in maintaining the traditional pattern of relationships within the family, and even in regulating the place of women in the labor force. Any consideration of moral issues was likely to be overshadowed by the fact that an unplanned pregnancy, within marriage or outside of it, would seriously complicate life both for the woman and for the man. Today, however, if they make proper use of contraceptives, people can freely engage in the sex relationship with little worry about the possibility of pregnancy. This development represents significant progress in the realm of morality, because decisions that once were made under the shadow of fear are now open to more important considerations.

Our sexuality is a part of who we are; it is basic to our being truly human. Sexual activity is not merely gratification; it is also expression. Our objective, therefore, is not to have fun but to enrich our lives through our sexuality. Although that cannot be achieved by imposing rigid taboos, neither can it be achieved by stripping sex of its significance. To every activity in which we engage we bring our total personality: our appearance, our mental ability, our interests, our sense of humor, our accomplishments, our ambitions, and so on. We cannot separate these elements from each other or from our sexuality. To realize that our personality has many facets that cannot be separated is to realize that we never act as a mind only or an emotional being only or a sexual being only but that everything we do involves our total personality. Our sexuality, therefore, is only one part of a cluster of human qualities. If the sexual crowds out all of the other aspects of a personal relationship, that relationship is seriously impoverished.

Sex and Love. We have said that coition is the most intimate way for a couple to express their love for each other. Does this mean that love should always involve a sexual relationship? In our modern mythology of romance we have tied sex to love, assuming that coition is thereby justified. Does the fact that two people are in love justify a sexual relationship whether they are married or not? Circumstances may prohibit a couple from marrying. They may still be in school, they may not be financially able to establish their own home, or their parents may object. One or the other may be married to someone else or may have financial, emotional, or legal obligations that at the moment make marriage impossible. Should they express their love in a sexual relationship?

This question is not easily answered, and several factors should be considered. First, love is not easily identified; that is, the distinction between being in love and not being in love is not a clear one. People do not really "fall" in love, or at least most people do not. They are often suddenly attracted to other people, who sometimes respond to them and sometimes do not. Sometimes they are quickly excited by a new relationship or by the possibility of one. Such attraction may result in a deep attachment or it may not. But love is not created instantaneously; it is developed over a period of time.

Another consideration is the fact that love does not always lead to marriage. Most people are in love with several different persons before they marry. More than half the engagements entered into in this country are broken because people who had believed that they were in love decided that they were not, or that in spite of their love their planned marriage could not succeed, or that they were not ready to marry at that particular time, or that other circumstances made marriage impossible. Being in love, therefore, is a tenuous basis on which to decide something as important as whether to engage in a sexual relationship.

A third consideration is the context in which two persons are in love. They do not exist in isolation from other people and their relationship is therefore not exclusively their own. They are son and daughter, brother or sister, students or workers. They have friends, are part of a community of faith, are children of God and disciples of Christ. They have past experiences from which they have benefited and from which they bear scars. They have a present in which they function with varying degrees of success and satisfaction and a future whose foundation is now being laid. Although each person decides in each situation what to do, the situation is not simply the fact that two people are in love. It includes the fact that each comes from a certain background, lives within a broad community, and has a future. To consider other relationships requires more than asking the question, "What would other people think?" It means recognizing that their lives and the lives of other people are profoundly affected by what they decide.

Sex and Marriage. In traditional Christian thought, sexual intercourse is to be reserved for marriage. This ideal is usually stated as "chastity before marriage and fidelity in marriage." Christians generally have affirmed this ideal even when they have not adhered to it. They have affirmed it in the face of clear evidence of increasing premarital and extramarital sexual activity in American society. They have affirmed it in the face of challenges mounted by sociological and psychological studies that question whether such activity threatens family life and endangers personal happiness.

The traditional Christian view draws strong support from both the Old Testament and the New. The Old Testament Law speaks of intercourse as appropriate only within the context of marriage. Prostitution was prohibited for Hebrew women, and the men were warned against patronizing prostitutes. A man who had intercourse with an unmarried woman was required to marry her, and one who had intercourse with a married woman was to be executed.

Jesus did not say a great deal about the sexual relationship, perhaps because the people among whom he lived had such high standards. When he spoke on the subject, however, his approach was unusual. John 7:53–8:11 (a passage not included in all ancient Greek manuscripts) reports that he spoke forgivingly to a woman taken in adultery rather than agreeing to the punitive requirement of the Law. In his interpretation of the law against adultery he focused on the essential inwardness of morality by speaking of lust rather than of the overt act (Matthew 5:27–28). He did not reject the ideal to which he was an heir but reinterpreted it, focusing on redemption rather than punishment.

Writing to churches located in the Gentile world, where the moral standards were quite different, Paul was much more articulate and specific in his affirmation of what was moral and what was not. Although he insisted that one is saved by grace and not by obedience to the Law, he regarded the Law as a sound guide to moral conduct. He understood it to prohibit all sexual relationships outside of marriage, which he labeled "sexual immorality" (*porneia*). To the Corinthians he said, "Do you not know that wrongdoers will not inherit the kingdom of God? Do not be deceived! Fornicators, idolaters, adulterers, male prostitutes, sodomites, thieves, the greedy, drunkards, revilers, robbers—none of these will inherit the kingdom of God" (1 Corinthians 6:9–10). He said the same thing, in other words, to the Galatians (5:19–21), the Ephesians (5:3), and the Colossians (3:5–6). Whereas he recognized the legitimacy of the sexual relationship within marriage, he considered sexual immorality an aberration. "The body is not meant for fornication," he said, "but for the Lord, and the Lord for the body" (1 Corinthians 6:13). He considered sex outside marriage so serious a matter that he affirmed that "no fornicator or impure person . . . has any inheritance in the kingdom of Christ and of God" (Ephesians 5:5).

Is this traditional and biblical ideal valid for today? An extensive body of research reveals that an increasingly large percentage of our population, including many Christians, no longer think so. Many people do not simply refuse to live by the traditional standard; rather they reject the standard itself as irrelevant to life in the modern world. They cite the fact that researchers have discovered no significant evidence of any relationship between premarital sexual activity and success or failure in marriage, and therefore they see no reason for accepting such a demanding ideal.

Yet the ideal remains a valid guide for Christians trying to make good decisions on moral issues. Sociological research can tell us what many, or even most, people do, but it cannot tell us what is the good or right thing for us to do. While we cannot use the Scripture as a rule book for sexual conduct, we can use it to inform ourselves about our relationships with one another and with God. Without dictating to us, the Christian community, with its history and its presence with us, offers support for our allegiance to values that transcend common practice. In that context we can base our judgments on our understanding of God's purposes for us in our relationships with others. And in that context we can discover the strength and value of personal commitment and of accepting responsibility for ourselves and for other persons. Only in a trusting and committed relationship can the unique quality and intimacy of the coition find its highest meaning.

What is the place of the sexual relationship within marriage? Is it at the heart of a marriage or is it secondary to other matters? Does a satisfactory sexual relationship signal a successful marriage and an unsatisfactory sexual relationship an unsuccessful one? As traditional Christianity has considered abstinence from premarital intercourse to be the moral course, so has it considered fidelity in marriage to be the correct one. The sexual relationship is appropriately reserved for the most intimate communion between husband and wife. On the one hand, to engage in it with someone other than one's mate is to deny the essential oneness in marriage of which the Scripture speaks. Fidelity, on the other hand, is the natural result of that oneness. The love between a man and a woman is actually an exclusive relationship in which there is no room for competition.

Sexual expression is intended for the mutual benefit of husband and wife. Paul showed surprising insight and clarity in his statement of this fact in 1 Corinthians 7:3–5. This insight into the mutuality of the relationship has not always been understood. In the past many women regarded sex as a burdensome responsibility of marriage, or if they enjoyed sex they were ashamed to admit it. It is both possible and desirable, however, for both the wife and the husband to find meaning in sex. For this reason the word *gratification* is not the best term to use because it implies an act of self-seeking. The word *expression* is better because in the sexual relationship, properly understood, each partner expresses love and commitment and seeks to please the other. Because it is the most intimate of all human experiences, it is the most complete expression of love and the most profound way of knowing another person.

A CHRISTIAN INTERPRETATION OF MARRIAGE

In modern American mythology, love, sex, and marriage constitute an inseparable trilogy. In fact, of course, the three are easily separated. Love does not always express itself in coition, and it does not always lead to marriage. Sex, in the form of coition at least, is entirely possible apart from love and apart from marriage. Marriages that are both loveless and sexless do in fact exist. Like all other myths, however, this one expresses a reality. There is a connection between love, sex, and marriage because all three are concerned with the basic human yearning for intimacy and acceptance. For this reason, it is appropriate to consider a Christian interpretation of marriage in connection with a Christian interpretation of sex.

At the outset it must be understood that marriage is not a uniquely Christian institution. Indeed, in some form it exists in virtually every culture. So varied are its forms that the word itself is exceedingly difficult to define. The 1995 report of the Council on Families in America call it "a relationship within which a community socially approves and encourages sexual intercourse and the birth of children" (David Popenoe, et al., *Promises to Keep*, p. 302). This report recognizes five dimensions of marriage in Western societies:

1. It is "a *natural* institution, meeting and guiding the primary human inclinations toward sexual expression, reproduction, and emotional intimacy."
2. It is "a *sacramental* institution," sanctioned by religious symbols and rituals.
3. It is "an *economic* institution," a unit of consumption, exchange, and production.
4. It is "a *social* institution, nurturing and socializing children and regulating the behavior of both husbands and wives."
5. It is "a *legal* institution, protected and regulated by a body of law." (p. 304)

Although we are primarily concerned about religious and moral issues, we do not deal with them in the abstract, but within the framework of our culture.

Most Protestant wedding ceremonies include phrases similar to the one in the *Book of Common Prayer* that affirms marriage as "an honorable estate, instituted by God." This affirmation is usually reinforced by the passage in which Jesus quotes the Old Testament statement that God instituted marriage: "Have you not read that the one who made them at the beginning made them male and female, and said, 'For this reason a man shall leave his father and mother and be joined to his wife, and the two shall become one flesh'?" (Matthew 19:4–5; cf. Genesis 2:24).

Human beings were created in such a way, therefore, that the coming together of a man and a woman, not merely sexually but in a personal bonding, is a normal experience. To ask, "What is the purpose of marriage?" is no more logical than to ask, "What is the purpose of sleep?" A more appropriate question is, "What are the functions of marriage?" Stated in ideal terms, marriage functions in two basic ways. First, it provides a setting for the full personal development of each partner in self-giving and affords a deep sense of security and acceptance. Although not all marriages function effectively in this way, the relationship uniquely holds this possibility. Second, it provides a supportive structure for the birth and nurture of children. Obviously some children are born and reared outside marriage, and obviously not all married couples have children. Yet socially and religiously marriage is regarded as the best setting for parenthood.

Three words traditionally used to describe the Christian concept of marriage are *monogamy, unity,* and *indissolubility*. In our society monogamy is firmly established in law, and few people seriously challenge it. The high rate of divorce and remarriage, however, has altered the pattern so that monogamy is not taken to imply a permanent marriage. It should be noted that the growing emphasis on the equality of women is thoroughly consistent with the concept of monogamy. Taken seriously, the ideal of monogamy leaves no room for the subordination of one person to another, for the well-being of one to be completely controlled by the other, or for the future of one to be at the mercy of the other. If monogamy is understood in any sense other than a legal one, it means an exclusive and mutual commitment of two persons to each other.

The concept of unity is currently challenged on two fronts. First, there is the question of whether it is possible. Can a real unity be created from two distinct persons, with different backgrounds, personalities, attitudes, tastes, and temperaments? However much they love each other, do they not always retain their own identity? Do they not always remain distinct individuals? The second question is whether unity is desirable. Does anyone really want to give up individual interests, ambitions, aspirations, possibilities? Should we not be more concerned with the development of individual potential than with its elimination?

If unity means the loss of individual identity, it is neither possible nor desirable. Marriage should nurture each partner so that the personality of each can be developed to the fullest. Personality never develops in isolation, however, but through interaction with other persons. Neither does it act in isolation but in relationship with others. Furthermore, our lives are never static or stationary; we never cease growing and developing. The concept of unity in marriage means that a husband and a wife contribute to the development of each other in such a way that their lives grow together. They depend upon each other and they support each other. They are always in tension between *I* and *we*, and in their efforts to resolve that tension they try to see the one in light of the other.

When is such unity achieved? Most marriage ceremonies include the quotation "What therefore God hath joined together, let not man put asunder," and the person officiating pronounces the couple "husband and wife." Obviously that pronouncement does not impose a unity in any sense other than a legal one. Many who go through the ceremony are never really united. Any unity that is achieved by a couple begins when they single each other out from all other potential marriage partners. Everything that they do together is a part of the unifying process, both before the ceremony and after it. The unity cannot be said to have been established at any specific point. Rather, as long as character and personality develop and grow, then the two are in the process of becoming one.

Yet the significance of the marriage ceremony should not be minimized. Rites of passage are important not only in signaling a change in status but also in establishing it. Thus ceremonies are associated with birth and death, with attaining maturity, with religious affiliation and status, and with marriage. It is not only in the eyes of the world that a marriage ceremony establishes a union between a man and a woman; it is also in our own eyes that our status is changed and we become husband and wife. A religious ceremony acknowledges the conviction that the union is, in a sense, an act of God. In Christian terms the ceremony is, at the least, an acknowledgment that one's status is changed in the eyes of God and, at the most, an acknowledgment that the creation of the union is the work of God.

The consummation of a marriage in the act of sexual intercourse also should not be minimized in the creation of the unity. Since this act gathers up and expresses the total personality, there is something profound and irrevocable about the commitment made in it. It is the consummation of love and self-giving. Beyond it there is nothing that can effect that union more perfectly nor express it more adequately.

The concept of indissolubility is closely related to that of unity. Most Christians, while acknowledging that some developments do in fact destroy a marriage, nevertheless insist that the ideal calls for a permanent union. Following the reports of Jesus's teachings on divorce in Mark (10:11–12) and Luke (16:18) rather than those in Matthew (5:31–32 and 19:3–9), the Roman Catholic Church teaches that no marriage that was valid and consummated can ever be dissolved. (The Catholic Church does sometimes annul marriages that were contracted in violation of certain regulations.) At one time Protestant churches generally followed Matthew's account and accepted the possibility of divorce on the ground of unfaithfulness. At present, most Protestant churches, while they uphold the ideal of permanence, nevertheless recognize a variety of causes for failure and permit the remarriage of divorced persons.

Are the Protestant churches ignoring the teachings of Jesus when they assent to the termination of some marriages? To answer this question we need to consider why Jesus taught what he did and try to determine whether he would say the same thing today. Although we cannot answer these questions certainly and completely, we do know that women of his day needed the protection that his position represented. The only Old Testament law on the subject permitted a man to divorce his wife if he found "something objectionable in her" (Deuteronomy 24:1). The intent of the word "objectionable" was debated in Jesus's day. Although some rabbis interpreted it to mean only sexual impurity, it was generally given a quite liberal interpretation. Divorce, therefore, though impossible for a woman, was quite easy for a man. A single woman, however, was in an untenable position in that society. A woman depended on her father until she was married and then on her husband. Because there were no legitimate ways for women to earn their own living, they needed the care and support of some man. To divorce a woman, therefore, was to deprive her of all security. Today most women are capable of fending for themselves, and indeed an increasing number are quite pleased to do so. Because they do not have to have husbands, they are not victimized by divorce in the same way that women were in Jesus's day. While the ideal of a permanent union remains and while the satisfactions of such a union remain important, the economic consequences of failure are not nearly so damaging to women.

Permanence is probably a better word than *indissolubility* to describe the ideal. Indissolubility has an extremely legalistic connotation, implying that there is no way out of a marriage no matter how bad it is. Permanence, however, implies an ideal that is closely related to unity. It suggests that the unity of a couple is not something that they are locked into but something that they work to achieve and to maintain.

In *Promises to Keep,* a collection of essays by lawyers, social scientists, and theologians dealing with the status of marriage in the United States, sociologist David Popenoe writes:

> Marriage in America is in trouble. A culture that once treasured the institution of marriage has been steadily displaced by a culture of divorce and unwed parenthood. In the past several decades the divorce rate has doubled and the percentage of unwed births has quintupled. Trends such as these have created tragic hardships for children, generated poverty within families, and burdened us with unsupportable social costs. At the same time, no one seems to be much happier. (p. ix)

In the interest of preserving the values of stable marriage in our society, in the concluding essay of the book Popenoe proposes "Seven Tenets for Establishing New Marital Norms." These proposals seem to retain much of the traditional American Christian ideal and at the same time to accommodate to the changes which took place in this country during the last two or three decades of the twentieth century:

1. "Girls, as well as boys, should be trained according to their abilities for a socially useful paid job or career."
2. "Young people should grow up with the expectation that they will marry, only once and for a lifetime, and that they will have children."
3. "Young adults should be encouraged to marry later in life than is common now, with an average age at time of marriage in the late twenties or early thirties."
4. Because people would live "for about a decade or more in a non-family, 'singles' environment, "young unmarried adults should be encouraged to save a substantial portion of their income for a 'family fund' with an eye toward offsetting the temporary loss of the wife's income after marriage and childbirth."
5. "Once children are born, wives should be encouraged to leave the labor market and become substantially full-time mothers for a period of at least a year to eighteen months per child."
6. "According to this proposal, the mother and not the father ordinarily would be the primary caretaker of infants." After the child reaches the age of

eighteen months, however, "it may be desirable for the father and not the mother to become the primary caretaker."

7. In later life, "some role switching occurs . . . in which women become more work-oriented and men become more domestic." (pp. 262–265)

HOMOSEXUALITY AND THE CHRISTIAN FAITH

So far the discussion has concerned heterosexual relationships. It is becoming increasingly apparent, however, that many people are homosexual. Just how large that number is cannot be determined, but estimates range between two and ten percent of the population.

The terms "heterosexual" and "homosexual" are by no means as precise as most people assume. "Heterosexual" is generally used to designate people who are attracted to people of the opposite sex, and "homosexual" to refer to people who are attracted to persons of the same gender. But some people are neither exclusively heterosexual nor exclusively homosexual in their erotic inclinations. A statement published by the American Psychiatric Association in 1997 affirms that "Sexual orientation exists along a continuum that ranges from exclusive homosexuality to exclusive heterosexuality and includes various forms of bisexuality" (Polaski and Eiland, *Rightly Dividing the Word of Truth*, p. 167). Although it is difficult to draw a sharp line, however, Fromer's characterization of homosexuality is helpful. He describes a homosexual person as one "who feels a strong erotic attraction to persons of the same sex, who has the ability to be sexually aroused by members of the same sex, and who prefers to engage in sexual activity with members of the same sex" (*Ethical Issues in Sexuality and Reproduction*, p. 81).

How do we explain the fact that a significant number of people feel "a strong erotic attraction to persons of the same sex"? One approach is to think of homosexuality as a completely natural phenomenon. According to this view, some people are born with this proclivity just as others are born with a heterosexual orientation. Although psychological factors are involved in the development of a person's sexual disposition, genes set the basic pattern. Any effort to deny or to alter a person's homosexual orientation is pointless because it is dictated by nature. A number of studies have been conducted to discover whether this is the case, and there is significant evidence to support a biological basis for homosexuality. Although the findings have not been entirely consistent, there is enough evidence to indicate that this hypothesis needs further exploration.

A second possibility is that a homosexual disposition is psychologically caused. Most students who take this approach consider it to be an arrested or distorted psychosexual development, which is the result of an abnormal relationship with one or both parents. Some people regard it as a mental illness, and indeed for many years the American Psychological Association classified it as such. In 1973, however, the Association removed it from the list of mental illnesses, although some psychologists still consider it to be such. If it is an illness, it is subject to treatment and perhaps cure.

A third approach to homosexuality stresses social and cultural conditioning. According to this view, the "accident" that leads an individual into his or her first homosexual experience, the conditioning effects of that experience, and the impact of prevailing social attitudes toward such sexual contact shape future behavior. One homosexual contact does not necessarily lead to homosexuality, as a large percentage of the people in our society know. Yet many people believe that in some instances the first sexual experience plays a significant role in the development of a pattern of homosexuality. Especially vulnerable, they think, are children of parents whose attitudes and discipline lead to an inhibition of normal sexual behavior. One who has been reared with the attitude that normal sexual relationships are dirty may develop an aversion to heterosexual relationships and thus lay the foundation for deviation from the usual pattern.

It may be that there is no one explanation for the fact that a given percentage of human beings are homosexual. Rather the explanation may be multidimensional: Biological, psychological, and sociological factors may combine with individual experience to bring about this result. This confusion makes our effort to look at the situation from a Christian perspective more difficult.

The very effort to explain the sexual orientation of gay and lesbian people implies that their orientation is abnormal, as contrasted with the normal orientation of other people. Furthermore, it tends to make objects of them, ignoring their emotions, their history, their personal struggle, and their status in society. Nearing the age of forty, formerly married, and the father of two children, Mel White, an evangelical Christian minister and theologian, came out as gay. With a personal letter dated December 24, 1991, written to Jerry Falwell, for whom he had been a ghostwriter, White responded to Falwell's widely circulated anti-homosexual letter. White said to Falwell, "I am gay. For the past eight years (which include all the time I've been in your employment) I have been in a loving, monogamous relationship with another gay man." He added, "We gay people are not 'perverts' nor 'degenerates' as the letter claims. My homosexuality is as much at the heart of what it means to be Mel White as your heterosexuality is at the heart of what it means to be Jerry Falwell" (White, *Stranger at the Gate*, pp. 292, 293). A year and a half later White wrote to another anti-gay minister:

> Like hundreds of thousands of your fellow Christian Americans, I spent twenty-five years trying to be an "ex-gay." Even after my conversion experience, I spent tens of thousands of dollars on Christian therapy. Repeatedly, I was counseled, exorcised, electric-shocked, medicated, and prayed for by the saints. Like the young people in your TV special, I began each new day really believing that God had "healed me," when in fact, I was simply refusing to face the facts.

Finally, I realized that my sexual orientation was permanently and purpose-fully formed in my mother's womb or in my earliest infancy. Because of sim-plistic, well-meaning, but uninformed teachings on homosexuality like your own, I wasted thirty-five years in guilt, fear, and personal agony. And though there were times I could not feel God's presence, God never left my side. God's Spirit was there always to comfort and to guide me. Now I have accepted my sexual orientation as a gift from my loving Creator. Finally, as our Savior promised, the truth has set me free to be a productive, responsible, Christian gay man. (*Stranger at the Gate*, p. 314)

Currently the legal status of homosexuality is changing. Laws concern-ing homosexual activity remain on the books in almost half the states, and the penalty for conviction of a "crime against nature" is imprisonment vary-ing from ten years to life. In addition, there are many local ordinances that are sometimes enforced and sometimes not. Even though the laws are rarely enforced, the criminalizing of homosexuality reinforces other forms of dis-crimination. The abolition of those laws is therefore a major concern for many people, and activists are exerting pressure to bring this about. They are meeting with some local success because public opinion is changing slowly, and many people now affirm that what consenting adults do in private should not be subject to legal regulation. As yet, however, there has been little change in state laws.

Court decisions have often upheld the right of both private agencies and the government to refuse to deal with gays and lesbians. For the most part, federal and state laws do not prohibit private employers from refusing to hire them, although some local governments have adopted regulations against such a policy. In most states there are no laws that prohibit landlords from refusing to rent to a prospective tenant whom they know or believe to be homosexual. In the past, persons known to be homosexual were not allowed to enlist in the armed forces of the United States, and people were discharged when the fact of their homosexuality was disclosed. The military regulations affirmed that "Homosexuality is incompatible with military service" and that the presence of a homosexual person "seriously impairs the accomplishment of the military mission" (Fromer, pp. 98–101). In 1993 the ban on gays and les-bians in the military was eased slightly by a policy that prohibited recruiters from asking about sexual orientation and prohibited gays and lesbians in the military from openly acknowledging their orientation. That change in policy has satisfied no one, however. Most of the military see it as creating serious difficulties within the armed services, and most gay and lesbian people see it as a grudging concession that in fact complicates their problems.

Gays and lesbians are often denied the courtesy and respect that other people take for granted. They are treated in ways "ranging from half-hidden scorn to open hatred," says Morton Hunt. "People avoid them, exclude them, whisper or joke about them, stare at them with open hostility" (Hunt, *Gay*, pp. 59–60). Some family members refuse to have anything to do with them, and others pretend not to know about their homosexuality. According to one survey, most Americans consider homosexuality morally wrong, and most think that gays and lesbians should not be allowed to serve as judges, schoolteachers, or ministers. Many people would deny them the privilege of being doctors or government officials, many think that they try to become sexually involved with children, and many say that they try to avoid associating with them (Levitt and Klassen, "Public Attitudes toward Homosexuality," in Levine, pp. 20–35).

This public sentiment parallels the attitude of the churches. Until about 1970, homosexuality was essentially ignored by the major religious groups. Both clergy and theologians said as little as possible about it. When they did speak it, usually they either condemned it as a sin or expressed a concern for it as an illness. In recent years, however, responding to an increasingly open and vocal homosexual population and to scientific investigations of the nature of homosexual orientation, many churches are giving new attention to this matter. Although the hierarchy of the Roman Catholic Church continues its vigorous condemnation of homosexuality, many priests and lay people challenge this ruling. Some Protestant churches, notably the Episcopal Church, the United Methodist Church, and the Presbyterian Church, are struggling with the question of the extent to which gays and lesbians may participate in the life and work of the church. Other denominations have not moved from the view that homosexuality is a sin, although a significant minority in those churches is urging the support for the civil rights of gays and lesbians and their acceptance within the church without restriction. Meanwhile, finding themselves unwelcome and uncomfortable in the mainline Protestant churches, many homosexual Christians have identified themselves with the Metropolitan Church.

In our attempt to consider homosexuality from a Christian perspective we begin with a look at biblical teachings. We are struck, however, by the rarity of pertinent biblical references. In the Old Testament, indeed, there are only three:

1. *Genesis 19:1–11.* The city of Sodom, sentenced to destruction because of its sinfulness, lost its opportunity for reprieve when the men of the city attempted the homosexual rape of God's emissaries who were visiting Lot. Was the offense homosexuality or gang rape? There is clearly no reference to consensual sexual activity of any sort.
2. *Judges 19:22–30.* In a situation similar to the event in Sodom, certain men of the tribe of Benjamin attempted the rape of a visiting Levite. This account, too, deals with sexual violence.
3. *Leviticus 18:22 and 20:13.* A part of the Holiness Code, these regulations include homosexuality in a catalogue of a variety of sexual offenses for which severe punishment is spelled out. These laws clearly refer to homosexual acts.

In the New Testament the only passage in which homosexuality is discussed is Romans 1:18–32. This passage is part of Paul's larger discussion of the entire world's need for Christ (Romans 1:16–2:29). Paul begins with the affirmation that all people, Jewish and Gentile alike, are sinful and that all are saved in the same way, by grace through faith (1:16–17). In Romans 1:18–32 he speaks of the Gentiles' need for Christ, and in 2:1–29 he speaks of the Jews' need for Christ. The sin of the Gentiles, from which they need redemption, is idolatry. Homosexuality, according to Paul, is one consequence of that idolatry.

It is not at all certain that the other New Testament passages commonly cited actually refer to homosexuality. First Corinthians 6:9–10 lists a number of types of sinful persons, including one that some translations render "homosexuals" but that the New Revised Standard Version renders "male prostitutes." The word translated "sodomites" in this passage is usually taken to refer to gay men but may just as well refer to those who engage in sexual violence. The same is true of the references 2 Peter 2:6–10, Jude 7, and 1 Timothy 1:8–11.

From a biblical perspective, then, is homosexuality to be considered a sin? Christian biblical scholars and ethicists are divided. Some unequivocally call homosexuality sinful. Edward Malloy, for example, after an examination of a wide variety of literature on the subject and after consideration of the psychological and sociological theories, concludes, "I am convinced that the homosexual way of life, as evolved in the social structures and practices of the homosexual sub-culture, is irreconcilable with the Christian way of life" (*Homosexuality and the Christian Way of Life*, p. 328). Lynn R. Buzzard says, "Both the specific injunctions of Scripture, the general teaching of Scripture and our general understanding of the nature of men and women makes homosexuality *ab*normal, *un*natural." According to Buzzard, the attitude of God toward the homosexual is that "God really cares about him and loves him" and also that "he/she ought to repent" ("How Gray is Gay?" in Twiss, pp. 51, 53). Buzzard assumes, as do many people, that even if homosexuality is not a deliberately chosen way of life, it can be deliberately rejected. "There is increasing evidence," says Buzzard, "that some, if not all, homosexuals can change if they really want to" (p. 53).

Others regard homosexuality as an abnormality with which certain persons must deal. This is the stance of Lewis B. Smedes, who says that "No homosexual, to my knowledge, ever decides to be homosexual; he only makes the painful discovery at one time or another that he is homosexual" (*Sex for Christians*, p. 54). Smedes consistently speaks of homosexuality as "abnormal" and "unnatural," and understands the pertinent biblical passages as teaching that "homosexual practices are unnatural and godless" (p. 51). He thinks of "normal" sexuality as (1) "woven into the whole character" of a person, (2) "an urge toward and a means of expressing a deep personal relationship with another person," and (3) moving a person "toward a heterosexual union of committed love" p. 29). Without assessing blame, Smedes says that homosexuality might (with great difficulty) meet the first and second criteria, but that it obviously cannot meet the third. He then makes three recommendations for "a responsible confrontation with one's own homosexuality."

First, he says, the homosexual person "should courageously face the abnormality of his condition" and "simply refuse to accept a burden of guilt for his condition." Instead, he "should recognize his own responsibility for what he does with his homosexual drives." Second, he should "believe that change is possible" and try to make that change. Third, if he cannot change he should either live a celibate life or "develop the best ethical conditions in which to live out his sexual life." "Within his sexual experience, he ought to develop permanent associations with another person, associations in which respect and regard for the other as a person dominate their sexual relationship" (pp. 55–58).

Still other Christian ethicists think of homosexuality as a fact of life within which some persons can function as Christians, just as heterosexuality is a fact of life within which other people can function as Christians. They do not regard one's sexual orientation, in other words, to be a determining factor in one's relationship to God. David Bartlett affirms this view in an essay first published in 1978 (in Twiss, *Homosexuality and the Christian Faith*) and reissued in 2000 (in Polaski and Eiland, *Rightly Dividing the Word of Truth*). In discussing Paul's statement about homosexuality (Romans 1:16–32), he says that the central idea is that no one is justified by his or her own goodness but by grace through faith. This passage is not about homosexuality but about the need of all people for salvation. "The discussion of a variety of sins, including idolatry and self-righteousness," Bartlett says, "is used to point toward everyone's need for God's gracious and redemptive mercy in Christ" ("A Biblical Perspective on Homosexuality," in Twiss, p. 31; Polaski and Eiland, p. 30). Bartlett uses the same method in discussing Paul's statement to the Galatians, "For in Christ Jesus neither circumcision nor uncircumcision is of any avail, but faith working through love" (Galatians 5:6). He suggests that for the words "neither circumcision nor uncircumcision" we could substitute "neither heterosexuality nor homosexuality" (Twiss, p. 39; Polaski and Eiland, p. 35). He believes that the recognition of homosexuality as an "unchangeable affectional preference" requires us to reject an ethic "which insists that homosexuals should either try to engage, unhappily, in heterosexual relationships, or remain celibate" (Twiss, pp. 34–35; Polaski and Eiland, p. 32). The gifts of God's Spirit, he says, are "equally available to heterosexual people and to homosexual people" (Twiss, p. 38; Polaski and Eiland, p. 34).

What, then, can we assume about homosexuality and the Christian way of life? Two observations are pertinent. First, since the best evidence suggests that people do not choose to be either heterosexual or homosexual, but rather are either born with a given sexual orientation or molded by psychological or sociological conditioning, there can be no credit or blame for either heterosexuality or homosexuality. One's sexual orientation is a matter entirely beyond one's control in just the same sense as is the color of one's eyes. It is simply a fact of life, which one accepts.

Second, the homosexual Christian has the same obligation to deal responsibly with his or her sexuality that the heterosexual Christian does. Here we must be a bit more tentative because Scripture, as we have seen, does not deal with homosexuality per se. We may assume, however, that except for procreation, sex functions in the same way in a homosexual relationship as in a heterosexual one. If this is true, can we not assume that gays and lesbians may commit themselves to each other in loving and caring relationships? That the ideal for such relationships is monogamy, fidelity, and indissolubility? That their union is one in which there is mutuality of responsibility and privilege? One that will help each partner to develop as a whole person? One to which the church may give its blessing? The idea of blessing was affirmed by the Alliance of Baptists in 1999, when they adopted a report which included the statement,

> We encourage the churches to lift up the ideal of covenant—that is, challenging persons, whether heterosexual or same-sex oriented, to express sexual intimacy within the covenant context of a committed, monogamous relationship. One example of that support could be a ritual of covenant-making between the couple, the couple and God, and the couple and the Christian Community. (*A Clear Voice: Report of the Task Force on Human Sexuality*, p. 5)

"Homosexual acts between persons who intend a genuine union in love are not sinful nor should the church consider them as such," says Norman Pittenger ("The Morality of Homosexual Acts," in Batchelor, ed., *Homosexuality and Ethics*, p. 139). He outlines the conditions under which such relationships are genuinely moral: The two persons must be committed to each other rather than using each other, there must be no element of coercion, the two must intend some loyalty to each other, each must welcome and appreciate the personality of the other, and the relationship must involve a union of lives in which the identity and the freedom of each is preserved (p. 140). This outline is in fact a description of an ideal marital relationship. We have no problem in assuming that although the ideal so described is difficult for a man and a woman to achieve, it is possible for them to do so by the grace of God. Can we also assume that by the grace of God two people of the same sex can achieve it?

LIVING-TOGETHER ARRANGEMENTS

One campus minister observed that every couple for whom he had performed a wedding ceremony during the past five years was already living together at the time of their marriage. Another campus minister challenged the obvious conclusion by saying that only a few of the couples for whom he had performed ceremonies were already living together. Who can say which minister was dealing with the more typical group? While no one knows how many unmarried couples are living together in this country, the practice is clearly increasing rapidly. In 1998 the U.S. Census Bureau reported approximately four million households with two unrelated adults of opposite sexes, as compared with approximately a half a million in 1970. In both instances, the figures are probably unrealistically low.

Why do unmarried people take up residence together? Obviously sex has something to do with it, but it cannot be the full explanation. After all, sexual activity is not restricted to people who are living together. Waite and Gallagher focus on the attraction of having certain benefits usually associated with marriage without making any commitment. They say:

> Cohabitation is a halfway house for people who do not want the degree of personal and social commitment that marriage represents, at least not now. As such, the cohabitation deal does offer some short-term advantages for both men and women. Men and women who live together can get some of the benefits of being married—a readily available sex partner who will share the rent and do some of the cooking—without making any long-term promises. And those who are anxious about marriage, either because they feel that they would not make a good spouse or that their partner would not make a good spouse, may decide to only live together. . . . Living together lets you keep your money separate, avoid responsibility for your partner's debts, and leave easily if things get too bad. (*The Case for Marriage*, p. 42)

Perhaps the most important reason for a living-together arrangement, however, is the common, if not universal, human characteristic of a yearning for intimacy, for a sense of belonging to someone else, for a sense of security in an exclusive personal relationship.

What happens to these relationships? After a time—the average lifetime of a living-together arrangement is approximately two years (Waite and Gallagher, *The Case for Marriage*, p. 38)—a couple is likely either to separate or to formalize their relationship in marriage. This does not mean that the arrangement is intended to be a "trial marriage." Upon entering into such arrangements, most couples do not look beyond the arrangement itself. They do not expect it to be permanent; if they did they would probably marry at the outset. They realize that marriage may follow, but they also realize that it may not. No statistics are available to indicate what is the most frequent development.

In several ways living-together arrangements are like a marriage. For one thing, there is a pattern of sexual relationship that involves more than the physical act itself. This relationship has meaning for both partners, though not necessarily the same meaning. It is a way of communicating, though what is communicated is not always understood and if understood is not always appreciated. Sexual behavior affects and is affecting and being affected by everything else in the relationship.

Another similarity is that, like marriages, living-together arrangements require agreement on certain economic considerations. Clearly there has to be some agreement on the financial obligations of each partner. Moreover, there are the routine affairs of housekeeping: preparing meals, washing dishes, housecleaning, taking care of clothes. What happens when one partner is ill? What about the acquisition of common property? Even more subtle are details in the relationship: What adjustments must be made about the time each partner owes the other? What consideration is due when the regular schedule is upset? How are differing opinions resolved? What about different preferences in food or television programs or the timing of certain activities? The list is infinite. Two people who begin living together must make a big adjustment, whether or not they are married.

A third similarity is that a living-together arrangement, like a marriage, entails a growing emotional involvement, one affected both by happy experiences and by unhappy ones, by conflict and by making up, by shared activities and communication about activities not shared. It is profoundly affected by the routines that develop and by any upset of them. For good or for ill, two people who live together, whether married or not, become a part of each other.

But these arrangements are not marriages. Unlike marriages, they have no legal sanction. Whereas marriage is defined by law, and to a certain extent is regulated by law, living-together arrangements are not. That fact becomes important in a consideration of the rights of both parties, both while the relationship lasts and when it is terminated. In some states, statutes have been enacted to protect the financial interests of the partners, particularly in the areas of inheritance rights and medical care. For the most part, however, the problems become serious and complicated when the couple begins to acquire property. Because the legal situation is so confused, some people suggest a written agreements that protect individual rights, with a particular focus on property. The legal status of such agreements, however, is unclear.

Neither do these arrangements have a religious sanction. Apparently this consideration is important to more people than is generally assumed. Even though only two-thirds of the people in this country claim membership in some religious group, more than ninety percent of those who marry look for a minister, priest, or rabbi to conduct the ceremony. And they usually want a religious ceremony, with vows, prayers, and Scripture, the whole works! While people do not suddenly become religious at the time of their wedding, most people do seem to value some religious sanction of their marriage. That sanction is missing from living-together arrangements.

Even more significant a difference is the lack of commitment that characterizes living-together arrangements. They are not entered into with the expectation that they will be permanent. The usual marriage ceremony contains the phrase "till death us do part" or the phrase, "as long as we both shall live." People who make that vow intend at the time to keep it. Although a high percentage of marriages do not turn out to be permanent, they are begun with the expectation that they will be. The couple promise themselves, the world at large, and even God that they will make it so. That commitment, realistic or not but clearly a part of marriage, is missing from a living-together arrangement.

Presumably Christian young people contemplating a living-together arrangement have already made their decision about sex outside marriage. If that decision was made without careful thought to the religious and ethical issues, they would do well to think about them before they take up residence together. If they have thought of them, however, and have decided that their faith does not require them to refrain from sexual intercourse before marriage, several other questions about other aspects of living together remain.

First, what spiritual and emotional resources do the partners have that will sustain the relationship under the inevitable pressures it will encounter? The simple fact of being together so much of the time places a strain on a relationship. The disruption of an accustomed way of life, the differences in personal habits, the eccentricities of each individual, the difficulty of making time for oneself, the impossibility of each meeting all the expectations of the other—all of these factors and many more create tension. The romantic involvement that we label "love," which is chiefly a physical attraction, is not adequate to deal with these tensions. Obviously a couple can learn to handle them if they choose to do so. But the question is, "What will make them want to do so?" In other words, what takes the place of the commitment that provides the framework within which a married couple deals with these matters?

Second, does it matter what other people think? Put another way, can a couple make their own decisions without regard to other people? One of the presuppositions that underlies ethics is that each individual has both the right of and the responsibility for decision making. For Christians, decisions are made within the context of the Christian community, and one source of guidance is the tradition of that community. Christians, therefore, should quite properly consider other people. How are our parents affected by what we do? How is our relationship with our parents affected by our decision? How do we relate to the church? How do we relate as individuals and as a couple to the broader community? To raise these questions is not to predetermine the answer; it is to say that in making these decisions Christians need to take into account all of the persons to whom they relate and how these relationships will be affected by their decision.

Third, and closely related to the second, is the question of the importance of "a piece of paper." If two people love each other, do they need a piece of paper to make them remain together? If they do not love each other, why should they remain together? The legal importance of the marriage contract has already been discussed, and its religious significance has at least been hinted at. But what of its emotional importance to the couple? Apart from such mundane matters as respectability and property rights, does the contract make any difference in their relationship? The contract might be compared to a sacrament. A sacrament is "an outward sign of an inward grace." Is it a necessary sign? Is it a helpful sign? Is the sign in any sense the vehicle of grace? Do we need the sign to confirm in our lives the experience of grace? These questions about sacraments are applicable to the piece of paper. Is there something within us that wants this confirmation (even if it does not require it)? Does the paper provide a sense of emotional security? Does it offer a challenge? Does it make the relationship more stable and more meaningful than it could otherwise be?

The final question that needs to be considered is how the living-together arrangement will be terminated. This is important because, as we have indicated, nearly all couples either marry or terminate the relationship after about two years together. Before entering into a relationship, therefore, one needs to contemplate the end. Some such arrangements lead to marriage, although there is no way to know what percentage do so. And some of those marriages turn out to be good and enduring. Apparently the couple came to believe that their relationship would be better if they were married, and their belief proved to be correct. Not all of those marriages turn out to be stable and happy, however, and many soon end in divorce. The failure of those marriages cannot be due to changing a relationship that was good and happy, because had the relationship been ideal, the couple would not have felt any need to change it. Apparently they married in an effort to prevent a breakup but failed in their purpose.

The other way a relationship is terminated is by separation. It is popularly assumed that the separation of a couple not legally married is easier than the divorce of a married couple because there are fewer legal entanglements and because only the two people are involved. That may be true of short-lived relationships, but the longer the couple live together the more complicated it becomes. One reason is that the two invariably begin to acquire joint property, and the more they have the more difficult its equitable distribution becomes when they separate. In addition, while it is assumed that each person would take out of the arrangement those items he or she brought into it, there are often conflicts concerning who owned what. Another, more serious problem, however, is the emotional difficulty of separation. What ties a married couple together is not so much the law as emotional involvement: shared experiences, shared concerns, shared conflicts. They have been related to each other in a highly complex way, and when that relationship is terminated by divorce, separation, or death, there is a profound sense of loss. The same thing is true of the involvement of those who live together without marriage; the longer they remain together the more their lives become intertwined. When they separate, even if the separation is mutually desired, they have the same sense of loss as do married people who divorce. And the problem is complicated by the absence of any kind of structure within which to deal with the loss.

QUESTIONS AND TOPICS FOR DISCUSSION

1. What is the relationship between love and sex? Between love and marriage? Between sex and marriage?
2. Discuss the ways in which marriage is defined. Can the term be used in our society without reference to the law? Without reference to religion? Without reference to a ceremony?
3. How is the ideal of unity in marriage affected by the changing status of women?
4. Can a marriage be established between two persons of the same sex?
5. What is the role in the church of gays and lesbians?
6. What is the role in the church of Christians who are in a living-together arrangement?

RECOMMENDATIONS FOR FURTHER READING

A Clear Voice: Report of the Task Force on Human Sexuality. Washington: The Alliance of Baptists, 2000. p. 5)

CAHIL, LISA SOWLE, *Sex, Gender, and Christian Ethics.* New York: Cambridge University Press, 1996.

COWAN, PAUL, and RACHEL COWAN, *Mixed Blessings: Overcoming the Stumbling Blocks in an Interfaith Marriage.* New York: Penguin, 1988.

GRENZ, STANLEY J., *Sexual Ethics: An Evangelical Perspective.* Louisville: Westminster John Knox, 1990 (1997).

JACKSON, CHRIS, *The Black Christian Singles Guide to Dating and Sexuality.* New York: Harper Collins, 1998.

McNEILL, JOHN J., *The Church and the Homosexual.* Boston: Beacon Press, 1988.

POLASKI, LeDAYNE McLEESE, and MILLARD EILAND, *Rightly Dividing the Word of Truth.* Washington: The Alliance of Baptists, 2000.

POPENOE, DAVID, JEAN BETHKE ELSSHTAN, and DAVID BLAKENHORN, *Promises to Keep: Decline and Renewal of Marriage in America.* Lanham, Md.: Rowman and Littlefield, 1996.

SIKER, JEFFREY S., *Homosexuality in the Church.* Louisville: Westminster John Knox, 1994.

SMEDES, LEWIS B., *Love Within Limits.* Grand Rapids: Eerdmans, 1990.

SMEDES, LEWIS B., *Sex for Christians,* revised edition. Grand Rapids: Eerdmans, 1994.

WAITE, LINDA J., and MAGGIE GALLAGHER, *The Case for Marriage.* New York: Doubleday, 2000.

8

Life and Death:
Issues in Biomedical Ethics

New methods of research and new technologies have resulted in dramatic developments in health care during the past fifty years. One consequence has been a shift of responsibility for decision making from the physician to the patient. We would like to be able to say to the physician, "You're the doctor. Do what you think best. I just want to get well." But increasingly patients are faced with such issues as choosing between two undesirable courses of action, choosing between two possible treatments, or deciding whether a treatment that can be done should be done. Should a pregnant woman who does not want to give birth to a child have her pregnancy terminated? Should a couple who want a child but cannot have one without following some extraordinary procedures resort to such measures? Should a person risk an organ transplant that offers the hope of prolonging life for only two or three years? What steps should be taken to prolong the life of a family member who is dying? Should we ask a physician to follow procedures that ease the pain but shorten the life of a terminally ill patient? Scientific and medical research have opened up a wide array of possibilities. Any one of us may be compelled to make agonizing decisions about medical treatment for ourselves or members of our family. In this chapter we shall consider six basic issues in biomedical ethics that individuals may face: abortion, biomedical parenting, cloning, responsible parenthood, organ transplants, and euthanasia. (The social issue of unequal access to health care is discussed in Chapter 14.)

ABORTION

On January 22, 1973, the Supreme Court of the United States handed down a decision in the case of *Roe* v. *Wade* that significantly altered the legality of abortion. For nearly a decade there had been signs that the change was coming. Through the mid-1960s the laws of every state had severely limited the right of a woman to have an abortion, most states permitting the procedure only when the life of the woman was threatened by the pregnancy. In 1967, however, legislation that was much more lenient but still maintained certain restrictions was adopted in Colorado, California, and North Carolina. In 1969 the legislature of New York State removed all restrictions, effectively making abortion legal for any woman who elected to have one. No change had been made in Texas, however, when in 1972 a single, pregnant woman challenged the state's law that prohibited abortion except when the life of the woman was in danger. The district court ruled in her favor, the decision was appealed, and in 1973 the Supreme Court upheld the district court decision, declaring that a decision about abortion should be made by the pregnant woman herself, not by some other agency.

Basing their decision on the Ninth and Fourteenth Amendments, the Court applied the right of privacy to a woman's decision on whether or not to have a child. The Court said that a woman's right to an abortion is limited by the state's appropriate interest in safeguarding the health of the woman, in maintaining proper medical standards, and in protecting human life. The last of these interests of the state is of particular importance. The ruling affirms that a fetus is not a person in the sense in which the Fourteenth Amendment uses the term. Yet the potential of the fetus and its state of development are recognized by the variance in the regulations based on the trimesters of pregnancy. According to the ruling, a state cannot prohibit abortion during the first trimester. In the interest of protecting the health of the woman, a state may insist that during the second trimester abortions be performed only by qualified medical personnel in proper facilities. During the last trimester, when the fetus is considered viable, the state may prohibit all abortions except those that are essential to protect the life or health of the mother.

The 1973 decision essentially invalidated all state legislation prohibiting abortions. It did not permanently resolve the legal issue, however, and in the next decade and a half a number of other cases made their way through the courts. Two were of particular importance. First, on July 3, 1989, in a five-to-four decision, the Supreme Court moved in the direction of a reversal of *Roe* v. *Wade* by upholding the constitutionality of a Missouri law that restricts the right to abortion. *Webster* v. *Reproductive Health Services* grants to the states wide authority to restrict abortion and leaves the door open to other test cases. Second, in 1992, ruling on *Planned Parenthood* v. *Casy*, the Court reaffirmed the basic direction of *Roe* v. *Wade*, but also supported the authority of the states to regulate abortion. While these rulings have not overturned *Roe* v. *Wade*, they have led to significant restrictions at the state level on a woman's right to have an abortion.

The nation itself remains so divided on the morality of abortion that often the issue becomes a major consideration in political campaigns. A number of anti-abortion organizations are quite active in working to bring about changes in the law. All of them hope to affect public opinion and private judgment. Pro-choice groups are equally active in defending the right of any woman to make a free decision to have an abortion if it seems best for her to do so. The issue is further complicated by the question of whether government funds can be used in any way to pay for abortions for poor women.

Whatever the legal situation, the question of whether to have an abortion is a major moral issue for the person who must deal with an unwanted pregnancy. No longer can one avoid the moral issue by falling back on the law or on medical concerns. Though the moral implications are thorny, from a Christian perspective they are important. In considering them, it is helpful to review the attitudes current in American society.

First, many people believe that abortion is morally wrong and that it should never be performed under any circumstances. This is the viewpoint of the Roman Catholic Church and of many Protestant Christians. The right-to-life movement, in which the Roman Catholic Church has historically taken the lead, draws support from a broad section of the American population. The people who subscribe to this view think of the fetus as a human being. As far as personhood is concerned, they make no distinction based on the stage of development of the fetus. From the moment of conception, the fetus is treated as having the same right to life as any other human being. These opponents of abortion consider the deliberate destruction of a human fetus to be murder. People who hold this view recognize that in some instances a choice must be made between the life of the unborn child and the life of the mother, that there is a life-for-life situation in which one must be sacrificed to the other. In these circumstances some people concede that the right decision may be to sacrifice the unborn child to save the life of the mother.

Second, some people argue that abortion is wrong except under a limited number of quite specific conditions. It can be justified, they say, only if (1) it is necessary to preserve the physical or mental health of the mother, (2) there is clear evidence that the child would be born with severe physical or mental handicaps, or (3) the pregnancy was the result of rape or incest. This approach implies that although abortion is sometimes the lesser of two evils, it is nevertheless evil. It can be justified only by demonstrating that a higher good is thereby served, that greater evil would result from not having the abortion than from having it. While this approach requires some decision making, it is not the woman who makes the decision. The decision that an abortion is indicated is made by the physician.

Third, many people believe that the decision concerning an abortion should be made by the woman alone. They believe that the Supreme Court's decision in 1973 was right not only because it is a correct interpretation of the Constitution but also because it is consistent with the dignity and responsibility of the individual. Any woman, they say, has an inherent right to choose to terminate a pregnancy when, for whatever reason, she judges it best for her to do so. They argue that a fetus is not in fact a human being but only potentially so and that the rights of a fetus should not be allowed to override the rights of a person. Only when the fetus has become viable, that is, when it is able to live outside the womb (a condition that emerges some time between the twenty-fourth and the twenty-eighth weeks of pregnancy) should its rights be equated with those of a human being. Before that time a woman has the moral right to terminate a pregnancy.

If abortion is murder, as those who hold the first view assert, then there is no moral issue to be decided. The distinction between right and wrong is clear and the only problem for the Christian is to take the difficult path of doing the right thing. If abortion is allowed under certain very limited circumstances, as the advocates of the second position insist, then the freedom and the responsibility of the pregnant woman are quite limited. It is the physician who must decide whether any of the conditions has been met. Only after the physician has determined that there is adequate cause does the woman have the option of an abortion. If the third view is correct, then the woman has sole responsibility, at least until the fetus is viable, for deciding whether to terminate a pregnancy.

From a moral perspective, the most important issue to be resolved is that of when personhood begins. The official view of the Roman Catholic Church is that it begins from the moment of conception. In *The Gospel of Life (Evangelium Vitae)*, his "Encyclical Letter on Abortion, Euthanasia, and the Death Penalty in Today's World" issued on March 25, 1995, Pope John Paul II reaffirmed that position by saying:

> Precisely for this reason, over and above all scientific debates and those philosophical affirmations to which the Magisterium has not expressly committed itself, the Church has always taught and continues to teach that the result of human procreation, from the first moment of its existence, must be guaranteed that unconditional respect which is morally due to the human being in his or her totality and unity as body and spirit: "*The human being is to be respected and treated as a person from the moment of conception;* and therefore from that same moment his rights as a person must be recognized, among which in the first place is the inviolable right of every innocent human being to life." (p. 108)

From this perspective, there is no distinction between killing a child before birth and killing one after birth.

Many Protestants agree with this view. The line of reasoning about abortion runs as follows: (1) Human beings do not have the right to take the lives of other human beings because all life is the gift of God. (2) Human life begins at the moment of conception. (3) Abortion at any stage in the development of the fetus is the termination of human life and therefore is always wrong. Some people, not quite willing to assume that personhood begins from the moment of conception, say that since we cannot be sure when it begins, to avoid terminating the life of a human being we must act as if it did begin with conception. The end result, therefore, is the same: Abortion is always wrong.

This line of reasoning focuses on the assumption that the fetus is a person. Is that, in fact, the case? Life clearly does not originate at the moment of conception because both the sperm and the egg are alive before they meet. Individuality, however, is established genetically at the moment of conception. From the time of conception through birth through maturation to death, that individuality develops as the potential is actualized. But this individuality is not the same in the various stages of development, and the fertilized egg is quite different from the newborn child. The Bible insists on the value of persons. Indeed, most of its moral teachings focus on safeguarding human rights, and among these rights the right to life is basic. These biblical teachings, however, speak of persons dealing with other persons who are functioning with an independence that unborn children do not have. Of course a fetus is alive; it moves, it shows sensitivity to pain, and early in its development it has a heartbeat and brain waves. Does that make the fetus a person? The lower animals also move, are sensitive to pain, have brain waves, and in addition are independent entities, but they are not persons. The potential of the fetus makes it different from anything else alive, but does that difference make it a person?

Unfortunately, the Bible gives little help in answering this question. Indeed, only one Old Testament regulation concerns unborn children. Exodus 21:22–25 prescribes a fine for a man who accidentally causes a woman to have a miscarriage. This law, however, reflects the importance of children to the Hebrew people rather than the sanctity of the life of the unborn child. Furthermore, it deals with a miscarriage that is the result of violence directed toward a third party, not toward the woman or the fetus, and therefore addresses the accidental rather than the deliberate termination of a pregnancy. It requires a rather vivid imagination to extend the Bible's stress on the worth of individuals and the value of human life to include a fetus at any stage of development.

This is not to suggest that the fetus is insignificant. It is not simply another part of the woman's body, as dispensable as the tonsils or a fingernail. The fetus has a potential that no other part of the body has. If nature is allowed to take its course, and the fetus develops normally, it will become a person. It must be respected for what it can become. Its right to life is not that of a fully developed human being, but its significance lies in its potential of becoming a person.

A second moral issue concerns a clash of values. This problem can be as thorny as the question of when the fetus becomes a person. A woman who is pregnant but wishes not to be does not have a simple choice between good and bad; rather she must choose one value to be sacrificed to another. On the one hand, there is the value of the fetus, which has the potential of becoming a person. On the other hand, there is the specific circumstance that makes the pregnancy undesirable. That circumstance may be the hardship of being a single mother, financial problems, disrupted career plans, difficult marital relationships, unsettled family circumstances, health problems for her or the unborn child, or even a threat to her life. What is to be sacrificed to what? Does the unborn child have absolute priority? How important is the health of the unborn child? Does the physical or mental health of the woman have absolute priority? How important are her career ambitions? How important are the personal relationships within her family? How important is her family's ability to take care of children? Whose best interests will be served, and whose damaged, by her decision?

A woman making a decision, therefore, is not choosing between having an abortion and maintaining traditional family values. Most people value the family quite highly. Most, though by no means all, expect parenthood to be a part of their lives. A woman does not necessarily reject motherhood for all time when she rejects motherhood at a particular time. Neither does she reject motherhood when she decides that one child, or two or three or any other number, is enough. She may indeed be acting in the interest of her family by choosing to have an abortion. Traditional family values are concerned not with the number of children but with the quality of life provided for all members of the family—mother, father, children, and perhaps members of the extended family.

These considerations lead to another important question: Who should be involved in the decision-making process? For obvious reasons the woman ultimately makes the choice. Although many pressures may be brought to bear, in the last analysis she determines what course to follow. In making her decision, should she consider the judgments of anyone else? One other person who should be involved in the decision-making process, if possible, is the father of the child. This is obviously true if the woman is married. After all, the child was conceived within the context of the marital relationship. Not only does the husband have rights and responsibilities, but the relationship between husband and wife is seriously affected by the decision. Moreover, the mutuality that has been described as the ideal in the husband–wife relationship would preclude a unilateral decision on such an important matter.

If, however, the woman is not married, the involvement of the father of the child is more difficult, if not impossible. An unwed father may be unwilling to take any part in the decision or even try to avoid his responsibilities. Sometimes at the initiative of the woman but more often at the initiative of the man, many unmarried couples break up when the woman becomes pregnant. The woman is then left with the full responsibility of deciding what to do and of implementing the decision. Even if the relationship between the man and the woman was a casual one, however, the man has both legal and moral rights and responsibilities.

Parents can give invaluable emotional support and practical assistance to a young, unmarried woman making this decision. Most young women are reluctant to discuss this problem with their parents. Some fear their anticipated reaction and some do not want to hurt them. Certainly it would be unrealistic to expect parents to be happy about the situation. Most would probably be both angry and hurt. But most would also be deeply concerned and want to help their daughter decide what to do and to follow through on her chosen course of action. A young, unmarried woman need not be alone in making and carrying out a decision either to have an abortion or to give birth.

Besides abortion, a number of viable alternatives are open to a pregnant, unmarried young woman. The first is marriage. Before the liberalization of the law on abortion and before the medical developments that made abortions fairly simple and safe, this was a frequently chosen option. It was often said of a couple that "they had to get married." They did not have to marry, of course, but that seemed the best option open at the time. Clearly a couple should not marry simply because the young woman is pregnant. If they were anticipating marriage, however, and were waiting because of educational status or economic circumstances or some other reason, it might be well to alter their plans and marry earlier than they had planned. A second option is for the woman to carry the child to full term and rear the child as a single parent. Many women have done so with happy consequences, and women in increasing numbers are choosing this option. A third possibility is to give birth to the child and give it up for adoption. Although it is usually difficult for a mother to give up her newborn child, this has proved to be a good decision for large numbers of people.

The availability of the drug RU 486 may inject a new element into the issue of abortion. Already legal in a number of European nations, in the year 2000 the Food and Drug Administration authorized its distribution and use in the United States. This drug prevents the implanting of the embryo in the uterine wall, and the uterus reacts as if a normal menstrual cycle were ending. If this drug is a contraceptive, it is the simplest and most effective yet devised, and it will relieve untold numbers of women of the necessity of deciding about abortion. If, however, a human being comes into existence at the moment of the fertilization of an egg, then the use of the drug is an act of abortion, and all of the moral issues are pertinent.

At any rate, it should never be assumed that abortion is an easy solution to a problem pregnancy. Although it may be the best alternative in a specific situation, it does not resolve all problems. Rachel Richardson Smith, who says of herself that she is both anti-abortion and pro-choice, writes,

Why can't we see abortion for the human tragedy it is?

No woman plans for her life to turn out that way. Even the most effective contraceptives are no guarantee against pregnancy. Loneliness, ignorance, immaturity can lead to decisions (or lack of decisions) that may result in untimely pregnancy. People make mistakes.

What many people seem to misunderstand is that no woman wants to have an abortion. Circumstances demand it; women do it. No woman reacts to abortion with joy. Relief, yes. But also ambivalence, grief, despair, guilt. ("Abortion, Right and Wrong," *Newsweek*, March 25, 1985, p. 16)

BIOMEDICAL PARENTING

While an unwanted pregnancy is a problem for some people, childlessness is a problem for others. Approximately one out of every ten couples in this country is infertile. In the past some have simply accepted the fact, and others have dealt with the problem by adopting children. The widespread use of contraceptive devices and the increasing resort to abortion are now reducing the number of infants available for adoption. The practice of adopting older children and children of different ethnic background, however, is increasing.

Modern medical technology offers another approach. In the nineteenth century there were some experiments with artificial insemination, a technique long employed with great success in breeding animals. After World War I the procedure, though uncommon, came to be accepted as valid. It has become quite common since World War II, and now it is estimated that each year more than ten thousand children are conceived in this way in the United States.

The technique itself is fairly simple. By means of instruments a physician introduces semen into the woman's uterus, where it may fertilize an awaiting ovum. If there is a physical difficulty on the part of the man, such as a low sperm count or impotence, semen from the husband may still be employed (artificial insemination by husband, or AIH). If the husband is sterile, however, or if there are medical or genetic reasons for not using his semen, semen from a donor may be used (artificial insemination by donor, or AID). While successful impregnation does not depend on the source of the semen, there are more moral questions about using semen from a donor than there about using semen from the husband.

Another technique for overcoming childlessness is in vitro fertilization. This involves removing a ripe ovum, or egg, from the woman's ovary and placing it in a laboratory dish with sperm from the husband. If, as hoped, one of the sperm fertilizes the ovum, the resulting embryo is cultured for a brief time and then returned to the woman's uterus. There the embryo may implant itself and develop as if conception had taken place in the normal way. About one in ten attempts at in vitro fertilization is successful. Its most common use is to overcome infertility in the woman.

Surrogate motherhood makes it possible for a couple to rear from birth a child who is the biological child of the husband but not of the wife. As far back as biblical days a childless woman sometimes gave a female servant to her husband so that he could have a child by her. The achievement of this result by artificial insemination, however, is recent. Exactly how long it has been practiced we do not know, but early in the 1980s it was done openly, as some physicians began to arrange such pregnancies and attorneys began to handle the legal arrangements. Clients entering into such arrangements knew the cost at the outset. The legality of contracts with surrogate mothers is still unsettled.

In discussing the morality of these procedures, several theoretical considerations are important. The first is the question of whether artificial insemination with semen from a donor is a violation of the husband–wife relationship. This question is equally applicable to the insemination of a surrogate mother. The position of the Roman Catholic Church, enunciated by Pope Pius XII in 1949, is that this procedure constitutes adultery because it is a violation of God's plan that husband and wife should have mutual, nontransferable rights to each other. It is an invasion of the wife's reproductive system by someone other than her husband. In fact, according to the Pope, even artificial insemination with semen from the husband is wrong because it substitutes another method for "natural sexual intercourse" and is therefore not a personal union of husband and wife.

Protestant theologians who oppose artificial insemination, although not speaking in such absolutist terms, are concerned about what they see to be a separation of procreation from the husband–wife relationship. Thus they see a problem even with artificial insemination with semen from the husband, AIH. They consider procreation in this way to be a matter of medical technology rather than of a loving relationship between husband and wife. Paul Ramsey, for example, speaks of these techniques as irreversibly removing "a basic form of humanity: the basis in our creation for the covenant of marriage and parenthood" (*Fabricated Man*, p. 130). He sees a necessary linkage between "the love-making and the life-giving 'dimensions' of this one-flesh unity of ours" (p. 133).

Not all Protestant theologians agree, however. Joseph Fletcher brushes aside any suggestion that artificial insemination is an adulterous act. He believes that to think of it as such is to think of marital fidelity as merely a legal relationship rather than a personal one (*Morals and Medicine*, p. 121). James Nelson likewise focuses on the intent of the man and the woman who resort to these measures. He says that when there is mutual consent, when it is chosen as an act of love, and when the child so conceived is accepted in the "parenthood covenant" of the husband and wife, it can hardly be considered adultery (*Human Medicine*, pp. 72–73).

A second consideration, important to many people, is that the semen used in artificial insemination must be secured by masturbation. The traditional teaching of the Roman Catholic Church is that masturbation is inherently sinful because it is a sexual act separated from the procreation intent, which is normative for every sexual act. Protestant ethicists who object to masturbation as sinful do so for other reasons. First, they think that in masturbation sex is separated from a personal relationship and thus is deprived of its fundamental meaning. And second, the sexual fantasy associated with masturbation, not tied in with a real partnership, promiscuously cultivates lust with a disregard for the personhood of other individuals.

Most ethicists do not spend a great deal of time discussing the morality of masturbation. It is probable that the traditional teaching of both the

Catholic and the Protestant churches that masturbation is sinful is rooted in the Old Testament attitude, which stressed the importance of procreation so much that it considered it wrong for a man to "spill his seed upon the ground." In discussing the issue of artificial insemination, therefore, most Protestant ethicists see no need to raise any objection on this point. Helmut Thielicke, for example, speaking of AIH, calls masturbation for this purpose "fundamentally and radically different" (*The Ethics of Sex*, p. 256). And speaking of artificial insemination with semen from a donor, James Nelson, although believing that the donor is "prostituting" his sexual functions, insists that unlike ordinary prostitution this act in no way damages anyone's marital union (*Human Medicine*, pp. 73–74).

A third consideration, relating to surrogate motherhood, is quite complicated. The legality of the practice, of paying one woman to bear a child for another woman, has not yet been fully resolved. Rightly or not, it has been compared with the illegal buying and selling of children who have been either kidnapped or purchased from people desperate for money. Indeed, courts in Kentucky and in Michigan have handed down decisions declaring surrogate motherhood illegal because it is a form of buying and selling babies. Although a court in New Jersey upheld in 1987 the validity of a surrogate mother contract, the New Jersey Supreme Court reversed that decision. At present it appears that the courts will not sanction such contracts.

Whether the practice is illegal, however, is not our major concern. What we are concerned about is whether the practice is in fact the buying and selling of children. What actually determines to whom a child so conceived and born belongs? Is it a contract between a childless couple and a woman who needs money? If so, parenthood is a matter of law. Is it a question of whose sperm and egg unite? If so, the child belongs to the man as well as to the surrogate mother, and he has all of the rights and responsibilities of fatherhood. If one woman bears a child for another, what difference does it make whether the semen came from the other woman's husband or from some other man, perhaps even the husband of the surrogate mother? What difference does it make whether the fertilization of the egg was in vitro or by artificial insemination with semen from a donor or by sexual intercourse? Is the problem that of one person handing over a child to another in exchange for money? Does that constitute treatment of the child as a commodity? Or are all of these questions unimportant in light of the fact that childless couples have found a way to satisfy their deep desire to have a child of their own?

Because these procedures for overcoming childlessness are relatively new, the implications have not yet been fully explored. There seem to be few moral problems with artificial insemination with semen from the husband; there are more when the semen is provided by a donor. The problems are even thornier in the case of surrogate motherhood. While these practices should not be avoided just because there are problems, anyone considering them should know the problems and be prepared to deal with them. Some of these issues are

1.   What are the parental rights of the husband whose wife was inseminated with semen from a donor? Of the woman for whom another woman was a surrogate? Of the surrogate mother? Are adoption proceedings necessary?
2.   Is it right to pay semen donors?
3.   Is it right to pay surrogate mothers?
4.   What steps should be taken to ensure that the donor or the surrogate mother did not transmit a disease or genetic defect?
5.   What kinds of records should be kept? Should children who later want to know about their biological parents have access to these records, as adopted children do in some states?

CLONING

In February 1997, Scottish scientist Ian Wilmut announced the successful cloning of a lamb, the first mammal to be cloned from adult body cells. The birth of "Dolly," as the lamb was called, was not only the culmination of a long process of research and experimentation; it was also the beginning of a new chapter in the human manipulation of the natural order. By definition, a clone is a genetic replication, by nonsexual means, of a single parent. The process by which Dolly was produced was far from simple, as evidenced by the fact that Wilmut had 276 failed attempts before he succeeded in producing her. If what was done to produce her were done to produce a human being, cells would be taken from an adult person, placed in a human egg from which the nucleus with the DNA had been removed, implanted in a woman, and the normal process of gestation and birth would take place. The child would have only one parent and genetically would be identical with that parent.

So significant were the implications of Wilmut's achievements that both scientists and laypeople reacted with excitement—and with some fear about what the next steps would be. Even before the announcement of the birth of Dolly, human cloning had been outlawed in Denmark, Germany, Great Britain, and Spain. Almost immediately after Wilmut's announcement, President Clinton took two steps in the same direction: First, he banned federal funding for attempts to clone human beings; and second, he appointed a National Bioethics Advisory Commission to consider the possible "abuse" of cloning human beings, asking them to make their report within ninety days.

The President's Advisory Commission reported in June 1997, with a number of conclusions and recommendations.

1.   Concluding that "at this time it is morally unaceptable" to attempt human cloning, they recommended:

   a.   The continued moratorium on federal funding for cloning projects.
   b.   The request that private agencies voluntarily comply with the moratorium.

2. They suggested that Federal legislation be passed to prohibit attempts at cloning for a period of three to five years, after which the situation would be reviewed to determine whether the moratorium should be continued.
3. They warned against legislation that might interfere with other important scientific research.
4. They asked that people of "different ethical and religious perspectives and traditions" consider carefully the "ethical and social implications of this technology."
5. They asked that Government agencies are urged to keep the public informed of significant development. (Cited in Howell and Sale, *Life Choices*, pp. 573–579)

It now appears that human beings *can* be cloned. But *should* that be done? Or is that undertaking, which the Commission called morally unacceptable "at this time," *permanently* unacceptable? This is a difficult question with which to deal because of the assumption by many people, both scientists and lay people, that questions of morality are irrelevant to scientific investigation. To be valid, science must be free to ask what it will, to use its own method of investigation, and to learn what it can about the way the natural order operates. Scientific questions, as such, are simply outside the realm of morality. From a moral perspective, however, no aspect of human life is exempt from critical evaluation. Just as there are valid moral questions about abortion, genetic screening, and organ transplants, so are there appropriate questions about cloning. Indeed, the questions are all the more urgent because the issue is even closer to the basic understanding of human life.

That is not to suggest that scientists are not concerned about moral issues. In personal life they may be guided by whatever moral considerations seem pertinent to them, and it is entirely legitimate for anyone to say, "I choose not to be involved in this activity." That can be a personally costly decision, of course, because so much is at stake for the individual, not the least of which are employment and personal standing in the professional community. Many scientists who were in one way or another involved in the development of nuclear weapons faced that issue and paid a great price for adhering to their personal convictions that that process should not continue. Yet that option is always open.

This difficulty is complicated by the fact that we are indeed dealing with something that is still in the exploratory stage. While we have learned a great deal about cloning both plants and animals, and while the cloning of Dolly represents a development of major proportions, our ignorance is still tremendous. We do not yet fully understand the possibilities, and we do not understand the dangers of further experimentation. That fact both challenges us to move ahead and urges us to be cautious. At this point, at least, it would seem that there should be some strong reason to proceed before we do so.

Is there such strong reason? In simple terms, why should we clone a human being? What good purpose would be served? Scott Rae has summarized six reasons that have been suggested, some of which seem more significant that others:

1. Helping to make infertility treatments more efficient and less costly
2. Providing embryos for research
3. Being able to provide a person with an exact tissue match should it be necessary to treat a life-threatening disease (as with a bone marrow transplant)
4. Being able to actually replace a child who had died prematurely
5. Offering organ farming, in which the cloned person is used as a source of biological spare parts
6. Making a profit from selling one's embryos on the open market in the case of people like athletes or supermodels (*Moral Choices*, p. 178)

It should be observed that all of these reasons focus on the needs of some other person, rather than on the intrinsic value of the child who would be born. A person would be created in order to serve someone else's needs. From a Christian perspective, however, persons are valued for their own sakes rather than for the sake of what they can do for someone else. Every person is a distinct, unique individual, created "in the image of God."

Is there any compelling reason, on the other hand, why we should *not* proceed? Are there considerations that demand that we refrain from doing something that apparently we *can* do? Most responses to this question have been quite positive. That is to say, most people have argued against cloning a human being. Indeed, Dr. Wilmut himself said, "We can't see a clinical reason to copy a human being. . . . We think it would be ethically unacceptable and certainly would not want to be involved in that project" (*New York Times*, February 24, 1997, p. B8). Only months after the announcement of Wilmut's work, a collection of essays was published under the title *Human Cloning: Religious Responses,* edited by Ronald Cole-Turner. The twelve authors, some from Great Britain and the others from the United States, were theologians and ethicists from widely varying Christian traditions. While each essay had its distinct emphases, there was a remarkable agreement. Abigail Rian Evans' summary of her own position is an excellent statement of that agreement:

> My answer is yes. We should refuse to practice human cloning because it is morally wrong. I will offer four reasons for opposing human cloning: (1) it is not a necessary solution to any human tragedy; (2) it fosters a reductionist rather than a holistic view of human nature while treating people as means not ends; (3) it undermines the structure of the family and human community; and (4) it creates a pressure to use this technology and make it a god. ("Saying No to Human Cloning," in Ronald Cole-Turner, editor, *Human Cloning: Religious Responses,* p. 25).

In other collections of essays, some of which presented both sides of the issue, these same objections were raised.

My own answer is tentative because we are in the early stages of scientific investigation into the possibility of human cloning, and we cannot yet be sure what the outcome will be. I do not think that it is possible to call a halt to scientific investigation into the possibility of cloning human beings, and I am not convinced that it is desirable to do so. While important moral questions must be dealt with, the need for answers does not require the halting of research; rather it requires honest and careful consideration and response. I venture several suggestions that, in my judgment, are pertinent. These are not offered as arguments on either side of the issue, but as ideas to be involved in the discussion.

First, the question of whether we should proceed with human cloning is not a scientific one but a moral one. The scientific question is, "Can it be done?" If the answer to that question is yes, then the scientific question becomes, "How can it be done?" The question "Should it be done?" calls for the examination of the issue on the basis of moral principles. As individuals, the scientists are appropriately involved in discussion of the moral issue. Indeed, their knowledge equips them to make unique and important contributions to the discussion. But the decision about the appropriate application of scientific knowledge to human life is a broader human issue and should be made by a broader group of people.

Second, there are failures in all experimentation, and the attempt to clone a human being would be highly risky. Wilmut made 266 failed efforts before he succeeded in producing Dolly. With continued experimentation the risk may be decreased. Yet the experiments would have to be done with human subjects. To experiment with human cloning in the way that Wilmut experimented with sheep, however, would be to ignore the fundamental distinction between human beings and the rest of creation. We do not ignore or denigrate the value of the rest of the created order when we speak of the uniqueness of humankind. Indeed, we acknowledge that there are serious moral problems associated with experimentation with other animals. Nevertheless, we affirm a difference between human beings and the other living creatures, a difference indicated by the biblical statement that humankind was created "in the image of God," and the statement that the human became "a living being" by receiving "the breath of life" from God. Experimenting with a human embryo, a risky undertaking, is therefore qualitatively different from experimenting with the embryo of a sheep.

Third, and closely related to the second issue, is the question of what would be done with the "left-over" embryos. Scott Rae, who views human cloning with great skepticism, says that cloning might possibly be justified as an infertility treatment "as long as there are no embryos left over at the end of the treatments and no embryos are destroyed in the process of cloning." He adds that using embryos for research is unethical "since either the research kills the embryo or it is discarded at the end of the experimentation." (*Moral Choices*, p. 178).

Fourth, every person is of worth in his or her own right, and no person should be treated as a means only. This, of course, is Kant's formulation of the principle that Christians find in the teachings of Jesus and exemplified in his actions. This conviction is important not only for the cloning process itself, but also for the person who is born in that process, and for the parent to whom the cloned child is born. To experiment with a person is to treat that person as an object, a tool that may be used to further human knowledge.

Fifth, while a clone is genetically identical with the parent, that is not the total identity of the clone. Personality is not merely a matter of genetics, but of environment and socialization as well. A clone, in other words, is not a total replication of someone else. We have some illustration of this fact in the case of identical twins. Technically, identical twins are "clones" in the sense that they both have the same genetic inheritance. Because of that, they look alike and, even as adults, often act and react in very similar ways. Yet they are not identical in personality, in character, in socialization, and so on. Therefore, the fear that cloning would produce identical persons is unfounded.

My own conclusion is that as of the present there seems to be no compelling reason to proceed with human cloning. It is entirely possible that circumstances may change and that at some time I may wish to revisit the question. Some of my concern is based on my faith, a faith that not all Americans share, and I cannot use my faith-based reasons to advocate legislation to prohibit human cloning. Others of my concerns, however, are integral to our American cultural and political ethos and may be an adequate basis for advocating careful legal regulation, perhaps even prohibition.

RESPONSIBLE PARENTING

Today most couples who marry plan eventually to have children. They expect to decide when they will have a child and how many children they will have. While many factors will enter into their decision, a major one should be their prospect of bringing a normal, healthy child into the world. This prospect is not at all certain. Seven percent of all children born in the United States have birth defects, which make necessary the hospitalization of over a million persons a year. In addition, there is evidence that genetic factors seem to be linked to a wide variety of illnesses.

On June 26, 2000, five years earlier than the projected date for the completion of a project begun in 1988, England's Prime Minister Tony Blair and the United States' President Bill Clinton issued a joint announcement that the human genome had been deciphered. In a widely read book, *Genome: The Autobiography of a Species in 23 Chapters*, Matt Ridley observes that "Scientists all over the world have deciphered the entire human genome, written down its contents and distributed them on the Internet to all who wish to read them" (p. 1). Among other things, that achievement ultimately will offer to prospective parents a wealth of information about the child whom they might bring into the world. For a number of years we have been able to iden-tify couples who are at high risk of producing a child with serious handicaps; now it is possible not only to know much more but also to take some thera-peutic measures. Even a healthy person may be a carrier of a disease. Tay-Sachs disease, for example, a disorder that leads to blindness, paralysis, and death, usually before the age of four, is common among Jews of Eastern European origin. Sickle-cell anemia, a painful and life-shortening disease, is found chiefly among African-Americans. Although only a minority of people in these groups are affected, people who are at high risk or who are carriers need to make informed decisions about whether to have children.

If a couple learns that any child they bring into the world may be born with handicaps, several alternatives are open to them. First, they can gamble, if they know or believe that the odds are in their favor. If the odds are one in four that their child will have sickle-cell anemia, for example, the odds are three in four that their child will not have that problem. They may even prepare themselves to take care of an afflicted child if that should be necessary. Second, they may decide not to have a child, by relying on contraceptives. This decision, of course, is essentially the choice not to have a child at this time, and it can be reversed at any time by simply ceas-ing to use contraceptives. It should be noted, however, that contraceptives are not altogether reliable. Third, they can decide that one or the other of the partners will be sterilized. Sterilization procedures are nearly 100 per-cent effective. The success rate for reversing the procedure for women is quite low, but the success rate for attempts to reverse vasectomies is better than 90 percent if done within the first seven or eight years after the initial procedure.

By a variety of tests, the most widely employed of which is amniocente-sis, it is possible early in a pregnancy to diagnose the health of a fetus. Couples who are already expecting a child and learn that there are serious problems have two options. First, they may decide on an abortion. We have already discussed the moral implications of this issue; it need only be said here that for some people nothing makes an abortion right, whereas for others the fact that the child would come into the world severely handicapped justifies an abortion. Second, they may decide to continue the pregnancy. Some prenatal treatment of the fetus is possible in some cases, and that possibility has been enhanced by the deciphering of the human genome. In addition, we are learning more about the treatment of some problems in infants. A couple may decide, therefore, to accept the responsibility of providing the best pos-sible treatment both before birth and after.

So far we have assumed that the decision is to be made by the couples alone. Society also has a stake in the decision, however. The direct financial costs of caring for handicapped people are sometimes great, and because few families can meet all of these costs, some responsibility falls on the state and on private agencies. In addition, the indirect costs for health care, education, and continuing support are immeasurable. Some efforts have been made, therefore, to pass legislation limiting or even removing the individual's right of decision in certain types of situations. For the most part, these efforts have failed because they have been seen as a violation of individual privacy.

Persons faced with the prospect of bringing a handicapped child into the world can be guided by three considerations. First, the best decisions require the most complete information possible. The prevention of a problem is far easier than its treatment. Obviously we cannot know everything about a child who has not yet been conceived or everything about an unborn fetus. We can know a great deal, however, and the more we know the better equipped we are to make a decision. Those who know that they are in a high-risk group, therefore, need to know as much as possible about themselves. Those who know that a fetus may be diseased need to know as much as possible about its condition and prognosis.

Second, we have a moral obligation to care for the helpless. Couples to whom a handicapped child is born, whether or not they had prenatal information about the handicap, are responsible for doing the best that they can for that child. This basic concept in Christian morality is reinforced by the fact that all human relationships involve responsibilities. This responsibility should not be romanticized. To care for a severely handicapped person costs a great deal in money and time, and even more in energy and emotion. In some cases the expenditure is required over a long period of time. It is emotionally draining, it is confining, and it seriously affects one's lifestyle. None of this detracts from the satisfactions that come from caring for one whom we love and who depends on us. The mother of one paraplegic child said, "We love her. We are proud of her accomplishments. We would not give her up for anything in the world. But I hope that no one else ever has to go through what she and her father and I have gone through." Those parents did not choose such a demanding way of life, but they did choose to do everything they could to meet the needs of their handicapped daughter.

Third, we have a moral obligation to all of the people affected by the birth of a handicapped child. Husband and wife have responsibilities to each other, and their relationship with each other will be affected by the care of a handicapped child. The lives of other children in the family are significantly altered. Each person has involvements and responsibilities outside the family, with work, school, the church, and community life in general. There are, therefore, broader implications for the investment of money, time, energy, and emotions. The needs of one person, even handicapped, cannot be allowed to destroy all other relationships.

ORGAN TRANSPLANTS

Medical history was made in 1954 when the first successful kidney transplant from a living donor took place. Since that time surgical techniques have advanced greatly, significantly facilitated by the development of new medicines to overcome the problem of organ rejection. Today approximately five thousand kidney transplants are done each year, and the success rate is about 90 percent. Many surgeons are well trained for the operation and hospitals are equipped for it.

This development is a part of a longer history of tissue transplants. The first successful cornea transplant took place in 1905. Skin grafts were first successful in the 1920s. The first liver transplant was performed in 1963, and the first pancreas transplant in 1966. Bone marrow, ovaries, and testicles have been successfully transplanted, and the prospects for further developments seem unlimited. Perhaps the operation that has claimed the greatest public attention is the heart transplant, first performed in 1967.

The phenomenal developments in the techniques of organ transplants should not blind us to the failure rate. Although tremendous strides have taken place in dealing with the problem of rejection, it has not been completely solved. Furthermore, other physical problems may be complicated by the surgery. All surgery, no matter how simple, involves some danger. Although the danger can be minimized, it cannot as yet be eliminated completely. The more complex the surgery and the more experimental it is, the greater the danger.

The medical profession is quite sensitive to the moral and ethical issues associated with organ transplants. Early in the development of the procedures, Dr. J. R. Elkinton and Dr. Eugene D. Robin suggested some ethical guidelines, which are still generally recognized as valid:

1. The physician must be concerned for the patient as a total person.
2. There must be a reasonable prospect for success.
3. Therapy must be the only goal.
4. Risk to the healthy donor of an organ must be kept low.
5. There must be complete honesty with the patient and his family.
6. Each transplantation should be done in a way to increase scientific knowledge.
7. There must be careful, intensive, and objective evaluation of results.
8. Publicity must be careful, accurate, and conservative. (Harmon L. Smith, *Ethics and the New Medicine*, p. 121)

In addition to the issues covered in this code, however, there are other moral concerns. One, which has to do with the use of organs from the body of a dead person, is the determination that the donor is actually dead. Under no circumstances is it considered right to remove a vital organ from a person who is still alive. Organs cannot be used for transplants, however, unless they are removed from a body immediately after death. At one time the line between life and death was sharply drawn. When the heart stopped beating and breathing ceased, the doctor could say that the patient was dead. But now breathing and the heartbeat can be restarted, and impaired functions can be assisted by artificial means. Brain death, considered by some to be the determining factor, is not an entirely satisfactory indicator because it can occur while other vital functions continue. At present the most widely accepted criteria for the determination of death are those stated in 1981 by the President's Commission for the Study of Ethical Problems in Medicine and Biomedical and Behavioral Research: "An individual who has sustained either (1) irreversible cessation of circulatory or respiratory functions, or (2) irreversible cessation of all functions of the entire brain, including the brain stem, is dead" (*Defining Death,* p. 73).

A second issue is the question of who has the right to decide that the organs of a deceased person may be used for transplants. Some persons use living wills to make that decision before their own death. Under what circumstances, however, is it right to remove organs from the body of one who has not made such a will? This question often arises in the case of accident victims. Because many such victims are quite healthy, their organs are ideal candidates for transplants. At present the next of kin may give permission. Does the body belong to them? On the one hand, is it right to remove organs from the body of someone who had not given approval? On the other hand, is it right to waste vital organs that could save the life of another person? As long as these questions remain unanswered, it seems appropriate to continue with the assumption that the next of kin may make the decision because they are the ones who have the greatest emotional involvement with the deceased.

A third issue is the allocation of scarce resources. There are many more people who need transplants than there are organs available. How is it to be decided which needy person is to be the recipient? It is taken for granted that an expressed wish of a donor will be respected. It is also assumed that if the next of kin express a desire, that will be respected. If there is no such expression, selection is generally made by a hospital committee. The usual procedure is to eliminate all candidates for whom the prognosis is not good. Then, from those who are left, the one who is first on the list is chosen. Every effort is made to eliminate such considerations as wealth, moral character, and social significance.

A fourth issue in organ donation is the risk to the patient. Medical canons require that physicians always act primarily in the interest of their patients and only secondarily in the interest of furthering medical knowledge and skills. This means, of course, that in the treatment of a patient a physician will employ methods known to have a high success rate. Only after those methods have failed may a physician properly try a less predictable treatment. The decision to move in that direction is not exclusively a medical one, and it certainly should not be made by a physician alone. The patient, too, must be involved. Of course no surgery can be performed without the consent of the patient or of someone legally authorized to make decisions for the patient. Physicians, however, can present the alternatives either in a persuasive manner or in an objective manner. The patient must have the option of carefully weighing the pros and cons. The patient must be informed of the odds, of the possible consequences both of having the operation and of not having it. In the last analysis it is the patient who needs to understand the risks because it is the patient who makes the final choice.

A fifth issue is a bit more difficult to delineate but nevertheless quite important: How is the person affected by the receipt of an organ? Harmon Smith, who is quite positive about organ transplants, comments, "In contemplating the personal dimension of organ transplantation, I have sometimes wondered how many organs from other persons could be transplanted into my body (presuming immunologic acceptance of them!) before I would no longer be myself" (p. 113). What does giving up an organ or receiving an organ from someone else, living or dead, do to the self? Clearly it does not make one more or less of a self. Yet, as Smith indicates, if one's personality is altered by forming a new friendship or by reading a book or by living in a different culture, can we expect our personality to remain unaffected by something as serious as this surgery?

Joseph Fletcher, however, equally concerned about human values, has written a passionate essay, "Our Tragic Waste of Human Tissue" (in Cutler, ed., *Updating Life and Death*). Human values are not something mystical, he says, but something very much connected with the body. They involve the health and well-being of living people and the possibility of helping people who are not healthy. To be moral is "to respond to human need, to answer a call for help in a concrete and particular situation" (p. 12). Paul Ramsey, who rarely agrees with Fletcher, is not far from him on this point. Commenting on an invitation he had received to present a theological definition of "the moment of death," he said that the determination of the time of death is a medical matter, not a theological one. The theologian, he said, "can only offer his reflections upon the meaning of respect for life, care of the dying, and some warnings of the moral complexities such as are set down here" ("On Updating Death," in Cutler, *Updating Life and Death,* p. 52). From a Christian perspective, then, the ultimate issue is not merely the treatment of bodies but a consideration of the quality of human life.

When we talk of a living donor, of course, we are talking of the donation of a paired organ. Although there have been successful transplants of testicles and corneas, the most commonly donated organ is the kidney. Whether it is morally permissible for a person to donate a paired organ has been questioned on the grounds of mutilation of the body. This question is more academic than real, however, for the almost universal conclusion has been that it is not only permissible but also commendable for one person to make such a sacrifice for another.

The question is more difficult when we ask whether it is the *duty* of one person to make that sacrifice for another. Does the general Christian duty to help other human beings extend to such an extraordinary action? On the other hand, does the fact that one is related to a patient, and that therefore the prospects for a successful transplant are greater, mean that one is obligated to make the sacrifice? Does the existence of a family connection impose undue pressure on a person to donate an organ? Does the urgency of one person's need have any bearing on another person's obligation? How can the need of a patient be balanced against the needs of other people who depend on the prospective donor? On the other hand, if pressure is exerted upon a relative, explicitly or implicitly, to donate an organ, how free is that person to say no? These questions cannot be answered in terms of a generalized duty. Each prospective donor, in the final analysis, must make an independent and unique decision.

THE CARE OF THE DYING

"Dad, how long does it take a person to die?" a child asked his father after a visit to an elderly friend dying of cancer. Commenting on this problem, Vincent Barry cites the "main currents in the experience of the dying: loneliness, fear, bitterness, self-doubt. Feelings of uselessness and desertion. Loss of self-governance, control, and participation. Indignity" (*Moral Aspects of Health Care*, p. 281). While facing death has always been a problem, it is intensified in our day by modern medicine's ability to delay death when it can no longer hope to cure or relieve pain or even prolong life at a worthwhile level. What do we do about a comatose person for whom there is no prospect of recovery? What do we do for an incurably ill person whose remaining days or months are certain to be increasingly, agonizingly painful? How are we to care for people who are surely dying?

We have already discussed the problem of determining when death occurs. More important from a moral perspective is an understanding of what death is. This understanding must be cast within the framework of understanding what life is. That human life is biological no one will argue. There is another side to human life, however, which we call personal; it includes self-consciousness, self-transcendence, the ability to relate. In biblical terms this is "the breath of life" and "the image of God." In defining death, therefore, we must distinguish between biological death and the loss of personhood.

Among those things for which there is an appropriate time, according to the author of the Book of Ecclesiastes, is "a time to die." In an earlier day we accepted that statement at face value. In light of the developments in modern medical science, however, we have begun to reject it. Instead, we take every possible step to avert death, both for ourselves and for those we love. Such efforts have enabled many people to live longer, more comfortably, and more productively. Sometimes, however, those measures seem inappropriate because, while they keep the body alive, they cannot keep body and soul together. And sometimes it seems that the soul (or at least the person) is trying desperately to leave. Historically the science of medicine has had three objectives: to cure the ill, to preserve life, and to ease pain. Modern medical practice succeeds remarkably well in the effort to ease pain, to heal, and to preserve life. Yet at times it seems that such priority is given to keeping a patient alive that the importance of easing the patient's pain is forgotten. Does there come a point at which extraordinary measures should cease and the patient should be allowed to die? If so, how do we know when that moment has arrived?

As a matter of fact, in recent years the medical profession has given a great deal of attention to the manner in which people die. Jonathan M. Mann, summarizing the thinking of physicians from fourteen countries involved in the Hastings Project's discussion of the goals of medicine, wrote about the pursuit of a "peaceful death":

> Since death will come to all, and the patients of every doctor must eventually die as surely as the doctor herself, medicine must give a high place to creating those clinical circumstances in which a peaceful death is most likely. A peaceful death can be defined as one in which pain and suffering are minimized by adequate palliation, in which patients are never abandoned or neglected, and in which the care of those who will not survive is counted as important as the care of those who will survive. (Howell and Sale, eds., *Life Choices*, p. 71)

Medicine must acknowledge the inevitability of death, he adds, affirming that when the time comes that life-sustaining treatment is futile, "the humane management of death is the final and perhaps most humanly demanding responsibility of the physician" (pp. 71–72).

A seriously ill person surely understands something of the situation, and a dying person often senses the imminence of death. People close to death are best served by an open and honest treatment of the facts. At a time when we are accustomed to talking about the responsibilities of physicians and nurses and about the love and care of family and friends, we will do well to consider the rights of the patients. These rights include, at the least,

1. The right to be treated as a living human being
2. The right to participate in decisions concerning care
3. The right to be cared for by caring and knowledgeable people
4. The right to express feelings and emotions freely
5. The right to be kept as free from pain as possible
6. The right to honest answers to questions
7. The right to die in peace and dignity

It should be noted that all of these rights *except for "the right to die in peace and dignity"* are, in one way or another, recognized in both the Patient's Bill of Rights adopted by the American Hospital Association and the statement of

Principles of Medical Ethics adopted by the American Medical Association (cf. Brody and Englehardt, *Bioethics*, pp. 388–389).

There is one notable omission from the above list: euthanasia, or what has come to be called "assisted dying." That was omitted because the issue is still very much subject to debate. Does one who is dying have the right to a quicker and easier death? Popularly defined as "mercy killing," euthanasia is far more than that. Literally the word means "good death," an idea that is especially important at a time when for many people there is no dignity in death but only pain, loneliness, bitterness, and fear. How can Christian love make death good?

Two facts of modern medicine combine to raise serious moral issues in caring for the dying: (1) our ability to keep comatose bodies biologically alive almost indefinitely and (2) our inability to relieve the suffering of many people who are approaching death. Three issues thus arise. The first concerns the way people currently die. Today 80 percent of Americans die in hospitals, as compared with 37 percent only thirty years ago. People die attached to machines, with relatives excluded from their rooms, with information withheld, and often with no one who can or will talk about what is occurring. What do Christian love and compassion require in this situation? What do they require of the medical personnel? Of the members of the family?

The second issue is whether one must simply wait for death to come, perhaps after long and intense suffering, or whether one may choose to hasten it. In more blunt terms, this is the question of whether one has the right to suicide. Does a terminally ill person have the right to choose death at a time and in a manner that seem best to that person? Or are such actions immoral because they disregard the sacredness of human life? Are they a usurpation of a right that belongs to God alone?

The third issue is whether someone else, out of compassion for a terminally ill patient, might morally help that patient implement a decision to end his or her own life. Are we obligated by love to resist death to the bitter end, regardless of the cost in suffering? Or does love permit us—perhaps even require us—to help the patient escape from the suffering? Long before Dr. Jack Kevorkian began to assist persons who wished to terminate their own life, both medical professionals and individuals caring for people whom they loved were dealing with the issue. Many Christians, observing the intense suffering of someone they love, have prayed for an end to it through death. If that patient were to ask for help in dying, would refusal be a greater act of love than compliance?

The difficult question is whether elective death, the choice of the time and the manner of dying, is sometimes morally valid or whether it is always wrong. There are two facets to this question. One is whether a patient who is conscious and capable of making decisions has the right to make this one and to implement it, either alone or with assistance from someone else. This decision may involve a prior declaration that life-support systems will not be employed to keep the body alive when hope of recovery is gone and that heroic measures will not be undertaken to resuscitate the body when breath and heartbeat have stopped. It may involve more direct steps to terminate life, taken by the patient who is capable of doing so or administered by someone else for the patient who is unable to do so. The other facet is whether someone caring for a comatose patient has the right—or the obligation—to make such decisions on behalf of that patient and to implement them.

Consider first the question of whether a terminally ill person has the moral right to refuse treatment, in the form of medication or surgery or life-support systems, that promises nothing more than a prolongation of the dying process. Is one obligated to allow everything possible to be done to lengthen life? The right of a person to refuse treatment is generally recognized in the laws of this country. Does one have the moral right to do so? If we accept the concepts of freedom and responsibility, the answer must be yes. Every person has the right to accept the inevitability of death.

The next question is whether someone else has the moral right to decide to withhold medication or to withdraw life-support systems from a terminally ill person. This question is much more complicated. Who should make the decision? The medical personnel? The family? How do we know that the time has come to take this step? Is there really a difference between withholding medication or withdrawing life-support systems, which we expect to result in death, and taking positive steps to terminate the life of a patient? If a patient is in a coma and death in a personal sense has already occurred, if therefore the only life remaining is biological, the moral problems of withdrawing life-support systems, if not eliminated, are greatly reduced.

If a terminally ill person decides, either because of intense suffering or because of the burden that long-term care imposes on the family or because of some other factor, that a quick death is to be preferred over a lingering one, is suicide justifiable? If so, and if a patient needs assistance in performing suicide, is a family member or a friend or a medical practitioner justified in providing it? Does one who is dying, in short, have the moral right to choose the time and manner of death? Does one have the moral right to choose a quick, painless death over a long, agonizing one? If so, does one have the right to help from medical personnel or from family or friends?

Although each of these situations has its own implications, the fundamental issue is the same: Do human beings have the moral obligation to struggle against death by every means possible, both for themselves and for other people, until the inevitable moment arrives? Or do human beings have the moral right to exercise some choice concerning the time and manner of death? Some important biblical and theological considerations can help us deal with this issue.

We begin with the biblical teachings on taking a human life. At the outset we must examine the commandment, "You shall not kill" (Exodus 20:13). All of the commandments of the Decalogue are concerned with the covenant community. This law protects its members from the threat of death at the hands of someone else. It is a prohibition of the deliberate slaying of one person by another, and other laws in the Old Testament reinforce it. In the Old Testament the word for *kill* covers both murder and involuntary manslaughter. The point of the commandment, therefore, is that people have a right to life that must not be violated either deliberately or accidentally. The law, in other words, deals with the right of the individual to live rather than with the attitude of another person toward that individual.

Jesus's comments on the commandment against murder (Matthew 5:21–22) must be read within the context of his general approach to the Law. Although Jesus rejected certain specific regulations, some in traditional rabbinic interpretation and some in the Scripture itself, he endorsed the basic moral teachings of the Old Testament. "Do not think that I have come to abolish the law or the prophets," he said; "I have come not to abolish but to fulfill" (Matthew 5:17). In his interpretation of the law, however, he often had a significantly different emphasis. He focused on responsibility rather than on rights: on the one who acts rather than on the one acted upon. Thus he internalized morality, making it a matter of motive and attitude rather than one of act and consequence. On the basis of this principle, he said about the law against murder,

> You have heard that it was said to those of ancient times, "You shall not murder"; and "whoever murders shall be liable to judgment." But I say to you that if you are angry with a brother or sister, you will be liable to judgment; and if you insult a brother or sister, you will be liable to the council; and if you say, "You fool," you will be liable to the hell of fire. (Matthew 5:21–22)

Acknowledging the validity of the law protecting the individual's right to life, then, Jesus talked about the attitudes of disrespect and hostility, seeing them too as violations of the life of other people.

Although the sixth commandment prohibits killing, Hebrew law does not prohibit everything that could be found under that term. Never was the law believed to prohibit killing in war, for example, presumably because their wars were understood as protection of the rights of the members of the covenant community. Indeed, the Hebrews are frequently described in the Old Testament as having proceeded, with the blessing of God, to the merciless slaughter of their enemies.

The law authorizes capital punishment for a number of offenses. The Code of the Covenant, of which the Decalogue is a part, specifies death as the penalty for striking one's father or mother, for kidnapping, for cursing one's father or mother, for murder, and for having kept an animal known to be vicious if it kills someone (Exodus 21:12–19). The **Deuteronomic Code** even prescribes execution for "a stubborn and rebellious son" (Deuteronomy 21:18–21).

In some circumstances, even suicide is considered by biblical writers to be legitimate. There is no Old Testament law against it. Without any censure the book of 1 Samuel (31:4–6) describes Saul's suicide following his defeat by the Philistines at Mount Gilboa. Presumably this course of action is more honorable than allowing oneself to be captured by the enemy. To allow oneself to be killed in support of a worthy cause, as in war, was recognized by the Hebrews, as apparently by people in all places and in all times, to be praiseworthy. It is implicit in Jesus's observation, "Greater love has no man than this, that a man lay down his life for his friends" (John 15:13).

Thus we cannot conclude that the Bible teaches either that under no circumstances is it valid to take the life of another person or that under all circumstances one's supreme moral obligation is to stay alive. The issue, therefore, is under what circumstances it is right to terminate either one's own life or the life of another.

A second theological consideration is the Christian and biblical understanding of personhood. We have already discussed this theological concept (see Chapter 4); here we need only review the fundamental ideas:

1. Persons are creatures made "in the image of God."
2. Persons are both body and spirit.
3. Persons are self-conscious.
4. Persons are rational beings.
5. Persons make moral decisions.
6. Persons relate to other persons.

A sound moral decision on whether assisting someone to die will have to come to grips with the question of respect for the person.

A third consideration in evaluating the morality of suicide is a Christian understanding of the nature of death. Is death always bad? Most people seem to think so. Their desire to avoid it is a combination of an unwillingness to lose their present relationships and an uncertainty about what lies beyond death. For people contemplating the death of someone they love, of course, the pain of bereavement is what they feel most. Christians share these concerns with all other people. And like other people, Christians are involved in those death-denying activities that include all our efforts to live to the last moment and our refusal to accept the certainty of death's approach. Also like other people, they engage in rituals that try to cover up the fact that death has indeed come to someone they love.

The people of biblical days were no less anxious about death than are we. They contemplated human frailty. They prayed for continued life and they mourned death. They were anxious about what they left behind, and they were uncertain about what was beyond the grave. In most of the history reported in the Old Testament, there was one significant factor in their understanding of death. Behind all references to death is the understanding that humankind was created by God and continues in the hands of God. Individual existence, however, was understood to cease with death. The dead simply resided in Sheol, and any continued existence that people had was in the memory of the survivors who honored them. In the later Old Testament documents, however, there was some speculation about the struggle between good and evil and about punishment and reward after this life. This speculation continued during the intertestamental period, so that by the time of Jesus the Pharisees, at least, affirmed the resurrection of the dead, with punishment for the wicked and reward for the righteous.

The New Testament writings consistently reflect the idea that the believer is in the hands of a loving God, both in life and after death. This presupposition of the Christian community, reflecting ideas from the late Old Testament period and the interbiblical period, was rooted partly in the teachings of Jesus and partly in the fact of the resurrection. In the synoptic gospels it is not taught directly but is assumed to be true, and certain implications are mentioned. In John it is talked about much more directly as the gift of "eternal life." In the letters of Paul there are frequent, forthright declarations of the expectation of a continuing personal, spiritual existence in the presence of God. Paul's most extensive discussion of the idea is found in the fifteenth chapter of 1 Corinthians, where he talks both of the resurrection of Christ and of the resurrection of the believer. His most moving affirmation is his insistence that nothing—not even death—can separate one from the love of God (Romans 8:35–39).

Among the "several principles" that Allen Page formulated from his study of what the Bible teaches about life after death, the following are relevant to our discussion:

1.   Life begins and ends with God.
2.   There is the growing hope in the biblical tradition among the faithful that they will be with God beyond death.
3.   Affirmations of hope for life after death are grounded in faith, in the experience of the individual and of the community of faith.
4.   The focus on continued personal existence is sometimes expressed with individual emphasis, sometimes with corporate emphasis. (*Life after Death: What the Bible Says*, pp. 84–87)

As we consider the morality of elective death in light of medical facts and Christian theology, we find ourselves struggling with several questions. First, are we usurping God's authority when we elect death either for ourselves or for someone else? God has final authority over human life. Although we have important decisions to make about our life, we do not own it. Do we, then, have the right to terminate it? That is a serious question. Basic human sin has been interpreted in a variety of ways, but one way to express it is as the attempt to take the place of God. Yet it must be said that we see no problem in interfering by trying to delay death. We take extraordinary measures to keep a body alive even after it is apparent that death can be delayed for only a short time. Few people raise any question about interfering with human life through capital punishment or through warfare. Why should it be a more urgent issue when a person is trying to die?

Second, what is the best way to demonstrate a sincere concern for the well-being of a patient? For most ill persons the ideal objective of treatment is recovery. If recovery is not possible, relief of pain is the next objective. Is the terminally ill person for whom there is no relief from intense suffering and no possible improvement best served by continued treatment or by euthanasia? What is the most loving thing to do in these circumstances?

Third, what makes us reluctant to administer euthanasia? Is it our fear of doing something wrong? If so, are we concerned for our own personal purity or for the well-being of the person who is in deep distress? Does our sense of guilt compel us to keep the patient alive no matter what the cost? This is not to suggest that a concern for our personal purity is irrelevant. After all, there is a strong biblical tradition that God is the source of right and wrong and that the moral obligation of the believer is to obey God. The issue, however, is whether the idea of the sanctity of human life requires us to take every measure to preserve that life or whether it requires us to take the awesome step of ending a person's life to provide escape from suffering.

Fourth, is euthanasia an act of mercy? We consider putting a suffering animal "out of its misery" to be an act of mercy. Does mercy, then, ever require this last desperate measure to relieve the suffering of a human being? Paul Simmons asks,

> Is it more harm to kill a patient who is (1) dying, (2) has no chance of recovery, (3) is in unrelievable pain, and (4) has requested help in dying, or to force that person to go on suffering, helpless to do anything about, and hopelessly frustrated at having earnest, sincere, and rational requests repeatedly denied? (*Birth and Death: Bioethical Decision-Making*, p. 149)

Scott Rae approaches the issue very cautiously by saying that "there is more to the sanctity of life than simply postponing an imminent death." He cautions against "using scarce and very expensive medical resources on treatment that is futile," saying that the principle of the sanctity of life does not demand "that every patient receive indefinitely the most aggressive treatment available." He concludes that "In many cases, treatment is clearly no longer helpful to the patient, is no longer desired by the patient, or is more burdensome than beneficial to the patient." Yet he does not affirm any measure other than withdrawing treatment (*Moral Choices*, pp. 204–205). John Cobb, however, who is also quite cautious, nevertheless takes that next step. Using the victim of Alzheimer's disease as an example of a person for whom assisted dying might be a possibility, he affirms the appropriateness of a physician helping that person die:

> But if one who is diagnosed as having this disease clearly and consistently expresses a preference to die rather than linger on for years in a decaying state, the argument of this chapter is that this person has the right to die. That implies that others have the duty to assist and that society has the duty to facilitate this process. Death with dignity requires that the acts can be public and approved and that the best wisdom of those who are best informed be at the service of those who need it. (*Matters of Life and Death*, p. 68).

Because of intense suffering, many people are unable to function as whole human beings, and many comatose persons have lost the faculties that distinguish them as human. Yet all human beings are children of God, are made "in the image of God." In the light of these two apparently contradictory facts, what does it mean to care for a dying person? It means acting in such a way as to demonstrate that that person matters. It means being with that person as he or she tries to cope with the dying process. It means sharing our attitudes about living and dying. It means an honesty that "speaks the truth in love" and bares our feelings as well. It means a respect for the dying person as one who thinks and feels, who desperately strives to hold on to relationships, and who both fears the unknown and longs for escape. In my judgment, it may ultimately mean helping that person make that escape.

QUESTIONS AND TOPICS FOR DISCUSSION

1. If you were to write a law regulating abortion in this country, what would it be? What arguments would you offer in support of this law?
2. Is it legitimate for anti-abortion groups to picket clinics where abortions are performed? Why or why not?
3. What restrictions, if any, would you place on biomedical parenting? Justify your answer.
4. What factors would you consider if you were asked to donate an organ to a member of your family?
5. If a member of your family could be kept alive indefinitely by a life-support system, how would you decide what to do?
6. If a member of your family were terminally ill and asked for your help in ending his or her life, what would you do?

RECOMMENDATIONS FOR FURTHER READING

COBB, JOHN B., JR., *Matters of Life and Death.* Louisville, Ky.: Westminster/John Knox, 1991.

COLE-TURNER, RONALD, ed., *Human Cloning: Religious Responses.* Louisville, Ky.: Westminster/John Knox, 1997.

HOWELL, JOSEPH H., and WILLIAM F. SALE, *Life Choices: A Hastings Center Introduction to Bioethics,* 2d edition. Washington: Georgetown University Press, 2000.

McGEE, GLENN, ed., *The Human Cloning Debate,* 2d, edition. Berkeley: Berkeley Hills Books, 2000.

MAY, WILLIAM F., *Testing the Medical Covenant.* Grand Rapids: Eerdmans, 1996.

MEILAENDER, GILBERT, *Bioethics: A Primer for Christians.* Grand Rapids: Eerdmans, 1996.

PALMER, LARRY I., *Law, Medicine, and Social Justice.* Louisville, Ky.: Westminster/John Knox, 1989.

PETERS, TED, *Genetics: Issues of Social Justice*. Cleveland: Pilgrim Press, 1998.

RANTALA, M. L., and ARTHUR J. MILGRAM, *Cloning: For and Against*. Chicago: Open Court, 1999.

SHANNON, THOMAS A., *An Introduction to Bioethics*, 3d ed. New York: Paulist, 1997.

SHANNON, THOMAS A , *Made in Whose Image?* Amherst, N.Y.: Humanity Books, 2000.

THOMASMA, DAVID C., *Human Life in Balance*. Louisville, Ky.: Westminster/John Knox, 1990.

TURNER, RONALD COLE, ed., *Human Cloning*. Louisville, Ky.: Westminster/John Knox, 1997.

9

Christian Ethics and Ethnicity

At the height of the Civil Rights movement of the 1960s, Howard Thurman said, "One of the central problems in human relations is applying the ethic of respect for personality in a way that is not governed by special categories" (*The Luminous Darkness*, p. 1). Special categories, however, have always been a part of the American scene. Although the United States was once called a melting pot, many groups in America remain separate from other groups—distinguishable in terms of beliefs, practices, appearance, or language. Some people have been attracted to the United States by the opportunities they believed were here, some have come to escape bad situations in their native land, and some were brought here against their will. Some immigrant ethnic groups have become completely assimilated, some have failed in their efforts to be accepted into the mainstream, and some have tried desperately to maintain or to rediscover connections with their past.

In any society the majority group shares a common tradition, a common language, and a common value system. It controls the economic and political structure in the society. For the whole of society it determines what is right and good, the proper procedures, the limitations under which various peoples work, and the manner in which people may participate in the process. A minority group, in contrast, is a subordinate segment of society, conscious of being a distinct group without having chosen that status and assumed to have certain physical or cultural traits by which members are identified. In the United States, African-Americans, Jews, Native Americans, Hispanics, and a significant number of other groups have such minority status.

STEREOTYPES, PREJUDICE, AND DISCRIMINATION

The lives of members of minority groups are profoundly affected by their membership in those groups. The chief instruments by which society exerts pressure upon them are stereotyping, prejudice, and discrimination. A **stereotype** is the attribution of certain characteristics to all members of a particular group of people. Most of us tend to create mental images to help us deal with the large numbers of people whom we encounter daily but cannot absorb as individuals into our life systems. By these images we decide what claim people have on us and how we are to relate to them. We learn from our culture certain ascribed characteristics of members of specific groups. Accurate or inaccurate, relevant or irrelevant, good or bad, complimentary or uncomplimentary, these pictures reflect common beliefs and affect interrelationships in society. Such stereotypes are invalid in a number of ways:

1. They highly exaggerate the importance of a few characteristics.
2. They fabricate some supposed traits and make them seem reasonable by associating them with other tendencies that may have a kernel of truth.
3. They either omit or insufficiently emphasize favorable personality traits.
4. They fail to show how other people share the same tendencies.
5. They give no attention to the reason for the tendencies of the minority group.
6. They leave little room for change.
7. They leave little room for individual variation within a group. (See Simpson and Yinger, *Racial and Cultural Minorities*, p. 100)

Prejudice is a rigid emotional attitude toward a group of people, a predisposition to respond in a certain way. In most cases, though clearly not in all, this response is negative. It leads us to expect all members of a particular group to think alike and to act alike, to have the same emotional reactions to situations, to have the same personal characteristics and the same values, even to have the same innate abilities. We tend to think that we know the most important things about a person, therefore, when we know the group to which he or she belongs. We see any personal difference as merely a variation of the same theme. Prejudice therefore makes it quite difficult for us to see members of the group as individuals with unique traits and characteristics.

Discrimination is the overt expression of prejudice. It refers to acts that are based on predispositions rather than reason. Judgments about employment, for example, about renting or selling property, about admission to schools, and about any number of other activities are often made on the basis of the applicant's membership in a group rather than on the basis of the applicant's qualifications. A garage owner, for example, prominently displays next to his cash register a sign saying, "No checks accepted." When a customer questions paying a large bill in cash, the owner answers, "No problem; I just use that sign to protect myself against some people." On what basis does he decide from which customers he needs to be protected?

Why is this pattern of stereotype, prejudice, and discrimination so widespread and why does it persist? Five explanations are commonly given:

1. It is culturally transmitted, and people learn to be prejudiced as they learn a language or as they learn manners.
2. Some personality types need this attitude to help them cope with their own problems.
3. Majority groups use the pattern to dominate minority groups for their own benefit.
4. People draw their identity from their group membership, and prejudice is a way one group distinguishes itself from another.
5. It is an expression of the sin that characterizes all human beings.

None of these explanations suggests that we must ignore the pattern, but rather that we must always deal with it in a constant struggle for justice.

In *Days of Grace,* Arthur Ashe wrote in an intensely personal way a chapter entitled "The Burden of Race." He described a conversation with a reporter who was preparing an article on the manner in which Ashe was coping with AIDS. The reporter had observed, "I guess this must be the heaviest burden you have ever had to bear, isn't it?" Ashe had replied, "No, it isn't. . . . You're not going to believe this, but being black is the greatest burden I've had to bear." Reflecting on that observation, Ashe said,

> Still, a pall of sadness hangs over my life and the lives of almost all African Americans because of what we as a people have experienced historically in America, and what we as individuals experience each and every day. Whether one is a welfare recipient trapped in some blighted "housing project" in the inner city or a former Wimbledon champion who is easily recognized on the streets and whose home is a luxurious apartment in one of the wealthiest districts of Manhattan, the sadness is still there. (p. 127)

Then he summarized what he saw as the achievements of segregation:

> It left me a marked man, forever aware of a shadow of contempt that lays [*sic*] across my identity and my sense of self-esteem. Surely the shadow falls on my reputation, the way I know I am perceived, the mere memory of it darkens my most sunny days. I believe that the same is true for almost every African American of the slightest sensitivity and intelligence. Again, I don't want to overstate the case. I think of myself, and others think of me, as supremely self-confident. I know objectively that it is almost impossible for someone to be as successful as I have been as an athlete and to lack self-assurance. Still, I also know that the shadow is always there; only death will free me, and blacks like me, from its pall. (p. 128)

CHANGES IN THE SOCIAL STRUCTURE

Current issues in minority group relationships cannot be understood without reference to the changes in American society that took place during the last half of the twentieth century. At the end of World War II the great majority of the people of the United States were classified as "white," though several other ethnic groups had been present in significant numbers for many years. The largest group were the African-Americans, who were concentrated in the South, though many African-Americans were living in the larger cities all over the nation. The Native Americans were concentrated in the West, though again many were living in small pockets in most of the other states. A large Mexican population lived in the Southwest, and communities of Asians were living in major cities all over the nation. Many of these minority peoples lived and worked under the restrictions of a fairly rigid segregation that was dictated by custom in some states and by law in others.

The ethnic picture of the United States changed drastically in the last half of the twentieth century, and particularly during the last three decades. In 1970, only 4.7 percent of the population was foreign-born, a decrease from 6.9 percent in 1950. But the percentage began to rise, and by 1998 it had almost doubled, reaching 9.3 percent. During that period some fifteen million people moved into the United States from other countries. A high percentage of those people came from Mexico, and many others came from other Spanish-speaking countries. A significant number of people came from Asian nations, and a small percentage came from Europe. Whites continue to be the majority group in the nation, and that is likely to continue to be the case for many years to come. The non-white and the non–English-speaking people have been particularly affected by the tendency of the majority to segregate and discriminate against minority peoples.

On May 17, 1954, the Supreme Court of the United States handed down a decision that proved to be a turning point in the life of African-Americans and that had profound implications for all ethnic minorities. For many years, the National Association for the Advancement of Colored People (NAACP) had been successfully challenging in the courts the validity of many of the laws sanctioning segregation. In 1950 it took to the courts the case of *Brown* v. *Board of Education,* which challenged the southern pattern of providing "separate but equal" educational facilities for blacks and whites. When that case reached the Supreme Court in 1954, the Court decided in favor of the plaintiffs. Although many years were to pass before significant changes were made, and although a great deal of pressure of many sorts was required to enforce change, it would be difficult to overemphasize the importance of that decision. The legal sanction for segregation on the basis of race had been destroyed.

Another major factor in the changing status of African-Americans was the activity of new protest groups. While there were several such groups, each with its own objectives and methods, the best-known and most effective was the Southern Christian Leadership Conference (SCLC), led by the Reverend Martin Luther King, Jr. For a decade the SCLC was virtually identical with the Civil Rights movement. King's "Letter from Birmingham City Jail," written on April 16, 1963, proved to be a highly influential statement of the philosophy of nonviolent resistance. Urging Christians to obey just laws but to disobey unjust ones, he distinguished between the two: "A just law is a man-made code that squares with the moral law or the law of God. An unjust law is a code that is out of harmony with the moral law" (p. 7). With that distinction, he called on Christians to "disobey segregation ordinances because they are morally wrong." In campaigns of nonviolent resistance, King and his followers challenged segregation in public transportation, in public facilities, in businesses, indeed in the whole fabric of society. There was violence, sometimes on the part of the onlookers and sometimes on the part of the police, but King and his followers refused to retaliate. While for many people nonviolence was merely a strategy, for King it was a way of life. The result of the movement was to effect major changes in the treatment of African-Americans and to alter the conscience of America.

The role of the government was critical in bringing about change. In June 1941, under pressure from African-American leaders, President Franklin Roosevelt issued an executive order prohibiting racial discrimination in defense industries and creating a Fair Employment Practices Committee. In 1948 President Harry Truman ordered an end to segregation in the armed forces. After World War II the NAACP went into the courts to force both state universities and the public schools to desegregate. Congress passed a civil rights act in 1957 and strengthened it in 1960. President John F. Kennedy encouraged civil rights legislation, and President Lyndon Johnson's support was crucial in passing the Civil Rights Act of 1964 and the Voting Rights Act of 1965.

Although the civil rights legislation of 1964 and 1965 marked the end of legal segregation, problems persisted for many African-Americans: unemployment and poverty; life in the slums, characterized by poor health and poor sanitation, fractured families, and a high crime rate; a lack of political power; and a pervasive sense of frustration and hopelessness. Martin Luther King, Jr., ceased to be recognized as the undisputed leader of African-Americans. Riots broke out in cities both in the South and in the North in 1963, and the same thing occurred again each summer throughout the remainder of the 1960s. When King was assassinated in 1968 his dream of a desegregated America seemed more impossible than ever.

During the 1970s and 1980s an approach labeled **affirmative action** was used to help establish the rights of minority peoples. The term was first used in the 1964 Civil Rights Act, and in 1965 President Johnson issued an order requiring all contractors who did business with the federal government to "take affirmative action" to ensure that they dealt with employees "without regard to their race, creed, color, or national origin." After that time the concept was used in congressional actions, executive orders, and court decisions. Such affirmative action involved disseminating appropriate job opportunity information among minority groups, keeping records to prove that there was no discrimination in hiring or dismissing employees, providing back pay to people who were victims of discrimination, and establishing training programs for minority groups.

Opponents of affirmative action called it "reverse discrimination" because preferential treatment was being given to members of groups that in the past had been discriminated against. Affirmative action did not require the hiring of unqualified applicants; it did require, in choosing between qualified applicants, that preference be given to members of minority groups. As this principle was enforced, employers were sometimes required to hire partly on the basis of the ratio of minority to majority employees. The purpose was to bring the minority group up to an appropriate level, and the method worked effectively to that end. Many people argued, however, that one consequence was the substitution of discrimination against one group for discrimination against another. Others insisted that employment partially on the basis of race is at least equally as fair as many other criteria, such as preference for veterans, seniority rights, the union shop, tenure in educational institutions, and so on. And they argued that it was necessary to break the cycle of inferior education, unemployment, and poverty. At best, however, preferential treatment was a temporary measure, a plan not to maintain racial balance but to eliminate the imbalance that existed.

In the early 1980s the Federal government reversed many civil rights policies that had been in effect for several years. The Justice Department, the Equal Employment Opportunity Commission (EEOC), the Office of Federal Contract Compliance, and the Office for Civil Rights in the Department of Education either slowed down or discontinued their enforcement activities. New guidelines that significantly modified the concept of affirmative action were issued in August 1981 by the Office of Federal Contract Compliance. Early in 1982 all civil rights enforcement measures were placed under the jurisdiction of the Justice Department, thereby eliminating the Labor Department's compliance programs and limiting the functions of the EEOC. This trend continued throughout the 1980s, and in the 1990s additional challenges were successfully mounted against affirmative action, busing to maintain ethnic balance in the public schools, government programs to improve the economic status of ethnic minorities, and the like. The result was that affirmative action was essentially invalidated.

In spite of the progress that has been made since World War II, ethnic minorities are still disadvantaged. The average income of black college graduates who are family heads, for example, is approximately $4,000 per year less than that of white college graduates; whites with fewer than eight years of schooling earn more than black high school graduates; and the unemployment rate of blacks is approximately twice as high as that of whites. A smaller percentage of blacks than whites graduate from high school, a smaller percentage attend college, and a smaller percentage earn degrees. Although segregated housing cannot be maintained by law, it is sustained by custom, and in most cities African-Americans are still concentrated in areas of substandard housing. Middle-class and upper-class African-Americans who can pay for better housing usually choose to live in predominantly or exclusively black communities. Although most churches claim to be open to people of all ethnic groups, in fact most Christians worship in segregated churches. The changes that have taken place during the past decades have been motivated partly by a desire of African-Americans to assimilate into the mainstream culture and partly by a desire to emphasize the distinctively African-American culture.

How successful has the effort been to desegregate our institutions and deal with the inequities in the structures of our society? Roy L. Brooks says that "racial integration has failed to work for millions of African-Americans" (*Integration or Separation?* p. ix) and calls "shackling African-Americans to racial integration at any cost simply another form of slavery" (p. x). Carefully documenting the failure of integration in education, in housing, in employment, and in politics, he calls for a program that he terms "limited separation." Although he does not want to abandon completely the goal of racial integration, he says, "I think it is necessary to make some form of racial separation available *as an option* for those African-Americans or others who need it to legitimately enhance individual opportunity" (p. 199).

Samuel DeWitt Proctor, on the other hand, praising the achievements of the efforts to desegregate our social institutions and arguing for the continuation of the programs says:

> As a people we still have tremendous societal deficits to overcome, particularly among marginalized youth without hope, but I believe that the glass is more than half full. As I write, millions of black people are leading productive, principled lives; forty blacks are in the Congress; a black woman is in the Senate; Riverside Church has a black pastor; five black Americans serve in the presidential cabinet; one has been chairman of the Joint Chiefs of Staff; another heads the Ford Foundation, the world's largest philanthropy; a black woman is America's poet laureate; one has directed the National Science Foundation; another directs the Center for Disease Control; and another has headed the TIAA, the largest pension fund in the world. (*The Substance of Things Hoped For,* p. xxiii)

Recognizing that there are problems within the African-American community and affirming the responsibilities of African-Americans for dealing with their own failures, he rejects everything that sounds like separatism. He believes that continued progress is tied in with the political system.

> Blacks have to assume responsibility for mending and restoring our own families and institutions. No one else can do this for us. At the same time, the federal government has responsibility for monotoring justice and due process, "secur-

ing the blessings of liberty" and "forming a more perfect union." The federal government is the only agent that can take initiatives to correct past discrimination, even to correct its evil consequences where possible, and remove barriers to equal opportunity. This has nothing to do with "Quotas" or promoting blacks who cannot perform over whites. It has to do with giving blacks equal opportunity to earn every social benefit, even to the extent of undoing previous gross offenses. Some call this reverse discrimination; it is simply redressing previous discrimination. (p. 176)

Cornel West sees the worst problem of the African-American minority in this country as rooted not in the structures of society but in what he calls "black nihilism," *"the lived experience of coping with a life of horrifying meaninglessness, hopelessness, and (most important) lovelessness"* (*Race Matters*, p. 23). Many of the social problems of African-Americans he describes as "the tragic response of a people bereft of resources in confronting the workings of U.S. capitalist society." "Saying this," he adds, "is not the same as asserting that individual black people are not responsible for their actions—black murderers and rapists should go to jail. But it must be recognized that the nihilistic threat contributes to behavior. It is a threat that feeds on poverty and shattered cultural institutions and grows more powerful as the armors to ward against it are weakened" (p. 25).

Like Proctor, West looks to continued direct governmental action for a part of the answer to the problem. He is particularly concerned that affirmative action be continued.

Given the history of this country, it is a virtual certainty that without affirmative action, racial and sexual discrimination would return with a vengeance. Even if affirmative action fails significantly to reduce black poverty or contributes to the persistence of racist perceptions in the workplace, without affirmative action, black access to America's prosperity would be even more difficult to obtain and racism in the workplace would persist anyway. (p. 95)

"In these downbeat times," he says, "we need as much hope and courage as we do vision and analysis." He adds, "We simply cannot enter the twenty-first century at each other's throats, even as we acknowledge the weighty forces of racism, patriarchy, economic inequality, homophobia, and ecological abuse on our necks."

A CHRISTIAN APPROACH

The presence of minority groups is a major fact of American society. Historically, some groups have been assimilated, whereas others have persisted as permanent, distinctive segments of the overall social structure. As long as there are distinctive groups, Americans will be required to deal with issues of majority-minority relationships. Although each group is distinct in terms of its history, its values, and its characteristics, there is a basic Christian approach to dealing with people that is directly relevant to the issues associated with all minorities.

Biblical Concepts

In Chapters 6 and 7 we discussed love (*agape*) as the appropriate way for Christians to relate to other people, and stressed the relationship of love and justice. With this approach in mind, let us now consider the implications of biblical teachings for dealing with minority groups. An honest study of the Old Testament compels us to recognize its ethnocentricity. The very concept of a chosen people makes a distinction between an in-group and an out-group. If one group has a unique relationship with God, there must be a difference between them and other peoples, who do not have that relationship. If one group is God's specially chosen people, the others are not. If one group is united by that covenant relationship, its members have obligations toward one another that they do not have toward people outside of the covenant. It is very easy to conclude that God loves the covenant group more than other people, that the covenant people are morally superior to other people, and that their relationship with God justifies doing what is necessary to sustain their privileged position. That disposition applies not only to enemy nations but also to outsiders who live in the territory of the chosen people. Clearly this way of thinking is a problem.

The Bible says nothing directly about race per se. A careful study of those Old Testament passages that some people interpret as sanctioning racial segregation and even discrimination (notably Genesis 4:8–16 and 9:25–27) reveals nothing that supports these views. The passages teach quite different ideas. The concept of race is a construct of the modern mind, an effort to classify the peoples of the world on the basis of certain relatively common inherited physical characteristics.

The Old Testament, however, does recognize the presence of minority groups who lived among the Hebrews throughout their history. Some who could not claim Abraham as their ancestor came with the Hebrews out of bondage in Egypt and into the promised land (Exodus 12:38). After they entered Canaan the Hebrews shared that land with many other distinct groups. After they became dominant, remnants of other populations remained. Some captives of war were held as slaves and even some Hebrews were impressed into slavery because of unpaid debts. At no point, however, does the Old Testament justify such minority status for anyone. Rather, recognizing that it exists, it records laws designed to protect the rights of minority peoples. The laws dealing with slavery, for example, restrict the power of the master and stress the obligation of the master to the slaves.

The theme of God's concern for all people, in contrast, is found in many places in the Old Testament. Both Isaiah (2:2–4) and Micah (4:1–4) dreamed of the day when universal peace among the nations would result from the universal worship of God. Deutero-Isaiah, though focusing on the imminent redemption of Israel from captivity, is permeated with the note of universalism forcefully expressed in the invitation, "Turn to me and be saved, all the ends of the earth" (Isaiah 45.22). The story of Ruth, set within the period of the Judges, protests the narrow nationalism of the Jews in the post-exilic period (see Ruth 4:18–22). And the prophecy of Jonah is a ringing, dramatic affirmation of God's love for Gentiles.

Several generalizations based on the Old Testament offer guidance for the consideration of minority groups in our society. First, the Old Testament teaches that the human race is one. Both creation accounts (Genesis 2:4b–2:25 and 1:1–2:4a) talk about the creation of one species of humankind, and other passages in early chapters of Genesis (4, 11) speak of divisions as the consequence not of God's will but of human sin. This wisdom is echoed in the prophetic dream of the reversal of the effect of Babel and the union of humankind in the worship of God and obedience to the word of God (see Micah 4:1–4; Zephaniah 3:9). Living in harmony with God's purposes, therefore, requires the removal of barriers rather than their maintenance. Second, justice requires a commitment to the protection of the rights of all persons, regardless of the groups to which they belong. No one's rights are lessened by accidents of birth or by social status or even by deliberate sinful choice. The rights of life, property, dignity, respect, and self-determination are unaffected by ethnic group, sexual orientation, social class, or any other way in which we classify people. And third, because God's love extends to all people, we may not exclude anyone from our concern. This is a particular emphasis of the prophets (see Isaiah 11:6–9, 45:22; Micah 4:2; Micah 5:2–9; Zechariah 2:10–11). If the love of God is inclusive, our practices must also be inclusive.

The New Testament is even more forceful in its judgment on group divisiveness. We have already examined Jesus's teachings on love as the basic moral imperative, stressing its universal character. A number of other statements are quite relevant to minorities. With a memorable and provocative story, for example, Jesus answered the question, "And who is my neighbor?" (Luke 10:25–37). In that story of the good Samaritan he dramatically confronted the sharpest division of his day, making a hero of a member of a hated minority group. Again, after he had healed the servant of a Roman centurion he commented on the man's faith, saying that he had not found that kind of faith even in Israel and adding, "Many will come from east and west and eat with Abraham and Isaac and Jacob in the kingdom of heaven" (Matthew 8:5–13). Yet again, in the parable of the great feast (Luke 14:16–24), Jesus taught that people who had been the recipients of divine favor could disqualify themselves by rejecting God's invitation and that others, despised by the chosen people, would be entertained at the heavenly feast. In quoting from Isaiah as he cleansed the temple, he sounded the note of the universal love of God: "Is it not written, 'My house shall be called a house of prayer for all the nations'? But you have made it a den of robbers" (Mark 11:17; cf. Isaiah 56:7). The Gospel of John reports an intimate conversation with the disciples in which Jesus asserted that barriers between groups of people have no meaning in the kingdom. "I have other sheep that do not belong to this fold," he said; "I must bring them also, and they will listen to my voice. So there will be one flock, one shepherd" (John 10:16).

By his example as well as by his words, Jesus demonstrated that discrimination on the basis of ethnic group was foreign to his religion. When he traveled between Galilee and Judea he usually went through Samaria, ignoring the Jewish custom of crossing the Jordan to avoid that area. On one such trip he talked at length with a Samaritan woman and consequently elected to spend two days in the nearby village (John 4:1–42). Several times he went into Gentile territory and ministered to people there (e.g., Mark 5:1–20, 7:24–30, 8:27–33). In Capernaum he talked freely with a Roman centurion, healed the man's servant, and commended the man's faith (Matthew 8:5–13). One can scarcely read the gospels intelligently without concluding that Jesus deliberately ignored the ethnic prejudices of some of his own people.

The Book of Acts makes it clear that the teachings and example of Jesus were taken seriously by the first-century disciples. Two striking passages bear directly on the subject of discrimination. The first is a dramatic experience in which Peter was led by the Spirit of God to ignore the Jewish restrictions and to go to a Roman centurion in Caesarea (Acts 10). Later, at the Jerusalem conference, where Paul's work with the Gentiles was being challenged, Peter vigorously and successfully defended his own innovation which had preceded Paul's action (Acts 15). The second is Paul's speech at the Areopagus in Athens (Acts 17:22–31) in which he declared, "From one ancestor he [God] made all nations to inherit the whole earth."

The apostle Paul insisted that the gospel removes all barriers between people and that all Christians are "one in Christ"; that is, our common relationship to Christ overrides all other differences, real or imaginary, between people. Within the Christian fellowship all differences of sex, language, culture, skin pigmentation, and the like fade into insignificance. Thus Paul insisted to the Corinthians that "just as the body is one and has many members, and all the members of the body, though many, are one body, so it is with Christ. For in the one Spirit we were all baptized into one body—Jews or Greeks, slaves or free—and we were all made to drink of one Spirit" (1 Corinthians 12:12–13). To the Galatians he wrote, "There is no longer Jew or Greek, there is no longer slave or free, there is no longer male and female; for all of you are one in Christ Jesus" (Galatians 3:28). In his letter to the Ephesians (2:11–22) he dealt with the subject at some length, stating that the terms "circumcision" and "uncircumcision" no longer have any real significance. Jew and Gentile have been made one in Christ, who "has broken down the dividing wall, that is, the hostility between us" (2:14). The decision at the Jerusalem conference (Acts 15) confirmed Paul's judgment and practice.

Power for Social Change

The struggle to ensure the civil rights of minority groups in this country has been led by members of those groups. Believing that they have been subjugated by the dominant society, they have taken steps to break those bonds. That they have had to struggle with little sympathy or assistance from the majority is a judgment on the nation. One could wish that the majority were sensitive to injustice, that they were concerned for the rights of the minorities, and that they would take the initiative to correct the abuses of power within the system. That, however, has not been the case. Furthermore, the minority peoples have become increasingly averse to granting to members of the majority group leadership roles in the struggle. Because the majority has often been viewed as the enemy, one from that group can hardly gain unquestioned acceptance.

The protest activities of the Civil Rights movement were essentially group efforts. Although individuals made unique contributions, the group provided the setting within which they worked. Rosa Parks's unwillingness to move to the back of bus, for example, mushroomed into a mass protest and led to the development of the Southern Christian Leadership Conference. The decision of some black students at North Carolina Agricultural and Technical College to try to eat at the lunch counter in a store in Greensboro led to the establishment of the Student Non-Violent Coordinating Committee. Many Christians, viewing morality as a personal matter and considering it their duty as individuals to struggle for justice, have been suspicious of organized group pressure. The problems of society, however, are too broad and too complex to be dealt with on an individual and personal basis only. They must be confronted by society as a whole, and it is entirely legitimate for Christians to involve themselves in group efforts to bring about a more just social order.

The Civil Rights movement was not a religious movement but a social one in which many Christians participated because of their religious convictions, and to which they provided significant leadership. As part of this movement, they were associated with many Jewish people whose motivations were rooted in their own faith and experience, and whose contributions of leadership and financial support were outstanding. In addition, there were people who had no religious faith but who were committed to the fundamental concepts of democracy.

The most dramatic and effective single instrument of the Civil Rights movement was nonviolent resistance to the policies of segregation and discrimination. Martin Luther King, Jr., a Baptist minister who was profoundly influenced by Ghandi, made this method central to his campaign for change. He took quite literally the words of Jesus, "Do not resist an evildoer. But if anyone strikes you on the right cheek, turn the other also" (Matthew 5:39). In *Stride toward Freedom,* his account of the Montgomery, Alabama, protest, marking the beginning of the civil disobedience movement he led until his assassination in 1968, he stated his philosophy of nonviolent resistance. He discussed six basic points:

1. Nonviolence "is not a method for cowards; it does resist."
2. Nonviolence "does not seek to defeat or humiliate the opponent, but to win his friendship and understanding."
3. Nonviolence directs its attack against forces of evil rather than against persons who happen to be doing the evil.
4. In nonviolent action there is "a willingness to accept suffering without retaliation, to accept blows from the opponent without striking back."
5. Nonviolent resistance "avoids not only external physical violence but also internal violence of spirit."
6. Nonviolent resistance "is based on the conviction that the universe is on the side of justice." (pp. 102–107)

In discussing the fifth point King insisted that the principle of love stands at the center of nonviolence. He described love (*agape*) as (1) "disinterested" in the sense of seeking the good of one's neighbor rather than of oneself, (2) not "discriminating between worthy and unworthy people," (3) making no distinction between enemy and friend, (4) springing from the need of the other person, and (5) not weak and passive, but active in seeking "to preserve and create community." He concluded by saying, "Love, *agape*, is the only cement that can hold this broken community together. When I am commanded to love, I am commanded to restore community, to resist injustice, and to meet the needs of my brothers" (*Stride toward Freedom*, pp. 101–107).

King realized that a dominant group will make no significant change in the social order unless it is forced to do so, and he sought to create a tension that would compel action. He therefore led his followers in mass rallies and protest marches to defy the laws that sanctioned segregation. On religious grounds he was unwilling to resort to violence, and on the same grounds he was convinced that nonviolent resistance was morally right. In his passionate and carefully reasoned "Letter from Birmingham City Jail," dated April 16, 1963, he described the actual practice of civil disobedience. He wrote in response to a letter addressed to him by a number of liberal white Protestant ministers in Birmingham. Sympathetic to the cause of civil rights, those ministers nevertheless had called the protest activities then taking place in Birmingham "unwise and untimely." King described what he and his associates had done to lead up to the activities and then outlined the process that had culminated in their nonviolent protest. According to King, "In any nonviolent campaign there are four basic steps: (1) collection of the facts to determine whether injustices are alive; (2) negotiation; (3) self-purification; and (4) direct action" (*Why We Can't Wait*, p. 78). To the first two steps no one could object, and if they succeed the next two steps are unnecessary. The third step is the necessary basis of the fourth, for it prepares participants to accept the consequences of their actions. The final step, the deliberate violation of the law that is seen as unjust, is intended to create tension that forces the community to face the issue. "One who breaks an unjust law," says King, "must do it *openly, lovingly,* . . . and with a willingness to accept the penalty." (p. 83).

This philosophy of civil disobedience is not a challenge to government and to the legal system per se. It is rather a challenge to unjust laws and to the unjust enforcement of law. That challenge, of course, requires making a judgment about which laws are just and which are not. King did that by defining an unjust law as "a code that a majority inflicts on a minority that is not binding on itself." He added, "An unjust law is a code inflicted upon a minority which that minority had no part in enacting or creating because they did not have the unhampered right to vote." He concluded that "an individual who breaks a law that conscience tells him is unjust, and willingly accepts the penalty by staying in jail to arouse the conscience of the community over its injustice, is in reality expressing the very highest respect for the law" (p. 7).

On religious and philosophical grounds, King rejected the validity of the use of violence in the effort to secure the rights of a group. Not all minority peoples, however, are willing to accept that concept. The riots during the long, hot summers of the 1960s are a case in point. They were not a planned effort; rather they grew out of the frustrations of poor residents in city ghettos. They resulted in some deaths, many injuries, and property damage in the amount of millions of dollars. They did not in any way improve the situation of African-Americans or better their relationships with whites. Had they achieved either of these results, however, would they have been justified? In retrospect, most whites now praise King's nonviolent resistance movement and condemn the violence of the riots. Do they, however, make the same criticism of violence in the service of other causes? If violence is wrong in the struggle of a minority group against a dominant majority in one country, is it also wrong in the struggle of a nation to establish its independence? Is it wrong in the struggle of one nation against aggression by another? Or is violence sometimes a proper tool in the struggle for right? If so, how do we know when the appropriate time for violence has come? Is it wrong to use violence in dealing with crime and criminals? Is violence always wrong, in other words, or is it sometimes right and sometimes wrong?

Violence, of course, is not the only form of power that minority groups can use. They can exert great pressure through group effort in education, in politics, and in economics. Is it right for a small group to act as a bloc in the interest of a single cause? Is it right for African-Americans, for example, to determine their support of a candidate for mayor or governor—posts in which the official makes decisions that affect the entire population—solely on the basis of the candidate's attitude toward African-Americans? In all fairness, we will have to admit that in our political system this is the way decisions are usually made. People are elected to public office who gain support for their stands on a variety of issues. One person supports a candidate for one reason, and another person supports that same candidate for another reason. Many groups use the power of the ballot to gain their objectives.

The same kinds of questions can be asked about other forms of power. Is it right for minority groups to boycott institutions or products? To picket business establishments? To hold mass rallies? Deliberately to flout traditional customs and practices? Deliberately to offend? Does the achievement of an objective justify the use of methods that otherwise one would not employ? Is a cause, in other words, more important than social custom and convenience? Does the end justify the means?

Affirmative action is one of the debated methods that has been used by government to deal with discrimination. Is this method morally right? In an objective sense, if it is wrong to discriminate against minority peoples it is also wrong to discriminate against members of the majority. Is a white victim of discrimination any less a victim than an African-American one? If we look at situations one by one, the answer would have to be that discrimination is wrong in any case. If, however, we look at the overall pattern, the answer may be different. The long history of discrimination has created a situation in which injustice to minority groups will persist until some step is taken to correct the imbalance. The majority of minority peoples will continue to have a disadvantaged status until something is done to improve their economic, educational, and political situation as a whole.

A Strategy for Christian Involvement

Questions of morality are always personal in the sense that they require personal decisions and actions. How can Christians bring their religious faith and their moral insight to bear on the divisions within our society? Several suggestions about personal involvement are offered here. First, we need to avoid the assumption that a person is good or bad in terms of the group to which he or she belongs. Truth is rarely on one side alone. We must maintain an objectivity that enables us to evaluate specific objectives, methods, and achievements. Further, we need to learn to respect people with whom we differ. If we cannot do so, we perpetuate divisions rather than heal them.

Second, we need to inform ourselves as fully as possible about history and about the current situation. People in the majority group need both to know what the facts are and to understand the feelings of members of minority groups. The latter need to know the same about the majority. We all need to know what is happening—and what is not happening. Without such knowledge and insight we are likely to accept the status quo and to assume that everyone else is satisfied with it. By doing so we will contribute to the perpetuation of a system in which injustice is done to large numbers of people. Without knowing it, we may contribute to the problems by subscribing to beliefs and ideas that are incorrect and practices that are unjust.

Third, we need to be meticulously careful about our language. Insidious stereotypes are perpetuated by terms used in ordinary conversation, by jokes, by the casual repetition of stereotypical concepts, and by attitudes and manners. A name, for example, is identified with a person; that is the significance of the commandment, "You shall not take the name of the Lord your God in vain." God's name is sacred because God is holy. By the same token, the terms we use to refer to groups of people are important; we should employ terms that the groups prefer, and we should never use terms of contempt.

Fourth, we need to raise questions about the status quo. Most of us tend to face an issue only when a crisis forces it upon us. If no trouble appears on the surface, we assume that all is well. The system may be unfair without either the majority or the minority being aware of this fact. The basic question is not whether people are satisfied, or even happy, with less than their full rights; it is whether justice is being done. To answer that question we must look at matters that other people are not looking at and raise questions that other people do not want raised. Christians in the majority group, in other words, should not wait for minority people to cry out for help; they should look for the hidden problems and try to resolve them.

Fifth, Christians should serve as a conscience for society at large. They need to challenge assumptions, criticize abuses, publicize facts. They need to correct mistaken ideas, protest injustice in business practices or in the courts, support public information programs, and resist the exploitation of others in employment.

These personal, individual activities, however, are the beginning of moral responsibility in these matters, not the end. The problems that we face are not merely personal but also are in the social structure. It may be true, for example, as has often been pointed out, that in an earlier day in the South there were warm, personal relationships between many African-Americans and whites, and even genuine affection. Those celebrated relationships, however, were not relationships between equals. Both parties knew that there were limits beyond which they could not go even if they wanted to do so. Both were governed by a superior–inferior mentality. The social structure isolated African-Americans from whites and kept them in an inferior position; no amount of goodwill on the part of individuals, black or white, could alter that situation. Only an alteration of the structure could effect improvement.

In dealing with the problems of any minority group, therefore, Christians must deal with the structures of society. Individual friendship and individual morality, as important as they are, are not enough. If better education is needed, the features of the institutions that provide education—the curriculum, the textbooks, the teachers, the social structure within the school, and the relationship of the school with the community—must be altered. If a law places a group at a disadvantage, it can be changed only by working through the normal political process. If the laws are enforced unfairly, public outrage can be directed against those responsible for the inequity. If there is discrimination in an industry it will not be corrected by individual protest; the pressure of the larger society will have to bring it about. The Christian who is concerned with observed injustices, therefore, will best work for improvement in cooperation with other concerned persons to alter the formal structures of society.

Fundamentally, Christian responsibility in the area of ethnic group relations is to exercise influence. Again, we are accustomed to thinking of influence as a personal, one-to-one matter, something that is most effective when it is done unobtrusively. It is that, but only in part. There are vast areas of our lives that are not intimate and personal but social, and it is in these areas that we can work most effectively to resolve the problems of minorities. We are citizens of local communities, states, and the nation, and through those government agencies we can work effectively for justice. We are a part of a church that needs to set its own house in order and then serve as a conscience for the community, and we have immediate access to that church and a voice in it. We are employed in business or industry or government or education, and through our work we have a means of effecting change. We are members of civic clubs and service organizations that have special interests, and we help to shape the policies of these organizations. We live in neighborhoods, where we meet other people on an informal basis, and we can help shape attitudes. We have, in short, far more influence than we realize, and we can therefore do far more than we dream. The nineteenth-century poet Shelley declared that "poets are the unacknowledged legislators of the world." Today Christians must fulfill the roles of both leaven and legislator.

QUESTIONS AND TOPICS FOR DISCUSSION

1. Discuss the involvement of ethnic minorities in campus organizations in your school.
2. Is it best for minority groups to maintain their identity or to be assimilated into the majority? Why?
3. Should Christians seek the merger of black churches and white churches? Why or why not?
4. How are you personally involved with people of other ethnic groups? How does that involvement affect the rest of your personal relationships?
5. How are you affected by discrimination in education, employment, the courts, and so on?
6. What evidence do you see that there is discrimination against minority people in your community? What is your responsibility in that situation?

RECOMMENDATIONS FOR FURTHER READING

America's Original Sin. Washington, D.C.: Sojourners, 1992.
ASHE, ARTHUR, and ARNOLD RAMPERSAD, *Days of Grace.* New York: Knopf, 1993.
BARNDT, JOSEPH, *Dismantling Racism.* Minneapolis: Augsburg Fortress, 1991.
DEYOUNG, CURTIS PAUL, *Coming Together.* Valley Forge, Penn.: Judson, 1995.

KING, MARTIN LUTHER, JR., *Stride Toward Freedom*. New York: Harper and Row, 1958.

KING, MARTIN LUTHER, JR., *Why We Can't Wait*. New York: Harper and Row, 1964.

KITANO, HARRY, and ROGER DANIELS, *Asian Americans: The Emerging Minority*. Englewood Cliffs: Prentice Hall, 1988.

McKENZIE, STEVEN, *All God's Children*. Louisville, Ky.: Westminster/John Knox, 1997.

RECINOS, HAROLD J., *Hear the Cry! A Latino Pastor Challenges the Church*. Louisville, Ky.: Westminster/John Knox, 1989.

ROBERTS, J. DEOTIS, *Black Theology in Dialogue*. Philadelphia: Westminster, 1987.

WEST, CORNEL, *Race Matters*. New York: Vintage, 1994.

10

The Status of Women

The subordination of women in our society is supported by the weight of long religious tradition. In an ancient prayer still in use, Orthodox Jewish men say, "Praised be God that he has not created me a Gentile; praised be God that he has not created me a woman; praised be God that he has not created me an ignorant man." In the traditional Christian marriage ceremony the minister asks, "Who gives this woman to be married to this man?" and the bride's father usually responds, "I do." Even when the response is, "Her mother and I do," the woman is nevertheless handed over to the man. In that same ceremony the bride used to be asked to promise to "obey" her husband. Only recently have the wedding vows been modified so that the woman and the man make the same promises of love, comfort, honor, and fidelity. Not for a long time, of course, have women really been regarded as the property of men, and not for a long time have wives really been expected to obey their husbands. But as yet their status falls far short of full equality.

Although the number of females in this country is slightly larger than the number of males, the power of women is far less than that of men. In the last chapter we defined a minority group as a subordinate segment of society, conscious of being a distinct group without having chosen that status and assumed to have certain physical or cultural traits by which they are identified. In that sense, women might properly be called a minority group in this country.

IMAGES OF WOMEN

Roles are a major factor in social interaction. We sort people by race, age, sex, marital status, occupation, religion, and so on, and we think that we know a

190

great deal about them because we can place them in these categories. Conversely we expect a person in one of these categories to act in a given way, and by our expectations we put pressure on people to conform. We expect southerners to act a certain way, for example. We expect Native Americans to be certain kinds of people and African-Americans and Jews and Asian-Americans and Chicanos to be certain other kinds of people. By the same token, we expect women to fit a specific profile.

In spite of the recent changes in the status of women in American society, the gender stereotypes have remained substantially the same. Nearly three decades ago (in 1975), Barbara Sinclair Deckard said that women were stereotyped as "emotional rather than logical," "passive and dependent," "naturally mothers," and "naturally subordinate to the male" (*The Women's Movement*, pp. 3–5). This image reflects a sexism that is still perpetuated in the home, in the schools, in TV programs and movies, in literature for children and adults, and even in the church. It teaches little children that girls play with dolls and boys play with guns, that girls may cry but boys may not, that girls must be pretty and boys must be strong. It teaches children that women are free to work outside the home if they wish, provided they can arrange for the care of their children, and that men must work to take care of their families. It sets patterns for home life that presume that housework is a woman's province and that yard work is the man's responsibility. Observing that such stereotyping is as costly for men as for women, Deckard described the stereotypical male as "aggressive, emotionally impassive, self-sufficient, athletic, brave in the face of danger, a natural leader, and competent at any task defined as masculine" (p. 53). Commenting on the pressure on men to succeed, she observed, "While to many men, women are sex objects, men are frequently success objects to women. Because career success is defined as central to masculinity in our society, men often sacrifice all other values in pursuing it" (pp. 53–54).

A decade later (in 1985), Ruth A. Wallace outlined what she considered to be our society's "underlying beliefs" about gender (*Gender in America*, pp. 43–55). First, there are "natural differences," in which men are strong, decisive, competitive, and not very emotional; women, by contrast, are smaller, softer, prettier, emotional, and poorly equipped to deal with the fierce competition in the business world. Second, God has given to men the right to command and to women the right to be protected by men. Third, man's characteristics push him into the public sphere, whereas woman's characteristics require her to concentrate on the private realm and limit her public activities to matters that are secondary, short-lived, and relatively unimportant. Fourth, work for wages is the primary responsibility of men and only secondarily a responsibility of women. Fifth, romantic love is the ultimate bond between a man and a woman. To win this kind of love, women must be physically attractive and men must be strong, assertive, and successful in work. Sixth, for men, education is directly related to work, their chief role in life. For women, however, whose chief interests are marriage and the home, education aims at "a set of useful and secondary relevancies."

Even in the fading years of the twentieth century, the stereotype appeared to be the same. In 1995 the authors of the Hunter College Women's Studies program identified five images of women that, they say, appear in many cultures around the world:

1. "Frightening females," the image of women as evil, dangerous, and powerful.
2. "Venerated madonnas," the representation of women as self-sacrificing, pure, and content.
3. "Sex objects," the focus on women as instruments for male sexual gratification.
4. "Earth mothers," the idea that women are closer to nature than men, and therefore consigned to a lower status.
5. "Misbegotten Man," the image, say the authors, that "emphatically denies women a place in culture, because we are neither threats, saints, sex objects, nor earth mothers; we simply are not there" (*Women's Realities, Women's Choices*, pp. 28–35)

While the authors do not give exclusive attention to the status of women in America, they do see these images as operative in our society.

How do such images function? On the one hand, they are the result of our effort to sort out what we see around us, to generalize about what we see going on in our society. Whether our perception is correct is open to question, as are the conclusions that we draw from what we see. But they are an attempt to give meaning to what we see. On the other hand, the generalizations that we make become instruments of regulation. We are shaped by those common images. The authors of *Women's Realities, Women's Choices* explain,

> Consider our appearance. In places where most people have an image of women as persons who wear makeup, jewelry, and skirts, women who are eager to be perceived as "feminine" do indeed wear makeup, jewelry, and skirts. Social constructs also influence more profound matters of conduct, personality, and intellect. To conform to a cultural representation of femininity, we may think of ourselves as being—and act as though we were—physically weak, incapable of understanding mathematics, and preoccupied with getting married and having babies. (p. 35)

This image of women, deeply imbedded in our culture, requires critical examination and evaluation from a Christian perspective.

WOMEN AND THE LAW

In spite of recent gains, women in the United States are so underrepresented in the political power structure that their influence on that structure is still limited. Although they vote in larger numbers than men do, and there make a major impact upon elections, most of the candidates for local, state, and national offices are men. The laws and policies that affect all the people are therefore made primarily by men and tend to reflect the interests of men. This does not mean that men conspire to keep women in a subordinate position; it does mean, however, that the self-interest of the more powerful group predominates. The authors of *Women's Realities, Women's Choices* observe,

> The law still acts to oppress women and treat us unfairly in many ways. Laws regulate women's reproductive rights. Lawmakers determine the respective priorities of health services, day care centers, education, job creation, and the defense budget. The government shapes welfare regulations that may force women to choose between husbands and money to feed our children. (p. 516)

The authors note that the private lives of men are also affected by the mores and the laws, but they point out that the difference lies in the fact that women have little power in the making and enforcing of the regulations (p. 503).

For two centuries the subordinate status of women in American society was clearly defined in law. "Under early common law doctrines of marital unity," says Deborah Rhode, "husband and wife were one, and, as a practical matter, the one was the husband" ("Justice, Gender, and the Justices," in Crites and Hepperle, *Women, the Courts, and Equality,* p. 13). Until late in the nineteenth century, women could not make contracts; engage in licensed occupations; own, inherit, or dispose of property; or participate in political activities. Although some women did find their way around certain regulations, most accepted and lived with the status assigned to them. Court action in the late nineteenth and early twentieth centuries brought about some changes, and legislative action brought about others. The passage of the Civil Rights Act in 1964, however, provided the framework for enforcing the rights guaranteed by the Fifth and Fourteenth Amendments to the Constitution. Pressure had already been building to bring about changes, and that legislation gave impetus to the movement. Because changes in law and in practice have been uneven throughout the country and throughout the various sectors of society, however, the present situation is in a state of flux.

Although the legal status of women is complicated, and although many laws are designed to protect women, on the whole women are still at a distinct disadvantage *vis-à-vis* the law. One of the most serious problems is the enforcement of the laws against rape. Far stricter standards of proof are required when rape is charged than are required in other crimes. A woman's failure to resist physically is often considered evidence that she consented; verbal protest is not deemed adequate resistance. A woman who brings a charge of rape may even be accused of provoking the assault. As a result, many rapes are not reported because for women the consequences of seeking justice are so painful. Since 1980 a number of states have amended their laws with the hope of making convictions of rape more likely. Under the theory that a conviction is more difficult to win when the death penalty may be imposed, some states now prescribe imprisonment rather than death as the penalty. In addition, some states have made it improper to introduce the victim's prior sexual activity as a factor in the case. As yet it is too early to know how effective these changes will be, but their purpose, at least, is to bring about a greater degree of certainty that rapists will be punished.

One legal advantage of a married woman is that she is entitled to financial support from her husband. Whether she works outside the home is irrelevant, and the support is not even conditioned on her functioning as homemaker. If a husband fails to support his wife, however, or if he provides only inadequate support, his wife actually has little recourse. In a dozen states she may get a divorce on the grounds of nonsupport, but otherwise there is no way of forcing a man to meet this obligation. As a matter of fact, in cases of divorce on any grounds, both alimony and child-support orders are often extremely difficult to enforce.

Property rights are determined by the laws of the state in which one lives. In most states each spouse controls both what he or she brings to the marriage and what he or she earns in the marriage. This means that a wife who does not work is totally dependent on her husband's decisions about the expenditure of money. In some states, however, marriage is recognized as a legal partnership in which the earnings of both parties are considered community property. At one time, lending agencies often refused to consider a wife's income in determining whether couples were eligible for a loan, assuming that her contribution was uncertain. In any credit transaction, however, it is now illegal to discriminate on the basis of sex or marital status.

Although by custom a woman assumes the name of her husband when she marries, the law does not require it, and an increasing number of women do not do so. Most jurisdictions, however, assume that a wife takes her husband's name in such matters as voter registration, the issuance of driver's licenses, and the receipt of some social service benefits. Most states allow a person to adopt any name he or she chooses and have established formal procedures for doing so. When she marries, however, a woman does not have to go through these procedures but may simply begin to use her "married name."

One of the greatest problems for women is sexual harassment. A number of court cases in the late 1970s brought this problem into the open, and in 1980 the EEOC issued strong guidelines in which it defined sexual harassment. According to the commission, "unwelcome sexual advances" and "verbal or physical conduct of a sexual nature" constitute sexual harassment when

> (1) submission to such conduct is made either explicitly or implicitly a term or condition of an individual's employment, (2) submission to or rejection of such conduct by an individual is used as the basis for employment decisions affecting such individual, or (3) such conduct has the purpose or effect of substantially interfering with an individual's work performance or creating an intimidating, hostile, or offensive working environment.

Although these guidelines seem clear, their violation is extremely difficult to prove. How can one convince a court that something is "implicit?" How can one deal with innuendo? How can one prove that an environment is "intimidating, hostile, or offensive?"

WOMEN AND EMPLOYMENT

Contrary to popular opinion, for many years a significant number of women have worked outside the home. They have worked with their husbands on the farms. They have been employed in manufacturing plants. They have been sales and clerical workers, teachers and nurses. For the most part, however, they have worked in order to supplement the income of their husbands. Few have had a sense of career, and few have had opportunities for advancement. Their employment has been secondary to their roles of wife and mother, and they have been identified in that way.

All of this is now changing as women in rapidly increasing numbers enter the labor force. In 1975, 44 percent of the married women in this country were employed; in 1980 the percentage had risen to 50, in 1990 it was 58.4, and in 1998 it had risen to 59.8. This increase has not occurred in those occupations in which women have traditionally been employed but in fields that heretofore have been essentially closed to them. Laura Crites and Winifred Hepperle say, "A greater proportion of women are employed than in any other peacetime period in our history, and are employed in a greater variety of occupations as a result of equal employment opportunities and affirmative action laws" (*Women, the Courts, and Equality,* p. 9). This broadening of opportunity has meant an improvement in the financial status of women. The fact that now they earn more money gives them independence and power that they have not had before, no matter how important they were at home and in the community.

The earning power of women, however, has not increased in proportion to their movement into the work force. The average income of women is only 76 percent of that of men. One reason for this difference is that women are still concentrated in low-paying occupations: More than half are secretaries, salespersons, waitresses, household workers, nurses, and public school teachers. Even equal education does not guarantee equal pay. On the average, a woman with a high school education earns less than a man who has not gone beyond the eighth grade, and a woman with a college degree is paid less than a man with only a high school diploma. Among white-collar high school graduates, women earn only a little more than half as much as men. Women employees are not promoted equally with men, and management and supervisory positions in industry, business, and government are most frequently filled with white males. The salary of women administrators and managers is gernerally only two-thirds of that of men on comparable jobs.

In the higher-paying and more prestigious occupations, women constitute a tiny minority. Only 8 percent of engineers in this country are women, 25 percent of lawyers, 22 percent of doctors, and 17 percent of architects. In higher education the picture is better, but equality has not been attained. Whereas nearly three-quarters of the elementary and secondary school teachers (a notoriously underpaid profession) are women, only 43 percent of college and university teachers are women, and most of them are employed in lower professional ranks. In virtually all the professions, then, women have more restricted opportunities than men, are paid less, and have more difficulty advancing.

Although for some time women had been moving into previously all-male occupations, the first federal prohibition of discrimination against them in those occupations was passed in 1963, when an amendment to the Fair Labor Standards Act required equal pay for women and men performing the same work. Title VII of the 1964 Civil Rights Act prohibits discrimination on the basis of race, color, religion, sex, or national origin in hiring, promoting, or discharging employees. Early efforts to enforce the act concentrated on racial discrimination, and attention was given to sexual discrimination only after concerned groups began to exert pressure on the Equal Employment Opportunity Commission (EEOC). Although court decisions have generally strengthened the case for women, progress has been slow and uneven.

THE FEMINIST MOVEMENT

The problem lay buried, unspoken, for many years in the minds of American women. It was a strange stirring, a sense of dissatisfaction, a yearning that women suffered in the middle of the twentieth century in the United States. Each suburban wife struggled with it alone. As she made the beds, shopped for groceries, matched slipcover material, ate peanut butter sandwiches with her children, chauffeured Cub Scouts and Brownies, lay beside her husband at night—she was afraid to ask even of herself the silent question—"Is this all?" (Friedan, *The Feminine Mystique*, p. 11)

With these words Betty Friedan sounded in 1963 the theme of modern **feminism**.

The movement was not born *de novo*. More than a hundred years earlier Lucretia Mott and Elizabeth Cady Stanton had campaigned for the rights of women, and in 1848 the Women's Rights Convention that they organized issued a "Declaration of Sentiments," which concluded, "Now, in view of this entire disfranchisement of one-half the people of this country, we insist that they have immediate admission to all the rights and privileges which belong to them as citizens of the United States."

The industrialization that took women out of the house and into the mills did not give them those rights and privileges; it merely transferred the scene of their labors. The early development of schools and colleges for the education of women benefited only a minority, and even for that minority it failed to open the doors to business and the professions. After a hard-fought battle women gained the franchise with the ratification of the Nineteenth Amendment to the Constitution in 1920, but the right to vote did not bring them into full and equal participation in the political arena. The most significant change in the status of women in America came during the Roaring Twenties:

> They drank, smoked, cut their hair, and engaged in the real sexual revolution of the twentieth century. Using the shortage of cloth after the war as an excuse, they also shed their heavy, confining dresses and crippling foundation garments in a dress-reform movement that many thought did women far more good than the vote. (Freeman, *The Politics of Women's Liberation*, pp. 19–20)

As early as 1923 the National Women's Party had managed to get an equal rights amendment introduced in Congress. Beginning in 1940, in every presidential election both parties included the amendment as planks in their platforms, though little attention was paid to it. In 1961 President John Kennedy established a Presidential Commission on the Status of Women. The commission's report was issued in late 1963, just before the publication of Friedan's *The Feminine Mystique*. It included recommendations that, if implemented, would have given women greater rights in employment and in the political process. It also stated, however, that the rights of women were adequately secured by the Fifth and the Fourteenth Amendments and that an equal rights amendment was therefore unnecessary.

The Civil Rights Act of 1964, originally written to prohibit discrimination in employment on the basis of race, was amended in debate to prohibit sexual discrimination as well. By this act the practices that disadvantaged women in the marketplace became illegal. Although the commission created to enforce the provisions of the act was more serious about dealing with racial discrimination than sexual discrimination, under pressure from a number of sources it did begin to fulfill its obligations to women.

The National Organization for Women (NOW) was formed in 1966, with Betty Friedan as its first president. Its purpose was "to take action to bring women into full participation in the mainstream of American society now, exercising all the privileges and responsibilities thereof in truly equal partnership with men." NOW set up task forces, introduced programs of education and publicity, became involved in sexual discrimination cases in the courts, and organized demonstrations. It began to work for the enforcement of anti-discrimination laws, for special consideration for working mothers, for abortion rights, and particularly for the equal rights amendment. The organization grew rapidly, forming chapters in more than 150 cities and at its peak claiming a membership of about 30,000. It suffered several splits; some women who considered NOW too radical formed more conservative groups, and others who considered NOW too cautious formed more radical organizations. The vast majority of American women, however, did not associate with any group, either because they disagreed with them or because they were indifferent or because they had no opportunity. Yet the groups publicized their cause so effectively that according to a Harris poll, by 1972 nearly half of American women favored efforts to change the status of women in American society.

The impact of the feminist movement inevitably was felt in the churches. Many Christians, accepting as permanently valid the patriarchal pattern reflected in the Bible, insisted that men and women have distinctive roles and functions within the family that have priority over all other social relationships. That does not mean, they said, that one group is inferior to the other, simply that there is a difference of function. This concept determines relationships in religious structures as well as in economics and in family life. Many women, however, challenged this way of thinking and began to seek full participation in the life of the church, even to the extent of ordination into the ministry or the priesthood. In spite of strong pressure, the hierarchy of the Roman Catholic Church has refused to make any concession that allows the possibility of the ordination of women. Some Protestant churches, however, have long ordained women, and others are beginning to do so. In most denominations the number of women ministers is increasing, although women serve for the most part in subordinate positions.

As the feminist movement grew, colleges and universities began to develop women's studies programs. A sizable literature was produced in the form of books and special-interest periodicals. Women moved in increasing numbers into political activity, not merely voting but also working within political parties and running for office both locally and nationally. On the whole, although at a slow pace, women are becoming a potent force in the whole formal structure of society.

In 1972 both houses of Congress overwhelmingly voted that the equal rights amendment be submitted to the states for ratification. The proposed amendment read, "Equality of rights under the law shall not be denied or abridged by the United States or by any State on account of sex." Both the supporters of the amendment and its opponents campaigned vigorously all over the country. Ratification required approval by thirty-eight states, but by the end of 1978 only thirty-five had approved it. Supporters persuaded Congress to extend the deadline for ratification until June 30, 1982. Even with the extension, however, the amendment died without the necessary three-quarters of the states approving. Had it passed it would have rendered unconstitutional all federal and state laws that treat men and women unequally and would have required significant changes in the ways in which most businesses and social institutions deal with men and women.

Without this legal action, however, important changes are occurring in the more informal structures of society. One such change is our use of titles and names. In our polite form of address for men we have never indicated marital status, using "Mr." for both single and married men, but we have indicated the marital status of women by calling single women "Miss" and married women "Mrs." In recent years, however, many women, both single and married, have begun to use the general title "Ms." Furthermore, in the past a single woman customarily took the full name of the man she married. "Miss Jane Roe," for example, became "Mrs. John Doe" when she married. Now, however, married women often continue to use their own given names: "Miss Jane Roe" becomes "Mrs. Jane Doe" or "Ms. Jane Doe." And some women do not change their names at all; "Jane Roe" remains "Jane Roe." These seemingly slight changes in designation reflect an increasing awareness that a woman is a person in her own right, not one whose identity depends on her husband.

Another example of increasing respect for women's rights is the emphasis on inclusive language, particularly in public discourse. By time-honored custom, generalizations that apply to everyone have been made using male imagery, as in "God created man in his own image," "All men are created equal," and "Man is a social animal." Of course it was understood that the word *man* was used in a generic sense and also included women. Nevertheless, the use of male terms in this way reflected the general attitude that men have a higher status than women. Many people insist, furthermore, that words do not merely reflect attitudes; they help to create them as well. For this reason they are seeking to make standard the use of language that is explicitly inclusive. The Prentice Hall *Author's Guide*, sensitive to this perspective, instructs writers that "Men and women should be portrayed as people rather than as male or female. Be careful to avoid sexist language that excludes men or women from any activity or that implies that either is superior or dominant in a particular role." The New Revised Standard Version of the Bible, published in 1989, reflects this same concern for inclusive language. In their preface, the translators state,

> During the almost half a century since the publication of the RSV, many in the churches have become sensitive to the danger of linguistic sexism arising from the inherent bias of the English language toward the masculine gender, a bias that in the case of the Bible has often restricted or obscured the meaning of the original text. The mandates from the Division specified that, in references to men and women, masculine-oriented language should be eliminated as far as this can be done without altering passages that reflect the historical situation of ancient patriarchal culture.

If this concern is taken seriously, it will lead to a long and perhaps difficult effort to purify public discourse by a new standard of language. It will make an impact on every phase of American life. The way our laws are written and enforced will be changed. The literature produced for our educational system will be affected. The concern will be reflected in worship in our churches. It will affect the way we do business and will be reflected in the communication media. It may, in fact, make a more profound change in the status of women than would have been brought about by the passage of an amendment to the Constitution.

WOMEN AND THE SCRIPTURE

So much is said in the Bible about women that it is impossible in this discussion to consider it all. We can, however, get a clear understanding of the biblical perspective by looking at general emphases and considering some specific illustrations.

Throughout biblical history the Hebrew family was patriarchal in form, and women were therefore subordinate to men. A man acquired a wife by presenting a gift to her family which some have considered to be a "bride purchase" price. The marriage of Isaac and Rebekah (Genesis 24) and the marriage of Jacob to Leah and Rachel (Genesis 29:15–30) illustrate this practice. At marriage a woman left her father's household and entered that of her husband. Although the interpretation of the tenth commandment is subject to debate, a man's wife is included along with his servants and his animals among those objects that, according to the law, "You shall not covet" (Exodus 20:17). A man determined where his family would live, when his family would move, and what his family would do with its property. A man found wives for his sons and husbands for his daughters. Whereas women had influence determined by their character and by circumstances, men had the authority determined by their status.

In biblical days the roles of men and women were distinct. They represented a division of labor and responsibility that sometimes functioned well and sometimes functioned to the disadvantage of one or the other. The woman was the childbearer and nurturer, a function of tremendous importance in the ancient world. Indeed, this was considered her chief reason for being. In the economic division of labor, she was responsible for preparing food and clothing for the family. In terms of religion, certain home rituals were her responsibility. The man was the provider of food and shelter, the protector, the religious leader, and the educator of the sons. In these roles, individual personality played a major part in the establishment of husband–wife relationships and in their expression. If we avoid the word *authority,* therefore, we can see that relationships were as varied then as now and that then, as now, some women had more freedom and more power than others.

Although the established roles were distinct, the attitudes toward women in the Bible are as varied as the authors of the books. On the one hand, the author of Ecclesiastes disliked and distrusted women: "I found more bitter than death the woman who is a trap, whose heart is snares and nets, whose hands are fetters; one who pleases God escapes her, but the sinner is taken by her." He concluded, "One man among a thousand I found, but a woman among all these I have not found" (Ecclesiastes 7:26, 28). The poetry in the Song of Solomon, on the other hand, voices appreciation for the beauty of a woman in an amazingly sensual manner. The inclusion of that book in the canon, made possible only by an allegorical interpretation, clearly indicates that such man–woman relationships were not objectionable to most people. In Proverbs woman is seen as an enticement to evil (Chapter 7), but in the same book wisdom is personified as a woman (Chapters 8–9). The poem on "A Capable Wife" (Proverbs 31:10–31), while it affirms the traditional roles in an idealized way, nevertheless injects praise for qualities of character that any person would do well to cultivate.

Jesus's attitude toward women does not fit the pattern that was firmly set in his cultural background. Although the gospels do not report any direct statement from him about women, they do offer a basis for some judgments about his attitude. The first thing to be noted is that whereas many rabbis of his day made harsh and derogatory statements about women, there is no record of Jesus ever having done so. Because such statements were common, their absence indicates an unusual kind of respect on his part. To that fact should be added a word about his relationships with women. Although none of the apostles was a woman, a number of women were numbered among his early followers (see Luke 8:1–3), and some were close friends (see Matthew 27:55–56; John 11:1–42). He seems to have dealt with women on the same basis as men, engaging in conversation with them and teaching them and on occasion performing some "mighty work" for them. In his teaching that every individual is of infinite worth in the sight of God, he made no distinction between men and women (see Matthew 6:25–33, 12:9–14; Luke 15). We can hardly escape the conclusion, therefore, that Jesus considered men and women to be on the same level.

A number of women were major figures in Hebrew history, and some occupied places of responsibility and authority. Moses's sister, Miriam, emerged as one of his chief advisers. Deborah, already functioning as a sort of civil judge for her tribe, became its military leader. Esther, thrust into an advantaged position, used her status as queen to save the Hebrews from an anti-Semitic pogrom. Judith, whose exploits are recorded in the apocryphal book that bears her name, used some rather questionable means to accomplish her purpose, but she destroyed the enemy who was besieging Jerusalem. Alexandra, widow of two Maccabean kings, herself ruled the Hebrews wisely and well for nine years. The achievements of these women are all the more remarkable because they occurred in a society in which women were not expected to function as leaders. It hardly seems possible, then, to think of Hebrew women as totally subordinate to men.

Women also played a significant role in the life of the early church. We have already observed that a number of women were disciples of Jesus: Mary, Martha, Mary Magdalene, Salome, and countless others whose names we do not know. It is not surprising, therefore, that in the early church women were active in leadership positions. Lydia, who was operating her own business, was the first Christian convert in her city, and her home became Paul's base of operations for as long as he remained in Philippi (Acts 16:11–15). In time two other women, Euodia and Syntyche, also became church leaders there (Philippians 4:2–3). Priscilla and her husband, Aquila, were early missionaries (Acts 18:2ff.). Phoebe was a deacon at Cenchreae (Romans 16:1). It is interesting that her title is rendered "deaconess" in older translations of the Bible. In the original, however, the word is the masculine *diakanon*, which everywhere else in the older versions is rendered "deacon." The New Revised Standard Version correctly recognizes her as a deacon, a properly accredited church official.

In addition to noting these general emphases, we must examine certain specific passages that are usually involved in a discussion of the status of women in general and the place of women in the church in particular. The first three chapters of Genesis are often cited in support of the subordination of women. In the older creation account (Genesis 2:4b–25), man was created first and placed in the Garden of Eden. Then, when none of the other animals that God had formed proved to be a fit "helper" for man, God made woman from one of man's ribs. Some people see in this passage the subordination of woman to man because man was created first and woman was created to be his helper. Neither being second in time nor being of assistance to another person, however, necessarily implies subordination; indeed, they sometimes imply exactly the opposite. The real point of the story is seen in the climactic statement concerning the unity of the man and the woman.

In the later creation account (Genesis 1:1–2:4a), the concept of the unity of man and woman is even more explicit. After the creation of all else, God made man and woman simultaneously, in one creative process (v. 27). Man and woman were not created as separate beings; humankind was created as one being. There is no hint that either man or woman exists without the other, that either is a unit apart from and independent of the other. No distinction is made between them. To them God gave dominion over the rest of creation, but to neither did God give dominion over the other.

The Garden of Eden story (Genesis 3) describes the sinfulness of humankind. In that account, the woman was enticed by the serpent to eat the forbidden fruit, and the man was enticed by the woman to do the same thing., All of the offenders—the serpent, the man, and the woman—were punished by a disorder in the natural process: The serpent was doomed to crawl on its belly, the woman was doomed to suffer in childbirth, and the man was doomed to be burdened by his work. By a strange logic, the fact that the woman sinned before the man did and was his agent of temptation has been interpreted by some people as justifying the domination of man over woman. This interpretation makes much of the fact that in the pronouncement of judgment on the woman she was told, "yet your desire shall be for your husband, and he shall rule over you" (Genesis 3:16). It is not at all clear, however, that this passage affirms a divine sanction for the subordination of woman to man. If it has any bearing at all on this point, it merely describes the situation and sees subordination not as a part of the divine order but as a part of the disorder that is the consequence of human sin.

Two of the most important passages in the New Testament concerning the status of women are found in Paul's first letter to the Corinthians. In Chapter 7, on the basis of his belief in the imminent return of Christ and his conviction that marriage distracts from service to Christ, Paul recommended that people not marry. Recognizing, however, that many Christians would not choose celibacy, he discussed the marital relationship as he understood it. Everything said in that chapter applies to both husband and wife. Each owes "conjugal rights" to the other (vv. 1–7), each should remain with the other even if the other is not a believer (vv. 10–16), and each will find marriage to be a distraction from service to God (vv. 32–35). If this idea of complete equality is surprising to us, how much more so must it have been in a patriarchal society.

A bit later in the same letter (1 Corinthians 11–14) Paul discussed some concerns about public worship, one of which is the conduct of women (11:2–16). Expressing a very paternalistic view, he said, "Christ is the head of every man, and the husband is the head of his wife, and God is the head of Christ" (v. 3). He continued with a statement about the propriety with which people were to pray and proophecy. He said, "Any man who prays or prophesies with something on his head disgraces his head, but any woman who prays or prophesies with her head unveiled disgraces her head," he said (1 Corinthians 11:4–5). He continued his argument by saying that man "is the image and reflection of God; but woman is the reflection of man. Indeed, man was not made from woman, but woman from man. Neither was man created for the sake of woman, but woman for the sake of man" (vv. 7–9). Then, recognizing the faulty logic, and perhaps also his inconsistency with positions he had stated elsewhere, he acknowledged the mutual dependence of man and woman and added that "man comes through woman" (v. 12). He tried to strengthen his argument by affirming that it is natural for women to have long hair and men short hair (vv. 14–15), an affirmation that he himself realized was weak. Consequently he concluded by asserting his own authority, saying, "But if anyone is disposed to be contentious—we have no such custom, nor do the churches of God" (v. 16).

In reading this passage we are usually so struck by Paul's stern affirmation that women should behave themselves properly in worship services that we overlook a crucial fact: The women were actually "praying and prophesying" in the services (vv. 4–5). They had leadership roles exactly as men did. Paul offered no rebuke for their participation in that way but merely said that when they prayed and prophesied they should do so in a manner that showed reverence and respect. Paul's acceptance of a socially approved practice should not blind us to the fact that women participated in worship services in exactly the same way as men.

In the letter to the Ephesians there is a passage (5:21–6:4) that describes the ideal relationship within the Christian family. We have already examined this ideal (Chapter 8), but we need to observe here that it involves mutual respect and responsibility and commitment. Here Paul (if indeed he wrote this epistle) did call the husband "the head of the wife" (Ephesians 5:23), but he did so within a context that called for each person to submit to the other. Furthermore, on the basis of this concept of mutual submission, he stressed the ideal of unity.

Rather than basing our understanding of Paul's view of women on these passages of Scripture alone, we need to consider also the implications of a principle that he enunciated on several occasions and that undergirded his entire ministry. He recognized that in the social order distinctions were made between groups of people. He insisted, however, that in the Christian fellowship those social distinctions are totally irrelevant: "There is no longer Jew or Greek, there is no longer slave or free, there is no longer male and female; for all of you are one in Christ Jesus" (Galatians 3:28; cf. Romans 10:12, Colossians 3:11). Although he used this phrase more frequently in speaking of the Jewish–Gentile matter, he did apply it to the male–female issue as well. We must not try to make a twentieth-century man of Paul. He probably would be quite uncomfortable with much of our "women's libera-tion"; he would be equally uncomfortable, however, with the exclusion of women from positions of service and leadership in the church.

Although the date of the writing of the Pastoral Epistles (1 and 2 Timo-thy and Titus) is debated, they clearly reflect a time later than that of Paul. At that time the church had developed a more precise organizational structure in which women were relegated to a subordinate status. In 1 Timothy 2:8–15 there are directions for public worship in which it is clear that "the men" are leading the services (v. 8). The women are directed to dress decorously (vv. 9–10) and to "learn in silence with full submission" (v. 11). That direction is followed with the statement, "I permit no woman to teach or to have author-ity over a man; she is to keep silent" (v. 12). In the next chapter the statements about the qualifications of the bishops and the deacons imply that these per-sons are men. The statements about "the women" may refer to a church office, but they probably refer to the wives of the officers.

A CHRISTIAN APPROACH TO CURRENT ISSUES

Much of what was said about a Christian approach to minority group rela-tionships pertains to women also. In both instances we are confronting the problem of dealing with people on the basis of their membership in certain groups rather than on the basis of their personhood. Here, however, we need to restate some basic principles that are relevant to the current status of women:

1. Because every individual is of infinite worth in the sight of God, our indi-vidual actions must demonstrate respect for all persons, and we must seek

to create a social order in which neither law nor custom sanctions any form of injustice.

2. Whatever may be the norm in the social order, in the Christian fellowship there can be no discrimination on the basis of sex.

3. All persons have the right and the responsibility to mature as individuals, to develop their own potential, and to employ their talents to the fullest extent possible.

On the basis of these principles we can say a word about several current issues. The first is the question of whether additional legislation is needed to guarantee women the right to full and equal participation in the social structure. Many people opposed the Equal Rights Amendment on the ground that equal rights are already guaranteed by the Constitution. They thought that all that was needed was the enforcement of the laws already on the books. It is true that enforcement is a problem and that women have not enjoyed the full benefits of the laws as they are written. But would enforcement be sufficient? Or do we in fact need an equal rights amendment? Do we need additional legislation to correct current problems? A review of the legal situation makes two things clear. First, there is confusion about the legal status of women because the laws vary so widely from one state to another. In particular there are problems with the laws dealing with sexual harassment, rape, and property rights. In addition, there is a need for protection for women in education, in employment opportunities, in career advancement, and in property rights. We may expect legislation to be introduced piece by piece, state by state. Perhaps a revised equal rights amendment will be proposed at some future date. At present, however, it seems clear that the law does not adequately safeguard the rights of women and that this is one area in which we need to work to implement the biblical concern for justice.

We have noted that the Civil Rights Act of 1964 prohibits discrimination on the basis of sex as well as race. We have also noted that the affirmative action policies adopted during the early 1970s and pursued until the mid-1980s encountered considerable resistance. These policies required employers doing business with the government to give evidence that in their hiring policies they did not discriminate on the basis of race or sex. The evidence was generally expected to show that the number of women and of members of minority groups among the employees was proportionate to their number in the general population. Where the number was disproportionately small, employers were required to show that they were trying to correct the imbalance. For a time this procedure was popularly understood to mean that a given number of women and of minority group members had to be hired. In 1979 the Supreme Court ruled that such a "quota system" was unconstitutional. In the same ruling, however, the Court upheld the validity of a more flexible plan of affirmative action. That same sort of affirmative action was required for educational institutions in their admissions policies. As we have seen, in the mid-1980s the process of reversing those policies was begun. The

1990s brought widespread reaction against affirmative action, particularly as related to race. But for women the far-reaching implications of this Act, and the implications of subsequent court decisions, have yet to be realized.

Is affirmative action an appropriate way to deal with discrimination against women in educational opportunities and in employment? Or can the inequalities of the past be overcome simply by employing the best-qualified person, regardless of sex, by promoting the best-qualified worker, by admitting the best-qualified applicants to the colleges and graduate schools? How can we be sure that a person's sex is neither deliberately nor subconsciously considered a qualification? If not by affirmative action, how can we guarantee women access to the best educational opportunities? How can we be sure that they are given equal consideration in hiring? In salary increases? In job promotion? How can we be sure not merely that we do not discriminate against individuals but also that in the educational world and in the business and professional world women have the same opportunities as men?

The leadership role of women in the church is an issue of great importance. In the Roman Catholic Church women are ineligible for ordination to the priesthood, and in spite of some strong sentiment in this country favoring their ordination, the situation is not likely to change in the near future. The Southern Baptist Convention, the largest Protestant organization in the United States, officially opposes the ordination of women and only a handful of women serve as Southern Baptist pastors. Indeed, in 1998 that group amended its historic "Faith and Message" statement with a section on "The Family" that affirmed that "A wife is to submit herself graciously to the servant leadership of her husband." All of the other larger Protestant denominations, however, including other Baptist groups, accept women as pastors. Of the smaller groups, some have historically accepted the leadership of women, but others have opposed it. In most groups acceptance has taken place only in recent years and only over significant opposition. In spite of the official positions of denominations, however, women pastors are in a distinct minority because at the local level there is often considerable reluctance to accept them. Some opponents to the pastoral leadership of women interpret Scripture as prohibiting it. More, however, are simply unwilling to accept women as leaders in any areas of life—politics, education, business, or religion.

We have observed that whereas much of Scripture is patriarchal in outlook, the basic doctrines of the Christian faith require the acceptance of persons as persons without regard to sex. We have observed that in spite of the patriarchal structure of society some women did indeed serve as leaders both in Old Testament days and in the New Testament church. It would seem, therefore, that in refusing to accept the leadership of women today we are following the dictates of social custom rather than the principles of Christian faith. And we are now in the surprising situation in which women are making greater progress in the social order, conservative as it is, than they are in the church. Is it not strange that it is easier for a woman to be our representative in Congress or our governor, to serve on the Supreme Court of our nation, to be superintendent of the public schools that our children attend, to own and operate businesses with which we deal, to be our doctor or lawyer, than it is for her to serve as our pastor? Rather than taking the lead on this basic issue, the church may be the last bastion of discrimination against women.

QUESTIONS AND TOPICS FOR DISCUSSION

1. How important is the use of inclusive language in public discourse? In personal conversation?
2. Discuss the status of women in your church.
3. What do you see to be the impact of the church on the status of women in our society?
4. Examine several issues of a weekly newsmagazine or several episodes of a television program, and evaluate the treatment of women.
5. Evaluate the adage, "When woman gained her equality with man she lost her superiority."

RECOMMENDATIONS FOR FURTHER READING

ADAMS, SHERI, *What the Bible Really Says about Women*. Macon, Ga.: Smyth and Helwys, 1994.

CRITES, LAURA L., and WINIFRED HEPPERLE, *Women, the Courts, and Equality*. Newbury Park, Calif.: Sage, 1987.

FEWELL, DANNA NOLAN, and DAVID M. GUNN, *Gender, Power, and Promise*. Nashville: Abingdon, 1993.

FRIEDAN, BETTY, *The Feminine Mystique*. New York: Dell, 1963.

HUNT, SUSAN, and PEGGY HUTCHESON, *Leadership for Women in the Church*. New York: Harper Collins, 1991.

MCKENZIE, VASHTI M., *Not Without a Struggle: Leadership Development for African American Women in Ministry*. New York: Pilgrim Press, 1996.

NEIL, ANNE THOMAS, and VIRGINIA GARRETT NEELY, eds., *The New Has Come*. Washington: Southern Baptist Alliance, 1989.

STETSON, DOROTHY MCBRIDE, *Women's Rights in the USA*. New York: Garland, 1997.

VALIAN, VIVIAN, *Why So Slow?* Cambridge, Mass.: MIT Press, 1997.

11

Citizenship in a Democracy

American citizenship is our birthright. Except for a small minority of people who have been naturalized, we are citizens by virtue of our parentage and our place of birth. We do nothing to earn our status, and whether we treasure it or ignore it we are not in jeopardy of losing it.

More than any other institution, the state determines the conditions of our life. It defines the family into which we are born, states the rights and privileges of its members, and designates their responsibilities to and for one another. It controls our education. It determines the conditions under which we work or operate our business. It regulates transportation and communication. It guards against the infringement of our personal rights. It protects us from criminals and defends us against foreign powers. It guarantees our individual freedom and defines its limitations.

In the practical affairs of daily life we operate in families and schools, in the workplace and the marketplace, and in the world of entertainment. We relate not just to persons but also to institutions, and through these institutions we affect the lives of other people. We have no option about working through the state. Whether by deliberate decision or by simply letting things take their course, we function as citizens. The question for Christian citizens is how to make this functioning the most effective expression of Christian concern.

AMERICAN DEMOCRATIC GOVERNMENT

The state, then, is a given within which we work. It may be defined as an organization that regulates the lives of the people of a particular geographic area and protects the integrity of that area from attack by outside forces. It is the final authority over all other institutions within its territory. It sets the limits within which they operate and exercises various kinds of power to enforce its regulations. Even though the form of government varies from one nation to another, the government is always the instrument for the establishment and maintenance of community. Even absolutist governments, which reflect little or no concern for the rights of the governed, nevertheless function as protectors and regulators in this sense.

The American form of government assumes that the community itself is the final seat of authority. The state is the instrument of the community, its agent in making and enforcing laws and in providing for its citizens all of those functions that are necessary for the well-being of the community as a whole as well as of individual citizens. The community itself, therefore, is involved in the governing process. This involvement is achieved through the selection of representatives who act for the community. Since unanimity of judgment on specific issues can never be achieved, we subscribe to the idea that the judgment of the majority shall prevail. At the same time, we try to be sure that the rights of the minority are carefully safeguarded. To make sure that the will of the majority continues to prevail, we choose representatives to serve for limited terms of office, we separate the powers of government (legislative, judicial, and executive), and we subject all officials to a wide variety of checks (regulatory agencies, special committees, recall, impeachment, and even nongovernment watchdog organizations).

The majority does not in fact always participate in the process, however. Through legal restrictions, group pressure, ignorance, or indifference, the participation of many groups of people in our country, such as women, African-Americans, the poor, and the uneducated, historically has been restricted. During the past three decades most of the legal restrictions have been removed, and the result has been greater involvement on the part of women and African-Americans. The poor and the uneducated, however, are still rarely involved.

A basic function of our democratic government is to maintain order and ensure justice for all its citizens. Although social justice cannot be defined in terms of law alone, the law is the basic instrument by which the state operates to this end. Laws that are general in scope and impartial in application provide the framework for social order and protect the rights of the whole society. The enforcement of the law necessarily entails the exercise of power. Christians, however, insist that the power of the state is limited, not absolute. They also recognize the danger that those who exercise power may try to hold on to it and use it in their own self-interest. Christians therefore insist that their highest loyalty is to God, not the state, and that in obedience to God they sometimes feel compelled to resist the power of the state. Thus they insist that the state holds power *under God*. A basic question, therefore, is what Christians should do when they become convinced that the power of the state is on the side of injustice.

The concept of justice, as it is understood in our democracy, presupposes the equality of all persons. One of the self-evident truths cited by our founding fathers was that all persons are "created equal." Obviously they did not mean equality of intelligence or wealth or power. They meant those "unalienable rights" of life, liberty, and the pursuit of happiness. The framers of the Constitution made these rights quite specific in the first ten amendments, which we call the Bill of Rights. These rights should be denied to no one because of race, sex, education, social status, wealth, or any other factor.

At all levels the activities of the government have become increasingly numerous and increasingly complex. We take it for granted now that the government will provide education, transportation, postal services, police and fire protection, protection against economic disaster, and so on. We take it for granted that the government should regulate matters of health, the environment, and natural resources. Although we agree that the government is properly engaged in a wide variety of activities that affect the lives of its citizens, we debate many of the specific programs and decisions involved. In deciding specific issues we make value judgments about the good or the right thing to do.

BIBLICAL TEACHINGS

We have said that the state claims final authority over all other institutions in its territory. Christians, however, are troubled by this claim. For us, the final authority is God, and even the state stands under the judgment of God. While few American Christians are aware of any conflict between the claims of the state and their allegiance to God, most would say that if there were a conflict, we should obey God rather than the state. This approach is solidly based on Scripture.

The Old Testament

The concept of government reflected in the Hebrew scripture is that of a **theocracy**, or government by God. This concept is quite different from American democracy. In a democracy the final seat of authority is the community; in a theocracy, the final seat of authority is God. While the basic function of government is to maintain order and ensure justice, and to function so the government makes and enforces laws, in a theocracy it is God who makes and enforces laws. Thus in the pre-monarchic days of the Hebrew people religious leaders were also the political leaders. Even after the establishment of the monarchy, the king did not have final authority; he was merely the instrument through whom God ruled. Although there were good kings and poor ones, devout kings and wicked ones, the theory persisted that the king was God's servant and was accountable to God.

In the Old Testament theocracy the state functioned as other states did. As in other nations, a primary responsibility of government was to ensure justice. The chief instrument of justice was the law, not thought of as dictated by the king or legislated by the people but as given by God. The laws that protected persons and personal property assumed a basic equality of men, so that the king was subject to the law to the same extent as his lowliest subject. As we have seen, while this theocracy offered some important protection to women, it did not assume their equality with men. Neither did it think of Gentiles as having the same rights as Jews, nor of slaves as having the same rights as their masters. Like all other legal systems, the Hebrew laws upheld a concept of justice that was at some points flawed.

The New Testament

Because the literature of the New Testament emerged from the experience of the early church, it reflects the struggle of that church for its own identity. A major factor was the attitude of the Jewish community, in which Christianity first appeared, toward the Roman government. Although the Jews were far from united in their attitudes toward Rome, there was a strong and popular resistance movement. The Zealots, as the resisters were called, were responsible for frequent outbreaks of violence in the first century, and the movement reached a climax in the ill-fated revolution of c.e. 66–72. One of Jesus's disciples was identified as Simon the Zealot (Luke 6:15), and James and John, nick-named "sons of thunder," might have been Zealots also. One interpretation of Judas Iscariot's betrayal of Jesus suggests that Judas may have been a Zealot disappointed in Jesus because he did not start a revolution. And although Jesus was not a Zealot, the charge on which he was convicted in the Roman court was insurrection. All of this suggests that many of Jesus's earliest followers were predisposed to be negative, if not overtly hostile, toward Rome.

Another factor in the background of the New Testament is the fact that Jesus was tried and executed by Roman officials. Although Jesus was a religious figure rather than a political one, although the gospels report no conflict with political leaders, and although his appearance in the Roman court was at the request of Jewish religious leaders, the crime with which he was charged was an offense against the state, the death sentence was pronounced by the Roman procurator, and the execution was carried out in compliance with Roman law. The New Testament writers do not play down the major role that the Jewish authorities played in the death of Jesus. Yet because the Romans executed Jesus, the writers viewed Rome as unfriendly.

Rome became increasingly unfriendly to Christians in the last half of the first century. In the earliest days of the church there was some local persecution of Christians, and there was one particularly severe episode in connection with the great fire that destroyed Rome in the days of Nero (c.e. 64). Widespread persecution of Christians broke out near the end of the first century and continued until well after the time in which the last book of the New Testament was written. The fact of persecution, therefore, is reflected in what the early Christians wrote.

Another, perhaps related, factor that influenced the attitude of the New Testament writers toward the state was the belief that the "end of the age" was imminent. This eschatological hope played a part in the teachings of Jesus and was therefore a prominent part in the life of the early church. Its impact on Christian thinking about social problems in general and about the state in particular is of great significance. Because they believed that the world was soon to end, the early Christians saw little value in trying to reform the institutions of the present order. Believing that the state was only a temporary and transitory structure, not one that would be a part of the new age, they accepted it and dealt with it as it was.

Jesus and the State.   Only once, according to the gospels, did Jesus speak directly about his disciples' responsibility toward the state. Mark 12:13–17 describes an incident in which the Pharisees and the Herodians, who differed radically from each other in their attitude toward Rome, teamed up to ask Jesus a question that they thought he could not possibly answer to the satisfaction of both groups: "Is it lawful to pay taxes to the emperor, or not?" Illustrating his answer with a coin bearing the emperor's image, Jesus replied, "Give to the emperor the things that are the emperor's, and to God the things that are God's." This answer affirms the validity of the claims of both the emperor and God on the individual. Although it says nothing about what one should do in case of conflicting claims, we can be sure that neither Jesus nor his questioners would have given priority to the emperor. What is clear from this answer is that Jesus did in fact recognize the legitimacy of the emperor's claims. While he did not accept the state as in any sense ultimate, he did accept it as a valid social institution and rejected the implication that it was necessarily hostile to God.

There is other evidence in the gospels that Jesus did not regard the state as the final authority. Not long before his arrest, for example, some friendly Pharisees warned him of Herod's hostility and cautioned him to change his plan to go to Jerusalem. Jesus, however, calling Herod "that fox," replied that his higher loyalty required him to carry out his plans (Luke 13:31–35). Again, in his conversation with the disciples on the eve of his arrest, Jesus contrasted the so-called "greatness" of those who exercise lordship over other people with the greatness of those who serve other people (Luke 22:24–27).

It is probably correct to say that Jesus did not spend a great deal of time thinking about the state. Rather he accepted it as a part of the environment in which he lived and worked. When he contemplated his own mission, he considered and rejected the way of the Zealots (Matthew 4:8–10; cf. John 18:36). His mission, he insisted, was spiritual in nature and his final loyalty was to God. When the forces of the state took him into custody he refused to allow his disciples to resist, and he accepted without protest the sentence that the state pronounced upon him. We might conclude from his example that even a miscarriage of justice is not an adequate reason for the destruction of the system. Oscar Cullmann summarizes Jesus's attitude toward the state:

> Jesus was in no sense an enemy of the State on principle, but rather a loyal citizen who offered no threat to the State's existence. Granted that on the basis of his consciousness of mission and his expectation of the kingdom of God he did not regard the State as a final, divine institution, even where it observed its proper limits. He regarded it as a temporary institution, toward which he maintained a critical attitude. He refused obedience only to the totalitarian State which was exceeding its limits, drawing the line always at the point where the State demanded what is God's—but only at that point. (*The State in the New Testament*, p. 54)

Paul and the State.   Paul was a Roman citizen and that fact served him well. At the time of his arrest in Jerusalem it saved him from a scourging and ensured him better treatment than that usually accorded prisoners (Acts 22:29). Because of his citizenship, when his life was threatened he was taken from the Jerusalem prison to Caesarea, where he pled his case before the governor. When after a time it appeared that he might be returned to Jerusalem, he exercised his right of appeal to Caesar and was taken to Rome (Acts 25:6–12). His freedom of activity there as he awaited trial (Acts 28) was doubtless due to his citizenship. We are not surprised, therefore, to find that in the letters he wrote while he was a prisoner and in which he referred to his impending trial he raised no question about the justice of the system. He seemed to take it for granted that the system would operate properly.

The chief passage in which Paul discusses the state is Romans 13:1–7. This passage should not be considered in isolation, however, but in its broader context. The preceding chapter begins a discussion of the pattern of conduct that Paul recommended to his readers. Citing love as the basic obligation, he advised them about how to get along with one another and with people in the broader community. Verses 14–21 speak of living in harmony with all persons. From that point Paul talked about living under the jurisdiction of the state. He concluded his discussion of the state with a statement anticipating the end of the age, implying that the present situation was a temporary one.

Within that context Paul affirmed that the state was instituted by God and used by God to maintain order. Law-abiding citizens, he said, have nothing to fear, but God uses the state to punish evildoers. Because the state is an instrument of God, it legitimately claims three things: obedience to the law, payment of taxes, and respect for authority.

For Paul, the state was the Roman Empire. Doubtless he knew that there were areas of the world not subject to Rome, but he had no contact with them. The empire was the world of his experience. When he wrote to the Romans he enjoyed the full benefits of his citizenship. Although he had had minor brushes with the authorities because of his missionary activity, he had no real basis for questioning the justice of the system. We cannot help wondering what he might have said had he written after he had received the death sentence. We are persuaded that he would have challenged the justice of the verdict. We are also persuaded that he would not have challenged the right of the state to make this decision. He acknowledged, in other words, the need for order and saw the state as God's instrument for meeting that need.

In his first letter to the Corinthians, Paul cited the lack of understanding that led "the rulers of this age" to crucify Jesus (1 Corinthians 2:6–8). He did not consider the crucifixion of Jesus to be the work of an illegitimate agency but rather the misguided judgment of a legitimate one. In that same letter he cautioned Christians against taking other Christians into the courts to settle issues between them (1 Corinthians 6:1–8). He did not challenge the authority of the state to handle disputes; he did challenge the propriety of Christians availing themselves of that service. As Cullmann says, Paul believed that "everywhere the Christian can dispense with the State without threatening its existence, he should do so" (p. 61). He affirmed the state as a necessary institution but rejected any suggestion that it has final authority.

The Literature of Persecution.   The Christian church expanded in a hostile world and at times was subjected to persecution. As a minority movement it was always looked down upon. When it grew, the opposition became more overt. A limited persecution of Christians was conducted during the time of Nero (54–68), and there was widespread persecution during Domitian's reign (81–96). After Domitian there were sporadic periods of intense persecution for the next two hundred years. Many of the documents that were written during those periods instruct Christians on how to deal with hostility, and some of them were written for the express purpose of encouraging Christians to be faithful in the face of persecution.

First Peter, for example, which was probably written during the time of Nero, makes an important point about Christians' relationship to the state (1 Peter 2:11–17). Regarding themselves as "aliens and exiles" in the world, and in spite of persecution, they are to conduct themselves "honorably among the Gentiles." They are to recognize the authority of the governing officials, conduct themselves as good citizens, and endure without complaint what happens to them. They are even to "honor the emperor." This passage reflects a view quite similar to that expressed by Paul in Romans 13.

A second document written to deal with persecution is Revelation. In this book the empire no longer is seen as an agent of God but rather as an instrument of Satan. Probably written at the height of the persecution under Domitian (81–96), this book views the empire as the very embodiment of evil. It is the Beast that challenges the power of God (Revelation 13) and seeks to destroy God's church. It has slain countless numbers of the faithful, and there is no sign of possible improvement. Indeed, this distress is seen as a part of that struggle of good and evil in which, though evil may have its temporary successes, the final victory of God is assured. The central theme is the assurance that no matter how bad the present conflict becomes, the ultimate victory is God's, and those who are faithful even to death will share in that victory.

The book of Revelation, then, has a radically different view of the empire from that of the other New Testament documents. The other writers viewed the empire as God's instrument in maintaining order—an instrument that makes errors of judgment but God's instrument nevertheless. In Revelation, however, it is seen as an instrument of Satan. How can we understand the difference in viewpoint? Cullman says that in the other passages "only the institution of the State as such was under discussion" (p. 71) but that in Revelation the state has become a Satanic power by demanding what belongs to God alone (p. 72).

THE CHRISTIAN AS CITIZEN

How do we move from an understanding of biblical teachings on the state to actual participation in the modern democratic political process? Do we go with Bible in hand and, ignoring the beliefs of those who are not Christian, try to impose our convictions on government structures? Or do we see biblical teachings as applicable to our personal lives but impossible for the nation? Do we search for some common ground other than religion for our pluralistic society? Or do we look for ways in which in this pluralistic society we can live out our faith, responding to God by being good citizens of a nation that is by definition not religious?

This issue is not an abstraction. We are talking about making down-to-earth decisions on matters in which everyone has a stake. We are talking about educating our children and young people, about making and enforcing laws, about dealing with AIDS or the connection between cigarette smoking and lung cancer or the industrial pollution of the natural environment. We are talking about national defense and international relations, about coal and oil and nuclear reactors, and about the care of the sick and financial security for the aging. In short, we are talking about involvement in decisions that affect every citizen.

As people of faith, we make those decisions as a part of the larger community. While we function as individuals, we do not function alone. H. Richard Niebuhr used the phrase "the responsible self" to indicate the interaction between the individual and the context of decision making on social issues. For him, the fundamental element in that context was God's relationship to humankind. That relationship is not abstract, however, but concrete and historical. It involves all of our social contacts, and in particular our political and economic activities. Niebuhr said that "for the ethics of responsibility the *fitting* action, the one that fits into a total interaction as response and as anticipation of further response, is alone conducive to the good and alone is right" (*The Responsible Self*, p. 61). In that sense, we can consider our place in the political order within the context of our Christian faith.

The Obligations of Citizenship

What are our responsibilities as citizens in a democratic society? All citizens have three basic obligations to the state. First, they owe respect for the law. This means that the law applies equally to all people, that individuals have no right to exempt themselves from its requirements, and that obedience is based not on the fear of being caught for violations but on respect. This is the idea that Paul expressed when he said, "Therefore one must be subject, not only because of wrath, but also because of conscience" (Romans 13:5). The only valid basis for disobedience is an allegiance to a higher law, what Peter meant when he said to the Sanhedrin, "We must obey God rather than any human authority" (Acts 5:29).

Second, all citizens owe intelligent, informed participation in the political process. Because democratic government is by nature participatory, it can succeed only to the extent that the citizens actually choose their representatives, help in the determination of policies, and accept the responsibility of running for office. The disfranchisement of any group, either through its own inertia or through exclusion from the system by a more powerful group, makes the process less than democratic. The greatest scandal of our government is not the misbehavior of any official but the failure of large numbers of people to participate.

Third, all citizens are responsible for conscientious criticism of persons and policies. We can never give absolute devotion to any system, since such devotion can be given only to God. We can never give absolute loyalty to any political leader, because all human beings are fallible. At all times, therefore, we need to measure actual practices by the stated ideals of our nation, by the concepts of honesty and justice, by the effects on all the people. This means that we must examine all proposals to understand their implications, constantly reevaluate what is already being done, and always be prepared to approve or disapprove.

None of these three responsibilities is uniquely Christian. Indeed, we cannot cite any responsibility that is exclusively the province of Christian citizens. What is distinctive about Christian citizenship is not any specific action that we take which others do not but the rooting of our obligation in God. For Christians, the exercise of our citizenship is one of the ways in which we relate to God. Paul said that "in him [Christ] we live and move and have our being." Christ, by this affirmation, is our environment, the world in which we live, the source from which we come. As our nature is shaped by Christ, our citizenship is an expression of that nature. As citizens we do the same things that other people do, but our action is an affirmation of our relationship to Christ.

The Contribution of Christians

Do Christians, then, have anything distinctive to offer in the political process? While we must be cautious about any claim to exclusive ownership of an idea or attitude, there are several important concepts that Christians bring to the political arena. First is our view of people. We have said that a belief in the dignity and worth of every person is fundamental in the Christian view of human nature. It is also basic in the democratic state. Those individuals whom many people regard as inferior—members of minority groups, the poor, criminals, victims of certain diseases—possess the same dignity and worth as those who look down on them. We Christians root this conviction in our belief in God and in God's dealings with people rather than in a faith in humankind. We affirm it in spite of the way in which both individuals and groups of people actually behave. We affirm it in spite of the complexity of social structures and the dehumanizing effects of group pressures to conform. We even affirm it in spite of the distinctions between people made in all social institutions, including the church. Our affirmation and our efforts to incorporate it into the social structure are a vital element in American democracy.

There is another side to the Christian view of people, however, that is essential to the democratic process. It is an awareness of the dark side of human nature, of what in religious terms is called sinfulness. It is because of this side of human nature that good people do bad things, that people do not always follow through on their promises, that graft and corruption are always with us, that people take advantage of the system and use it for their own benefit, that no system works perfectly, that group conflict is always a possibility. For this reason it is necessary for the people to impose limitations on the power of their representatives and to find ways to hold them accountable.

Second, Christians bring an emphasis on the concept of community to the democratic process. The concept of community, of course, is fundamental in the understanding of the church. The church is a community of faith, a group of people bound together by their relationship to Christ. The members do not think of this community as rooted in or sustained by their activities or their feelings of unity, but rather in the work of Christ. It is a community in which people recognize a responsibility to and for one another, care for one another, and share experiences. When this concept of community is carried over into the nation, it counterbalances the extreme individualism that at best ignores other people and at worst sets persons and groups against one another. A national sense of community will ensure a concern for the rights of minorities, for the care of the helpless, and for respect for the individual, as well as a concern for the common good. This is not to suggest that the unity of the nation is or should be the same as the unity of the church. The two are different in nature and in function. At the same time, the idea that the nation is in some sense a community has a positive effect on the operation of our democracy.

What is the basis for our national sense of community? Both national-ism and the philosophy of enlightened self-interest play a part. It cannot be these alone, however. Our nationalistic spirit is somewhat limited by the fact that we are such a diverse people. In addition, nationalism fosters a spirit of hostility toward other nations, a spirit alien to the democratic philosophy. Enlightened self-interest is limited in that it requires the protection of the rights of others only when it is clearly to our own advantage to do so. J. Philip Wogaman suggests that the concept of "covenant" is the basis of national community. Although this concept is somewhat similar to the old "social contract" theory, it does have a distinctively biblical and Christian flavor. Wogaman says about God's covenant with the Hebrew people that it both reinforces the sovereignty of God and creates the community of Israel. Then he adds the Christian concept that "in Jesus Christ we understand that the covenant is universal; it is with and for everybody; it is not limited to a par-ticular historical community" (*Christian Perspectives on Politics*, p. 167). Applying that idea to modern government, he says,

> The suggestion here that the community of reference for all people is the inclusive, universal community has political consequences on the face of it. No people can be understood as aliens—not even clearly political adversaries. All political divisions based upon city, nation, or empire are relativized by the covenantal notion when it is applied in this universal sense. (p. 167)

Third, Christians bring to our democratic society the element of hope. The dream of a better world is a persistent theme in the Bible. We are deeply moved when we read Isaiah's words,

> they shall beat their swords into plowshares,
> and their spears into pruning hooks;
> nation shall not lift up sword against nation,
> neither shall they learn war any more. (Isaiah 2:4)

Christians think of themselves, in a sense, as already living in this context because they are members of a community that transcends race and nation and class and sex. Even though they know that as it exists now that commu-nity is flawed, they are moved by their vision of perfection. Even though they project the full realization of that dream into the eschatological age, they live as if that age were breaking in on this one and transforming it.

The dream of an ideal social order is not exclusively Christian. Lit-erature and philosophy contain a great deal of it, from Plato's *Republic* to Skinner's *Walden Two*. From nineteenth-century Utopian communities to twentieth-century communism, people have experimented with institution-alizing the dream. Nearly every political figure who comes into power does so by promising to lead the nation into a brighter future. The ideal age has never come, however. Old hostilities are not forgotten. New divisions are created by new circumstances. The struggle for power goes on between individuals, between groups, and between nations. Even the church, which sees itself as already living in the new age, is torn by conflict.

Yet Christians are committed to and drawn by an ideal of community. Knowing that it will never be fully realized on earth, they nevertheless do not project it entirely into another world. Rather they hold out to this world the constant possibility of approximating the ideal. In every political situation they hold out the hope that things can be made better.

Suggestions for Involvement

How can we effectively involve ourselves in the political arena? At the outset we need to set out deliberately and systematically to inform ourselves. On the surface that would not seem to be difficult. Between the media, which try, with varying degrees of success, to report the news objectively, and the partisans who flood us with propaganda, it would seem that we have more information than we can use. The problem, however, is distinguishing between fact and fiction, between reporting and special pleading, between accuracy and distortion. Our task is to sort through and evaluate all that we see and hear and, on the basis of what we learn, to make our decisions about persons and issues.

Once we have committed ourselves to a person or a program, we can begin to exert our influence through our conversation with others. Talk can be cheap, but not always. Whether in casual conversation or in deliberate and sustained discussion, words make an impact. They convey ideas and emotions, both of which are involved in most decisions. By our words on the job, in the marketplace, at the ballpark, on the street, or with friends in our living room, we can help to create a climate and to shape public opinion. In addition, we can influence some people who have not as yet made up their minds how they are going to vote. In most campaigns a strikingly large number of people do not make their decisions until quite late in the season, and they are often the deciding factor in the election. They are likely to respond to the influence of people whom they know and whose judgment they respect.

In the long run, the most effective way to influence public policy is through direct involvement in the political structure. Most decisions of social significance are not made through personal interaction but through group interaction. Candidates vie with each other for the nomination of a political party, and they run for office on party platforms. The party system functions at every level of government. In any given campaign, local or national, the people of influence are not likely to be newcomers to politics but those who have worked faithfully within the system. The most effective criticism of a person or a policy comes from within the system, not from the outside.

The practice of politics always involves compromise. Although we tend to regard compromise as undesirable, it is in fact essential for any group cooperation. No one person has either the wisdom or the power to make all decisions. Certainly there are some matters that we cannot approve and some matters that we must approve. Most political decisions, however, are not between such absolutes but between alternatives that are a mixture of good and bad. In politics, as in other activities, we must work within restrictions for the best possible outcome. If perchance we face an issue on which we cannot compromise, it is entirely possible to make an impact while going down to defeat.

In addition to political parties, we may also exercise influence through special-interest groups. People of different political parties may be united in a concern about local issues such as street construction or recreational facilities or matters before the school board. They may be united in a concern about national questions such as the safety of nuclear energy or the pollution of the environment or the spread of AIDS. By working through such groups we can help make progress toward goals that we consider desirable. We do need to be careful, however, not to spread ourselves too thin. Because we have limited time, energy, and money, we will do well to concentrate on a limited number of concerns.

How are we to decide which concerns? We need to work with other people and other groups whose objectives are consistent with our own ideals. Here we need to be very careful not to seek, through political activity, our specifically Christian objectives. We live in a society that includes people of many other faiths and people of no faith, and with many of them we share a concern for the welfare of all people. So we need to ask: Are the objectives sufficiently inclusive? Are they important enough to claim our limited time and energy and money? What are the possibilities of achieving these objectives? Are the methods employed consistent with our ideals? Do we have confidence in the people who are in positions of leadership?

Effective work in the political arena calls for the best use of all available means of influencing thought. Jesus once urged his disciples to be "wise as serpents and innocent as doves" (Matthew 10:16). Packaging is as important in the selling of ideas as it is in the selling of products. Whether we are trying to convince the people in our group or are trying to help our group convince the public, we need to learn the techniques of presenting what we believe in ways that will compel people to listen. Honesty, sincerity, and integrity are basic to our efforts; we must begin with them, and they must permeate all that we do. But if we are to have an impact, we must use the techniques of communication that are known to be effective.

All of this takes money. Most of us have limited resources and feel that we cannot invest a great deal in political campaigns of any sort. Yet one way to be involved in the political arena, to support causes in which we believe and persons whom we trust, is to make financial contributions. Jesus said, "For where your treasure is, there your heart will be also" (Matthew 6:21). This applies to politics as well as religion. Since conducting a political campaign of any sort requires money, we can make an impact through our contributions.

In the periods between political campaigns, it is important to remain alert to issues and to express our views to elected representatives. There is a sense in which we elect persons to do certain jobs and should therefore leave them free to fulfill their responsibilities. Unfortunately, they often need to be reminded of our expectations. Furthermore, as specific issues arise, our elected officials must decide where they stand. This is true of the local school board and the city government, and it is true of the Congress of the United States and the president of the nation. As they make their decisions, people in office want to know what their constituency is thinking and are influenced by what they learn.

How much impact does the average person have in the political arena? Not very much if acting alone. But acting in concert with other people and through groups, the average person compounds his or her strength. Working through social, civic, and political organizations and through special-interest groups in which they are allied with a wide variety of people, Christians find in politics an important way of expressing their commitment to Christ.

QUESTIONS AND TOPICS FOR DISCUSSION

1. What are legitimate methods of protesting government action?
2. What are legitimate ways to force the government to take actions that you believe to be right?
3. Is it legitimate to try to legislate on moral issues? For example, on sexual behavior? On abortion? On pornography?
4. Discuss Paul's words, "Let every person be subject to the governing authorities."
5. Discuss Jesus's words, "Give to the emperor the things that are the emperor's, and to God the things that are God's."

RECOMMENDATIONS FOR FURTHER READING

BROWN, ROBERT MCAFEE, *Saying Yes and Saying No*. Philadelphia: Westminster, 1986.

GEYER, ALAN, *Christianity and the Super Powers*. Nashville: Abingdon, 1990.

MESSER, DONALD E., *Christian Ethics and Political Action*. Valley Forge, Penn.: Judson, 1984.

NEUHAUS, RICHARD JOHN, and MICHAEL CROMARTE, *Piety and Politics*. Washington: Ethics and Public Policy Center, 1987.

WOGAMAN, J. PHILIP, *Christian Perspectives on Politics*, revised edition. Louisville, Ky.: Westminster/John Knox, 2000.

12

Punishment for Crime

We have said that one basic function of the state is to maintain order. The state therefore makes laws to regularize social relationships and enforces those laws through a police force and a court system. In our pattern of government the words *just* and *legal* are virtually synonymous. Indeed, the word *justice* comes from the Latin *jus,* which means "law." We do acknowledge that there are certain moral standards by which even the law of the land is to be evaluated, however, so that at times in the name of justice certain laws or their application may be challenged. If we find a law to be unjust, we attempt to revise it; and if we find the law to be unjustly applied, we attempt to correct the miscarriage of justice.

THE CONCEPT OF PUNISHMENT

Basic to our system of justice are two principles. The first is equal treatment. We believe that no person should be given preferential treatment because of such matters as status in the community, personal influence, or personal wealth and that no person should be treated harshly because of not having such an advantage. This principle, of course, is not absolute, for some differences in particulars are appropriately considered in the determination of a case: motives, circumstances, mental competence, and the like. To the question of whether an individual actually violated a law, in other words, certain external factors are considered relevant and certain others are not. Relevant factors are taken into account, but irrelevant factors must not be allowed to influence legal action.

The second principle is that in the legal process people should be punished in proportion to the seriousness of their crime. People should get what they deserve; punishment should be neither too light nor too severe. This principle recognizes that certain crimes are more serious than others, that some inflict greater distress or cause more damage. The more serious the crime, the greater should be the penalty.

This idea of punishment is integral to our system of law enforcement. Punishment is defined as causing a person to experience pain, loss, or suffering because of his or her wrongdoing. The purpose of punishment is to make the offender worse off than before. Although we may sometimes make mistakes in our judgment about a person's guilt or innocence, we do not punish anyone until that person has been convicted of criminal action. If a person has not been found guilty, inflicting hurt on him or her is itself a crime. Administering punishment is a function of the state alone. No one has the right to take the law into one's own hands, to usurp the role of either the police or the courts. Within our system there is no place for vigilante groups and no place for an individual to act alone to enforce the law. Only those people duly commissioned by government authority and functioning for that authority have the right to decide guilt or innocence and to punish the guilty.

These two principles lead us to the question of why society punishes wrongdoers. What is the purpose of punishment? The oldest and most common answer is summed up in the word *retribution*, which means that because someone has done something bad, something equally bad should be done to the offender. This concept reflects the idea that crime is an offense against the moral order, that it creates a moral imbalance that must be corrected.

Our modern legal system, however, does not assume that justice lies in doing to an offender exactly what that person did to someone else. Requiring an offender to return what has been stolen, for example, cannot even the balance; something more has to be done to force the offender to suffer as the victim suffered. Consequently our system requires that the criminal be fined, sent to prison, or made to pay some other penalty over and above any attempt at restitution. It assumes that an offender deserves punishment. This approach concentrates on the criminal rather than on the victim, and it therefore involves no compensation for any damage done to the latter. It is deeply ingrained in our system of justice, however, and may be rooted in that desire for vengeance which seems to be part of us all.

A more recent theory of punishment is the utilitarian approach that considers the consequences of the penalty. Its basic question is, "What do we hope to achieve by taking action against the offender?" This approach, of course, acknowledges the nature of punishment as the inflicting of pain on a criminal. But it demands that such pain be justified by some anticipated positive impact on the offender, the victim, or society as a whole. Will the punishment undo any damage done to the victim? Will it improve the character of the criminal? Will it deter the criminal from committing other crimes in the future? Will it deter other people from committing criminal acts? Will it protect society from further criminal actions by the offender or by people influenced by the offender? Punishment cannot be justified merely by the achievement of some theoretical balance, but only by some improvement in the situation. For the individual offender, this means reformation, so that he or she can return to society as a normal and well-adjusted individual. For society, it means protection from future crime.

Both the retributive and the utilitarian concepts have serious flaws. On the one hand, the idea of retribution assumes a kind of moral balance, which we cannot really quantify. We do not know how much pain is required to even the score for any offense and thus how large a fine or how long a prison sentence is called for. The utilitarian idea, on the other hand, assumes that we have found a system that will produce good results. Yet the threat of punishment is really not very effective in reducing crime. We may refrain from speeding or from parking illegally because we are afraid that we might be caught and fined. Psychiatric and sociological studies, however, show that this kind of threat does not prevent such serious crimes as murder, rape, or trafficking in drugs. In addition, inflicting suffering on some people in order to teach a lesson to others presents serious moral problems. Nor does a period of imprisonment often reform a criminal. John Hospers says,

> We put a man in prison for two years for a theft, five years for armed robbery, and twenty years to life (or the electric chair) for homicide, assuming smugly that these penalties will lessen his tendency to repeat his crime. We assume that being behind bars with nothing to do but build up resentments or go mad will make him emerge from prison a better man, renewed and chastened, and that when he does emerge from prison after the five years or the twenty, he will be able to resume his role in a society that refuses to employ him, spiritually prepared at last to conform to the moral ideals of middle age and the middle class. (*Human Conduct*, p. 390)

Hospers proposes a "compromise view," which actually combines the two approaches of retribution and reformation by saying that punishment should meet two conditions: It should be deserved, and it should do some good to someone: the offender, the victim, society, or all three. To meet the second condition, he suggests, the penal system should not focus on punishment but on treatment (p. 387). Although he does not use the word *Christian*, his suggestion is in line with basic Christian concepts. Many years ago Emil Brunner discussed the theory of punishment in terms of the biblical concept of expiation (*The Divine Imperative*, pp. 474–478). The idea of achieving a moral balance by punishing the criminal is similar, he said, to the Christian concept of atonement for our sins. In theological terms, Christ has "expiated" our sin and thus reconciled us to God. Applied to crime (in contrast to sin), this concept suggests that something must be done to provide satisfaction for the offense. Presumably that satisfaction reconciles the criminal to society. What must be done is not necessarily what we are now doing, for that system, as we have seen, is flawed. But in human nature there is that which cries out for justice. We feel that the guilty person must make expiation for his or her offense.

This idea of expiation can be saved from the spirit of vindictiveness only by society's recognition that it shares in the responsibility for crime. Of course all persons are responsible for their decisions. Our decisions, however, are influenced by the circumstances in which we live and function. Some options are simply not open to some people because of heredity, social environment, or history. Some pressures are so powerful that an outside observer might even be able to predict what choices a person will make. In that sense, therefore, society shares in the responsibility for that person's crime. This does not mean that society should ignore the criminal actions of someone who is poor or who comes from a broken home or whose education is limited or whose aspirations are frustrated or who has no good role models. Society must recognize its responsibility for allowing such conditions to exist, however. Just as an individual criminal pays the price at the hands of the penal system, so must society pay the price of correcting these dangerous and destructive situations.

In an important work, *Crime and Justice in America,* L. Harold DeWolf attempts to describe from a Christian perspective a consistent, defensible philosophy to undergird our criminal justice system. He lists a set of "ethical norms of criminal justice" by which he thinks our system should be evaluated (pp. 154–156):

1. Consistency and coherence with realities
2. Benevolent good will and respect toward all persons
3. Equal rights for all persons
4. Presumption of innocence
5. Special care to protect the poor, weak, and unpopular from unfair treatment
6. Restoration of community when disrupted
7. Responsibility of all individuals for the community

DeWolf calls his approach to criminal justice "a philosophy of social defense and restoration" (p. 173). Thinking of crime as alienation from other people, he sees no place for retribution in a valid philosophy of criminal justice. He recognizes the necessity of incarcerating some offenders to give temporary protection to society, and he acknowledges that punishment may have some value as a deterrent. He warns, however, that such measures, "when taken against people who already feel frustrated, deprived, and outside of any real participation in the good opportunities of society, are almost certain to aggravate the problem of crime in the community" (pp. 168–169). Cut off from all meaningful family relationships, prisoners reach the point at which their most meaningful social relationships are with other prisoners.

Society does need to protect itself against criminal activity, and as yet we have found no more effective way of dealing with criminals than imprisonment. But society also needs to find some way to transform a criminal into a responsible citizen. To operate a criminal justice system with this objective in mind, we need to be realistic about the persistence of evil in all persons and the consequent difficulty of effecting a change. We need also to take seriously the possibility of redemption and wholeness and restoration, the truth which is at the heart of the Christian gospel.

THE RIGHTS OF VICTIMS

For the most part, our criminal justice system has been concerned with the protection of society, the maintenance of order, and the punishment of criminals. The victims of crime, however, have largely been ignored. In some cases victims may seek recourse through private lawsuits for damage, but the responsibility for initiating a suit falls upon them, as does the cost of prosecuting the cases. Most people do not have the financial resources to avail themselves of this option, even if they are aware of it. Consequently, the rights of the majority of victims are simply ignored.

This has not been the case in all the legal systems that are in the background of our practice. In the law codes of the Old Testament, both restitution and compensation were often required for offenses against persons or their property. The law of Saxon England required criminals to make payment to their victims for certain kinds of personal violence. The Germanic states of the Middle Ages required a person who injured or killed another person to make payment to the victim or the victim's family, as well as a payment to the ruler who had jurisdiction over the parties involved in the conflict. Although payment to the victim has been abandoned in most places, in some European nations the law provides for restitution either by the offender or the state.

In this country it is generally believed that the best way to deal with the problem of crime is to make things hard on the criminal. Consequently many people want to strengthen the police force, get quick court action, and impose long prison terms with little opportunity for parole. Many people think that life is too easy for people in prison and that simply shutting convicts off from society for a time is inadequate punishment. They think that convicted offenders should be made to suffer for their crimes. However valid or invalid this attitude may be, we cannot adequately deal with the problem of crime by concentrating on the criminal and ignoring the victim. A criminal justice system that ignores the people most immediately and seriously affected by a crime can hardly be said to be equitable. It is certainly inconsistent with the tradition in the Christian faith that emphasizes ministry to people in need, and it falls far short of the social application of the principle of love for all people. Justice is not done when victims are left alone to cope with the physical and emotional damage done to them.

What the victim of a crime needs most is a correction of the damage that has been done. In the case of loss of property, however, it is not always easy to calculate everything that has been lost. In addition to the item that has been stolen or destroyed, there is the inconvenience, the loss of time, and perhaps the expenditure of money entailed by the original loss. The loss may also have caused emotional trauma, on which no price can be set. In the case of personal violence the damage is even more difficult to calculate because the emotional impact is so much greater and so much more complex. Much of the damage, in other words, is such that it is impossible to determine what compensation might be adequate. Yet some of the damage can be repaired, and some compensation can be made.

The questions of who should make the compensation and how it should be done are woven together. Obviously justice would be best served if the offender could be required to make the appropriate restitution. One way in which this can be done is through a work-release program in which the offender is employed on a job nearby and leaves the prison a few hours each day to go to that work. A part of the wages is used to support the prisoner's family and a part is used as payment to the victim of the crime. While full compensation to the victim may never be complete, such a plan is a step in the right direction.

Should the state itself make restitution to the victims of crime? Most states do not recognize any such obligation, though a few make some limited legal provision for compensation for bodily injury. When states do acknowledge such a responsibility, they assume a financial obligation that requires an increase in taxes. Is it not an obligation that the state *should* assume? The only alternative is the system under which most of us now live, the system that leaves us all at great risk and offers no help to those who fall victim. Acknowledging the responsibility of the state to deal with criminals and spending a great deal of money to meet that obligation, we do not acknowledge the responsibility of the state for helping the victim. Is the victim of crime any less in need of help than the victim of natural disaster or the victim of disease? DeWolf says that, ". . . we should simply emphasize that when a community has been wounded by a crime, the community has not been made whole while its living members who have most grievously suffered from the crime are uncompensated" (*Crime and Justice*, p. 195).

CAPITAL PUNISHMENT

On January 17, 1977, convicted murderer Gary Gilmore was executed by a Utah firing squad, the first person to be executed in the United States in ten years. Five years earlier, in *Furman* v. *Georgia,* the Supreme Court had declared unconstitutional any law that left the imposition of the death sentence to the discretion of the judge or the jury. This decision was based on the possible unequal imposition of the sentence. The Court, however, did not rule for the petitioners that the death sentence itself constituted "cruel and unusual punishment" and was therefore a violation of the Eighth and Fourteenth Amendments to the Constitution. Consequently thirty-six states, seeking to ensure equality in sentencing, rewrote their laws to require, rather than simply to permit, the imposition of the death sentence for persons convicted of certain crimes. Between 1977 and 1997, 432 persons were put to death. During 1997 alone, 74 persons were executed in 23 states, and at the end of that year more than 3,335 persons were under the sentence of death in 34 states. Gilmore's execution, the first to take place under these new laws, sparked fresh debate on the issue of capital punishment. The usual questions were raised: For what crimes should the death penalty be administered? How can we be sure that it is fairly imposed? By what means should people be executed? How public should the execution be? Underlying all of these questions, however, is a more basic one: Should the penalty ever be imposed? Or is it fundamentally immoral?

Let us focus on this basic question. While we may refer to statistics, to the differences among the states concerning what crimes are capital ones, to the factors (other than the crime itself) that apparently influence court decisions, and so on, our concern is whether the state should ever resort to this form of punishment. We need first to consider the teachings of Scripture. Because the Old Testament reflects the changing circumstances and beliefs of the Hebrew people for a period of more than a thousand years, we should not be surprised to discover that its teachings on capital punishment are not entirely consistent. Basic to all such teachings, however, is the conviction that everyone is made in the image of God and that we must therefore treat all human life with respect. We have already discussed this concept (Chapter 6) and at this point need only to note its importance. This belief in the worth of human life is not unique to the Jewish and Christian faiths; other peoples of the ancient world expressed a similar view of human beings. But the distinctly biblical idea is that the transcendent worth of human life is not due to any individual talent, effort, achievement, or merit but to a unique relationship to the divine. For Christians, this fact is basic in all dealings with other people.

The sixth commandment, "You shall not murder" (Exodus 20:13), affirms respect for human life. It is in the form of apodictic law; that is, it states the obligation without specifying any penalty for its violation or giving consideration to circumstances. It prohibits murder and makes no direct reference to any other form of killing, such as accidental killing, killing in war, or capital punishment. Yet as an affirmation of our responsibility to respect human life, it may properly serve as a touchstone in a discussion of any of these matters.

Some passages are often cited to support the idea of exact retribution. As mentioned, Exodus 21:23–24, for example, says, "life for life, eye for eye, tooth for tooth, hand for hand, foot for foot, burn for burn, wound for wound, stripe for stripe." The larger context in which such phrases are found, however, is usually "case law." That is, distinctions are drawn on the basis of the extent of the damage, whether the offense was premeditated, the circumstances under which it took place, and so on. Furthermore, as in Exodus 21, provisions are often made for substituting some form of payment (money or property) for the infliction of physical damage on the offender.

In spite of the principle of respect for human life, the Old Testament does prescribe death as the penalty for a variety of offenses. According to the Code of the Covenant, "Whoever strikes a person mortally shall be put to death" (Exodus 21:12). The code specifies the same penalty for striking one's father or mother, for kidnapping, and for cursing one's father or mother (Exodus 21:15–17). To this list of offenses the next chapter adds sorcery, bestiality, and idolatry (22:18–20). The Deuteronomic Law calls for execution as the penalty for a large number of offenses including the worship of other gods (Deuteronomy 17:2–5), the refusal to accept the judgment of the priests in a case appealed to them (17:8–13), premeditated murder (19:11–13), adultery (22:22), rape (22:25–27), and kidnapping (24:7). It even commands the execution of a son for being "stubborn and rebellious" (21:18–21). In the Old Testament, therefore, the question is not whether the death penalty should be used but what offenses call for it.

Although the Old Testament prescribes execution for what strikes us as a rather large number of offenses, its regulations actually represent a restriction on the spirit of vengeance that characterizes all people. By carefully specifying the crimes for which a person was to be executed and by describing acceptable substitutes for execution in a number of cases, the Law guards against the human tendency to go to extremes of cruelty in retaliation for personal offenses. That this tendency to minimize the death penalty was in operation among the Jews is evidenced by the fact that by the time of Jesus most of those crimes were being dealt with by the imposition of fines.

Only one New Testament passage refers directly to capital punishment. John 7:53–8:11 concerns a woman found in the act of adultery, one of the offenses for which the Law specified execution. While this passage was not originally a part of the Gospel of John, it is generally regarded as an authentic story that was preserved independently by the Christian community and at some point inserted in that Gospel. When Jesus was asked what should be done to the woman, he indicated his disapproval of the imposition of the death penalty. His answer, "Let anyone among you who is without sin be the first to throw a stone at her," and his words to the woman—"Neither do I condemn you. Go your way, and from now on do not sin again"—are completely harmonious with everything else that he taught about the worth of every individual in the sight of God, about forgiveness, and about the possibility of reformation of character and conduct.

In considering the morality of capital punishment as it is administered in America today, we need to begin with our objectives. What are we trying to achieve by the execution? We have already noted that one reason for punishment is to provide the balance that a concern for justice requires. With such a concern, the penalty must be designed to fit the crime so that a person receives the punishment that he or she deserves. Clearly the state should not take the life of a person except for the most extreme offense. No one, therefore, would think today that disobedience, idolatry, bestiality, or adultery should be punished by execution. But are there some crimes so heinous that justice requires the death of the offender? Is capital punishment a just retribution for premeditated murder? For forcible rape? For kidnapping? How is the balance evened by the death of the criminal?

Another way of stating the concern for justice is to think in terms of what the offender deserves. The idea is that each person would receive his or her due, that a person would be rewarded or punished in proportion to the good or evil done. The question, therefore, is this: Do people who have committed certain crimes deserve to die? Is death the only penalty painful enough to equal the harm caused by murder, rape, or kidnapping? We need to consider whether all offenders against all laws should always be given penalties that balance their offenses. We need to consider further whether a particular case should be decided on the basis of the crime alone, or whether consideration should also be given to other factors, such as background, previous record, mental condition, impact on other persons related to both the victim and offender, and so on.

A second frequently mentioned objective of punishment is to prevent a criminal from committing other offenses. The expectation is that offenders will suffer enough from fines or imprisonment to make them decide not to run the risk of repeating such behavior. Statistics on recidivism, however, indicate that this is not the case. Repeat offenders are responsible for a high percentage of crimes. Indeed, we cannot know whether such preventive measures ever work because there is no way to gather statistics on crimes not committed. Yet according to this argument we know no better way to deal with criminals. Since we cannot predict whether murderers or rapists would repeat their crimes, or whether they are more likely to commit another such crime than are other people, the only way that we can be sure that they do not do so is to execute them. We must question, however, whether it is valid to execute people because of what they might do in the future.

The idea that criminals can be deterred from repeating their offenses is closely related to the idea that we might be able to prevent people from committing a first crime. If persons who are tempted to commit crimes know that punishment is certain and severe, it is argued, they may refrain from criminal behavior. Obviously not everyone responds to the threat of punishment. Some people are mentally incapable of making logical judgments, and some people are self-destructive. Most people, however, have a strong will to live and are unwilling to risk death unnecessarily. If execution is a real possibility, potential criminals may refrain from committing a crime entailing that penalty. Of course, merely having the law on the books does not serve as a deterrent; only actual executions will do so. The death of one condemned individual, with its accompanying publicity, is a warning to all that the penalty is not an empty threat but a real possibility.

This line of reasoning is challenged by many people who marshal figures to demonstrate that there is no correlation between the crime rate and capital punishment. Because the incidence of murder in states with capital punishment is not necessarily lower than in states without it, they conclude that the fact of capital punishment does not in itself affect the rate of the crimes for which it is administered. We cannot be sure at present whether the threat of capital punishment does or does not deter further criminal action. From our point of view, however, there is a more important issue at stake: Is it proper to execute one human being in order to teach a lesson to others? Is it just to make an example of one offender in the hope that other possible offenders will decide not to take the risk?

The right to life is a serious issue in the discussion of capital punishment. We have discussed the biblical and Christian concept of the worth of the individual, that every person is to be respected and that the personal rights of every individual are to be guarded. The most basic of these rights is the right to life. The Declaration of Independence affirms that life, liberty, and the pursuit of happiness are unalienable rights. If we believe that some persons should be executed, we have concluded either that some other consideration is even more important than the right to life or that some persons forfeit that right by some actions of their own. If we conclude the former, we must decide what consideration is more important than the right to life. Is it property? Is it the body or life of another person? Is it the well-being of society as a whole? If we conclude the latter, we must decide whether our rights depend on our behavior. Does misbehavior, particularly misbehavior of a serious nature, eliminate these rights? If we conclude that someone ought to die, we are forced to the conclusion that our rights are not derived from our nature but from our conduct.

Considerations of prevention and deterrence have a bearing not merely on individual criminals and individual victims but also on society at large. All crime is in a sense an attack on the social order. Most people assume that individuals have the right of self-defense, that when attacked they have the right to use whatever means are necessary to protect themselves. While they do not have the right to use excessive force, they do have the right to use effective resistance. By the same logic, concern for justice and for the well-being of other people justifies the use of necessary force. Does this same right extend to the state? It is sometimes said that capital punishment is for the state what self-defense is for the individual. By this logic it is assumed that the state has the right to do what is necessary to protect itself (that is, not only its existence but also its proper functioning). Certain laws, such as those protecting life and property, are necessary for people to live and work together.

To violate these laws is to threaten the very existence of society, and society therefore has both the right and the responsibility to do what is necessary to protect itself. As it is true for the individual, so is it true for society that excessive force should not be used. The question concerning capital punishment, therefore, is whether it is necessary or whether there are alternative methods for dealing with the threat to the state.

The question with which we are struggling is whether capital punishment is ever right. If we conclude that it is sometimes the right action, we have certain other important issues to decide. For what crimes is it right? To what extent should the circumstances of the crime be taken into consideration? In what manner should persons be executed; that is, should the execution be as humane as possible or should the criminal be made to suffer? What steps can we take to be sure that the process of conviction for a capital crime functions fairly, without regard to race, sex, or financial resources? If we conclude that it is never right, we must find an appropriate alternative for dealing with heinous crimes. What does justice require? Is long-term or even life imprisonment a greater or lesser punishment than execution? How can we be sure that the process of conviction operates fairly?

In this discussion nothing has been said about the victims of the crimes because no effective restitution can be made to a victim. In the case of murder, nothing can bring the victim back to life, and nothing can ease the pain of the survivors. In the case of violence to a person, nothing can undo its results. We do need to find ways of helping victims cope with the consequences of the crime, which no punishment of the criminal will accomplish. This problem, however, is not the same as dealing with the criminal.

My own conclusion is that capital punishment is wrong. I am influenced by the demonstrable fact that our best efforts to be impartial in the administration of the justice system have failed and almost certainly can never succeed. The chances of execution after conviction for a capital offense are far greater for men than for women, for blacks than for whites, for the poor than for the affluent. I am influenced by the lack of conclusive evidence that the threat of execution has any bearing on the rate of capital crimes and, therefore, that it is an effective preventive measure. I am influenced by my disposition to look to the future rather than to the past and, therefore, to be more concerned with reformation and restoration than with balancing the scales of justice. But my conclusion is based primarily on my understanding of the Christian doctrine that every human being is of infinite worth in the eyes of God and that my responsibility as a disciple of Christ is to deal with every person, no matter how unworthy, on that basis. I do not believe that any person ever ceases to be a child of God, no matter what crimes he or she may commit. Although crime must be dealt with if the social order is to survive, as I believe it must, we cannot deal with crime in any way that violates the fundamental element in that social order, the nature of the people who constitute it.

QUESTIONS AND TOPICS FOR DISCUSSION

1. What does society seek to achieve by the punishment of criminals?
2. What factors should be considered in determining the punishment for a given crime? Explain your answer.
3. For what offenses, if any, should criminals be executed? Justify your answer.
4. What rights should prisoners have?
5. How are the victims of crime helped by the punishment of the offenders?

RECOMMENDATIONS FOR FURTHER READING

BEDAU, HUGO ADAM, *The Death Penalty in America*. New York: Oxford, 1998.

LIFTON, ROBERT J., and GREG MITCHELL, *Who Owns Death?* New York: Harper Collins, 2000.

POJMAN, LOUIS P., and JEFFREY REIMAN, *The Death Penalty: For and Against*. Lanham, Md.: Rowman and Littlefield, 1977.

PREJEAN, HELEN, *Dead Man Walking*. New York: Random House, 1993.

STASSEN, GLEN, *Capital Punishment*. New York: Pilgrim Press, 1998.

13

War and the Quest for Peace

The quest for peace seems always to be overshadowed by the threat of war. The ever-present possibility of war distorts the lives of people everywhere and constantly threatens the survival of humankind. All over the world people live with either the possibility or the actuality of conflict within their own nation. Nations fear the expansionist ambitions of neighbor nations. They stockpile weapons—conventional, nuclear, chemical, and biological—that can be unleashed at any moment. Everywhere people fear that the surprise attacks of a terrorist group or the deliberate aggression of some national leader might set off the final holocaust. All over the world people wait anxiously as their leaders negotiate for peace and arm for war. With international relations always in flux and scientific and technical developments constantly bringing new pressures, we seem unable to find a balance in which the peoples of the world can live in peace. How are Christians, motivated by love and concerned for justice, to function in a world always on the brink of war?

THE BIBLE AND WAR

Since the beginning of the church, Christians have struggled with the question of the morality of warfare. As might be expected, they have looked to Scripture for guidance. In the historical material in the Old Testament, however, they have found little evidence of any moral concern with warfare. The Hebrews regarded themselves as God's chosen people, as a nation for whom God had a special purpose. The fulfillment of that purpose involved conquering a land already occupied by others, establishing a kingdom there, and blessing or punishing the nation on the basis of its loyalty to God. When the people were faithful, God gave them victory over their enemies. When they were not faithful, God used enemy nations to punish them. Their methods of warfare were no different from those of other people and their treatment of their enemies no more humane. We are not surprised, therefore, to find in many of their hymns (the Psalms) angry imprecations against their foes.

Many of the Hebrew prophets saw warfare as a tool of God in the historical process. On the one hand, Amos, Isaiah, Jeremiah, and others spoke of oppression by foreign powers as God's punishment of the Hebrews for their unfaithfulness. Obadiah, on the other hand, gloated over the destruction of Edom, calling it God's vengeance on a nation whose crime was war against God's people. In the same vein, Nahum gloated over the anticipated destruction of Nineveh, the capital of the Assyrian empire, which had long oppressed Judah. Yet in the Prophets there are passages in which the note of God's love for all people is sounded and the expectation of universal peace is proclaimed. Both Isaiah (2:4) and Micah (4:3) anticipated the time when all the nations "shall beat their swords into plowshares, and their spears into pruning hooks; nation shall not lift up sword against nation, neither shall they learn war any more." And it was Isaiah who described what has been called "the peaceable kingdom":

> The wolf shall live with the lamb,
>   the leopard shall lie down with the kid,
> the calf and the lion and the fatling together,
>   and a little child shall lead them.
> The cow and the bear shall graze,
>   their young shall lie down together;
>   and the lion shall eat straw like the ox.
> The nursing child shall play over the hole of the asp,
>   and the weaned child shall put his hand on the adder's den.
> They shall not hurt or destroy on all my holy mountain;
>   for the earth shall be full of the knowledge of the Lord
>   as the waters cover the sea. (Isaiah 11:6–9)

Even in a nation in which war was not a moral problem, whose God indeed was "mighty in battle," the dream of peace never died.

Although the New Testament says little about war, those who oppose participation in any war find strong support in Jesus's teachings on love. They cite particularly his summary of the moral law in the words, "You shall love your neighbor as yourself" (Mark 12:31) and his exhortation to "love your enemies" (Matthew 5:43–48). They quote the beatitude, "Blessed are the peacemakers, for they will be called children of God" (Matthew 5:9). They pay special attention to Jesus's teachings about nonretaliation:

> You have heard that it was said, "An eye for an eye and a tooth for a tooth." But I say to you, Do not resist an evildoer. But if anyone strikes you on the right cheek, turn the other also; and if anyone wants to sue you and take your coat, give your cloak as well; and if anyone forces you to go one mile, go also the

> second mile. Give to everyone who begs from you, and do not refuse anyone
> who wants to borrow from you. (Matthew 5:38–42)

Pacifists find the essence of Jesus's teaching in the Golden Rule: "In everything do to others as you would have them do to you" (Matthew 7:12).
Acknowledging that these teachings were intended for personal relationships, they argue that the concepts are equally valid for social relationships.
They do not build their case simply by citing specific passages, however.
Rather they focus on Jesus's teachings on love and the way of the cross and
on his general spirit and disposition toward others. In that way they find him
to be utterly opposed to any possibility of participation in armed conflict.

Other people find in the gospels evidence that Jesus was not in fact a
completely nonviolent person. They cite his apparent use of some force in the
cleansing of the temple (Matthew 21:12–3; John 2:13–6); his statement, "Do
not think that I have come to bring peace to the earth; I have not come to bring
peace, but a sword" (Matthew 10:34); and his words to the disciples on the eve
of his arrest, "And the one who has no sword must sell his cloak and buy one"
(Luke 22:36). It must be admitted that in none of these instances, as in none of
the instances cited by pacifists, was Jesus talking about war. To apply them to
war, therefore, is to extend them beyond Jesus's obvious intent.

Perhaps more to the point is Jesus's apparent nonjudgmental acceptance
of the fact of war. He praised the faith of a Roman centurion without saying
anything about the man's profession (Matthew 8:5–10). He warned his disciples
not to think of "wars and rumors of war" as signs of the end of the age because
these conditions persist in the present age (Mark 13). He frequently used military figures of speech as if the military were a normal part of life. This is not to
suggest that he approved of war but that he accepted it as inevitable.

As we have seen, Paul was a disciple and interpreter of Jesus. His recommendations for dealing with other people sound very much like Jesus's
sayings:

> Bless those who persecute you; bless and do not curse them. Rejoice with those
> who rejoice, weep with those who weep. Live in harmony with one another; do
> not be haughty, but associate with the lowly; do not claim to be wiser than you
> are. Do not repay anyone evil for evil, but take thought for what is noble in the
> sight of all. If it is possible, so far as it depends on you, live peaceably with all.
> Beloved, never avenge yourselves, but leave room for the wrath of God; for it is
> written, "Vengeance is mine, I will repay, says the Lord." No, "if your enemies
> are hungry, feed them; if they are thirsty, give them something to drink; for by
> doing this you will heap burning coals upon their heads." Do not be overcome
> by evil, but overcome evil with good. (Romans 12:14–21)

Little is said elsewhere in the New Testament that can be interpreted as
pertaining to war. As we have seen, much of the New Testament was written
when Christians were being persecuted. Most of the documents anticipate
the time when the end of the age will come with a great upheaval, perhaps

some final conflict between the nations. The New Testament simply does not deal directly with the issue of war. Its overall emphasis, however, clearly fosters the ideal of peace.

CHRISTIANITY AND TRADITIONAL WARFARE

Can we translate the biblical dream of peace into the realities of modern political relationships? Since the New Testament period, the Christian church has constantly struggled with this question. For some three hundred years after the time of Christ there was a strong pacifist leaning in the church. Many early Christians believed that the teachings of Jesus totally prohibited the use of the sword and refused to serve in the Roman army. After Constantine made Christianity the state religion of the empire in the early fourth century, and after the stability of the Roman Empire was threatened by the invasion of barbarians from the north, theologians debated for centuries the question of whether Christians should sometimes wage war. Out of that debate emerged the theory of a "just war," developed by Augustine (354–430) and refined by Thomas Aquinas (1224–1274). According to this theory, to be just a war must meet six conditions:

1. It must be conducted by a legitimate authority which explicitly serves notice that it intends to use military power to attain its objectives.
2. The cause must be just; that is, the action must be intended for the advancement of good or for the avoidance of evil.
3. It must be undertaken only as a last resort.
4. The good anticipated from the war must outweigh the evil done in pursuit of the war.
5. There must be a reasonable expectation of success in the effort.
6. It must be conducted according to the internationally accepted rules of warfare, never going beyond certain agreed-upon moral constraints.

Under this last requirement such actions as attacks on nonmilitary targets, unnecessary destruction, looting, and massacres are prohibited.

Today we can delineate three distinct positions regarding the participation of Christians in war. First, many people see participation as a responsibility of Christian citizenship. This position draws support from Paul's exhortation, "Let every person be subject to the governing authorities" (Romans 13:1). Resistance to the state would be justified only if the state were to claim ultimate authority and thus assume the place of God. Otherwise our Christian duty is to support the state. When our nation is involved in war it is acting to protect itself against a foreign power and to safeguard the well-being of all its citizens. All citizens, of course, retain the right of conscientious criticism of specific policies and actions, even the right of refusal to participate in military service. In the last resort, however, we know that the use of force in world affairs is necessary because oppressive and tyrannical powers are at work in many places. If we do not prevent them from doing so, these powers will extend their control until they dominate the rest of the world. Decisions about when the exercise of force is necessary are not individual decisions; they can be made only by the leaders of the nation.

Second, some Christians believe that their commitment to Christ prohibits any involvement in armed conflict. In the 1930s some Christians in this country and in Europe adopted pacifism as a strategy to achieve a warless world. Most contemporary pacifists, however, do not see refusal to participate as a strategy but as the way God intends people to live. They are pacifist not in order to achieve peace but in grateful obedience to the God of love. They are aware of persistent evil in the world and they work to overcome it. They are realistic about oppression and aggression and the danger that in any situation nations may resort to force to achieve their purposes, good or bad. Nevertheless, they believe that discipleship to Christ requires them to love rather than hate and that war can never be an expression of love.

Third, some Christians believe that war is sometimes the lesser of two evils. Recognizing the horrors of war, they believe that worse occurrences may result from a failure to resist the activities of an evil government. The term currently employed to identify this view is "agonized participation." People who take this approach believe that it is their responsibility, not to give unconditional support to the government, but to evaluate the situation for themselves and to support the government in those wars that they believe to be necessary. This, of course, is very close to the "just war" position. In *War and Conscience in America*, written during the Vietnam War when our nation was divided on the morality of our involvement, Edward LeRoy Long characterized this view in the following way:

a. *This position believes that while war can never be an act of justice it may sometimes be necessary for the prevention of a greater evil that would result from permitting morally perverse power to gain political dominance.* (p. 41)
b. *The agonized participant insists that war must be conducted with contrition and kept free of vindictive hatred for the enemy.* (p. 44)
c. *Military victory, while necessary, is but a negative attainment that clears the way for subsequent political and social programs designed to reestablish reasonable justice and order.* (p. 45)
d. *Lastly, the agonized participant acknowledges the right and privilege of conscientious objection to war even though he disagrees with those Christians who consider themselves called to this witness.* (p. 46)

CHRISTIANITY AND MODERN WARFARE

The development of nuclear weapons has introduced a new factor into the consideration of warfare, and the development of chemical and biological weapons has significantly intensified the possibility of mass destruction. In the foreword to a work by Paul Ramsey, John Hallowell wrote in 1961, "Not only must we come to terms with the fact that all civilized life upon this planet may come to an end but that this is possible through human decision and action" (*War and the Christian Conscience*, p. vii). Twenty-five years later Joseph Nye began his book, *Nuclear Ethics*, by saying,

> The prospect of a nuclear war is horrifying. It brings us face to face not only with death, but with destruction of the civilization that makes our life meaningful. It might even destroy our species. There is no precedent for the challenge that nuclear weapons present to our physical and moral lives. (*Nuclear Ethics*, p. ix)

Traditional Christian eschatology, as Gordon Kaufman says, has thought of the consummation of history as God's climactic act, which we could anticipate with hope. But now it appears that the end of history may be our own doing, not God's, and that it will not mean the salvation of the world but the extermination of life on earth (*Theology for a Nuclear Age*, pp. 3–4).

Although our concern here is not the scientific and technological aspects of the development of nuclear weapons, we do need to be aware of their potential for total destruction. In a much discussed book, *The Fate of the Earth*, published in 1982, Jonathan Schell vividly described the effects that would result from an in-air explosion of a single bomb of the sort that is now considered "medium-sized" (one megaton). He said that the initial radiation would kill immediately every unprotected human being within an area of six square miles and in the next ten seconds the heat would cause second-degree burns on exposed persons within a radius of nine and a half miles. The blast would flatten all buildings within a radius of four and a half miles. A large portion of the radioactive dust created by the explosion would fall back to the earth within a day, but most of the remainder would be pushed by the winds and fall in lethal quantities over an area of a thousand square miles.

The presence of nuclear weapons in the arsenal of any nation presumes the possibility that under some circumstances they will be used. From the end of World War II until the dissolution of the Soviet Union in 1991, the possession of nuclear weapons by both the USSR and the United States was a dominant factor in world politics. Since that time there have been reductions of nuclear weapons in both the United States and Russia. In that context J. Philip Wogaman said,

> But this must not lead to complacency. Vast nuclear weaponry remains in parts of the former Soviet Union and in the United States, even a small fraction of which is capable of inflicting awful destruction. If any major nuclear power should fall into the hands of an irresponsible government, its use or sale to other countries (to help with economic problems) is always a possibility. Moreover, the number of countries possessing nuclear capabilities continues to grow. Of late, both India and Pakistan have acquired some capability, and neither has shown much restraint in brandishing the sword as a chilling threat in the long-standing and bitter dispute over Kashmir. (*Christian Perspectives on Politics*, revised edition, pp. 351–352)

American Christians have struggled on the horns of this dilemma. In 1983 the Roman Catholic bishops of the United States issued a pastoral letter, *The Challenge of Peace: God's Promise and Our Response*, in which, within the context of the "just war" tradition, they addressed the issue of nuclear weapons. In 1986 the bishops of the United Methodist Church likewise issued a pastoral letter, *In Defense of Creation*, in which they demonstrated the inconsistency of nuclear warfare with a Christian vision of God's purposes for the world. In the years that followed, a number of Christian theologians and ethicists wrestled with this question: Robert F. Drinan in *Beyond the Nuclear Freeze* (1983); Edward LeRoy Long, Jr., in *Peace Thinking in a Warring World* (1983); Stanley Hauerwas in *Against the Nations* (1985); Robert McAfee Brown in *Religion and Violence* (1987); James W. Walters, ed., in *War No More?* (1989); Alan Geyer, *Christianity and the Super Powers* (1990); and a score of others.

In political circles in our country two main approaches to the use of nuclear weapons were debated during the Cold War era. The first was the idea of "mutual assured destruction," which assumed that both the United States and the Soviet Union had the capability of launching massive nuclear attacks. If either nation were to attack the other, the attacked nation would launch a massive retaliatory strike. In such an exchange thousands of nuclear warheads would be employed and the losses on both sides would be incalculable. Because neither side could "win" such a war, it was argued, no rational leader or group of people would intentionally start it. By this line of reasoning, therefore, we were required to keep our nuclear defenses equal to those of the Soviet Union to ensure that neither it nor the United States would resort to their use.

The second line of thought entertained the possibility of the limited use of nuclear weapons. Both the United States and the nations of Western Europe feared that the Soviet Union might invade West Germany. The Soviet Union had a large military force within quick striking distance of the West German border and could have launched a sneak attack that would have overrun the conventional defense of that nation. The only option open to West Germany and its allies, other than surrender, it was argued, would be the use of the intermediate-range nuclear weapons that were maintained throughout Europe. The members of the North Atlantic Treaty Organization (NATO) were committed to this policy, although such action by NATO surely would have been met with retaliatory action by the Soviet Union and a full-scale nuclear war would have been launched. The treaty signed in 1987 by the United States and the Soviet Union represented a movement away from this line of reasoning, and the unification of the two German states in 1990 virtually ended it.

The collapse of the Soviet Union in 1991 eased the world's fear of a nuclear conflict between the two great world powers and set the stage for a reduction in the nuclear arsenals of both. But the world was still not free from the fear that some nation might use nuclear weapons—the United States, one of the four republics of the former Soviet Union that had such weapons, or one of the many other nations that possessed them or that might be able to manufacture them.

In addition to nuclear weapons, the development of chemical and biological weapons and a raft of other scientific and technological developments have made modern warfare qualitatively different from anything in the past. As in the case of nuclear warheads, the impact of such weapons cannot be limited to military targets but inevitably inflicts untold suffering on civilians and irreversible damage to the ecological balance. The possibility of manufacturing and using these new weapons has altered the political decision-making process in our government, leaving to experts the determination of what is needed, how much is needed, and when and where the weapons will be used. The result has not been a greater sense of security but a greater sense of fear.

According to Robert McAfee Brown (*Making Peace in the Global Village*), the distinction between traditional warfare and modern warfare is not simply the possession of more powerful weapons of destruction. Rather it is a complex of factors:

1. The automated battlefield, by means of which those using the weapons are miles away from the damage inflicted
2. The refinement of antipersonnel weapons, which destroy human beings rather than military targets
3. The extensiveness of destruction, which involves widespread devastation from bombs, defoliants, herbicides, and various gases and may ultimately upset the ecological balance
4. The breakdown of clear distinctions between civilian and combatant
5. The increasing erosion of moral constraint, not only on the part of those who participate directly but also on the part of those who set policies
6. The increasing attractiveness of the use of military means to solve political problems
7. The increasing power of the military in the political and economic decision-making process
8. The concentration of enormous power in the hands of the executive branch of government
9. An increasing tendency of governments to curtail the right of dissent
10. The increasing tendency to think in terms of individual nations rather than of the global village
11. The increasing willingness of policy makers to engage in deliberate public deception (pp. 48–53)

In light of these factors, it appears that now, more than ever, Christian responsibility for peacemaking requires much more than a decision to participate or not to participate in armed conflict. It requires careful attention to the things that make for peace in the world.

THE QUEST FOR PEACE

Whenever our nation has been involved in a declared war, our citizens have been compelled to make individual decisions, and conscientious Christians have responded in different ways. Debating the political and economic aspects of the situation, most have responded in the spirit of "agonized participation" to the demands made upon them by the government. Some who have been called upon for military service have chosen, after great personal struggle, to follow procedures established by the government to allow them to register as conscientious objectors. Others, believing that their witness for peace would not be heard if they followed established procedure, have refused even to register. Still others have taken direct and dramatic action to protest the military system. While each person must respect the decisions of others, each must also face the issue and make an individual decision in response to the Spirit of God.

When our nation is not involved in war, all of us have the opportunity to think about national policy, and ultimately all of us can be involved, in a small way at least, in its formulation. This fact is particularly relevant to the question of nuclear, chemical, and biological weaponry. For many years our thinking was shaped by fear of the Soviet Union and by the simple conviction that we must be stronger than that nation. We believed that its objective was world conquest and that ours was world security. We were conditioned to think that we did not wish to interfere in the affairs of other nations and that we would never take aggressive action against them. Now that the USSR no longer poses a threat, we may be able to examine more carefully these assumptions about ourselves.

At the outset, we must be realistic about the human condition. Specifically, we must acknowledge the persistence of evil in the life of the world. In our earlier discussion of human nature (Chapter 6) we affirmed the conviction that although humankind was created in the image of God, the image is flawed by our sinful choices, the consequences of which will always plague us. The problem is compounded when the choices are not those of individuals but of corporate entities, such as the nations of the world. The biblical writer's juxtaposition of a statement about the great steps forward in civilization with the bloodthirsty Song of Lamech (Genesis 4:17–24) suggests that progress in technology is not accompanied by a change in human nature. The development of more powerful weapons only makes us more effective in slaughter. Jesus's parable of the tares makes the same point concerning the persistence of evil along with good (Matthew 13:24–30). This means that as long as history lasts, war will always be a possibility. We will not be able to create a world in which the outbreak of war is impossible. We can certainly hope to improve international relations, and we can certainly hope to resolve specific issues as they arise. In no crisis is war inevitable; in every crisis conflict may be averted. But the resolution of one crisis does not prevent another. We will move from problem to problem.

Thus we have to come to grips with the fact that the creation of nuclear weapons has made a qualitative difference in warfare. In the past, new weapons were simply more efficient ways of killing, but it remained possible to control them, at least to an extent. Even bombs dropped from airplanes on specific targets destroyed lives and property only in the immediate area. When the bombing ended, the damage had been done. It was possible to destroy one area and one group of people without damage to other areas and other people. But the destruction wrought by nuclear weapons persists long after they are unleashed. Their effects are spread by the wind to distant places and by the genes to future generations.

Our quest for peace is complicated by the fact that the difference between war and peace is not clear-cut. Are we at peace when our country maintains military bases in friendly nations all over the world? When our armed forces are participating in "peace-keeping actions" in troubled regions of the world? When our naval vessels sail in waters that we consider to be international but that other nations claim as their own? When our ships and planes in international space defend themselves from attack by the ships and planes of other nations? When we supply equipment and personnel to a nation defending itself against insurgents? When we supply equipment and personnel to insurgents in a nation whose government we consider unfriendly? When we impose an economic boycott on a particular nation? This is not to suggest in any of these situations that we are right or that we are wrong. It is only to point out that the distinction between war and peace is not always clear.

The world situation clearly calls for a reexamination of our assumption that greater military strength is the key to peace. The need for a new approach is even greater now than it was when Robert McAfee Brown said,

In the name of trying to be "realistic," we have lost touch with reality. We have the military capability to kill everybody in the world twelve times, so we want to increase that killing capacity to fifteen or sixteen times. We have 30,000 nuclear weapons in our stockpile, and Russia has at least half that many, and yet we accede without quibbling when military men, whose way of life depends on it, tell us that we need still more nuclear weapons. We are told that building more weapons will make our situation safer, when each weapon we build actually makes it more precarious. (*Making Peace in the Global Village*, p. 62)

Brown concludes that we operate on the basis of a logical madness that says, "The more weapons we build, the less secure we are; therefore we will build more weapons." We must respond to this madness by refusing to conform to this "recipe for disaster." "We need the brashness to affirm that whatever we know, or do not know, about God's will, we know at least that it is not God's will that, having created this earth, God is now urging earth's children to destroy it and one another" (p. 64).

The greatest potential for war today may lie in the desperate struggle for power in the developing nations. Apparently the major powers have not grasped the explosiveness of this situation. After World War II many countries that had been colonies of Western powers won their independence and established themselves as sovereign nations. Other nations regained their independence with the breakup of the Soviet Union. Many of these nations have been torn apart by internal power struggles and by the resurgence of ancient ethnic conflicts and territorial struggles. At issue in many of these struggles are some beliefs that we Americans take for granted: that in free elections the majority can and will express their will, that elected officials will act in the best interests of their constituents, and that the power of the police is on the side of justice. In some places racial factors complicate the problems because a white minority controls most of the wealth and power, and people of color live in poverty. In light of our history and in light of the problems of the poor and of ethnic minorities in our country, we should not be surprised that the peoples of developing nations do not automatically regard the United States as friendly and benevolent.

Poverty plagues many developing countries. Many have few natural resources, and they may lack the technology and financial resources to develop what they have. Consequently two-thirds of the world's people never have enough food to satisfy their basic needs. One-fifth of the world's population controls four-fifths of the world's resources, and that one-fifth is white. As long as this radical discrepancy between the haves and the have-nots continues, the possibility of a violent explosion will continue. It is difficult to convince deprived peoples that they must not resort to violence to correct this imbalance. This being the case, would not money allocated to the resolution of this problem be more moral and make a greater contribution to world peace than money spent on arms?

Continued physical violence appears to be inevitable unless other and better means are found for dealing with the desperate needs of the struggling peoples all over the world. Part of the solution is to find some way to share our wealth with the rest of the world. It may take the form of direct relief in emergencies or technological assistance in the development of resources. In the long run it may mean a less comfortable lifestyle for us. It will involve the surrender of power, the risk that people will not do what we wish or what we think is wise. It will mean that we cannot ask other peoples to surrender the right of self-determination as the price for receiving our help.

Can we as a nation move in this direction? The democratic process to which we are committed assumes the possibility of change in policies and procedures in response to the expressed will of the people. Our elected officials do remain sensitive to our expression of our beliefs and wishes, and their actions in office can be influenced by the concerted effort of concerned members of their constituency. We will not be able to achieve all that we wish in a changed national emphasis, but we will be able to achieve something.

Another aspect of making peace is the cultivation of a sense of world community. A community is a group of people who live so near one another that they know one another well, who live so intimately that they care for one another, and who are so involved with one another that what each person does affects the life of everyone else. If the world is not, by this description, a community, it is rapidly becoming one. This sense of community is being forced on us by the fear of a war in which nations utilize terrifying new weapons, by the fear of violent civil war in nations where the poor are oppressed, by the eruption of ethnic conflict within nations and between nations, and by the fear of economic and political chaos in newly independent nations. We are made aware of it by the news media, which force us to see hunger, anger, fear, and greed all over the world. It is facilitated by the spread of scientific and technological knowledge. It is expressed in the interaction of people who travel for business or pleasure and who learn to appreciate other cultures. Most important, for Christians at least, this sense of world community is the consequence of a commitment to God's purposes for humankind.

The cultivation of a sense of community involves practical, even materialistic, concerns. It requires concentrated efforts to help the peoples of the world achieve their goals of nationhood and self-determination and to cope with their poverty. It requires structuring relationships among nations so that differences can be resolved in an orderly fashion. Furthermore, it requires abandoning our reliance on military supremacy and instead attending to basic human rights all over the world. As Brown says, peacemaking does not merely involve keeping us out of war:

> It also involves seeing to it that people have enough to eat; that they are not undernourished or malnourished; that they can go to bed at night without fear that someone will spirit them off to prison; that the society will be so planned that there is food enough to go around; that the politics of the country (and of the world) are so arranged that everybody's basic needs are met. (*Making Peace in the Global Village*, p. 14)

For building the concept of world community, Christians have a model in the church. In ideal terms the church is a world community, transcending nation, race, and class. To a limited extent, it is that in fact as well. Not only do we proclaim a universal gospel, but we also have a sense of unity with Christians everywhere. We regret the actual divisions that we see in the church along the lines of race, class, and nation, and we are troubled because we allow differences of doctrine to separate us. But in our faith we have a common bond. A starting point in working to establish world peace, therefore, is to make the church conform more fully to its ideal. This is the starting point, not the ultimate objective. From there we can challenge the divisiveness of the world and work for a world community that does not ignore or exclude any of its members.

Wanting to demonstrate the validity of the teachings of Christ for the kind of world in which we live, Reinhold Niebuhr spoke of "the relevance of an impossible ideal." Perhaps the dream of a world community is unrealistic.

Moved by that dream, however, we can take many practical steps. We can, for example,

1. Begin to think of ourselves not as Americans or whites or rich or middle-class but as members of the world community.
2. Search for nonmilitary approaches to the resolution of national differences.
3. Work for the relief of disaster-stricken areas of the world.
4. Cooperate in the spread of resources and technology for the long-term improvement of the economy of developing nations.
5. Encourage our government to base its military posture on our domestic and foreign policies rather than allowing the former to dictate the latter.
6. Deal with the reality of sin as a part of the social structure and not merely as an individual matter.
7. Work for changes in those structures of society that perpetuate our human problems.

These steps do not constitute a strategy for establishing permanent peace in the world. Rather they are ways in which Christians can deal with present problems with the hope of making a better future. They are ways in which we can respond to our calling to be disciples of Christ in a world driven by lust for power and torn by greed, injustice, inequality, and fear. And they are based on the belief that rather than leaving us alone, God works through us to accomplish justice and peace in the world.

QUESTIONS AND TOPICS FOR DISCUSSION

1. Under what circumstances, if any, do you think it is morally right for a nation to go to war?
2. In 1991 a coalition led by the United States entered oil-rich Kuwait to drive out the invading Iraqi forces. Was that action morally justifiable? Why or why not?
3. How do the moral issues of nuclear warfare differ from those of traditional war-fare?
4. On December 7, 1993, in a dramatic protest against American preparation for war, four disarmament activists, led by Philip Berrigan, illegally entered Seymour Johnson Air Base in North Carolina and used hammers and blood to "disarm" one nuclear-capable jet plane. What do you think about such symbolic actions?
5. Can we realistically expect to prevent war? Why or why not?

RECOMMENDATIONS FOR FURTHER READING

BROWN, ROBERT MCAFEE, *Religion and Violence*, 2d ed. Philadelphia: Westminster, 1987.
BROWN, ROBERT MCAFEE, *Saying Yes and Saying No*. Philadelphia: Westminster, 1986.

BUTTRY, DANIEL L., *Christian Peacemaking*. Valley Forge, Penn.: Judson, 1994.

CARTER, JIMMY, *Talking Peace*. New York: Dutton, 1993.

HAUERWAS, STANLEY, *Against the Nations*. New York: Harper and Row, 1985.

HOLLENBACH, DAVID, *Justice, Peace, and Human Rights*. New York: Crossroad, 1988.

WALTERS, JAMES W., *War No More?* Minneapolis: Fortress, 1989.

WILL, JAMES E., *A Christology of Peace*. Louisville, Ky.: Westminster/John Knox, 1989.

14

Work, Property, and Community

A person being interviewed for employment will be asked a number of questions: What are your qualifications? What experience have you had? Why did you leave your last position? What references can you give? The applicant, in turn, will ask questions: What will be expected of me? What salary is offered? What are the fringe benefits? What are the working conditions? What security will I have on the job? What are the opportunities for advancement? All of these questions are important, but do they have anything to do with morality?

All of us are profoundly affected by economic forces totally beyond our control. The interest rate on home mortgages fluctuates for reasons that none of us seems to understand. The price of gasoline is five cents a gallon higher in our town than in the town twenty miles away. A manufacturing plant closes in one city and people lose their jobs for reasons totally beyond their control. A new industry opens in another city, and new jobs are created, again for reasons beyond the control of the new employees. The stock market plunges, and even people who own no stock are somehow affected. All of these developments are matters of very great concern, but are they moral issues?

What should determine the price a customer pays for a product? Should a business or industry be concerned about anything other than making a profit for its owners or investors? On what basis should an industry make a decision about waste disposal? About the release of pollutants into the atmosphere or soil or water? What are the moral responsibilities of a corporation that manufactures and distributes products known to be dangerous to human health? What are the responsibilities of a person who works for such a corporation? What are the obligations of manufacturers to provide a safe and healthful work environment for their employees? What recourse do endangered workers have?

In the relatively simple economy of early America the moral factor was not nearly so complicated. Most people were self-sufficient farmers and artisans whose moral responsibility was essentially that of honest labor and helping one another in times of crisis. In 1776 no one took exception to Adam Smith's "invisible hand" theory, which said that if everyone worked diligently for his or her own good the result would be as if some invisible hand were working for the good of society as a whole (*An Inquiry into the Nature and Causes of the Wealth of Nations*, Book 5, Chapter 2). Today, however, our employment is affected by fluctuations on the stock market, by war in the Near East, by the government of South Africa, by Japanese investments in this country. Our security is affected by the unemployment rate, problems between labor and management, industrial development, and international politics. In these circumstances, how can we talk about moral responsibility? How can we function as responsible Christians in an essentially impersonal system?

Yet Christians must talk about moral responsibility in the economic order. Even the derivation of the word economy suggests this necessity. It comes from the Greek word *oikos*, which means "household," and *nomos*, which means "law," "rule," or "management." Thus *economy* literally means "the orderly management of the household." A household is the arena within which one operates to meet the basic needs of life. Now, more than ever, a person's household is not simply one's immediate family but the wide community of one's interaction with other people. The orderly management of this larger household is a fundamentally religious matter because the human family, or household, is the family of God. The *nomos* of God directs the activities associated with the human need for food, clothes, and shelter.

No one economic theory can properly be called Christian, however. Although the Bible expresses great concern about economic matters, it does not in any sense deal with theory. Throughout its history the church has functioned within a wide variety of economic systems. Neither capitalism nor socialism nor any other economic system is totally good or evil, and none operates fully on Christian principles. The very independence of Christianity from all systems distinguishes it from them and imposes upon its followers the obligation to criticize those systems from the perspective of their faith.

Living within a capitalistic system, then, Christians properly give serious and careful attention to determining what their faith requires of them as regards the economic values and commitments and practices of their society. Accepting individual responsibility for helping the poor and the oppressed, for welcoming the stranger, for visiting the sick and those in prison, Christians realize that individual action does not resolve the broader problem. They find it necessary, therefore, to look for more inclusive and effective ways to influence social policies and political mechanisms and to establish new and sound social structures. "If we are to build such structures," say Prentiss Pemberton and Daniel Finn, "we must do nothing less than gain a new vision of what it means to be a twentieth-century good Samaritan."

Let us concede that we are no longer good Samaritans if, for example, we visit those sick with malaria but do not help to structure community health programs, to deal with the mosquitoes that spread the disease. We are no longer good Samaritans if we complain about big government with its bloated bureaucracies and behind-the-scenes pressure groups but do not also help to structure more nonpartisan, general-interest lobbies that work resolutely to reduce inefficiency and secrecy in what should be public areas of government. . . . Have we in the churches really thought through what will be required of us if we are to structure new efficiency and fairness? (*Toward a Christian Economic Ethic,* p. 3).

It is important, then, for Christians to evaluate the economic system within which we live and to offer constructive criticisms about its operation. It is necessary to raise questions: How can we function morally within this structure? How do we need to change our way of doing things? How can we make the system more just, more caring, more respectful for the created order? How can we broaden the scope of our concern to reach all the members of the household of God?

THE CONTEXT: CAPITALISM

The economic system that prevails in the United States, as well as in many other nations of the world, is capitalism, or the free enterprise system. It is not capitalism in the classic sense, for it has undergone such radical changes since its rise with the Industrial Revolution that modifying adjectives are often used, as in democratic capitalism, welfare capitalism, people's capitalism, regulated capitalism, and monopoly capitalism. Perhaps a better phrase to describe the American economic system would be *mixed economy.* Yet while the system has changed and is changing rapidly, the fundamental ideology has not been significantly altered.

Capitalism in the classic sense is defined as the private ownership of the instruments of production, distribution, and exchange and the use of these instruments, with a minimum of government regulation, under a plan of individual initiative and open competition to earn private profit. The system rests on four main concepts. The first is the right of the ownership of private property. Property includes not only material goods, such as land, tools, dwellings, and the like, but also the instruments of production and distribution. Ownership entails the right to determine what use shall be made of property, subject only to the restriction that the use must not interfere with the rights of other people. Some moral problems associated with ownership focus on the question of whether there are restrictions other than the legal ones on the acquisition and use of property. They become more complicated when, as is often the case, great wealth, and therefore great power, is concentrated in the hands of a few individuals. They become even more complicated when ownership is not in the hands of individuals but rather in the hands of corporations. These complications, however, do not invalidate the assumption that individuals have the right to own property; they only make the solution of the problems more difficult.

The second basic concept in capitalism is free enterprise, the freedom to pursue one's own interests without interference by the government except when such interference is necessary to protect the rights of others. It assumes that all people naturally pursue their own self-interests and that such pursuit is entirely legitimate. One should be free to make as much money as possible and to spend it however one chooses. In its most extreme form this view holds that government restrictions should be kept to an absolute minimum. Few people today would agree with the dictum that "that government is best which governs least" because we want protection from crime, defense against foreign enemies, compulsory education, government regulation to guarantee minimum quality in goods, and so on. Yet we assume that within the limits of social responsibility, free enterprise is basic to our economic system.

The third fundamental idea in capitalism is competition in the production and distribution of goods and services. Capitalism assumes that in the long run the best results for all persons involved depend on free competition. Competition among buyers and sellers will regulate quality, set prices, establish wages, and determine what goods will be produced. In this connection it should be noted that the chief threat to competition today is not from the government but from large corporations absorbing smaller ones or forcing them out of business and thus gaining a virtual monopoly.

The fourth capitalistic principle is that the profit motive is the most effective incentive in the economic system. The same hope of personal gain that drives an individual to do good work impels a giant corporation to produce high-quality goods or services; that is, people work hard when it is to their advantage to do so. The success of an individual or a corporation, therefore, is gauged in terms of the profit earned. The commonly used phrase "the bottom line" suggests that while other matters may be important, the deciding factor in all economic activity is the size of the profit.

The philosophy of capitalism assumes that human beings are essentially rational creatures who, for the sake of their own individual interests, can and will manage their own economic affairs within the framework of an automatically self-regulating system. This system will provide for the best possible allocation of resources to meet the needs of all the people. The demand of consumers will determine what is produced and how it will be priced. It will regulate the wages of the labor force. It will provide the incentive for the improvement of quality and for efficiency in production. No outside intervention is needed because the system itself provides incentive, promotes efficiency, penalizes the incompetent, and guarantees that all basic needs are met.

The modified capitalism that prevails in the United States involves a great deal of government regulation and direct action. The government necessarily takes certain actions that are essential to our well-being. It is responsible for national defense, law enforcement, and equal educational opportunity for all people. In addition, we believe that we are better served by having the state responsible for some functions that could be done by private enterprise: building and maintaining roads, delivering the mail, and providing financial help to those unable to meet their own needs. We need government regulation of industries that are by nature monopolies, government enforcement of minimum standards in businesses and professions, and government assistance to individuals and businesses during crises or natural disasters. We find it unwise, in other words, to leave the economic function entirely in private hands. Yet we are wary of too great a concentration of power in the hands of the government. We have therefore a mixed system in which, on the one hand, we cling to the principle of private enterprise and, on the other hand, we affirm the principle of public control of functions that are genuinely public in scope. In between these two distinct areas are many functions that are semiprivate and semipublic, some of which are performed by the government, some by private enterprise, and some by voluntary group activity.

A CHRISTIAN PERSPECTIVE ON PROPERTY

The ownership of property is a right defined by society. Because social orders have differed significantly throughout history, there has been great variety in the meaning of ownership and in the designation of the kinds of things that an individual may claim as private property. Classical capitalism assumes that one has the right to all the property to which one can gain legal title and to use or dispose of that property in whatever manner one desires. In our system, some restrictions are set on the ownership and use of certain property because of the larger interests of society. Within such limitations, however, our economic order takes as a given the concept of private property.

Although the Bible teaches no theory of economics, it reflects a view of property that we can employ in our evaluation of our economic responsibilities. At the heart of the biblical understanding of property is the recognition that ultimately all things belong to God. "The earth is the Lord's and all that is in it, the world and those who live in it," said the Psalmist (24:1), voicing a conviction that underlies all statements about ownership. The appropriate conclusion, therefore, is that property is never owned absolutely by human beings but is held in trust. People are responsible to God for the use they make of the property over which they have only temporary control.

Within that perspective, the Old Testament supports the idea of the private ownership of property. The commandment "You shall not steal" (Exodus 20:15) is the basic protection of this right. The wide variety of laws providing for restitution for damage done to the property of another person, even accidental damage, supports that right, and the laws of inheritance assume it. The prophets denounced persons of wealth and even the nobility, not for ownership, but for violating the property rights of others and ignoring the needs of others.

Jesus forbade theft and fraud, he denounced those who practiced extortion, he condemned wealth gained by improper means, and he praised restitution of ill-gotten gains as evidence of repentance. Rather than stressing ownership, however, he talked a great deal about the responsible use of wealth. He spoke of people as "stewards" of their possessions, responsible to God for the manner in which they use them (Matthew 25:14–30; Luke 19:11–27). While he seems to have assumed that it is appropriate for us to use wealth to meet our own needs, he taught directly that we should share our possessions with the poor and the helpless (Matthew 6:3, 25:31–46; Luke 18:22). Indeed, although the words that he quoted from Isaiah do not speak directly of wealth, they show that his sense of mission focuses on meeting the needs of other people:

> The Spirit of the Lord is upon me
>   because he has anointed me to bring good news to the poor.
> He has sent me to proclaim release to the captives
>   and recovery of sight to the blind,
>   to let the oppressed go free,
> To proclaim the year of the Lord's favor. (Luke 4:18)

In addition, Jesus acknowledged the responsibility of supporting the government (Matthew 22:21; Mark 12:17; Luke 20:25) and the institutions of religion (Matthew 17:24–27; Mark 12:41–44; Luke 21:1–4) and the legitimacy of spending money to express affection (Mark 14:3–9; John 12:2–8). He recognized, in other words, that wealth is a necessary tool by which people live and work in the world as children of God.

At the same time, Jesus warned against the dangers of wealth. He spoke of the false sense of security that wealth brings (Luke 12:19–21); of the insensitivity to the needs of others that often accompanies wealth (Luke 16:19–31); of "the lure of wealth, and the desire for other things," which choke out the gospel (Mark 4:19). Because the passion for wealth tends to crowd out all other considerations, he urged his disciples to lay up "treasures in heaven" rather than "treasures on earth" (Matthew 6:19–21). His most extreme statement was the warning that "it is easier for a camel to go through the eye of a needle than for someone who is rich to enter the kingdom of God" (Matthew 19:24).

The early church had a sense of community, of belonging together and being responsible for one another, which expressed itself in a variety of ways. One striking incident was the sharing of wealth by the members of the congregation in Jerusalem (Acts 2:44–45, 4:32). Although this way of life apparently did not last long and was not adopted by the church in other places, it did express in a profound way a sense of responsibility for the entire community of faith. Other expressions of that same sense of community are seen in the Epistles in their frequent references to stewardship, their directions for ministering to the poor, and in their instructions about the collection of gifts for that purpose.

We can summarize the biblical teachings on property by making four generalizations. First, people have a right to own private property. This right is important because the management of property is one of the most significant ways in which human beings express their own nature and their relationship to God. In a sense, one's property is an extension of one's being. Second, people are responsible to God and to one another both for the manner in which they acquire property and the manner in which they use it; that is, they have the obligation to manage property, within the context of the whole of creation, in the manner most appropriate to the purposes of God. Third, acquiring and retaining more property than one actually needs entails great spiritual danger. Fourth, people who manage to acquire property are responsible for helping people who are unable to do so.

A CHRISTIAN PERSPECTIVE ON WORK

Although nature provides basic materials, people must gather and transform them into what is necessary to live, and to live well. The Bible interprets this reality in terms of the plan of God for the created order and for the place of humankind within it. The older creation narrative says, "The Lord God took the man and put him in the garden of Eden to till it and keep it" (Genesis 2:15). While work is sometimes burdensome because of human sin (Genesis 3), it is never regarded as an option. Furthermore, there is a connection between work and reward. When Jesus commented to his disciples that "the laborer deserves to be paid" (Luke 10:7), he was quoting a popular proverb. In stressing the responsibilities of his disciples he observed, "The reaper is already receiving wages" (John 4:36). In dealing with a problem that had arisen in the church at Thessalonica, Paul suggested, "Anyone unwilling to work should not eat" (2 Thessalonians 3:10). Even the belief that the end of the world was imminent was no justification for the cessation of labor.

We tend to identify ourselves in terms of our work. Asked what we *do*, we usually respond with the words "I *am* a . . ." We know biblical characters in the same way. We know Jesus as a carpenter, Peter as a fisherman, Matthew as a tax collector, Paul as a tent maker, Lydia as a merchant. Some biblical characters are not even named, but identified only by their work: a shepherd, a Roman centurion, a priest, a jailer. While Scripture is concerned about matters other than occupation, it reflects this idea that one is what one does. Many of our surnames are derived from the occupations of our ancestors: Baker, Smith, Cook, Fisher, Farmer, and so on. This close identity between doing and being is involved in the recognition that work is not merely something that one does to earn a living; it is also something that one does to develop as a full human being.

The word *career* is sometimes used to refer to our life's work, the means by which we earn a living. It comes directly from a French word that means "road" or "racing course" and indirectly from a Latin word that means "wagon." The implication is that a career is the route that our lives take, or the vehicle by which we carry ourselves through life. An older term, now used less frequently but perhaps more appropriately from a Christian perspective, is *vocation* or *calling*. This term implies that what we do with our lives is a response to the call of God. The Bible usually uses this term to refer to the call of God into the life of faith. Paul, for example, in rebuking the Corinthian Christians for certain failures, reminded them of their "call" (1 Corinthians 1:26). Because of the centrality of our daily work in our lives, Christian tradition came to affirm that what we do to earn a living is a part of our response to God. For some Christians this means that they choose their careers on the basis of what they believe God leads them to do. For others it means that their career is one way in which they serve God. In either event, their effort to serve God by serving one's neighbor is a compelling motivation.

PERSONAL ISSUES IN AN
IMPERSONAL ECONOMIC ORDER

The person who wishes to live as a Christian within our economic system faces a wide variety of problems. The first has to do with a concept that is at the heart of capitalism. We have said that capitalism assumes that the profit motive is the most effective incentive for economic activity. This means that the system operates on the assumption that each of us is out to meet our own needs, that we do what we think will be most profitable for us, and that ultimately we are responsible for ourselves. We operate businesses to make money, not to serve the needs of other people. That does not necessarily entail unbridled competition, and it does not suggest that we have no responsibilities beyond our own needs and desires. The basic appeal, however, is to our acquisitive nature. Christians therefore feel a tension between that appeal and the command of Christ to love our neighbor as ourselves. Taught by our faith that we should love our neighbor as ourselves, we live in a society that expects us to put our own good ahead of that of our neighbor.

A second problem is that of maintaining a sense of vocation. Certain occupations can easily be seen as ways of serving God because they offer direct and immediate benefit to others—service careers such as medicine, teaching, and social work. Others offer less direct and immediate benefit but might ultimately be construed as service—careers such as plumbing, road building, scientific research, and statistical analysis. Still others are even more remote from service to God and other people—typing and filing documents, archaeological research, and work on an assembly line, for example. Thus some people may have a sense of vocation, a sense that in their work they are responding to God; but many, perhaps most, people do not see any real connection between their faith and the way they earn their living.

A third problem for Christians in our economic system is the depersonalizing character of the work that large numbers of people are required to do in an industrialized society. The techniques of mass production, which require routine work and demand little or no skill and even less thought, do not permit workers to function as whole persons. To use an old term, people are regarded as "hands." Even the most benevolent manufacturer, who provides the best working conditions and offers the greatest financial benefits, cannot eliminate the deadening effect of such routine labor. Yet a central consideration in Christian faith is the worth of the individual, a consideration that requires each one to be dealt with as a whole person and not as a tool or an object.

A fourth problem lies in the choice and pursuit of a career. This idea seems consistent with the Christian understanding of free will, by which we are capable of making choices. It is also consistent with our image of our country as a land where people may choose to be and do what they like. The fact of the matter, however, is that our opportunities are restricted. Young people with limited educational opportunities do not have a wide range of choices. People who live in certain areas of the country are also limited, as are those making their decisions at a time when few jobs are available or when they are under the constraints of family responsibilities. They are limited by the expectations of family and friends and by public judgments about what careers are prestigious or challenging. They are limited by stereotypes and role expectations, by the personal drive for security, and by social pressure for success. One does not make career choices in the abstract but within circumstances that significantly narrow the options.

A fifth problem is the fact that many people find themselves trapped in work that they find personally deadening. For a wide variety of reasons, many people can find employment only in mass-production facilities where the work is routine, repetitive, and completely impersonal. Other people, with more options, often make ill-advised decisions, or fail to prepare for a challenging career, or prepare themselves for a career in which they have no real personal interest. Others find that their work situation changes, or they experience changes within themselves. Some are frustrated with being unable to accomplish what they set out to accomplish or by reaching a dead end regarding promotions or achievements. Some find that they have to work with people with whom they are incompatible. Some learn too late that their job offends their sensibilities or clashes with their ideals and values. For any of a dozen reasons, then, many people have no sense of satisfaction in their work. Yet they may not be qualified for any other occupation. If they were to move into another situation, they would have to start at the bottom again. Because of personal or family responsibilities, they cannot surrender the financial security granted by their present job. In such a situation they have difficulty appreciating the virtues of free choice.

A sixth problem is that of being involved in work that requires questionable practices. Many people in merchandising know that some of the products they deal with are of inferior quality and that false claims about them are made in advertising. Some salespersons have to persuade consumers to buy things that they do not need or cannot afford. People in management positions find themselves at odds with the labor policies of the company for which they are working. Teachers must support school policies that they think violate the best interests of the students or the community at large. Attorneys, physicians, engineers, and social workers—people in all sorts of occupations—become aware of basic flaws in the very system for which they have prepared themselves and on which their success depends. It is too simple a solution to suggest that they should get into another kind of work. They have invested time and money in preparation, and they have already gotten a start in a career to which they remain attracted. But they are troubled by the requirements of the system of which they are a part.

SOCIAL ISSUES IN AN IMPERSONAL ECONOMIC ORDER

Citizens of capitalist countries enjoy the highest living standards in the world. In housing, food, and clothing, as well as in the extras that enhance the quality of life, Americans are rich in comparison with people in noncapitalist countries. We must not allow this comparative success, however, to blind us to serious moral problems within the economic structures of our society.

The first and most obvious problem is the unfair distribution of wealth. *Unfair*, of course, does not simply mean that wealth is unequally distributed. It could hardly be called unfair to reward an industrious worker more highly than a lazy one. It is appropriate to reward preparation, diligence, efficiency, and faithfulness and to value work that contributes significantly to the well-being of society as a whole. People are not equal in ability, they are not equal in preparation, they do not make an equal effort, and they do not value the same things equally. A fair distribution of wealth must take into account these various factors. Unfortunately, however, in our system people are rarely paid on the basis of what they deserve. Many are paid on the basis of contracts that allow no variation. Pay is often based on the number of available workers, on competition for the job, or on custom. The wages of some people are affected by whether they are male or female, black or white, old or young. Many factors, in other words, other than job performance are involved in the determination of pay.

The problem of unfair distribution, however, is far more complex than a matter of wages. Our system permits the accumulation of great wealth by a relatively small number of individuals and corporations. Since, in our system, wealth means power, wealthy persons often gain control over the lives of others. A relatively small number of people, for example, control our main sources of energy and the communication media. The same is true of providing public transportation, producing automobiles, marketing food, and manufacturing arms. The decision to close a manufacturing plant that provides employment for a thousand people, to move the manufacturing operation to another community, or to introduce new methods of manufacturing that call for different skills is made by executives whose job is to increase the profits of the corporation. Whether they are the most benevolent or the most insensitive of persons, the system requires them to act in the interests of the industry no matter how the lives of the workers are affected.

Another aspect of the unjust distribution of wealth is the poverty of a large segment of our population. *Poverty*, of course, is a relative term and difficult to define. By the standards set by our own government, however, the enormity of the problem is dismaying. Although the figures fluctuate a bit with each yearly report, the U.S. Bureau of the Census has regularly revealed that 13 to 15 percent of our population, or 33 to 40 million people, live below the poverty level. Throughout the 1990s between 5 and 7 percent of the people in the labor force—some 7 to 9 million persons—have been unemployed. This means that vast numbers of persons are ill fed, ill housed, and ill clothed. Vast numbers of others live at or just above the poverty level. In spite of the great wealth of our nation, we have not learned how to deal adequately with this problem.

A second moral issue in economics, closely related to the first, is the limitation on access to institutional and social services, such as education and health care. The operation of these services is quite costly. Workers must be paid, facilities must be built and maintained, and supplies must be bought. The normal way of meeting these costs is to charge those who benefit from the services. And herein lies the difficulty. We assume that all people have the right to these services, and we try to make them available to everyone. As yet, however, we have failed to find equitable ways to deliver these services to people whose ability to pay is limited. This is not only a problem for the poor; it is also a problem for people whose income is adequate for the normal expenses of daily living but not for dealing with crises. The fact is that accessibility to services is not related to need so much as it is to ability to pay.

One persistent problem is the distribution of health care. On one level, this is a matter of the very high cost of medical service. People who have medical insurance are usually able to get the care they need without undue difficulty. But large numbers of people do not have any form of medical insurance. Many do not receive the treatment they need, and others are burdened with tremendous bills, which they cannot pay. Government efforts to deal with this inequity have not yet been successful.

On another level the problem is even greater. Whereas many people avail themselves of the benefits of preventive medicine, those with low incomes deal only with emergencies. They see a doctor only when they need to, although their health would probably be better if they were able to receive more comprehensive care. They cannot afford elective health care, treatment that is not necessary for survival but prevents health problems and contributes to a more comfortable life.

Another facet of health-care distribution is the location of doctors and facilities. For sound economic and professional reasons, medical institutions and personnel are usually located in densely populated areas. Consequently hospitals, clinics, physicians, and nurses are in short supply in many places, where the problem for residents is not money but the absence of services.

Another service to which there is unequal access is public education. Some unevenness in the quality of public educational institutions is inevitable. Yet there are patterns of equality not caused by the normal differences between individuals or by the choices of those associated with the institutions. In some areas the public school systems are inferior to those in other areas, and children from minority groups have limited access to the better schools.

Inequality of opportunity is seen also in higher education. Tuition at universities, colleges, and technical schools is an insuperable barrier for some people. Tuition, books and supplies, and living costs, manageable expenses for some people, are beyond the means of many. In addition, the benefits of a college or university degree are unequal because both the employment rate and the pay scale of graduates are different for different groups.

In our society, even legal service is related to the ability to pay. Guilty or innocent, those who are charged with a crime need legal services, as do those who are involved in civil suits, are engaged in some business transactions, or have domestic difficulties. The more serious the problem, the greater the demands on the time of the attorney and the larger the fee. There are some provisions to help people who cannot pay, but the extent of these services is limited.

A third moral problem with our economic structure is the contrast between our affluence as a nation and the poverty of much of the rest of the world. By the most conservative estimates, 400 million people do not get the daily food necessary for a normal, healthy life. Consequently they are not only constantly hungry but also suffer from diseases and infections that they would be able to resist if they had a better diet. Children are the most seriously affected, and every year more than 15 million children under the age of five die from malnutrition.

The problem is not that the world cannot produce enough food for its people. Although an unchecked growth in the world's population may bring us to that point, we have not reached it yet. Rather the problem is what we do with what we produce. There are two aspects of this issue. First, our methods of consumption in this country are unbelievably wasteful. When we feed grain to animals and then convert it into meat, milk, and eggs, we waste up to 95 percent of its food value. If the people of our nation were to take the simple step of eating more vegetables, grains, and fruits, and less meat, the amount of food saved would be enough to reduce significantly the hunger of the world.

Second, we have not devised adequate methods of distributing to the needy peoples of the world what we have learned to produce so abundantly. We have not been totally indifferent to this problem. With varying degrees of success, some groups have made some efforts to deal with emergencies. Some affluent nations have tried to help developing nations, although many of these efforts have been considered as interference and have thus been seen as a form of imperialism. No well-to-do nation has made a major effort to deal with this issue, however, nor has any existing effort been free from problems of administration.

The issue here is not whether affluence in itself is immoral, or even whether waste in itself is immoral. Rather it is the fact that one part of the world wastes what another part of the world desperately needs. Christians generally acknowledge their responsibility for helping those in need. They are moved by Jesus's words in the parable of the last judgment: "Just as you did it to one of the least of these who are members of my family, you did it to me" (Matthew 25:40). What they have not generally acknowledged is the necessity of extending this kind of ministry beyond the range of personal relationships. It is difficult to avoid the conclusion, however, that the most effective way of feeding the poor, particularly those vast numbers of poor in distant areas of the world, requires an alteration in our patterns of consumption and the development of some techniques to help other nations meet the basic needs of their own people.

Once we acknowledge our responsibility to help, our task then becomes one of finding the most appropriate ways of doing so. Raising the living standards of poor nations may involve encouraging land reform measures, sharing technology, improving education, and helping to liberate women from a purely child-bearing role. All such assistance will have to be recognized as just that, assistance to people dealing with their problems and not the imposition of an alien culture.

A fourth moral issue in economics is the relationship between capital and labor in establishing working conditions. This matter was not a problem in the early days of this country because our methods of production and distribution were essentially individualistic. But the methods of modern technology have centralized production and distribution. Consequently the economy is dominated by big business, big labor, big agriculture, and big professional organizations, all of which tend to be highly impersonal.

The rise of big business has created a new situation with new problems. Does an employer, whether an individual or a corporation, have the exclusive right to set wages, benefits, and working conditions? Is an employer free to exercise complete control over the business? Or do the employees have the right to bargain with the employer? If so, must it be done individually or can it be done collectively? If it is done individually, the employer has a distinct advantage because the loss of one worker is unlikely to cripple an operation. A worker who has no job, however, may have difficulty finding other employment. If it is done in concert with other employees, that is, through a union, the workers have an advantage because they can in fact cripple an enterprise.

Although the first labor unions in the United States appeared about the time of the Revolutionary War, their significant growth began only with the industrialization that followed the Civil War. The movement has always been controversial. In 1894, the same year that Congress made Labor Day a legal holiday, President Cleveland called out federal troops to keep order during the Pullman strike in Chicago. Union membership was highest during the years of World War II, reaching a peak in 1945 and claiming 35.5 percent of the labor force. Since that time there has been a gradual decline in membership, and in 1998 it was just under 14 percent. Unions are stronger in certain sections of the country than in others, and strong in certain industries but virtually nonexistent in others. Transportation workers and public utilities employees are the most highly organized, with more than 35 percent of workers being union members.

Beyond the general requirements of love and consideration for all people, are there religious considerations that might have a bearing on the relationship between capital and labor? The ideal of respect for the rights of others is relevant. We have affirmed that individuals have the right to private property, and it seems appropriate to extend that concept. Property held by corporations, therefore, merits the same respect as property held by individuals. By the same token, the labor of the worker is a valuable asset, his or her property in a sense, that merits the same respect. Negotiations between management and labor should be conducted in such a manner as to safeguard these rights.

The matter of justice, or fairness, is also pertinent. We have observed that power is concentrated in the hands of management when negotiations are on an individual basis. When management negotiates with representatives of a larger group of employees, however, both sides have significant power. Of course power can be abused by either group. It does seem more fair, however, for each side to negotiate from strength than for one side to be strong and the other weak.

Related to this consideration is the conviction that all people should be free to make significant choices. No one ought to be at the mercy of another; no one should be victimized by another. Each person should have a voice in determining his or her future. It is not quite adequate to say that someone is never forced to accept or to keep a job. There really is no choice if the only options are either to have this particular job or not to have one at all. Neither is there any choice if the job is available only on unacceptable terms. Real freedom is the ability to be involved in decisions affecting what one does and how one does it.

Also related to the idea of fairness is the concept of honesty. Christians have long been taught that they should give "an honest day's labor for an honest day's pay." The reverse is also true: They should be given an honest day's pay for an honest day's labor. Granted, the determination of what is "an honest day's labor" and "an honest day's pay" is difficult. How intensely can we be expected to work, for example, on an assembly line or in an office? How much time do we need for a coffee break or for lunch or for going to the restroom? What determines the value of the work that an individual does? The intensity of the work? The skill required? The number of people in the labor pool? The market value of the finished product? As difficult as these questions are, the generalization holds true. The worker and the employer have mutual responsibilities. If there is disagreement about them, it should be dealt with on the basis of mutual respect and concern.

We have noted that people have a strong tendency to identify themselves by what they do. We have noted also that Christians incorporate their work into the belief that their life is to be an expression of their faith. Today, however, employees of large enterprises, particularly those whose work is of a routine nature, understandably have some difficulty in thinking of their work in this way. The difference may not lie so much in the nature of the work as in the lack of a sense of ownership. In earlier days, the person who gathered raw materials and fashioned them into a chair could take pride in the skill and craftsmanship that were involved; no matter who purchased it, the worker could say, "That is one of my chairs." Can modern assembly-line workers, who place one part on each of hundreds of chairs every day, think in the same way? They may be able to do so if they are involved in some way in decision-making processes, if they feel secure with their company, and if there are ways in which their workmanship is recognized. While this approach is good business, it is more than that; it recognizes employees as persons who express themselves in their work.

A fifth moral issue for Christians in our economic system is the relationship between business and the consuming public. The profit motive is basic to the capitalistic system, but it may lead businesses and industries to take unfair or inappropriate advantage of the public. Often it is difficult to determine what individual or group is responsible for these practices because the responsibility is shared by many people at many levels of operation. Sometimes the practices develop gradually without anyone making a single, deliberate decision. Yet when stated in simple terms, it is easy to identify as unethical such practices as

1. Misleading labels and misrepresentation of merchandise
2. Adulteration of products with inferior materials

3. Advertising that is false and misleading
4. Corruption in the form of price fixing
5. Improper methods of influencing legislation related to the business
6. Planned obsolescence

Government regulations are established to protect the public, but there is always a tension between the interests of the public and the needs of the business. Although professional organizations of businesses and industries establish certain standards of operation, these organizations function in the interest of their members, not the general public. Consumer protection organizations try to educate the public, but they are unable to deal with all the products available and are unable to reach the majority of the public. Although the problem may be inherent in our system, we need to find more effective ways of dealing with it.

IDEALS AND ECONOMICS

When Jesus said, "You shall love your neighbor as yourself," he did not command us to love ourselves. Rather he recognized the depths of our self-love and proposed it as the standard by which we are to measure our love for our neighbor. He understood that we naturally seek our own good and he did not say that we should not do so. He did say, however, that we should seek our neighbor's good with equal concern and he gave us some dramatic examples of how we can do so by the use of our material possessions. He spoke to a people driven by competition for property and power, torn by differences between the haves and the have-nots, troubled by the misfortunes of widows and orphans and social outcasts, victimized by corruption in business and government. He addressed his message to people in high places and low, to some who made foolish investments and some who were more prudent, to people whose sense of values was misplaced. He taught in a world in which nations went to war against one another, where the powerful nations exploited the weak ones, and natural disasters wrought death and destruction. His teachings, therefore, were not intended for people living in a perfect society. They were intended for people living in a world beset by human weakness and human sinfulness—a world like the one in which we live. They were intended for people who are by nature grasping, self-centered, indifferent, hostile, jealous, afraid, and materialistic. In that context Jesus said, in effect, "Let the way you seek your own good be the standard by which you seek the good of other people."

Two facts determine the parameters within which we function in the economic realm. First, we live in a capitalistic society, certain aspects of which are quite in harmony with our Christian faith and certain aspects of which are not. It is a cohesive system, however, and we must live with all parts of it. Second, we live in a world that is in upheaval, in which rival economic systems clash as people who are desperately poor struggle for the physical necessities for survival. While we feel a strong impulse to respond to the needs of the world, we do not know what is the best thing to do and we are not sure how much we are willing to sacrifice to do it.

We have said that the basic element in the Christian understanding of our relationship to the material world is stewardship. If we regard God as the owner of all things and ourselves as entrusted with the management of certain goods, we may be guided by several considerations. First, the economic factor is elemental in human existence. Perhaps the founders of modern communism overstated their case when they said that economic forces determine all our attitudes and shape all our social institutions, but in our world the economic factor, if not determinative, is at least highly influential. On the one hand, we find it impossible to operate without money, we find it impossible to have money without working for it, and we demonstrate what we think is important by the way we spend it. On the other hand, forces beyond our control set rather precise limits on what we can earn and how we can earn it.

Second, we are interested in people, not systems. What Jesus said about the Sabbath can be applied to any economic system: "The system was made for people, and not people for the system." We are not therefore primarily interested in defending capitalism. We are interested in making the system operate effectively to meet people's needs. We are not primarily interested in attacking any other system; we are interested in holding up all systems to the test of how well they serve the people who live within them.

Third, economic activity is a major area in which we can implement Christian love. This statement is quite general, of course. It does not tell us how to earn our money or how to spend it, how to take care of the poor in our own country or anywhere else in the world, or how to deal with the threat of environmental pollution or industrial disputes. It does not guarantee success in any of our efforts to meet human needs. It does say that as disciples of Christ we must be actively concerned about the distress of the world around us.

Finally, we must deal with specific issues. Many of us may feel like the character who "flung himself upon his horse and rode madly off in all directions." Troubled about many things, we are effective in dealing with none of them. We implement Christian love most effectively by choosing specific problems and doing everything we can to deal with them. That choice may be dictated by a crisis: a natural disaster in some distant land or an industrial dispute in our own city. It may be the result of a gradually developing awareness of the needs of a developing country or of the powerless and the impoverished in our own society. It may be the result of the study of such current problems as environmental pollution and occupational health hazards. In any event, we do well to choose our targets and concentrate on them rather than fragmenting our efforts.

No one of us can do everything, but all of us can do something. No system works properly, and even the best can be ruined by the activities of self-centered, dishonest, uncaring people. Our system can be made to work better to the extent that we heed the command, "You shall love your neighbor as yourself."

QUESTIONS AND TOPICS FOR DISCUSSION

1. What do you do when the economy of your area depends on a product that you believe is harmful? Or when you believe that the methods of growing or processing that product are harmful?
2. What can you do when your work involves activities that you believe to be immoral? For example,
   a. You are a gynecologist who believes abortion to be wrong.
   b. You are a defense attorney who knows that your client is guilty of a serious crime.
   c. You are in advertising and are required to promote an inferior product.
   d. You are a teacher who disagrees with commonly accepted standards or values in your community.
3. What is your responsibility for the policies of businesses, industries, and professions in your area in which you are not personally involved?

RECOMMENDATIONS FOR FURTHER READING

BEHRMAN, JACK N., *Essays on Ethics in Business and the Professions.* Englewood Cliffs: Prentice Hall, 1988.

DONALDSON, THOMAS, and PATRICIA H. WERHANE, *Ethical Issues in Business.* 3rd ed. Englewood Cliffs: Prentice Hall, 1988.

MEEKS, M. DOUGLAS, *God the Economist.* Minneapolis: Fortress, 1989.

MOUNT, ERIC, JR., *Professional Ethics in Context.* Louisville, Ky.: Westminster/John Knox, 1990.

VELASQUEZ, MANUEL G., *Business Ethics*, 2d ed. Englewood Cliffs: Prentice Hall, 1988.

15

Ecology and
Moral Responsibility

The only known surviving spotted owls, officially designated an endangered species, live in national forests in northern California, Oregon, and Washington. Their continued survival requires old-growth forests, forests that are at least 200 years old. To protect the species, in 1991 the courts banned logging on millions of acres of national land in those states. The ban deprived logging companies of millions of dollars in profit and resulted in the loss of thousands of jobs. In simple terms, the issue appears to be one of owls versus jobs. In more complex terms, however, it is a question of short-term goals versus long-term goals, human manipulation of the natural order, and the place of both owls and humankind in the ecological system.

Hog farming became one of North Carolina's major industries during the 1990s. As the technology for improving the production and processing of these animals outdistanced the technology for disposal of the waste, environmental pollution became a major problem. As people in the affected areas lobbied for legal protection of the environment, the voices of those with greater economic resources seemed to be heard more readily than those with less power. While regulations were being debated, the industry protested that the sewage disposal from cities was a far greater problem than the industrial waste. Environmental groups, drawing support largely from urban areas and a relatively affluent population, expressed concern for the rivers, wetlands, forests, and endangered species. The grass-roots groups, usually made up of rural and small-town people with less economic and political power, tended to be anxious about what was happening in their own neighborhoods. One resident of a small community complained that the recently adopted law of the state allows swine operations to locate closer to wells that people used for drinking water than to golf courses. "It's a reflection of the system that ends up saying that golf courses are more important than people," he said. "We can't just protect the trees and the forests and the water-ways and the animals. We also have to protect the people" (Raleigh *News and Observer*, November 24, 1997). In simple terms, the issue appears to be individual interests versus industrial development. In more complex terms, however, it is a question of the profitable production of enough food to feed a growing population versus the quality of life for the people for whom the food is produced.

Consideration of these complex questions is relatively new. We have long been accustomed to manipulating nature to suit our own purposes. We have thought of scientific investigation and technological application as beneficial and have relied on them to make life easier, more comfortable, and more satisfying. We have long understood that new social problems result from new methods of production and distribution, and we have tried, with varying degrees of success, to cope with these problems. But we have not been prepared to deal with any disruption of the natural order. In fact, it was not until 1970 that our nation established the Environmental Protection Agency (EPA).

Raising ecological issues has been prompted by unanticipated problems in public health, growing public discomfort, unexpected shortages in desirable goods, and a growing awareness by social and physical scientists of the potential for disaster. Consequently the environmental movement has been dominated by the threat of greater problems to come, such as shortages of pure water, air, and food, natural disasters resulting from deforestation, global warming, acid rain, and hazardous waste materials. So serious are the problems that failure to take drastic measures, many people believe, may result in the destruction of life on earth. Human survival, indeed, is at stake.

The ethical issue, however, is not whether humankind will survive but rather its proper relationship to the entire created order. Are we at the center of this order? Does the environment exist for our purposes—our survival, our comfort, our use? Do we manipulate it with concern only for human well-being? Or is this order a total system of which humankind is a part? Do all elements of the system interact with one another? Do all of them—animate and inanimate, human and nonhuman, matter and energy—have value in themselves that must be respected?

For Christians the consideration of the natural order goes one step further. We see this order as ultimately theocentric. We are accustomed to thinking of our responsibilities to one another as the result of our relationship to God. We understand that all human values issue from the value of all persons to God. Thus we ask whether the value of the entire natural order is determined by its relationship to God.

To be sure, as we deal with moral issues related to the natural order, we will be concerned with all three approaches. Human survival is properly a concern for all of us, and the quality of human existence does depend on the

way in which we use the natural order. Although we will not be apocalyptic
in our approach, we will nevertheless talk about the practical effects of scientific and technological developments on human existence. In addition,
because we understand that we are creatures, a part of a created order that is
not of our making, we will be concerned with respect for everything that
exists. Ultimately, however, we will recognize that in this created order we
function within the purposes of the Creator.

THE ECOLOGICAL PROBLEM

The ecological problem is that of sustaining a growing population with finite,
limited resources. Can it be done? Late in the eighteenth century Thomas
Malthus, in his "Essay on the Principle of Population," said that it cannot,
that the constant tendency in all animated life is to increase beyond the
capacity of the earth to sustain it. As population grows, food shortages are
inevitable. War, famine, and disease are therefore inevitable phenomena,
necessary to prevent too great an increase in the population.

In the first half of the twentieth century Americans were not nearly so
pessimistic. Most scholars seemed committed to the idea that there were no
real limits to the possibilities of growth and expansion. The Western world
moved rapidly and without fear into the production of more and more goods
for a growing population whose appetites never seemed to be satisfied. Early
in the second half of the twentieth century, however, ecological problems
began to force themselves upon the attention of the public. Five days of smog
killed twenty people and injured more than fourteen thousand in Donora,
Pennsylvania, in 1948. In 1952 smog was blamed for the death of more than
four thousand people in London. An explosion of nuclear wastes in the Ural
Mountains of the Soviet Union in 1957, twenty-nine years before the accident
in Chernobyl in 1986, spread radioactive contamination over thousands of
square miles. Acid rain, produced by the release into the atmosphere of gases
from industrial plants and automobiles, began to damage animal and plant
life. Rachel Carson's *Silent Spring*, published in 1962, became a best-seller
and a rallying point for the ecology movement. From time to time Congress
enacted legislation to deal with specific environmental ills, but in 1970 the
crucial nature of the problem was recognized by the creation of the EPA.

Although we have been alerted to the problem, however, we have
never agreed on the proper approach to its solution. Some people argue that
in spite of the ecological damage produced, economic growth is necessary to
the well-being of the nation, and indeed of the world. Without it, they say, we
cannot hope to improve the conditions of the poor in our country and elsewhere and there can be no adequate provision for a growing population.

Others argue that we are not producing too much but producing in the
wrong way. They believe that a proper application of technology can increase

production without damage to the ecological system. They insist that the earth can accommodate an ever-increasing population if we increase urbanization and industrialization on a world scale. Environmental problems are seen as susceptible to a scientific solution. Still others see hope for the future in a return to a more simplified lifestyle, or a "return to Eden," by foregoing many of the benefits of science and technology. Regardless of these different approaches, however, we are compelled to acknowledge the fact that, as Robert Paehlke states it, "our society has tended to prefer wealth to health" (*Environmentalism and the Future of Progressive Politics*, p. 37).

Three closely related factors are involved in our ecological crisis. The first is the rapid growth of the world's population. It is estimated that in 1995 the total population was 5.7 billion, nearly four times the population in 1900 and an increase of 1.3 billion since 1980. The rate of growth apparently has reached its peak and is expected to decline fairly rapidly. But continued growth at a decelerating rate is anticipated until about the year 2075. In the so-called developed countries of Europe, North America, and the former Soviet Union, the growth has been declining for a number of years and now is quite slow. But about 1950 the rate began to explode in the developing countries of Africa, the Middle East, Latin America and the Caribbean, and most of Asia. The growth rate in these areas is now dropping also and is expected to decline rapidly until the end of the next century. If this projected decline does not occur, the consequences may well be a radical disruption of the balance of nature and irreparable damage to the order that sustains life on earth.

The growth rate of the world's population is directly related to a number of factors: birthrate, infant mortality rate, death rate, food supply, and lengthening life expectancy, which results from the improvement of all factors related to public health, the improvement of direct medical care, and the conquest of disease.

The distribution of the world's population is an important facet of the problem. The most densely populated areas are the developing nations, which, at present at least, are the least capable of producing the goods needed to sustain life. The developed nations that are capable of the greatest production are more sparsely populated. As a consequence, the developed nations are wealthy, and most of the people of the developing nations live in poverty. The distribution of surplus goods produced in the developed nations to the rest of the world is a problem involving not merely technology but also politics, economics, and even religion. It is a matter, therefore, that has no obvious, clear-cut solution.

The second factor in our environment crisis is the depletion of certain natural resources. In our nation we have had a long history of exploiting non-renewable resources. For decades our forests were stripped from the land without concern for replacement and without attention to flooding and soil erosion. Farmland was cultivated in ways that destroyed its future productivity. We are now destroying wetlands that sustain certain species of plants and animals and that are directly related to the health of the seas. Minerals are extracted from the earth with little consideration to the impact of mining methods on the surrounding area. Oil and coal are extracted, processed, and used as if the supply were inexhaustible. But the fact is that these resources are finite and limited, and if we continue to use them at the present rate, within the foreseeable future there will be none left. And while we are exploring other sources of energy, we give more attention to the development of nuclear energy, which itself is laden with tremendous dangers, than we do to solar energy and wind power, which we cannot deplete and which do not pollute.

The third aspect of the ecological problem, and the one that is most discussed in our day, is the pollution of the natural environment. Most apparent is what is happening to the air we breathe. Immediately after World War II we began to become aware of the smog that affected many of our major cities, such as New York, Los Angeles, Chicago, and Washington. Now almost no region of the nation is free of air pollution. Everywhere gases, dust, soot, smoke, and liquid droplets are released directly into the atmosphere by factories, power plants, cars, construction projects, and even natural erosion. Many people suffer directly from a variety of respiratory difficulties caused by the pollution, and others find that their chronic problems are compounded.

The land is being polluted in two major ways. One is the use of certain chemical fertilizers, fungicides, and insecticides. Not only are these chemicals absorbed into our foods, but also they are washed into streams and lakes and ultimately into the sea, affecting all that lives in the water. The other major type of land pollution is the disposal of waste. We produce more waste than ever before, not only because there are more people but also because each individual produces more waste materials today than in past generations. We have to deal with municipal waste and industrial waste, solid waste and liquid waste, natural waste and manufactured waste. We have hazardous waste materials, which pose particularly perplexing problems. To dispose of all this waste we use landfills, we dump waste into streams and lakes and seas, we incinerate, and we release waste directly into the atmosphere. And we store some of the hazardous waste in the ground, often in leaky containers; and we have yet to learn how to dispose of it safely. The combination of our methods of extracting materials from the earth, the runoff of chemicals used in our methods of production, and the use of the land, water, and air for the disposal of waste result in severe damage to the food supply. This, in turn, poses both an immediate threat to the health of the population and a long-range threat to the balance of nature.

BIBLICAL CONCEPTS

The people of the Bible lived much closer to nature than we do. They saw the beauty of the mountains and the sea, the flowers and the birds, the animals and those who cared for them. They saw the cycles of the seasons and the movements of the heavenly bodies. They knew the awesomeness of the storm and the tragedy of famine. They lived and died knowing how dependent they were on the world around them and on the God who controlled it.

Reflection on the relationship of humankind to the natural order was fairly common to the writers of the Old Testament. One looks in vain in the New Testament for such a discussion, however. Jesus and his earliest disciples assumed without question the validity of the basic Hebrew views. They were much more concerned about the relationship of human beings with one another than with the rest of creation. Jesus clearly lived close to nature and rejoiced in it, and in his teachings he used illustrations from it. But he apparently felt no need to reiterate what his contemporaries all knew and approved.

That basic Hebrew perspective is radically different from the modern concept of natural law, of a system that operates through self-sustaining forces and regulating principles. The Hebrews believed not in natural law but in a God who was in direct, immediate control of all things, who indeed normally operated in orderly, predictable ways but who also might alter this regularity at any time. In Hebrew thought, therefore, both the usual and the unusual, the "natural" and the "miraculous," were God's doing.

It is from this perspective that the ancient stories in Genesis 1 through 11 speak. The two creation accounts (Genesis 1:1–2:4a, 2:4b–2:25) affirm a number of beliefs about the nature of the earth and humankind's place in the created order. Properly understood, these accounts are not descriptions of a process that must be believed to be accurate in spite of scientific thought. Neither are they childlike stories that must be rejected by modern thinking people. Rather they are faith affirmations that, taken seriously, offer important guidance and hope for a world in an ecological crisis.

First, God is the creator. It is important to remember that in Hebrew thought God is not identified with nature. Whatever exists was brought into being by divine activity, but the creature is not identified with the creator; it is the handiwork of the creator. God is sovereign over all that exists. God is not *in* the wind or the rain, *in* the cycle of the seasons, *in* the fertility of the land or of animals or of people, or *in* the movements of the heavenly bodies. God is *behind* these things; God causes them to take place. They are not divine; they are the work of the Divine. Thus, in Old Testament thought, even that which appears to humankind to be evil, such as famine or flood or earthquake, is ultimately the work of God.

Second, humankind is a part of the natural order. We were created in the same process that brought all else into being (Genesis 1:1–31). Indeed, according to the older account, God created humankind from "the dust of the ground" (Genesis 2:7). We are creature, as everything else is creature. We are therefore at one with the rest of existence—with all other life, animal and plant; with all other matter, animate and inanimate; with the land and the water and the air.

Third, humankind has a uniquely important place in God's creation. On the one hand, the older account (Genesis 2:4b–2:25) affirms that God formed humankind at the beginning of the creative process and that this particular creature became a "living being" only after God breathed into it "the breath of life." The later account (Genesis 1:1–2:4a), on the other hand, portrays the formation of humankind as the last stage of creation, the climax of the whole process, almost as if bringing humankind into existence was God's ultimate objective. This passage, indeed, affirms the uniqueness of humankind by making the astounding affirmation that God created humankind "in the image of God."

Fourth, humankind is responsible to God for the care of the rest of creation. The older account says, "The Lord God took the man and put him in the garden of Eden to till it and keep it" (Genesis 2:15). (The word *man* is used here because, according to this account, woman had not yet been formed.) A prime element in this responsibility is the naming of the animals. In the later creation account this responsibility of humankind is seen in God's instruction to the human beings, "Be fruitful and multiply, and fill the earth and subdue it; and have dominion over the fish of the sea and over the birds of the air and over every living thing that moves upon the earth" (Genesis 1:28).

Fifth, everything that God made is good. The author of the later account concluded the description of each stage in the creative process with the words, "And God saw that it was good." At the conclusion of the final stage of the creative process, the writer observed that "God saw everything that he had made, and indeed, it was very good" (1:31). In neither the older account nor the later one is there any hint of a dichotomy of matter and spirit. There is no suggestion that one is hostile to the other, no dualism in which one is a demonic force and the other an angelic one. Creation is good because it is the work of God.

The story of the Garden of Eden (Genesis 3) deals with the dark side of human nature and with its impact on God's good creation. This account affirms the universality of human sin. All human beings are the man and the woman in Eden who choose to defy the clearly stated command of God. All human beings act on the basis of self-interest even as they try to deny their responsibility for their own choices and actions.

Of particular importance for our purposes is the consequence of the sin of the man and the woman. Their punishment is a disruption of the natural order. Whereas ideally the creatures that God has made should live in harmony with one another, there is now enmity between them. Whereas human beings, like all other creatures, are intended to "be fruitful and multiply," the natural experience of childbearing is disrupted by pain. Even worse, there is conflict between the man and the woman, who were made in the image of God, and one dominates the other. And finally, the cultivation of the delightful garden in which God placed humankind has become a burden, a task at which people must labor against great odds until death. Human sin disrupts the harmony of God's good creation.

The flood story (Genesis 6–9) affirms God's redemptive work in a society that has gone wrong. Although the idea of punishment seems to dominate the story, it is not punishment in the sense of vengeance but in the sense of redemption and restoration. Through Noah and his descendants God is moving to a re-creation of the world. God's commands to Noah when the flood had ended were much like God's commands to the man and the woman in the Garden of Eden (Genesis 8:17–19; 9:1–3). The new covenant, of which the rainbow is the symbol, is to be an "everlasting covenant between God and every living creature of all flesh that is upon the earth" (Genesis 9:16).

These themes from Genesis 1 through 11 are reiterated constantly throughout the rest of Scripture. The historians, the prophets, and the poets of the Old Testament all had their own emphases and their distinctive ideas. They focused, of course, on God's self-disclosure in the history of the Hebrew people. And in their work these convictions about God and humankind and the world keep reappearing. The writers of the New Testament focused on the person and work of Jesus. They dealt with the origins and the expansion of the church as extensions of that presence and that work. But they too, nearly all of them Jewish by birth and rearing, accepted the validity of this ancient understanding of the relationship of God to the world in which they lived.

THEOLOGICAL REFLECTION

To what extent is the treatment of the natural order that characterizes Western society, with all of its beneficial results and all of its concomitant problems, an outgrowth of the Hebrew-Christian tradition? Some writers trace what they call "the myth of human dominance" to the biblical idea that humankind was instructed to "subdue the earth" and "have dominion" over it. Clearly it is true that the scientific methods by which we have come to know more about the natural order and the technologies by which we have exploited it have developed in the region of the world known as Christendom. The extent to which this approach has been fostered by religious teaching and tradition, however, is subject to debate. Recognizing, at any rate, that we face the present situation from the perspective of our own faith, let us consider the religious implications and look for helpful directions.

We might begin with the fundamental biblical insistence that God is not to be identified with nature but rather works in and through nature. We properly talk about respect for nature, perhaps even about reverence for nature, but we do not deify nature. The natural order is not absolute; it is derivative, conditional, and subordinate to God. In traditional terms, this means that God is transcendent. God is the power behind the existence of the world and the continued operation of the world. God alone is the source of value, and God alone directs the whole world toward the realization of its possibilities.

Yet this God who is behind the natural order is also at work in it. In traditional theological terms, this is the **immanence** of God in nature. God interacts with all of nature, including humankind, in the movement toward redemption, restoration, wholeness. God cares, loves, suffers, and struggles with the whole of creation. God is still creating and still redeeming.

The natural order is not an undisturbed, utopian world in which all creatures live together in peace and harmony. The lion and the lamb do not in fact lie down together, and they never have. One lives at the expense of the other. Throughout history various species of plant and animal life have come into being, have survived for a time, and then have been destroyed by changes in the natural order. The surface of the earth has been altered by the forces of wind and rain, by volcanos and earthquakes, by the constant shifting of the matter that constitutes the earth. In many of these changes there have been destructive violence and disaster. Flood, famine, windstorm, extremes of cold and heat, disease, pestilence, and the like have forced people in all ages and in all climes to realize that nature is not always benevolent.

Yet the elements of nature—earth, water, air, the various species of life—are important to God and therefore must be respected by humankind. Perhaps this attitude was easy in biblical days. Then, people had no concept of natural law; rather they believed that everything that happened was caused by God's direct action. Psalm 19 is a wonderful expression of reverent awe of nature, which is seen as a reflection of God's presence in the world. With that attitude, the biblical writers could regard even natural disasters as the work of God, intended to protect the children of God in some instances and to discipline them in others, but always under God's control.

Respect for nature is more difficult to maintain in our world, where we see far more of the artificial, more of the work of humankind, than we do of the natural. For most of us, the natural world seems remote because of the way we interfere with nature, the way we use it and the way we protect ourselves from it. We have little opportunity to see the sun and the moon and the stars, the mountains, and the rivers and the seas. We see buildings, automobiles, grocery stores, amusement parks, and television. We see the works of God only as they have been modified by the work of humankind. Humankind, however, needs to look beyond the work of human hands and recognize the intrinsic worth in everything that God has created. This does not mean that we must reject science and technology. It does mean that we need to learn to use the scientific method and technological facilities in ways that respect and preserve the entire created order.

Respect for the created order, however, cannot ignore the fact that in the world of nature one species uses another, preys on another, or lives at the expense of the other. Nature is a hierarchy in which generally the more complex forms of life use the less complex ones. Human beings, the most complex of creatures, manipulate the whole of creation in their own effort to survive and to live in comfort. This fact is not challenged by Scripture. The

Bible assumes that humankind is at the crown of creation, only "a little lower than God." This does not justify the wanton destruction of anything that exists or even the reckless use of the things around us. Much of Scripture places restrictions on our use of the land and its resources. It assumes that within appropriate bounds humankind may "subdue the earth," may, in other words, make use of other forms of life and existence.

This kind of thing must be said with great care. We are in fact an integral part of nature and kin to all other creatures. Like all else that exists, we are finite and limited. There are energies at work in all other forms of life, as in us, that we do not understand and that we do not own or control. Although Scripture speaks of a "breath of life" in human beings, which it does not attribute to other creatures, it also speaks of human beings as created from the "dust of the ground," the same material from which all other living beings are created. Scripture implies therefore that we are appropriately as concerned about the right to life of other animals and plants as we are about that right for humankind.

If we focus on the high place in creation that is occupied by humankind, we must recognize it as one of responsibility and not ownership. In dealing with the natural order, human beings are not dealing with something over which they have an absolute claim. They are dealing with something that belongs to God, over which God has total authority, which is to be used in a way consistent with God's purposes and interests. The final word in what we do is not ours but God's. That purpose may include our own survival and well-being, but it is not limited to that.

We are accustomed to speaking of creation as if it were something that occurred eons ago and was completed at a specific point in time. It is more accurate, however, to understand creation as an ongoing process. God is still at work creatively in the world and in the universe as a whole. In scientific terms, this means that the world is still evolving, that some forms of life are disappearing and others emerging, indeed, that the entire universe is pulsing with life. Human beings may properly view their place in the world as one of cooperation with God in this creative process. A fundamental moral implication is that in the universe a struggle is going on between the forces of creativity and the forces of destruction. If the creative process is the work of God, human involvement in that work is a fundamental moral issue.

We must therefore take seriously the biblical understanding of human sinfulness. It is entirely possible that some, perhaps even much, of what we human beings have done and are doing is in opposition to God's creative purposes. In 1972 John B. Cobb, Jr., raised that possibility in a book entitled *Is It Too Late?* Like many other writers of the period, he was a bit apocalyptic in discussing the ecology of the earth, suggesting that we were in grave danger of bringing the total process of life to an end. He was not nearly as pessimistic as some, however, for his answer to his own question was no. The question remains important, nevertheless. Although it is not yet too late, we may still do irreparable damage to the natural order. That possibility is rooted in our sinful nature—in our tendency to regard all creation as ours, to act on the basis of self-interest, to take the short-term view, to ignore the rights of others, and to ignore the purposes of God.

Because humankind does not stand apart from nature but exists as a part of it and in solidarity with it, our sinfulness affects all of nature. As Henlee Barnette says, "Both biblical and biological views of nature see the interconnection and interdependence of man and his environment. Man is so intrinsically related to nature that when he sins against God, nature suffers; and when he obeys God, nature rejoices" (*The Church and the Ecological Crisis*, p. 37).

In our approach to other problems, we have operated on the assumption that love (*agape*) is the fundamental requirement. Those other problems, however, have involved relationships between human beings. Is it possible to extend the concept of *agape* to our relationship to nonhuman existence? The answer is yes because God is the source of all that exists, and the nature of God is love. It was said of all creation, not just of humankind, that "God saw that it was good." Jesus said that not a sparrow falls without God knowing about it and that God feeds the birds, which "neither sow nor reap nor gather into barns." Jesus talked about God caring for "the lilies of the field" which "neither toil nor spin." He was reassuring people, of course, about God's care for them. Nevertheless, he gave that reassurance by citing God's care for the more helpless parts of creation. Was St. Francis, then, really too simplistic in his devotion to birds and animals, or was he showing a Godlike love for creation? It certainly would appear appropriate for modern people, scholars and laypeople alike, to operate on the assumption that the created order is a valid object of concern not merely because of our own self-interest but also because of the inherent value of everything that exists.

Of course one good often has to be sacrificed to another. The lion is not evil because, rather than lying down with the lamb, it feeds upon the lamb. The lion, after all, is doing what is natural for lions and indeed is necessary for the survival of lions. Presumably the lion never thinks about what it ought or ought not to do or about the inherent value of the lamb, which unfortunately must be sacrificed so that the lion can live. But human beings, so Scripture teaches, are blessed with a quality that apparently nothing else in creation has a sense of morality. Human beings do raise the question of right and wrong. They ask whether it is appropriate for them to kill lions, and if they conclude that it is appropriate, they consider the circumstances that make it so. They can ask about the value of the lion in a way that the lion cannot ask about the lamb. Only human beings can relate to other beings on the basis of love. Thus it may be appropriate for human beings to use other parts of creation—animals, plants, inanimate objects—but not appropriate for them to abuse or wantonly destroy them. To use other parts of creation is not necessarily to say that they have no worth on their own; it is only to recognize that one good is sacrificed on behalf of another.

SUGGESTIONS FOR INVOLVEMENT

We begin with the recognition that concern for the ecology is a fundamental moral issue. We are not accustomed to thinking in this way. We tend to believe that given the resources available, there is no limit to the possibilities of scientific research and technological development. And we have assumed that we are free to do anything that we have the know-how to do. The fundamental question, however, is not what we can do but what we ought to do. The answer to this question depends on our basic beliefs about the universe and our place in it. Scott I. Paradise has suggested the following revision of certain common religious beliefs which he thinks is necessary for a satisfactory solution to our ecological problems ("Rehabilitation for Cosmic Outlaws," in Stone, ed., *A New Ethic for a New Earth*, pp. 133–142):

1. "Only man and the things he treasures have any value" must be replaced by "All things have value."
2. "The universe exists for man's exclusive and unconditional use" must be replaced by "Man has been given responsibility for the earth."
3. "In production and consumption, man finds his major fulfillment" must be replaced by "In producing and consuming, man finds only a small part of his humanity."
4. "Production and consumption must increase endlessly" must be replaced by "Improvement in the quality of life takes precedence over increasing the quantity of material production."
5. "The earth's resources are unlimited" must be replaced by "Material resources are limited and are to be used carefully and cherished."
6. "A major purpose of government is to make it easy for individuals and corporations to exploit the environment for the amassing of wealth and power" must be replaced by "A major purpose of government is to regulate the exercise of property rights and to supervise a planning process that will prevent the impairment of the quality of the environment."

The problems we are discussing are essentially social and therefore must be dealt with by society as a whole. The conservation of natural resources—forests, wetlands, minerals, water, the atmosphere—depends on public policy. Standards for the safe use of chemicals in pest control and in increased production must be set and enforced at the public level. The disposal of the waste produced in homes, businesses, and industries of the nation has to be accomplished with the interests of the entire population in mind. Individuals working alone, and even industries working alone, cannot accomplish these tasks. Even with the best of intentions, no individual or corporation can deal with the massive issues that affect the entire population and the resources on which the world depends.

If it is society as a whole that must deal with the issues, effective action can be taken only through the structures of power in society. Specific businesses and corporations are required by their own self-interest to maintain certain standards. In addition, the persons responsible for corporate decisions may act responsibly and with great concern for the welfare of the public. Many businesses and corporations, therefore, can and do have policies designed to safeguard the public and preserve natural resources. But their primary purpose is to make a profit, and they cannot continue to operate if they do not do so. Consequently, for them the bottom line ultimately determines policies; that is, while they may try to operate with the broader interests of the public in mind, that is not their primary concern.

No structure of power is more important in dealing with environmental concerns than government. At all levels of government, from the local to the national, legal regulation of the use of natural resources is necessary for the common good. Although legislation and policing are not the entire solution, they are powerful and indispensable elements of it. The government is concerned with the interests of all the people, as no business or corporation is. The government has a comprehensive view of all the issues, as no business or corporation does. In dealing with environmental concerns, of course, the government must not only respect but also guard the rights of individuals. Yet it can and must take actions that are in the interests of the group as a whole. Individuals who are concerned about ecological issues may properly work through the government to arrive at relevant policies.

Other structures of power may also be used effectively by people concerned with the ecology. No agency of our society reaches more people and has a more profound impact on them than does the educational system. Although knowledge does not necessarily lead to action, wise action cannot be taken without a good understanding of the problem and possible approaches to rectify it. Courses in the schools to educate children and young people on ecological concerns can be of great value. More valuable, however, would be the inclusion of appropriate information in courses that are already part of the curriculum. Such information is clearly directly pertinent to social studies and the sciences but also might appropriately be incorporated in other subjects such as the humanities and the arts.

The power of the communications media is subject to debate. Many people argue that television and radio and the press do not shape public opinion but only reflect public taste. If that is the case, businesses and industries are wasting their money on advertising. Most people realize that although the media do not necessarily shape public opinion, they do affect it. Their effectiveness can be seen in successful appeals for help for those in disaster areas or in personal crises. Support for long-term projects may be more difficult to secure, but it is both possible and necessary.

Religious institutions are another well-established and influential structure. Because of their voluntary nature, they do not reach as many people as do the government and the schools. Yet also because of their voluntary nature, their influence on the people involved in them may be even greater. To religious people the concepts of reverence, stewardship, and duty are important. If they come to see the relationship of these ideals to ecological issues, they will begin to act together for a solution. This is not a matter of using the church for partisan concerns; it is a matter of churchpeople expressing their faith through concerted action on a fundamentally moral issue.

There are, of course, other voluntary agencies through which interested persons can and do work, such as organizations concerned with wildlife, pure energy, disease control and relief, and other numerous causes. These agencies have an outstanding record of effectiveness in alerting the public to specific issues and helping to arrive at meaningful solutions. While no one can be effectively involved in every agency that invites support, everyone can choose certain agencies through which to work. As people work through these special-interest groups, they need to keep a broad perspective. Ultimately what we are concerned with is not the spotted owl, the bobwhite, the manatee, the California condor, the bald eagle, or the mission blue butterfly. What is at stake is the whole complex of which all these species are a part. When we claim that "the whole earth is the Lord's," we are affirming not so much that every species belongs to the Lord but that the entire world in its wholeness is God's. Harold K. Schilling notes that this understanding involves the recognition that

1. The entire world constitutes one integrated ecosystem.
2. Each entity in the world exists in and is defined by interrelationships with all other entities.
3. In all of the entities of the world there is a drive toward unity. Without that drive, "there would be no parenthood, brotherhood, friendship, citizenship; no language and literature, no science and philosophy, no jurisprudence and economics; no knowledge, or wisdom, or loyalty and love. All of these qualities are strictly social in kind, and they are not available or possible to the isolated individual who is not 'in community.'"
4. Mind and spirit are not unique to humankind but are characteristic of the entire ecosystem. ("The Whole Earth is the Lord's: Toward a Holistic Ethic," in Ian Barbour, ed., *Earth Might Be Fair,* pp. 104–106)

Our approach to nature, then, must be holistic; that is, we must recognize that it is not merely the parts of the system that matter but also the whole, the system of interrelationships itself. Whatever maximizes wholeness is morally responsible and right, and whatever breaks or destroys wholeness is wrong. Inevitably, of course, there will be some conflict between what is best for the individual and what contributes to the common good. In other words, there is always tension between the immediate needs of individuals and the group's need for the preservation of natural resources. Our efforts, therefore, must be directed toward *the individual in community.*

Cooperative involvement with other people working within the structures of power is an essential expression of our sense of moral responsibility. But there is another side to the ecological issue. Individual decision and action are vital to personal integrity. At the same time, they may make an impact on the community at large. Even though they may not be effective in bringing about immediate social change or determining the fate of any specific element in the environment, they are important expressions of faith and concern. Individual activism may include the following:

1. Learning as much as possible about problems and policies, both on a local and on a national scale
2. Examining one's own lifestyle and adjusting one's own behavior by

    a. Buying and using nonpolluting products
    b. Recycling
    c. Using mass transit, carpooling, bicycling, or walking
    d. Economizing on the use of energy and of water in the household
    e. Buying and using reusable materials and avoiding throwaway products

3. Participating in the government process by voting and by influencing elected and appointed officials
4. Working through voluntary environmental organizations

The ultimate moral issue for Christians is not whether the spotted owl will survive. It is not whether humankind will survive. It is not even whether the world itself will survive. The ultimate moral question concerns the relationship of human beings to God. When Jesus was asked, "Which commandment is the greatest of all?" he emphasized the love for God. From that fundamental relationship comes all responsibility to God. As related to the natural order, our basic moral duty to God is the responsible care of all of God's creation.

In practical terms this does not mean that we use God to support our concern for nature. Rather it means that our love for God expresses itself in our concern for the vitality and the wholeness of the created order. It means that we cooperate with God, the Creator and Redeemer, in God's acts of love. As we see God's presence in the natural world and as we experience God's redemptive work, we respond through our own efforts to show that "the earth is the Lord's, and all that is in it."

QUESTIONS AND TOPICS FOR DISCUSSION

1. Suppose the unemployment rate in your area is four times the national rate. An industry proposes to build a manufacturing plant that will employ many people but will pollute the atmosphere and the major river of the region. Will you encourage or oppose the industry? Why?
2. Is the right to life of human beings greater than the right to life of nonhuman beings? Why or why not?
3. Should the survival of humankind be our ultimate goal in deciding how to treat the natural order? Why or why not?

4. Should smoking be prohibited where people work in groups? In public transportation? In public meetings? Explain your reasons.
5. Should the government take steps to encourage the use of public transportation? To limit the use of gasoline in private automobiles? Why or why not?

RECOMMENDATIONS FOR FURTHER READING

COBB, JOHN B., *Sustainability*. New York: Orbis, 1994.

HESSEL, DIETER T., ed., *Theology for Earth Community*. New York: Orbis, 1996.

LINDZEY, ANDREW, *Christianity and the Rights of Animals*. New York: Crossroad, 1987.

McDANIEL, JAY B., *Of God and Pelicans*. Louisville, Ky.: Westminster/John Knox, 1989.

NASH, RODERICK FRAZIER, *The Rights of Nature*. Madison: University of Wisconsin, 1989.

RASMUSSEN, LARRY L., *Earth Community, Earth Ethics*. New York: Orbis, 1996.

VANDYKE, FRED, DAVID C. MAHAN, and JOSEPH K. SHELDON, *Redeeming Creation*. Downers Grove, Ill.: InterVarsity Press, 1996.

Glossary

Affirmative action. Giving preference in employment to members of minority groups in an effort to overcome the impact of past discriminatory practices.

Agape. "Christian love"; a deep-seated, active concern for the good of another person.

Apocalyptic. Having to do with a sudden revelation or sudden unveiling of God's power; usually associated with the end of the present world order.

Autonomous. Self-governing; undertaken or carried on without outside control.

Christocentric. Religious belief that focuses on the person of Christ.

Covenant. Agreement entered into by two or more parties; the promises God makes to God's people and the demands God imposes on them.

Decalogue. Ten Commandments.

Deontological. Referring to movement from a basic obligation. Deontological ethical systems teach that some acts are morally obligatory without regard to their consequences for human welfare.

Desegregation. Elimination of separate institutional services for different ethnic groups.

Deuteronomic. Having to do with "the second law;" having to do with the reinterpretation of the Law in the first half of the sixth century B.C.E.

Duty. Conduct required on moral grounds.

Ecclesiastical. Having to do with institutional religion.

Ecology. Relationships between living organisms and their environment.

Eschatology. Doctrine of "the end"; teachings concerning the end of the world or the end of history.

Ethical monotheism. Belief that there is only one God who rules the entire world and who makes moral demands on humankind.

Ethics. Study of good and bad, right and wrong, in human conduct.

Euthanasia. Literally, "good death"; mercy killing; deliberate termination of the life of a person who is suffering great pain from an incurable disease.

Evangelicalism. Theological perspective in Christianity that emphasizes a conversion experience, the authority of the Bible, and the acceptance of the miraculous and supernatural in Scripture.

Feminism. Movement seeking full freedom and equality for women in society.

Fundamentalism. Theological perspective in Christianity that focuses on biblical literalism.

Gemara. A compilation of the discussions, interpretations, and explanations of the Jewish oral law.

Gentile. Non-Jewish.

Grace. God's spontaneous, free, unmerited love for human beings; God's activity in and on behalf of human beings.

Halakah (Halacha). Literally, "the way to walk"; traditional Jewish legal code of moral and ethical behavior.

Heteronomous. Subject to external control; governed by an external force or power.

Immanence. God's presence or action in the natural order.

Incarnation. The doctrine that in Jesus Christ God entered fully into experience, that Jesus was uniquely "the Son of God."

Inerrancy. The teaching that there are no errors of any kind in the Bible; the insistence that all biblical statements, not only about religious and spiritual matters, but also about history and science, are entirely correct and reliable.

Integration. Blending of two or more distinct ethnic groups; dealing with people without regard to group distinctions.

Koinonia. Greek word variously translated as "community," "fellowship," and "church."

Law. Torah (Jewish); the first five books of the Old Testament; sometimes called the Books of Moses.

Literalism. Belief that Scripture was given directly by God and that its teachings and narratives must be accepted exactly as they are presented.

Liturgy. Ceremony of worship.

Messiah. "The anointed one"; the one to be sent by God to lead the Jewish people (and the world) toward a time of peace and restoration.

Mishnah. The first compilation of the Jewish oral law.

Morals. Literally, "custom" or "way of life"; codes of conduct of individuals and groups.

Moral theology. The systematic study of ethics.

Natural law. In Roman Catholic thought, the unchangeable regularity that can be observed in nature.

Prophets. Second division of the Old Testament; those books that report the messages of the persons who "spoke forth" for God.

Restrictive covenant. Agreement not to sell or rent property to persons of a minority group.

Sexism. Discrimination against women.

Stereotype. Standardized mental picture that represents uncritical acceptance of an oversimplified opinion.

Synoptic gospels. The first three gospels of the New Testament, which have a great deal of material in common and which often contain similar phrasing.

Talmud. The authoritative body of Jewish tradition, consisting of oral law (Mishnah) and discussion (Gemara).

Teleological. From **Teleology**.

Teleology. Literally, "theory of the end or the purpose"; belief that there is a design or purpose operating in the universe as a whole.

Theocentric. Literally, "God-centered"; teaching that God is actively involved in the historic process; teaching that God, not humankind, determines process and value.

Theocracy. Government by God.

Torah. The Law; the first five books of the Bible; sometimes used to include also other sacred literature and tradition.

Transcendence. God's separateness from the natural order; God's superiority to the natural order.

Value. Intrinsic worth; that which is desirable or worthy of esteem for its own sake.

Vatican II. Second Ecumenical Council of the Roman Catholic Church, convened by Pope John XXIII, meeting from 1962 through 1965, to deal with a wide variety of theological, ecclesiastical, and moral issues.

Wisdom literature. Portion of the Writings of the Old Testament; contains practical, down-to-earth advice on life.

Writings. Third section of the Old Testament; all the books that are neither Law nor Prophets.

Bibliography

Adams, Sheri. *What the Bible Really Says about Women*. Macon, Ga.: Smyth and Helwys, 1994.

Albrecht, Gloria. *The Character of Our Communities*. Nashville: Abingdon, 1995.

Alliance of Baptists. *A Clear Voice: Report of the Task Force on Human Sexuality*. Washington: Alliance of Baptists, 1999.

America's Original Sin. Washington, D.C.: Sojourners, 1992.

Arthur, John, ed. *Morality and Moral Controversies*. 4th ed. Englewood Cliffs: Prentice Hall, 1995.

Ashe, Arthur. *Days of Grace*. New York: Knopf, 1993.

Ashmore, Robert B. *Building a Moral System*. Englewood Cliffs: Prentice Hall, 1987.

Barndt, Joseph. *Dismantling Racism*. Minneapolis: Augsburg Fortress, 1991.

Barnette, Henlee. *The Church and the Ecological Crisis*. Grand Rapids: Eerdmans, 1972.

Barry, Vincent. *Moral Aspects of Health Care*. Belmont, Calif.: Wadsworth, 1982.

Bates, Ulku, et al. *Women's Realities, Women's Choices*. New York: Oxford University Press, 1995.

Beach, Waldo. *Christian Ethics in the Protestant Tradition*. Atlanta: John Knox, 1988.

Bedau, Hugo Adam. *The Death Penalty in America*. New York: Oxford, 1998.

Behrman, Jack N. *Essays on Ethics in Business and the Professions*. Englewood Cliffs: Prentice Hall, 1988.

Bloesch, Donald G. *Freedom for Obedience*. New York: Harper and Row, 1987.

Boff, Leonardo, and Clodovis Boff. *Introducing Liberation Theology*. New York: Orbis, 1987.

Bornkamm, Gunter. *Jesus of Nazareth*. New York: Harper and Row, 1960.

Borowitz, Eugene B., ed. *Reform Jewish Ethics and the Halakhah*. West Orange, N.J.: Behrman House, 1994.

Brody, Baruch A., and N. Tristam Englehardt, Jr. *Bioethics*. Englewood Cliffs: Prentice Hall, 1987.

Brooks, Roy L. *Integration or Separatism?* Cambridge: Harvard University Press, 1996.

Brown, Marvin T. *The Ethical Process*. Englewood Cliffs: Prentice Hall, 1998.

Brown, Montague. *The Quest for Moral Foundations*. Washington: Georgetown University Press, 1996.

Brown, Robert McAfee. *Liberation Theology.* Louisville, Ky.: Westminster/John Knox, 1993.

———. *Making Peace in the Global Village.* Philadelphia: Westminster, 1981.

———. *Religion and Violence.* 2d ed. Philadelphia: Westminster, 1987.

———. *Saying Yes and Saying No.* Philadelphia: Westminster, 1986.

Bruggemann, Walter. *Interpretation and Obedience.* Minneapolis: Augsburg Fortress, 1991.

Brunner, Emil. *The Divine Imperative.* Philadelphia: Westminster, 1947.

Buttry, Daniel. *Christian Peacemaking.* Valley Forge, Penn.: Judson, 1994.

Cahill, Lisa Sowle. *Between the Sexes.* Philadelphia: Fortress, 1985.

———. *Sex, Gender, and Christian Ethics.* New York: Cambridge University Press, 1996.

Cahill, Lisa Sowle, and James F. Childress. *Christian Ethics.* Cleveland: Pilgrim, 1996.

Cannon, Katie G. *Black Womanist Ethics.* Atlanta: Scholars Press, 1988.

Carter, Jimmy. *Talking Peace.* New York: Dutton, 1993.

Cauthen, Kenneth. *The Ethics of Assisted Death.* Lima, Oh.: CSS Publishing Company, 1999.

Cobb, John B., Jr. *Is It Too Late?* Beverly Hills, Calif.: Bruce, 1972.

———. *Matters of Life and Death.* Louisville, Ky.: Westminster/John Knox, 1991.

———. *Sustainability.* New York: Orbis, 1994.

Cochran, B. H., et al. *Task Force Report on Same-Gender Covenants.* Raleigh, N.C.: Pullen Memorial Baptist Church, 1993.

Cohon, Samuel S. *Judaism—A Way of Life.* Cincinnati: Union of American Hebrew Congregations, 1948.

Cole-Turner, Ronald, ed. *Human Cloning: Religious Responses.* Louisville, Ky.: Westminster/John Knox, 1997.

Cone, James H. *A Black Theology of Liberation.* Twentieth Anniversary Edition. New York: Orbis, 1986.

———. *For My People.* New York: Orbis, 1984.

———. *God of the Oppressed.* New York: Seabury, 1975.

Council of Bishops of the United Methodist Church. *In Defense of Creation.* Nashville: Graded Press, 1986.

Countryman, L. William. *Dirt, Greed, and Sex.* Philadelphia: Fortress, 1988.

Cowan, Paul, and Rachel Cowan. *Mixed Blessings.* New York: Penguin, 1988.

Crites, Laura L., and Winifred L. Hepperle. *Women, the Courts, and Equality.* Newbury Park, Calif.: Sage, 1987.

Cullman, Oscar. The *State in the New Testament.* New York: Scribner, 1956.

Cutler, Donald R., ed. *Updating Life and Death.* Boston: Beacon, 1969.

Dailey, Robert H. *Introduction to Moral Theology.* New York: Bruce, 1971.

Daly, Herman E., and John B. Cobb, Jr. *For the Common Good.* 2d ed. Boston: Beacon, 1994.

Daly, Lois K., ed. *Feminist Theological Ethics.* Louisville, Ky.: Westminster/John Knox, 1994.

Deckard, Barbara Sinclair. *The Women's Movement.* 3d ed. New York: Harper and Row, 1975.

DeLangue, Nicholas. *Judaism.* New York: Oxford, 1986.

DeWolfe, L. Harold. *Crime and Justice in America.* New York: Harper and Row, 1975.

————. *What Americans Should Do about Crime*. New York: Harper and Row, 1976.

DeYoung, Curtiss Paul. *Coming Together*. Valley Forge, Penn.: Judson, 1995.

Donaldson, Thomas, and Patricia H. Werhane. *Ethical Issues in Business*. 3d ed. Englewood Cliffs: Prentice Hall, 1988.

Dosick, Wayne. *Living Judaism*. New York: Harper, 1995.

Drinan, Robert F. *Beyond the Nuclear Freeze*. New York: Seabury, 1983.

Emerson, Michael O., and Christian Smith. *Divided by Faith*. New York: Oxford University Press, 2000.

Englehardt, H. Tristam. *Bioethics and Secular Humanism*. London: SCM, 1991.

Erickson, Brad, ed. *Call to Action*. San Francisco: Sierra Club Books, 1990.

Eskridge, William N., *Gay Law*. Cambridge: Harvard University Press, 1999.

Farley, John E. *Majority-Minority Relations*. 3d ed. New York: Simon and Schuster, 1995.

Fewell, Dianna Nolan, and David M. Gunn. *Gender, Power, and Promise*. Nashville: Abingdon, 1993.

Fletcher, Joseph. *Morals and Medicine*. Boston: Beacon, 1960.

————. *Situation Ethics*. Philadelphia: Westminster, 1966.

Freund, Richard A. *Understanding Jewish Ethics*. San Francisco: Edward Mellen, 1990.

Friedan, Betty. *The Feminine Mystique*. New York: Dell, 1963.

Fromer, Margot Joan. *Ethical Issues in Sexuality and Reproduction*. St. Louis: Mosby, 1983.

Funk, Robert W., and Roy W. Hoover. *The Five Gospels*. New York: Macmillan, 1993.

Gensler, Harry S. *Ethics: A Contemporary Introduction*. New York: Routledge, 1998.

Geyer, Alan. *Christianity and the Super Powers*. Nashville: Abingdon, 1990.

Gonsalves, Milton A. *Fagothey's Right and Reason*. 8th ed. St. Louis: Times Mirror/Mosby, 1985.

Grenz, Stanley J. *Sexual Ethics: An Evangelical Perspective*. Louisville, Ky.: Westminster/John Knox, 1990 (1997).

Guroian, Vigen. *Life's Living Toward Dying*. Grand Rapids: Eerdmans, 1996.

Gustafson, James M. *Ethics from a Theocentric Perspective. Vol. 1, Theology and Ethics*. Chicago: University of Chicago Press, 1981.

————. *Ethics from a Theocentric Perspective. Vol. 2, Ethics and Theology*. Chicago: University of Chicago Press, 1984.

————. *Protestant and Roman Catholic Ethics*. Chicago: University of Chicago Press, 1978.

Gutierrez, Gustavo. *A Theology of Liberation*. Rev. ed. Maryknoll, N.Y.: Orbis, 1988.

Haring, Bernard. *The Law of Christ*. Westminster, Md.: Newman Press, 1966.

————. *Toward a Christian Moral Theology*. Notre Dame, Ind.: University of Notre Dame Press, 1966.

Harmon, Gilbert. *The Nature of Morality*. New York: Oxford University Press, 1994.

Hauerwas, Stanley. *A Community of Character*. Notre Dame, Ind.: University of Notre Dame Press, 1994.

————. *Against the Nations*. New York: Harper and Row, 1985.

————. *Character and Christian Life*. Notre Dame, Ind.: University of Notre Dame Press, 1994.

Hauerwas, Stanley, and William H. Willimon. *Resident Aliens*. Nashville: Abingdon, 1989.

Hayes, Diana L. *And Still We Rise*. New York: Paulist, 1996.

Hayes, Richard B. The *Moral Vision of the New Testament*. New York: Harper Collins, 1996.

Hessel, Dieter T., ed. *Theology for Earth Community*. New York: Orbis, 1996.

Higginson, Richard. *Dilemmas*. Louisville, Ky.: Westminster/John Knox, 1988.

Hollenbach, David. *Justice, Peace, and Human Rights*. New York: Crossroad, 1988.

Hospers, John. *Human Conduct*. New York: Harcourt Brace Jovanavich, 1972.

Hovannisian, Richard G. *Ethics in Islam*. Malibu, Calif.: Udena Publications, 1985.

Howell, Joseph H., and William Frederick Sale, eds. *Life Choices*. Washington: Georgetown University Press, 2000.

Hughes, James W., and Joseph J. Seneca. *America's Demographic Tapestry*. New Brunswick: Rutgers University Press, 1999.

Humanist Manifestos I and II. Buffalo, N.Y.: Prometheus Books, 1973.

Hunt, Arnold D., Robert Crotty, and Marie Crotty. *Ethics of World Religions*. Rev. ed. San Diego: Greenhaven, 1991.

Hunt, Morton. *Gay*. New York: Pocket Books, 1973.

Hunt, Susan, and Peggy Hutcheson. *Leadership for Women in the Church*. New York: Harper Collins, 1991.

Hunter College Women's Studies. *Women's Realities, Women's Choices*. 2d ed. New York: Oxford, 1995.

Jackson, Chris. *The Black Christian's Guide to Dating and Sexuality*. New York: Harper Collins, 1998.

Jacobs, Louis. *Jewish Personal and Social Ethics*. West Orange, N.J.: Behrman, 1990.

Jacobs, Michael. *The Politics of the Real World*. London: Earthscan, 2000.

John Paul II. *The Gospel of Life [Evangelum Vitae]*. New York: Random House, 1995.

Kaufman, Gordon D. *Theology for a Nuclear Age*. Philadelphia: Westminster, 1985.

Kidder, Rushworth M. *How Good People Make Tough Choices*. New York: Simon and Schuster, 1996.

Kilner, John F., Nigel M. de S. Cameron, and David L. Schiedermayer, eds. *Bioethics and the Future of Medicine*. Grand Rapids: Eerdmans, 1995.

King, Martin Luther, Jr. *Stride toward Freedom*. New York: Harper and Row, 1958.

————. *Why We Can't Wait*. New York: Harper and Row, 1964.

Kitano, Harry, and Roger Daniels. *Asian Americans: The Emerging Minority*. Englewood Cliffs: Prentice Hall, 1988.

Kung, Hans, and Karl-Josef Kuschel, eds. *A Global Ethic: The Declaration of the Parliament of the World's Religions*. New York: Continuum International Publishing Group, 1994.

Kurtz, Paul. *In Defense of Secular Humanism*. Buffalo, N.Y.: Prometheus, 1983.

Lammers, Stephen E., and Allen Verhey, eds. *On Moral Medicine*. Grand Rapids: Eerdmans, 1987.

Lehmann, Paul. *Ethics in a Christian Context*. New York: Harper and Row, 1963.

Levine, Martin P., ed. *Gay Men*. New York: Harper and Row, 1979.

Lifton, Robert, and Greg Mitchell. *Who Owns Death?* New York: Harper Collins, 2000.

Lincoln, C. Eric. *Race, Religion, and the Continuing American Dilemma*. New York: Hill and Wang, 1999.

Linzey, Andrew. *Christianity and the Rights of Animals*. New York: Crossroad, 1987.

Loesch, Judi. "Unmarried Couples Shouldn't Live Together." *U.S. Catholic,* July 1985, pp. 16–17.

Long, Edward LeRoy. *War and Conscience in America.* Philadelphia: Westminster, 1968.

McDaniel, Jay B. *Of God and Pelicans.* Louisville, Ky.: Westminster/John Knox, 1989.

McGee, Glenn, ed.. *The Human Cloning Debate.* Berkeley: Berkeley Hills Books, 2000.

McKenzie, Steven L. *All God's Children.* Louisville, Ky.: Westminster/John Knox, 1997.

McKenzie, Vashsti M. *Not Without a Struggle: Leadership Development for African American Women in Ministry.* New York: Pilgrim Press, 1996.

McNeill, John J. *The Church and the Homosexual.* Boston: Beacon, 1988.

McQuilkin, Robertson. *An Introduction to Biblical Ethics.* Rev. ed. Wheaton, Ill.: Tyndale House, 1989.

Malloy, Edward A. *Homosexuality and the Christian Way of Life.* Washington, D.C.: University Press of America, 1981.

Mastsuoka, Fomitaka. *The Color of Faith.* Cleveland: Pilgrim Press, 1998.

May, William E. *An Introduction to Moral Theology.* Huntington, Ind.: Our Sunday Visitor, Publishing Division, 1995.

May, William F. *Testing the Medical Covenant.* Grand Rapids: Eerdmans, 1996.

Meeks, M. Douglas. *God the Economist.* Minneapolis: Fortress, 1989.

Meilaender, Gilbert. *Bioethics: A Primer for Christians.* Grand Rapids: Eerdmans, 1996.

Mott, Stephen Charles. *Biblical Ethics and Social Change.* Part 1. New York: Oxford University Press, 1982.

Mount, Eric, Jr. *Professional Ethics in Context.* Louisville, Ky.: Westminster/John Knox, 1990.

Nash, Roderick Frazier. *The Rights of Nature.* Madison: University of Wisconsin, 1989.

National Conference of Catholic Bishops. *The Challenge of Peace: God's Promise and Our Response.* Washington, D.C.: National Conference of Catholic Bishops, 1983.

————. *Economic Justice for All.* Washington, D.C.: National Conference of Catholic Bishops, 1986.

Neft, Naomi, and Ann D. Levine. *Where Women Stand.* New York: Random House, 1997.

Neil, Anne Thomas, and Virginia Garrett Neely, eds. *The New Has Come.* Washington, D.C.: Southern Baptist Alliance, 1989.

Nelson, James B. *Human Medicine.* Minneapolis: Augsburg, 1973.

Neuhaus, Richard John, and Michael Cromartie. *Piety and Politics.* Washington, D.C.: Ethics and Public Policy Center, 1987.

Neusner, Jacob. *World Religions in America.* Louisville, Ky.: Westminster/John Knox, 1994.

Niebuhr, H. Richard. *The Responsible Self.* New York: Harper, 1963.

Niebuhr, Reinhold. *An Interpretation of Christian Ethics.* New York: Meridian, 1956.

————. *Love and Justice.* New York: Meridian, 1967.

————. *The Nature and Destiny of Man.* 2 vols. New York: Scribners, 1941–1943.

————. *Selected Writings.* Edited by D. B. Robertson. New York: World, 1957.

Noss, John B., and David S. Noss. *Man's Religions.* 7th ed. New York: Macmillan, 1984.

Novak, David. *Jewish Social Ethics.* New York: Oxford, 1992.

O'Connell, Timothy E. *Principles for a Catholic Morality.* Rev. ed. San Francisco: Harper and Row, 1990.

Paelhke, Robert. *Environmentalism and the Future of Progressive Politics.* New Haven, Conn.: Yale University Press, 1989.

Page, Allen F. *Life after Death: What the Bible Says.* Nashville: Abingdon, 1987.

Palmer, Larry I. *Law, Medicine, and Social Justice.* Louisville, Ky.: Westminster/John Knox, 1989.

Perrett, Roy W. *Hindu Ethics.* Honolulu: University of Hawaii Press, 1998.

Petersson, Geoffrey. *Conscience and Caring.* Philadelphia: Fortress, 1982.

Pojman, Louis P., and Jeffrey Reiman. *The Death Penalty: For and Against.* Lanham, Md.: Roman and Littlefield, 1997.

Polaski, LeDayne McLeese, and Millard Eiland. *Rightly Dividing the Word of Truth.* Washington: Alliance of Baptists, 2000.

Plotkin, Albert. *The Ethics of World Religions.* Lewiston, N.Y.: Mellen, 1993.

Popenoe, David. *Promises to Keep.* Lanham, Md.: Roman and Littlefield, 1996.

Prejean, Helen. *Dead Man Walking.* New York: Random House, 1993.

President's Commission for the Study of Ethical Problems in Medicine and Biomedical and Behavioral Research. *Defining Death: A Report on the Medical, Legal, and Ethical Issues in Determination of Death.* Washington, D.C.: U.S. Government Printing Office, 1981.

Proctor, Samuel DeWitt. *The Substance of Things Hoped For.* New York: Putnam, 1995.

Ramsey, Paul. *Basic Christian Ethics.* Louisville, Ky.: Westminster/John Knox, 1993.

———. *Fabricated Man.* New Haven, Conn.: Yale University Press, 1970.

———. *War and the Christian Conscience.* Durham, N.C.: Duke University Press, 1961.

Rand, Ayn. *Capitalism: The Unknown Ideal.* New York: Penguin Books, 1967.

———. *For the New Intellectual.* New York: Random House, 1961.

———. *The Virtue of Selfishness.* New York: American Library, 1964.

Rasmussen, Larry L. *Earth Community, Earth Ethics.* New York: Orbis, 1996.

Rae, Scott B. *Moral Choices.* Grand Rapids: Zondervan, 2000.

Recinos, Harold J. *Hear the Cry! A Latino Pastor Challenges the Church.* Louisville, Ky.: Westminster/John Knox, 1989.

Ridley, Matt. *Genome.* New York: Harper Collins, 2000.

Roberts, J. Deotis. *Black Theology in Dialogue.* Philadelphia: Westminster, 1987.

Robson, Ruthann. *Gay Men, Lesbians, and the Law.* New York: Chelsea House, 1997.

Sanders, Cheryl J. *Empowerment Ethics for a Liberated People.* Minneapolis: Fortress, 1995.

Schell, Jonathan. *The Fate of the Earth.* New York: Knopf, 1982.

Shannon, Thomas A. *Bioethics: Selected Readings.* 4th ed. Mahwah, N.J.: Paulist, 1993.

———. *An Introduction to Bioethics.* 3d ed. New York: Paulist, 1997.

Siker, Jeffrey S. *Homosexuality in the Church.* Louisville, Ky.: Westminster/John Knox, 1994.

Simmons, Paul D. *Birth and Death: Bioethical Decision-Making.* Philadelphia: Westminster, 1983.

Simpson, George E., and J. Milton Yinger. *Racial and Cultural Minorities.* 5th ed. New York: Plenum, 1985.

Skinner, J. B. *About Behaviorism.* New York: Knopf, 1974.

———. *Beyond Freedom and Dignity.* New York: Knopf, 1971.

Smedes, Lewis B. *Choices.* New York: Harper and Collins, 1991.

————. *Love Within Limits*. Grand Rapids: Eerdmans, 1995.

————. *Mere Morality*. Grand Rapids: Eerdmans, 1983.

————. *Sex for Christians*. Rev. ed. Grand Rapids: Eerdmans, 1994.

Smith, Adam. *An Inquiry into the Nature and Causes of the Wealth of Nations*. Chicago: University of Chicago Press, 1976.

Smith, Harmon L. *Ethics and the New Medicine*. Nashville: Abingdon, 1971.

Smith, Huston. *The World's Religions*. New York: HarperCollins, 1991.

Smith, Rachel Richardson. "Abortion, Right and Wrong." *Newsweek*, March 15, 1985, p. 16.

Stassen, Glen H. *Capital Punishment*. New York: Pilgrim Press, 1997.

————. ed. *Just Peacemaking: Ten Practices for Abolishing War*. New York: Pilgrim Press, 1998.

Stetson, Dorothy McBride. *Women's Rights in the USA*. New York: Garland, 1997.

Stone, Glenn C., ed. *A New Ethic for a New Earth*. New York: Friendship, 1971.

Storer, Morris B., ed. *Humanistic Ethics*. New York: Prometheus Books, 1988.

Stout, Jeffrey. *Ethics after Babel*. Boston: Beacon, 1990.

Tachibana, Shundo. *Ethics of Buddhism*. Richmond, Surrey: Curzon Press, 1994.

Taylor, Paul W. *Respect for Nature*. Princeton: Princeton University Press, 1986.

Thielicke, Helmut. *The Ethics of Sex*. New York: Harper and Row, 1964.

Thomasma, David C. *Human Life in the Balance*. Louisville, Ky.: Westminster/John Knox, 1990.

Thurman, Howard. *Luminous Darkness*. New York: Harper and Row, 1965.

Tillman, William M.. *Understanding Christian Ethics*. Nashville: Broadman and Holman, 1994.

Trull, Joe E.. *Walking in the Way: An Introduction to Christian Ethics*. Nashville: Broadman and Holman, 1997.

Twiss, Harold L., ed. *Homosexuality and the Christian Faith*. Valley Forge, Penn.: Judson, 1978.

Umbreit, Mark. *Crime and Reconciliation*.Nashville: Abingdon, 1985.

Valiar, Vivian. *Why So Slow?* Cambridge, Mass.: MIT Press, 1999.

VanDyke, Fred, David C. Mahan, and Joseph K. Sheldon. *Redeeming Creation*. Downers Grove, Ill.: InterVarsity Press, 1996.

Velasquez, Manuel G. *Business Ethics*. 2d ed. Englewood Cliffs: Prentice Hall, 1988.

Waite, Linda J., and Maggie Gallagher. *The Case for Marriage*. New York: Doubleday and Company, 2000.

Wallace, Ruth A. *Gender in America*. Englewood Cliffs: Prentice Hall, 1985.

Walters, James W. *War No More?* Minneapolis: Fortress, 1989.

Weeks, Louis B. *Making Ethical Decisions*. Philadelphia: Westminster, 1987.

Welch, Sharon D. *Communities of Resistance and Solidarity: A Feminist Theology of Liberation*. New York: Orbis, 1985.

Wellman, Carl. *Morals and Ethics*. 2d ed. Englewood Cliffs: Prentice Hall, 1988.

Wennberg, Robert N. *Terminal Choices: Euthanasia, Suicide, and the Right to Die*. Grand Rapids: Eerdmans, 1989.

West, Cornel. *Race Matters*. New York: Vintage, 1994.

White, Mel. *Stranger at the Gate*. New York: Penguin, 1994.

White, R. E. O. *Christian Ethics*. Macon, Ga.: Mercer University Press, 1996.

Wilkins, Steve. *Beyond Bumper Sticker Ethics*. Downers Grove, Ill.: InterVarsity Press, 1995.

Will, James E. *A Christology of Peace*. Louisville, Ky.: Westminster/John Knox, 1989.

Williams, Bernard. *Morality: An Introduction to Ethics*. Cambridge, Mass.: Cambridge University Press, 1993.

Willimon, William H., and Stanley Hauerwas. *The Truth About God*. Nashville: Abingdon, 1999.

Wogoman, J. Philip. *Christian Perspectives on Politics*. Philadelphia: Fortress, 1988.

Yount, Lisa, ed. *Cloning*. San Diego: Greenhaven Press, 2000.

Index

McQuilken, Robertson, 38–39
Making Ethical Decisions (Weeks), 59
Making Peace in the Global Village (Brown), 241, 243, 245
Malloy, Edward, 134
Malthus, Thomas, 268
Man-woman relationships
  AIDS and, 117
  changing status of women and, 116–17
  contraception and, 117
  Paul on, 120–21
Marriage
  ceremony, 127–28
  Christian interpretation of, 118–19, 125–30
  indissolubility of, 126, 128–30
  Jesus on, 126
  monogamy in, 126
  permanence in, 129
  sex relationship in, 124
  unity in, 126–28
Martha, 201
Mary, 201
Mary Magdalene, 201
Masturbation, 150–51
Mature manhood, Paul on, 98–99
Mere Mortality (Smedes), 39–41
Messianism, 13
Miriam, 201
Modern warfare, Christianity and, 238–41
Monogamy in marriage, 126–27
Moral Aspects of Health Care (Barry), 162
Moral Choices (Rae), 154
Moral Man and Immoral Society (Niebuhr), 33
Moral theology, 28–33
"Morality of Homosexual Acts, The" (Pittenger), 136
Morality, Old Testament, 67–72
Morality, worship and, 101–02
Morals and Medicine (Fletcher), 150
Morals, distinguished from ethics, 4
Mott, Lucretia, 196
Murder, 42, 51–52, 79, 121, 166
Mutual assured destruction (MAD), 240

National Association for the Advancement of Colored People (NAACP), 175
National Bioethics Advisory Commission, 152–53
National Organization for Women (NOW), 197–98
National Women's Party, 197
Natural law, 29, 32, 271
Nationalism, 218
Natural order
  humankind as part of, 94
  theological reflections on, 273–76
Natural resource depletion, 269–70

Natural sciences, 1, 2
Nature, holistic approach to, 279–80
Nature and Destiny of Man, The (Niebuhr), 33
Neighborly love, 81–82
Nelson, James, 151
Neusner, Jacob, 12, 16, 18
New Ethic for a New Earth, A (ed. Stone), 277
New life in Christ, Paul on, 89–91
New Revised Standard Version of the Bible, 199
Niebuhr, H. Richard, 215–16
Niebuhr, Reinhold, 33–34, 245–46
Nineteenth Amendment, 197
"Noble Eightfold Path" (Buddhism), 18
"Noble Truths, the Four" (Buddhism), 18
Nonretaliation principle, 88, 235–36
Nonviolent resistance, 183–86
North Atlantic Treaty Organization (NATO), 240
Novak, David, 13–14
Nuclear Ethics (Nye), 239
Nuclear warfare, 239–41
Nuclear waste explosion, 268
Nye, Joseph, 239

Obedient love, 34, 79–80
Objectivism, 21–24
O'Connell, Timothy E., 30–33
Office for Civil Rights, 177
Office of Federal Contract Compliance, 177
"On Updating Death" (Cutler), 161
Orderliness in universe, 6
Ordination of women, 198, 206–07
Organ transplants, 159–62
"Our Tragic Waste of Human Tissue" (Fletcher), 161
"Overcoming the Biblical and Traditional Subordination of Women" (Bennett), 48

Pacificism, 235–36, 238
Paehlke, Robert, 269
Page, Allen, 168
Paradise, Scott I., 277
Parenting, responsible, 156–58
Parks, Rosa, 183
Pastoral Epistles, 204
Patient's rights, death and, 163–64
Paul on
  covenant community, 56–57
  death, 168
  love, 88–89
  mature manhood, 98–99
  minority groups, 182
  new life in Christ, 89–91
  nonretaliation, 89, 235
  responsible freedom, 86–88
  resurrection, 168

Stereotypes, 173–74
  of women, 190–92
Sterilization, 157
Stewardship, 264–65
Storer, Morris B., 19, 21
Stranger at the Gate (White), 131–32
Stride toward Freedom (King), 183–84
Student Non-Violent Coordinating
      Committee, 183
Substance of Things Hoped For, The (Proctor),
     178
Suicide, morality of, 166–67
Surrogate motherhood, 149, 151–52
Syntyche, 201

Talmud, 12
Tay-Sachs disease, 157
Teleological approach, 4
Ten Commandments, 37, 39, 68–69. *See also*
     Decalogue
Theocentric ethics, 41–43
Theocracy, 210–11
Theology for a Nuclear Age (Kaufman), 239
Theology of Liberation, A (Gutierrez), 43
Thielicke, Helmut, 151
Thomas Aquinas, 237
Thurman, Howard, 172
Torah, 12, 68, 69
Toward a Christian Economic Ethic
     (Pemberton & Finn), 250
Traditional warfare, Christianity and, 237–38
Transmigration of souls, 16
Truman, Harry S., 176
Twiss, Harold L., 135

Understanding Jewish Theology (Neusner), 12
United Methodist Church, bishops of, on
     nuclear warfare, 240
Unity in marriage, 126–28
Updating Life and Death (ed. Cutler), 161
Utilitarian approach
  to ethics, 2
  to punishment, 223–24
Utilitarianism, humanism and, 20

Value, 2, 4
Value judgments, 5
Vasectomy, 157
Vatican II, 28, 30
Victims' rights, 226–27, 232
Violence to achieve good ends, 7–8, 185
Virtue of Selfishness, The (Rand), 22–23
Vocation, 255–56
Voluntary agencies, ecological concerns
     and, 279
Voting Rights Act (1965), 176

Wait and Gallagher, 137
Walden Two (Skinner), 218
Wallace, Ruth A., 191
Walters, James W., 240
War
  agonized participation in, 238, 242
  Bible and, 234–37
  Christianity and
    modern warfare, 238–41
    traditional warfare, 237–38
  developing nations and, 244
  individual responses to, 237–38
  just war theory, 238
  lesser of two evils, 238
  quest for peace, 242–46
War and Conscience in America (Long),
    238
War and the Christian Conscience (Ramsey),
    239
War No More? (ed. Walters), 240
Warfare, chemical and biological, 241
Watson, J.B., 24
Wealth
  Jesus on, 253
  unfair distribution of, 257–58
Webster v. *Reproductive Health Services*,
    143
Weeks, Louis B., 59
Welch, Sharon, 46
West, Cornel, 179
Westminster Confession of Faith, 53
"What is Feminist Ethics?" (Haney), 46–47
White, Mel, 131–32
White, R.E.O., 83
"Whole Earth is the Lord's: Toward a
    Holistic Ethic, The" (Schilling),
    279
Why We Can't Wait (King), 184
Williams, Delores S., 48
Wilmut, Ian, 152, 154
Wisdom literature, 71–72
Wisdom of experience, 113
Wogaman, J. Philip, 218, 239
Womanism, 48–49
Women
  affirmative action, 205–06
  changes in status of, 190–91
  Christian approach to current issues
    regarding, 204–07
  churches, leadership in, 206–07
  Civil Rights Act, 193, 197, 205
  employment and, 195–96
  Equal Rights Amendment, 198, 205–06
  feminist movement, 196–99
  images of, 190–92
  inclusive language and, 199
  income of, 195–96
  law and, 192–95, 196, 205–07
  ordination of, 198